BREAKFAST WITH THE DEVIL

BREAKFAST WITH THE DEVIL

L. WAYNE CARLSON

INSOMNIAC PRESS

Edited by Lee Shedden
Copy edited by Catherine Jenkins
Designed by Mike O'Connor

National Library of Canada Cataloguing in Publication Data

Carlson, L. Wayne, 1942-
    Breakfast with the devil: the story of a professional jail breaker

ISBN 1-895837-18-9

1. Carlson, L. Wayne, 1942- .2. Prisons - Canada. 3. Prisoners - Canada - Biography. 4.
Escapes - Canada. 5. Escapes - United States. 6. Automobile thieves - Canada - Biography.
I. Title.

HV9505.C37A3 2001   365'.44'092   C2001-930387-4

The publisher and the author gratefully acknowledges the support of the Canada Council,
the Ontario Arts Council and Department of Canadian Heritage through the Book
Publishing Industry Development Program.

Printed and bound in Canada

Insomniac Press, 192 Spadina Avenue, Suite 403,
Toronto, Ontario, Canada, M5T 2C2
www.insomniacpress.com

This book is dedicated to my wife, Hilde Schlosar, whose love, support, and sense of humour have been the energy carrying me into a new life.

And to her most accepting family:

Dylan, Jennifer, Brittany and Emily Tetrault, Adam, Candy and baby Tetrault, Frank Schlosar, Elizabeth, John, Paula and Carl Ayer, Christine, Richard, Alex and Katherine Louie, John, Carol, Jillian, Jay and Tamara Schlosar

Without their kindness and generosity of spirit I would never have been able to produce this book.

The love, support, and encouragement of friends and family are paramount to making a new life in the community. I want to thank those special people in my life:

The Samaritans of Southern Alberta, Jane Carlson, Deanna, Robin and Donnalene McKerricher, Mom, Jeff and Brandon Barchuk, Cory and Nadine Barchuk, Roger Carlson, Donald Carlson, Debbie and Jeff Magson, Moira Farr, Erna Hood, Debbie Atkinson, Pat and Lynda Quinn, Dan, Maureen and Kerri Campbell, Lance Pettman, John and Denise Thompson, Nancy, Stephen, Dorothy and Eileen Graham, Rick Levesque, Sister Esther, Mike Burden, Tom Fedora, Randy Tymchuk, Brian Kreutzer, Rick and Wendy Burton, Morris Karp, Bob and Karen Purdue, Peggy Doyle, Tim Holt, Bill O'Malley, Morton Molyneaux, Tom Anderson, Dennis and Shirley Maday, Stephen Reid—who recognized me as a writer and didn't hesitate to tell me so, Lee Shedden—a superb editor—and his wife Fiona, The Sams of Drum Pen, past and present.

The people to whom I owe my freedom: Larry Simonson, Tim Fullerton, Donna Geer, and the National Parole Board.

And to the men who shared the dark years with me inside, some of whom still live there—thank you for your friendship. I will always remember you.

And finally, in remembrance of my friends who are gone, but not forgotten:

Dennis Atkinson - meningitis; Chris Hood - suicide; Roly Paton - suicide; Ronnie Westadt - illness; Gunther Cordes - brain hemorrhage; Bill Peachy - death by misadventure; Norm Beckman - car accident; Willie "Potatoes" Daddano - heart attack; Angelo Ruggiero - cancer; Sammy Wood - stabbed to death; Art Newman - death by misadventure; Gary Vance - overdose; Gary Allen - stabbed to death; Spencer Briltz - stabbed to death; Tim Collins - stabbed to death; Murray Boyd - killed in a shootout with police; John McGarry - overdose; Andy Cluckie - suicide; Herman Labelle - overdose; Robbie Pelletier - overdose.

FISH

My nineteen-year-old partner and I were in handcuffs and our legs were shackled with heavy links of chain that dated back to the nineteenth century. The solid oak door had large steel hinges with black bolts that looked as if they had been there since the beginning of time. In the center of the door was a recessed, three-inch glass peephole covered on the inside with a metal plate. As quick as the shutter on a camera the metal plate moved. An eye owlishly peered at us, then just as quickly disappeared and the shutter fell silently back in place. A moment later the door began to slowly open, like a castle drawbridge being lowered on chains. We'd arrived at the penitentiary.

The two RCMP escorts became busy stripping the metal from our hands and legs and the shackles fell clanking to the floor. The inside of the front door had a locking mechanism run by a polished spoked wheel on the side of the wall and beside it was a lock-box with a gear poking out its side. The gear could be locked into a gear on the wheel and the door could only be opened by unlocking and hand-turning the wheel. Leading to the interior there was another door made of steel bars, behind which I could see other guards moving about.

"Just these two?" asked the guard who stood watching, clipboard in his hand, as the restraints were being removed. *No, there's a dozen of us,* I wanted to say, but fear made me bite my tongue.

"Just these two," agreed the escort. The paperwork quickly changed hands and the man at the locking wheel reached up to grab it. With a flick of his powerful wrist it began to spin, silently and smoothly, like the wheel of a submarine hatch just before it dives, and the door was quickly and silently clamped shut.

"You been here before?" asked the guard with the clipboard. All four men laughed. There was the ratchet sound of handcuffs being folded for storage.

"No, never," I replied. The pen in his hand made a flick on the paper. He turned to Bill, my partner.

"You?"

"No," Bill answered. Another flick of the pen and the guard turned his head toward the barred steel door in front us, cupped his mouth with the clipboard and shouted into the recesses of the prison, "Two Cherries comin' through!"

We had arrived to serve our sentences in the Prince Albert Penitentiary. It was September 12, 1960. I was eighteen years old.

The cells were small. I could touch the walls on either side just by stretching out my arms, but the frame of the bed was hinged on one side, folded against the wall, and held with a large green butterfly hook so the most could be made of the space. The chair was wooden, and it too folded up. The cupboard was a wooden box made of one-inch board, attached to the wall, and like the bed and chair, it had hinges and could be folded to give more space. The light was a bare bulb surrounded by a small, green tin shade and the electrical cord was rolled up and tied in a loose knot so the light could be moved around the cell if it was unravelled. There was a sink and a toilet, and the front of the cell was barred, the bars so closely spaced a man's hand could not fit beyond the wrist.

There were twenty-eight cells on a range. Each cell appeared identical, and the range we were on was split in two by a wall and a doorway. I'd heard the guards refer to us as fish and we understood we were on the fish range; fish were those prisoners who had not previously served time in the federal prison system. The prison was now home to me, to Bill, and to the seven hundred other men serving time in the P.A. Penitentiary.

Prince Albert Penitentiary was officially opened as a federal prison in 1917, according to a plaque on the outside wall of the entrance. However, the buildings had been used as a jail when the Prince Albert area was first settled. The graveyard outside the walls held more than just the numbers of men who died inside; there were rumours that three North West Mounted Police killed in a battle with Metis at Duck Lake were also buried on the prison grounds.

When we flew in on the plane the wings had tipped to afford me a window-seat view of the prison below. A square red-brick wall surrounded red-brick buildings with bars over each entrance and window. The gun towers on each corner of the wall, and the peaks of the buildings, were fashioned like the turrets of castles. The place was silently imposing, and with the Union Jack fluttering on a pole in front, it looked like a fortress squatting on the edge of a small town in northern Saskatchewan.

"Hey Wayne!" shouted Bill. He was four cells down the range from me. His voice brought me down from my aerial view and dropped me back in my cell.

"Yeah?" I shouted back.

"Have you tried the cap?" I looked at the bundle of clothing I had been given. Everything was stamped with a large number in fresh black ink. I quickly found the cap and unfolded it. It was grey, with a strip of white cloth sewn to its front. My number was 8329Y. I tried it on and found it was too big. The bill was so long that I had to tilt my head to look straight ahead.

"Yeah, I've tried it," I answered. It seemed quiet on the range, and I could hear the steam pipes of the heating system along the wall creaking as they expanded or contracted. I couldn't tell which.

"Dummy up!" shouted a voice on the other side of the divider wall. The voice sounded mean, like someone shouting at a barking dog in the middle of the night. It confused and frightened me.

"There's no talking now," said a voice from the cell next to me.

"Did you hear that, Bill?" I almost whispered, keeping my voice down.

"Yeah, " Bill whispered back, doing the same.

"We'll talk later," I said.

"Okay," he replied. I unfolded my chair, sat down, and began searching through my pillowcase.

The pillowcase served as a bag which held my newly issued toothbrush, toothpaste, comb, four stamps, a long pen with two nibs, a small bottle of ink, four pieces of writing paper and four envelopes, one package of tobacco, a book of Vogue cigarette papers and one Zippo lighter. There were two pairs of home-made wool socks that had been shrunk so badly I doubted I would get them on my feet. I pulled out a light green shirt with no collar and pants of the same material, and I guessed they passed as pajamas. Next came two pairs of shorts, two new grey and white pin-striped shirts, and two pairs of pants, all of which had my number stamped on them, even the shorts. There was an old grey horse blanket, in good shape but well washed and worn, and two new bedsheets made of coarse linen as stiff and as abrasive as burlap. At the bottom of the bag was a set of headphones dating back to World War II. Last I saw a sheet of paper I had almost missed. It was a typed sheet of rules and regulations. I set it on top of the pile of clothes and decided to make my bed.

I flipped the butterfly hook and the bed came down on legs made of flat iron that were loosely riveted to the frame, which, as the bed was lowered, automat-ically flopped down and fell into the well-worn holes they had created in the cement floor over the years; it was a crude but effective system. I put the pil-lowcase on a pillow made from a piece of flat material which felt like, but was-n't, a folded blanket beneath its striped covering.

The mattress was very old and made of a straw-like material, and the many men before me who had lain on it had left their sagging imprint on it exactly in the center. The springs were not really springs at all, but small circular links of steel which had long since suffered metal fatigue. It was like lying in a rigid ham-mock, quite uncomfortable, but I settled my body into it and read over the basic rules.

Each convict was allowed to write one letter home each week, free of charge. Writing was allowed on one side of the paper only, and the words had to be between the lines with no overlap or the letter would be returned to the sender. If the convict forgot to put his name on the letter it would not leave the prison.

No unacceptable language could be used and if it was, those sentences would be censored out with black ink or the letter would be returned to the sender. Each convict had to put his name and number at the top of the page. A letter could only be sent to his family or someone on his approved list, and no convict could write to any person who was not twenty-one years of age. I felt my heart sink as I read that, because my girlfriend was only eighteen. *Maybe I can lie about that,* I thought.

I glanced up and saw at the back of the cell a funnel-like recess with a small hole in the centre; it was in fact a peephole through which a guard could observe a prisoner without his being aware of it. Later I learned there was a rule against masturbation; if a prisoner was caught doing it, he would be charged with self-abuse.

The sudden sound of a steam whistle split the air like an air raid siren and I almost leapt from the bed. It sounded like a train whistle and it seemed to last a long, long time. Was it some sort of signal?

I didn't remember dozing, but I found myself waking to the sound of a ringing bell. It had a high, reverberating quality to it, like the ringside bell at a boxing match. I was still worried about the owner of the mean-sounding voice and wondered if he knew who I was. If he did know I was the one who had been speaking, what would he do? How would I react? I rose to my feet, stood close to the bars and looked as far as I could see both ways. The bell was somewhere to my right, beyond the door and divider wall, and I thought I could hear movement from that direction.

There were large, barred windows in the wall across the hall; they extended beyond the ceiling and seemed to go up forever. Directly above me was another range and I later learned that D Block, where I was, was the only cellblock that was sectioned off. The other cellblocks were four tiers high and a convict could look up from the lowest range and see someone standing on the top range.

Each cell had an abutment and each cell door was recessed. The locking mechanism consisted of two flat bars bolted to the top of each abutment and which ran the length of the range. As the bars moved in the groove, the holes lined up with the locking bar on each cell, and once in line each cell door could be opened by pushing the locking lever up and through the hole.

Suddenly I heard a metal-on-metal grinding noise and I saw the locking bars in front of my cell begin to move. Banging came from the cells around me, as if the men were pounding on their bars, then men were moving quickly past my cell and through the open doorway to my right, as if they knew where they were going. Bill appeared in front of my cell. As he lifted the locking lever, I pushed the door and it swung open easily on its machine-tooled hinge.

"It's suppertime," he said, stepping aside to let me pass. We nervously followed the men in front of us. The man next door, who had told me there was no talking, fell in beside us as we walked across the dome and turned down F range, where a large stencilled sign proclaimed Feed Line.

The man with us was also named Bill, and he explained that we were going to pick up our trays from a food slot, which was called "blind feeding," and then return to our cells to be locked up while we ate. He counselled us not to peer into the other convicts' cells when we walked down the ranges for our food; that would be considered an invasion of privacy and confrontational. We would be released to return our trays to the slot in the wall of the kitchen, after which we would return to our cells and be locked up for the night. Breakfast was at 7:00 A.M., at which time the same procedure would be followed, the difference being we would go to work after returning our trays to the kitchen. There were close to fifteen men in our group and we were all labelled fish, regardless of our ages. Neighbour Bill's number was lower than mine and we learned he had arrived two weeks before us.

Under the Feed Line sign a doorway led behind the end of the cellblock, and as we walked through, we picked up our steel trays from a stationary slide onto which the trays were funnelled through a food slot just big enough for the tray. A dozen feet away in another slot, were heavy, pint-sized steel mugs full of milky tea. The hallway was so narrow it only allowed for a single file of men, and as we picked up our trays, we moved forward to pick up our tea mugs. At the end of the narrow hallway we walked out to enter E range where a wagon and table was set up to hold the bread. A guard was stationed at each end of the line and anyone who attempted to take more than one portion of anything would be charged with an offence. I could feel some of the men on F and E ranges watch us as we passed by. I tried not to look at them, and I tried to not let my nervousness and insecurity show on my face. When one of the fish behind me glanced into one of the cells, a harsh voice barked, "What the fuck are you lookin' at?" There was no response. I felt grateful to Bill for his timely advice.

The food trays had been stamped out of one piece of stainless steel, similar to cafeteria trays, and our meals were placed into its sections. The meat was thinly sliced. I later learned that each man was allotted two ounces of meat per serving and that a scale was used in the kitchen to ensure this rule was applied. It wasn't long before I heard the term "belly robber" used to describe a kitchen worker.

"Them fuckin' belly robbin' cocksuckers," I heard a man say, unhappy with the portion of meat on his tray. But on my first day I heard little else; I was much too intent on learning how to pick up my meal and return to my cell through the maze of corridors. Although the procedure was simple, and the walk was not far, I felt disoriented, half lost, and very vulnerable. This feeling was to persist for the next couple of days, but like everyone else, I quickly learned that a man can get used to anything. When we all arrived back on our part of D Block, a guard stood watching from the end of the range, and just before we walked into our cells and closed our doors, I asked Bill what the whistle meant.

"Nothing as far as I know," he answered.

"Nothing? You mean they just blow it whenever they want to?"

"No, it blows twice a day, every day, at exactly twelve noon and four o'clock in the afternoon."

"Maybe something to do with the count?"

"Maybe," he replied, but I could see he was distracted by the supper on his tray, so I let him go. I learned later some of the townspeople set their clocks to the sound of that whistle.

"See you later," I said.

"Right," he replied. I walked into my cell, and because I had not yet lowered the shelf on my cupboard, I placed the supper tray on my chair. When I closed my door I stood to watch how the locking mechanism worked and saw how simple it would be to cut the locking bar and open the door.

I put down the shelf and sat to eat everything on the tray, even the pudding, which didn't taste like any pudding I'd ever tasted. I also thought back to my first experience with prison pudding.

I was fifteen years old and had been sent to Regina Gaol by a Saskatchewan Provincial Court judge, for a 30-day pre-sentence evaluation. For some reason jail was spelled gaol, the English spelling of the word. Many prisoners would say "goal," not realizing the difference. I had been there for three days, just long enough to hear the prisoners on the other ranges talk about their lives of crime; we men on remand status did not get to interact with many of the men actually serving time. Remand prisoners exercised together, went through the meal line together, and talked among ourselves. Jock was the cleaner of our range— "cleaner" being the Canadian equivalent of the American "trustee"—and he would pick up our food trays after we pushed them into the hallway through the slot in the bottom of our doors.

One day at lunch, just after we'd returned to our cells from picking up our trays, I heard someone talking in a quiet voice to my next door neighbour, and a moment later Jock appeared in front of my cell.

"Don't eat the rice pudding," he murmured, conspiratorially. He was a slim, dark-skinned man of medium height and he had an ingratiating, confident way of speaking. I looked at the rice pudding on my tray.

"No?" I asked. It looked fine to me.

"No, don't eat it—they found maggots in it but they fed it to us anyway—

but leave it on the tray," he whispered, and was gone to deliver his message to the next cell. I sat there looking at the pudding and though I couldn't see any maggots, the white rice could be camouflaging a hundred of them. Just thinking of what might be hiding in the pudding cost me my appetite. I pushed my food-filled tray into the hallway and picked up one of the pocketbooks I'd been reading.

Fifteen minutes later Jock came by with a tray full of rice pudding, and as he bent to scoop the pudding from my tray to his, he caught my inquisitive glance.

"I'm collecting this for evidence," he whispered.

"Good," I replied, grateful that someone was going to do something about the bad food. Before he left for the next cell I told him I didn't think anybody should have to eat contaminated food.

"You're right," he said, "we'll do something about this." And again he was gone.

My Prince Albert Penitentiary meal finished, I opened my package of tobacco and rolled myself a smoke. *This is the kind of life Jean Valjean lived for so many years,* I thought. Jean Valjean is the central character in Les Misérables, a convict who escaped from a French prison and lived on the run. As the smoke filled my lungs and my body absorbed the nicotine, my thoughts turned to escaping, just as Jean Valjean did so many times. But I had no idea where in the prison I actually was. I looked at the large, rusty steel bars covering the windows and I knew it would be no easy task cutting through so much steel. While I was looking around, I remembered the headphones.

There was a small box on the wall above the bed, and two holes which would fit the jack on the headphone cord. I hesitantly plugged it in and when there were no sparks, I put the headphones on. Within a minute I learned the weather in the province was cool, that rain was expected for the next couple of days, and that the news, with an update on Hurricane Donna on the east coast, would be coming on in less than a minute. If I wanted to stay tuned I would learn more about Cassius Clay's gold medal win at the Olympics. It was almost five o'clock, my first meal in the penitentiary was digesting in my belly, and I had only four hundred-ninety suppers to go. If I didn't escape.

Thirty minutes later the locking bars went through their opening cycle and Bill and I found ourselves returning our trays. As we walked to and from the kitchen ranges, men from the other ranges called out to men from the "fish tank" they seemed to know, and I gathered from the conversation they were getting reacquainted. Once back on the range, before we were locked up for the night, I asked my neighbour if he had anything to read. He walked into his cell and returned with a ragged pocketbook. I was grateful for the gift.

After a few minutes of listening to a couple of prisoners talking about someone they knew from Fort Saskatchewan provincial jail and had seen on the kitchen workers' range, I lay back on my bed to read my book. Reading allowed me to escape from the present into another world. Ever since I was able to read I had done so—I thought everybody in the world could read and a life without the world of literature was inconceivable to me. That night I read for a few hours, slept for a few hours, then awoke and read until the words began to run into each other on the page, and then went back to sleep again. Every hour a guard walked by peering into the cells on the range, and all around me I heard the sounds of the men in their cells, snoring, coughing, grunting and groaning, and one man talking in his sleep. The steam pipes along the wall would crack when they expanded and contracted with the heat and cold, and my first night was full of unease and restlessness.

The next morning I awoke to the same bell I had heard the night before and in a minute I was up, dressed in my new prison clothes, and waiting for the door to open for breakfast. It was then I caught the odour of full toilets. When the doors opened and I commented on it, my neighbour told me it was unacceptable to flush the toilet in the night because the sound would disturb everyone on the range.

McCudden, a tall guard in charge of orienting the fish to the ways of prison life, would lead us through the prison routine over the next few weeks.

"If you're offered anything by one of the convicts, don't take it," he said. We would take out the folding chairs from our cells and sit in the range hallway while he stood in front of us on the fish range, lecturing like a school teacher. He explained what the prison administration expected of us. We were to work each day; if we didn't, we would be charged with refusing to work. If we reported to the hospital too sick to work, and the doctor had a second opinion, we would be charged with malingering. If we got into a fight with another prisoner we would go to the hole, and if we got into a fight with a guard it was an assault and we would be paddled for it. McCudden also led us on tours of the work and recreation areas of the prison and as we walked across the yard convicts would call out to him, and to us.

"Don't believe a fuckin' word he tells you."

"They're gettin' younger all the time."

McCudden would sometimes respond in a jocular fashion, but generally he simply ignored the comments.

Within the red-brick walls were a wide variety of shops and service departments, and we visited them all. There was the laundry, the shoe shop, the tailor shop, paint, maintenance, plumbing, the machine shop, carpentry, automotive, the print shop, and others, and there were convicts working in every area. As I became more familiar with some of the seven hundred men serving time in the prison, many of them would offer me advice.

"What do you do?" a man asked me.

"What do you mean?"

"Well, everybody has an expertise—what's yours?"

"Well I drove a caterpillar..." There was much laughter over my response.

"Look kid, you're either a can man, a con man, you go with a gun, or you hang paper—or you boost for a living," I was told. I had no idea what any of it meant, but I learned quickly. A can man was a safecracker, going with a gun meant armed robbery, a paper hanger was a cheque scam artist, and a booster was a professional shoplifter. And there were "skinners," or "rape hounds" and "baby fuckers" as they were called among us. As time went on I became able to identify the cell of a skinner, just by glancing into it; their cells were almost always devoid of any family pictures, or personal photos and instead they put up religious articles: crosses and pictures of Jesus, and bibles prominently displayed on white linen. They were also the most ingratiating and friendly of people. As time went on I learned a basic rule: if I looked at a man and couldn't picture him committing one of the acceptable crimes, he was probably a sex offender and should be avoided.

There was a considerable amount of conversation among the prisoners about the recent riot, which had been in 1956. Most prisoners are concerned with the past, and I learned what it means to have a long memory.

My arrival in the penitentiary corresponded closely with John Diefenbaker's rise to power, and because he was a lawyer of note in the Prince Albert area, many people seemed to feel they knew him. And because of his stance on prisons and prisoners, there were rumours of impending changes in the federal penal system. Those changes would forever change the way serving prisoners were allowed to do their time, including their leisure time; group night exercise for the whole of the prison population; prisoners wearing their personal clothing and jewelry, including watches; and being allowed to purchase small radios for their cells. The guards were vehemently opposed to prisoners exercising en masse; they believed we would violently attack each other, destroy prison property, and wreak general mayhem once we were in one large group.

There was also talk among the prisoners and guards about the upcoming annual prison Christmas concert and we fish were asked by a variety of people if we played instruments, if we could sing, tell jokes, or had any sort of entertainment abilities. The annual Christmas concert consisted of a group of the more talented prisoners putting on a show for the guards and their wives. Comedians, musicians, and actors were in demand and because my partner and I had no obvious talent at the time, we did our time as observers with the majority. It was the Christmas concert that first brought home to me the role environment plays in how human beings think, feel, act and react, but it would be many years before I fully appreciated the extent of that role.

The violent death of my dog when I was fourteen was, I believe, the major factor in cementing my hatred of authority, and would have repercussions for years to come.

He was scruffy and sorry-looking and looked like he would never amount to much. His hair was matted with grease, he had a smell which came from going too long without a bath, and if it wasn't for his innate friendliness I might never have come to know him. We came into each other's lives at the exact moment when we needed each other, and our gratitude for each other's company assured we would have a long-lasting relationship of mutual affection and trust. He was lonesome for his family, and I was still grieving over the loss of a very good friend who had been murdered less than six months previously.

On the day I met him I was at home with my parents, my two sisters, Deanna and Jane, and my brother Roger, when my father asked me to go to the garage and take a look around.

"Look around?" I asked. It was after supper, my mother and sister were busy with the dishes and Roger and I were ready for the hockey game. My sister Jane, being too small to do the dishes, was busy doing something with the remnants of the food on her plate.

"Yes," he said, casually. "I heard something in the garage. Maybe you can find out what it is." I put on my rubbers and my toque, shrugged myself into my parka and walked into the freezing temperatures to investigate.

I found him lying under the oil pan of the caterpillar, curled up with fright and cold. I asked him to come out but he only whimpered. I had to use the wheeled crawler to go under the machine myself to get him.

I took one of his front legs and literally pulled his protesting body out from his hiding place. He was a greasy, matted, cold and hungry, black and white, curly-haired, floppy-eared, one-month-old retriever pup.

I picked him up in my arms and as he squirmed into my parka and tried to lick my face, he wriggled his way deep into the most tender part of my heart. With him in my arms I ran back to the house, forgetting about lights and locks, and even the hockey game. My brother and sisters were delighted, but my father's voice cut through our enthusiasm.

"He can't stay in the house," he said.

"But he's cold..." we began, but were cut off by our mother.

"I don't want that dog in the house," she said.

"It's so cold in the garage," I entreated, "he'll freeze..."

"He won't freeze," stated my father with finality.

Roger and I found an old parka whose zipper had been ripped, and though the outside was grease-stained, the orange lining inside was clean and warm. We made a comfortable bed for him in a corner of the garage, lit a fire in the stove and returned to the house and begged my mother for food scraps. That night Roger and I played hockey enthusiastically, each scoring a goal for our team.

We needed a name for the newest member of our family, and we quickly decided on Pooch, as it was the first word to which he had responded.

Pooch explored the countryside with me, and he didn't seem to need the training other dogs did. I personally thought he was just born smart. He was with me when I discovered the small cluster of tiger lilies on top of the hill on the outskirts of town, and he knew instinctively not to bite at them like he would at the blue crocuses that covered the hills by the railroad tracks. He sniffed at them, just like I did, and I didn't have to tell him that tigers, though at one time abundant and plentiful, were now protected because their population had dwindled to a very few. They had become so scarce that to find a bouquet of them growing wild was considered very lucky indeed. I was convinced he could tell time as well. When school was out for the day, he would always be there, sitting in front at the bottom of the stairs waiting for my brother and my sister and me, and he would happily walk us home.

Time went on and my father purchased a dairy farm, complete with all the buildings and a new garage with a room in its attic that I claimed as my own. Pooch and I had our own place; we could come and go as we pleased, and we made the most of it.

Roger and I hatched a plan to raise wild ducks. Pooch's retriever instincts served us well when we set out to capture ducklings from the sloughs around our farm. Pooch would form one point of a triangle, my brother and I the others, and together we would catch them in the middle of the slough. The ducklings would dive and swim underwater, and with their elongated necks and heads pointed straight out, their webbed feet working behind them like tiny propellers, they looked like small, chubby arrowheads moving beneath the surface of the algae-covered water. We would reach into the murky depths and scoop them up and in a week we had captured two dozen of them.

"Those birds are going to die," my father told us one sunny, early-summer day in front of our large pen. Like most kids we believed we knew better than the grown-ups. We believed it was only a matter of time before they would grow hungry enough to begin eating, and we kept them in the pen until we learned for ourselves that some things cannot be caged.

On the fifth day we found that two small teals had died overnight, and that afternoon we found two others dead, both pathetically lying in tiny heaps in the grass. The only movement was their feathers as they were ruffled by the summer breeze. We decided we would let the rest of them go. We carried them to the shore of a large slough a half mile from our home and set them down. It took them a few minutes to realize they were free and make their way tentatively into the water. Seeing them swim, flapping the water over their small bodies as if washing away their captivity, did wonders in washing away some of our guilt.

The summer passed and we moved back into town for the winter months. Pooch and I waited impatiently for spring to come so we could once again live in what we came to think of as the wild. The next summer disaster struck, and changed forever the way I looked at myself and perhaps life itself.

My father was an entrepreneur, a legacy from his father and grandfather; we were involved in municipal road building in summer, logging in winter, and we also had a farm where we raised two hundred chickens.

On July fourth there is an annual Sports Day in my hometown and we didn't get back until dawn of the next day. When we pulled up in front of the house, Pooch was there with his happy barks and wagging tail to welcome us all. None of us noticed anything untoward and we all went to bed to rest for a few hours. Pooch went with me to our loft above the garage and within moments we were sound asleep, him on his rug and me in my bed.

It seemed I had no sooner closed my eyes when my dad's loud and angry voice woke me.

"What?" I answered. Pooch was on his feet.

"Get your ass down here!" he shouted. I had learned early that when my father was angry my life could become a painful, bruising experience.

"Okay!" I shouted back. As I quickly dressed I wondered if he had somehow found my stash of Vogue cigarettes behind the garage. "I'm in trouble, Pooch," I whispered to my buddy. Like all boys I had learned that when one was in trouble, or sad, or lonely, a boy's dog would listen to him. But it wasn't the cigarettes; it was something far worse.

"Look at what your dog did!" my dad shouted when I approached him. He was standing behind the garage and with a large hand he pointed to four dead hens lying in a clump of white feathers. I couldn't believe my eyes.

"It wasn't him," I said, defensively. I turned to look at Pooch who stood quietly watching us. "It wasn't you, was it Pooch?" He looked at me and licked his lips in puzzlement.

"Yeah, right," said my father with disgust, "he'll tell you won't he?" I stood looking at the dead hens, and the others who were very much alive, hunting and pecking nearby as if nothing had happened. I looked at Pooch who calmly looked at me in return.

"He wouldn't do this..." I started, but my father cut me off.

"You and your brother get rid of these birds," he demanded, "and after that I want you to tell me how many he killed." He walked into the house and a moment later my younger brother appeared, still rubbing the sleep from his eyes.

We counted thirty-two dead chickens, some of whom had no visible signs of damage. Many of them were still warm. As the count mounted so did our fear.

I chastised Pooch, who still looked puzzled. He didn't seem to understand that his antics had resulted in so many deaths. We piled the birds on the stoneboat, and though my brother and I whispered conspiratorially about lying about the count to my father, our fear of him was too great, so we walked into the house to tell him the truth. He was sitting at the table with a cup of coffee in front of him. His twelve-gauge Winchester pump-action shotgun rested ominously against the wall.

"Well?" he asked me. My fear was so strong I could hardly speak. The look on his face was calm, yet as cold and as brutal and as unforgiving as a Saskatchewan winter night.

"Thirty-two," I answered truthfully.

"Roger?" He asked my brother for confirmation of the figure.

"Thirty-two," answered my brother in a small vulnerable voice. My father slammed his cup on the table, spilling coffee on the table cloth. He stood to his feet, picked up the shotgun and angrily strode out the door. My brother and I stood frozen in fear, our eyes locked on one another in horror. A moment later we heard my father's voice bellow, "Wayne, you get out here!" Roger and I walked into the sunshine of that beautiful July day to face one of the blackest moments in our lives.

Pooch had bounded away from my father, for he was no fool and could sense anger and hatred in people. He stood fifty yards away in the shade of the lane leading from our house to the dairy barn. My father ordered us to come to him.

"Call your dog," he demanded.

"Dad, he won't do it again," I promised. My mind was racing as fast as the horses on the track at the sports day the day before. Could I run off with Pooch—just the two of us—across the fields and into the woods that stretched across three provinces?

"Call your dog," he said with finality.

"We can tie him up when we leave—he never did anything like this..."

"Goddamn it! Shut up and call your dog!" He jacked a shell into the chamber, and I'll never know if it was the fear that the shotgun would be turned on my brother and me if I didn't call my dog, or if it was only that innate instinct inherent in all sons to obey their fathers. I only know I called his name.

"Here Pooch," I said quietly, "come here boy." He didn't hesitate. Wasn't I his best friend and companion? Wasn't I the one he could trust with his very life? He came to within ten feet of my father, who brought the shotgun to his shoulder, and as my father leaned forward slightly to absorb the kick of the explosion, Pooch growled low in his throat. That was the only time I had ever heard him growl.

The shotgun pellets literally exploded his chest into flying clumps of hair and bloody flesh. As his front legs buckled, he coughed out his last ragged breath into the leafy carpet of the lane. Roger and I were moaning in a heart-wrenching agony that matched Pooch's, and, though his pain ended a moment later, ours continued for many more years.

"Put his body in the stoneboat with the chickens," my father curtly ordered, jacking out the spent cartridge from the shotgun. I watched it twirl slowly in the air, then fall and bounce in the leaves. He looked at me and said, "Get rid of them." He walked back into the house and went to bed, leaving my brother and I standing there frozen in shock and disbelief, the smell of gunpowder, blood, and earth in our nostrils. It was so quiet I could hear the rustle of each leaf on the branches of the trees around me. I felt the breeze in my hair, and off in the southern distance a crow called to one of his brethren. Another answered from the east. Time and life seemed suspended. It was many moments before we could move to obey my father's orders.

Roger and I hooked up the tractor to the stoneboat, gently lifted Pooch's body onto it, and after piling dead chickens around him, we hauled away the victims of a dog's loneliness and my father's rage into a far-off field, where we quietly buried them in separate places. My brother and I spoke not a word then, and we never spoke about Pooch's death with anyone, including each other. But I know in my heart it was at the moment my father pulled the trigger of his shotgun, that I never saw him or heard his voice, or any other voice of authority in the same way again. For years after that I would relive the moment when Pooch died, and I would always think I could have saved him by helping him to escape into the woods with me by his side. In later years I fought authority on many occasions, and I became very adept at escaping and running through the woods.

My partner Bill and I were in fact in the penitentiary for escaping from Regina Gaol. Bill and I had worked in the kitchen in the jail. He was the baker and I was the second cook, which meant we were both out of our element and hating our lot in life. I had been sentenced to a year for car theft and Bill was doing two years less a day for cashing a string of bad cheques near his home-town of Rockford, Saskatchewan.

Both the prisoners and the guards regularly mentioned the hole, and I always had the idea the hole was a hole in the ground. I was soon to learn first-hand what the term meant.

We prepared the food for prisoners who'd been placed in the hole, and though the food was regular fare, no desserts or sweets were allowed on the trays, just meat and potatoes, and a prisoner couldn't smoke while undergoing punishment. But a "good con" always did what he could to make the stay in the hole easier on his comrades. One day, one of the kitchen workers added some tobacco, papers, and matches to the mashed potatoes. In a few minutes all the trays came back untouched. The kitchen steward was enraged that someone would attempt to smuggle something to someone in *his* food, and he wrote up the man who'd prepared the delivery. This caused the smuggler more than a little concern, because he only had a few days left to serve on his sentence and a charge would most probably result in his losing some of his "good time."

I was nominated as the one to cop out as the guilty party.

"Wayne, you're doing a year, and this is your first charge so they won't do anything to you," said Brian. Brian was a veteran of Regina Gaol, having served more than a couple of bits there. He was held in high esteem by all of us, solely for that reason.

"Yeah," said the smuggler, "they won't do a fuckin' thing to you—maybe a reprimand—besides, I'll do you a favour sometime."

He looked sincere and I could see it would be the right thing to do. I approached the steward and confessed to the institutional crime. The steward was tall and extremely skinny and bony, and his skin was so tight and white that he looked like a skeleton and, like a skeleton, I think it would have been impossible for him to smile. He was at the chopping block, cutting up chickens for the next meal. The meat cleaver cleanly split a chicken, and as he paused, his piercing eyes bore into mine.

"Bullshit," he said.

"No," I said, again, "I did it."

"Do you know somebody down in the hole?"

"No."

"Then why did you do it?"

"I just did it."

"Bullshit," he said again. Then he added, "But you are now charged." He went back to chopping chicken carcasses and I went back to the freezer area to tell my new friend he was off the hook.

The next day I was taken to the administrative area and placed on a bench while I waited for a caseworker to deal with my breach of the rules. I wasn't worried because I knew I would only suffer a reprimand.

Mr. McCllullen was a pleasant, kind-looking, red-faced man, who wore a blue suit, and he spoke quietly as he informally dealt with my case.

"So you put the tobacco in the potatoes?" he asked. He held a sheet of paper in his hand, which I thought probably had the charge written on it.

"Yes," I said, "I did."

"Why did you do it?"

"Well, I know how much I like to smoke."

"So it was a matter of doing unto someone else what you would have done unto you?"

"Yes," I replied. It did rather fit, I thought, because I was now doing what I was doing with the idea that it was the right thing.

"Have you been in trouble in here before?" he asked. He opened a file folder, but the way he held it did not allow me to see its contents.

"No."

"Well, in that case, I'm going to send you to the hole for three days," he stated.

"Oh."

"I would ordinarily put you there for at least five days, but this is your first time so I'm only giving you three," he said. It was as if the light in the room had suddenly shifted, and I was now seeing him more clearly—he was no longer the kind man I had thought he was.

"Three days?" I asked. Three days without a cigarette was a long time, but I knew my kitchen buddies would send me some tobacco. I only had to look in my potatoes.

"Yes, three days. Do you have any more questions?" he asked.

"No," I replied.

"I'm putting you in the death cells area," he said.

"Oh."

"That's where Louis Riel was held before they hanged him in the city," he stated, quietly.

"I know who he was..." I began, but he cut me off.

"They say his ghost is still there," he said, "but he probably won't hurt you."

"I know who Louis..." I began, but again he cut me off.

"Okay—we're done." He made a check mark on the paper, put it into the brown file folder and turned in his chair to open the cabinet behind him. While he was putting away the folder, I walked out the door to find a guard waiting for me.

The death cells were at the far end of the hallway of the hole behind a large green steel door, and we walked past a dozen cells, only four of them occupied. Nobody spoke to the guard and me, and we didn't speak to them.

There were three death cells, and they were larger than the ordinary ones on the range. The guard made me empty my pockets and he took my pouch of tobacco and my lighter. I was placed in the cell at the very end, and after closing the barred cell door, the guard walked away. I heard, rather than saw, the green door close and I was left in silence. As I stood there, I thought about the song Green Door, written by Marvin Moore, which my friend Donny used to play on his piano.

There's an eyeball peeping through a smokey cloud behind the green door, and when I said "Joe sent me" someone laughed out loud behind the green door...

We'd heard that the song had been written by a condemned man in a death house in the States, but we never could determine if that was true or not.

The cell appeared clean and there was such a strong odour of disinfectant permeating the air that it felt as if the lining of my nostrils were burning, but it didn't seem to bother the large number of flies buzzing about. I noticed there were no signs of graffiti on the walls. Unlike other cells in the jail, which had prisoner artwork and the odd magazine picture pasted to the walls, this cell was almost sterile. There was nothing else to do but walk, or as I'd heard other prisoners say, pace the floor. I could step six paces lengthwise across the floor, and four steps back and forth the other way, and as I developed a system of pacing, I remembered an obscure book I'd once read, called *Four Steps to the Wall.* Though I tried to count my steps in order to determine how far I would have walked if I was doing so in a straight line, I always lost count and had to begin all over again.

There were windows in the wall across the hallway, but they were opaque and I couldn't see through the glass. Later in the day I heard men exercising in the bullpen, but I couldn't see them so I didn't call out to them. My craving for a cigarette was strong, and I wished for my meal so I could dig one out of my potatoes.

I walked until I was tired and I lay on the floor and placed my head in the crook of my arm. Though the flies were numerous, crawling into my ears and nostrils, I still managed to doze off.

The sound of the green door opening woke me up. It was my meal. I was disheartened to see it was stew on my tray, with no potatoes at all. I ate almost everything, but I saved a small piece of meat and a gob of gravy to attract the flies. After the tray was picked up I took off my shirt and sat in a corner and watched while the flies gathered at my bait. When a cloud of them settled down to feast I would pounce on them, swinging my shirt like a club. The gravy stains didn't bother me—I knew they'd dry—and it became a game to see how many of the nasty little creatures I could kill with one blow. Of course my bait didn't last long; it was quickly pulverized, and when I tried to sleep the flies seemed more determined to make my life miserable, as if torturing me for doing away with some of their comrades.

I examined the cell from top to bottom, half hoping to find some sign that Louis Riel had occupied the cell. I had tried to explain to the man who had sentenced me to the hole that I knew who Louis Riel was, and what's more, that he wasn't a man to be feared by me or anyone else. My teachers in grade school had always given me the impression that he was just a teacher who tried to bring enlightenment into Saskatchewan and Manitoba. They may have identified with him because he had been a teacher. There was no sign of Riel, but I still felt a kinship with him. After all, he was an innocent man who was hanged for doing the right thing and I was an innocent man being punished for doing the right thing. Louis Riel may have lived in this very cell before being driven into the city to his death. The way I looked at it, if his ghost did appear in front of me, he would probably have said, "Be strong, young man, don't let them get you down."

The three days passed slowly and I found the nights were worse than the days. The bare one hundred watt light bulbs hanging high on the ceiling outside the cells were never turned out. And though I did my best, I don't think I made a dent in the fly population. Though I had more than a couple of meals of mashed potatoes, I never did find anything in them to help relieve my craving for nicotine.

In the normal course of our jobs, one of which was to bring in the boxes of bread from outside one of the main doors of the jail each evening, Bill and I would talk about our lives in the free world, and we began to trust each other.

The guard stationed in the main square would open the door with one of his many keys, and we would step outside and carry in the bread. One day we realized it would be a simple thing to just keep going, climb the one fence surrounding the property and run off into the dark of the night, leaving the bread for someone else to carry in. We talked about it the next day and decided we would do exactly that. We left that very night.

The fence didn't pose a problem for us; we were up and over it in a few seconds. Bill had been a cadet in the paratroopers and I had been climbing and jumping off trees all my life.

The run through the wheat fields was truly exhilarating, and though the jail guards made an attempt to follow us, at night it was impossible to stay on our trail for long. Whenever the lights of their vehicles came close, we moved at a right angle and soon lost them. Once we were off jail property their hot pursuit became cold and we left them driving in circles in their fields.

Bill and I lasted a week, and in that week we accumulated a large number of charges, from car theft, to breaking and entering, and theft. We were finally arrested by the RCMP following a high-speed chase during which we rolled a stolen 1958 Chev into a slough, while doing close to a hundred miles an hour. One minute we were flying down a country road and the next we'd run out of road and rolled the car attempting to make a right angle turn. Then the car was on its roof and Bill and I were breathing in swamp water.

Back in Regina Gaol we were placed in the death cells for security reasons, and together we killed flies. After one of our flurries of blows into our buzzing nemeses we decided we would start counting the dead.

"How many did you get?" Bill asked.

"Four I think, with at least four more badly wounded," I said.

"Not bad," he replied, "I think I got seven—all dead."

"Seven?"

"Yeah."

"Just like the story, Seven in One Blow?"

"Yeah," he laughed.

We also made an attempt to turn out the lights ourselves by using paper cups of cold water to shock the elements in the bulbs, but the lights didn't stay out long. The bulbs were quickly replaced by irate guards, and when we burned out the new ones, we were handcuffed with our backs to the bars, our hands so high above our heads that we were forced to stand on our toes for many hours. After the first night, we decided to leave the lightbulbs alone, devoting our energies instead to killing flies and talking about our lives in the free world. We did this for the next couple of weeks before we went to court, where another year was added to our sentences. It was then we were sent off to Prince Albert penitentiary.

The pay we received was small; we were able to look after our tobacco habits and once in a while buy food from the canteen. One payday a man named Fulstrum asked to borrow a jar of peanut butter. He was a miner from Flin Flon, Manitoba, and he looked as if he could haul sixteen tons without breaking a sweat. He was a large man, weighing in at two hundred thirty pounds, and he always seemed pleasant enough. However, the old adage to "neither a borrower nor a lender be" was not something I paid much attention to, so I lent him the peanut butter.

When two paydays came and went and I still hadn't received my due, I asked him to pay it back. He was leaning over the railing on the range above me, and instead of the quiet apology I expected, I received a clear rebuke.

"Fuck you, Carlson," he said belligerently. He glared at me as though daring me to say anything in response. I was never one to turn down a dare. Of course I was more than a little afraid of him, but I remember what one of my school-teachers, a man named Armstrong, had told me about bravery; a man can't be brave unless he's afraid—having courage is having the ability to overcome fear, and an act of bravery follows. So I dug deep.

"Pay me, you fuckin' asshole," I replied. I could see the shock on his face; after all, he outweighed me by close to a hundred pounds.

"I'll fuckin' come down there," he threatened. He straightened from a slouch to his full height, and lifted a leg onto the rail as though making a move to jump, but he paused to glare at me, as if to intimidate me into folding.

"If you come down here, bring my fuckin' peanut butter with you or I'll kick your ass," I said. Again I could see the shock and dismay in his face. He never expected to be called out. He climbed over the range and hung by his fingertips for a moment, just long enough for me to step forward and deliver a left hook into his exposed belly, which was soft and flabby. The blow didn't even slow him down.

He wheeled around and charged me like an angry bull, and if he hadn't wrapped his arms around me and literally lifted me off my feet, I would've been trampled and stamped into the concrete floor like a bug. He threw me high against the wall and when I landed, it was against the radiator. I was on my feet in an instant, unhurt. He tried to hit me, but I was a lot lighter and a lot faster, so I caught him with a couple of punches. It didn't faze him at all.

Suddenly there were two guards between us, and it wasn't until they were present and the adrenalin had slowed, that I heard a number of voices encouraging me to lay a beating on him.

"Both of you—into the dome," commanded one of the guards. We walked with them to where the Keeper waited for our arrival. The guards had seen everything.

"What's the fight about?" asked Wilson, the main man in charge of the dome, and that part of the prison. Fulstrum responded before I could say a word.

"He started it—he got me mad—I had to do..." His voice was whiny, and he sounded like a boy caught doing something wrong in the schoolyard. Wilson cut him off.

"What about you?" he asked me.

"What about me?" I replied.

"Is the fight over?"

"I wasn't fighting," I said. He looked at me, and I could see a small smile attempting to break through on his face.

"No? Then what was all that about?" He pointed with his hand to the range where the scuffle had taken place.

"Well, I think I made a fool of myself," I said.

"Okay, is it over?" he asked.

"Yeah," I responded, "it's over." He turned to Fulstrum.

"Is it over?" Wilson asked him. Fulstrum hung his head and began making excuses for his behaviour. Wilson cut him off.

"Look—either it's over or you're both going to the hole." Fulstrum finally realized the point of all this.

"Oh, yeah, it's over," he said.

"All right, get back to your cells," commanded Wilson.

We both walked away, but Fulstum had stairs to climb and I waited for him to arrive at his cell door above me. When he did I said, "I want my fuckin' peanut butter." Fulstrum paused to look at me before he entered his cell, but there was no longer any attempt at intimidation in the glance. I went to work in the afternoon, and when I returned there was a jar of peanut butter in front of my door.

The fight with Fulstrum had not gone unnoticed by others. Through that incident I came in contact with two men, Don Kolot and Roy Holland, and shortly after I met them, they escaped from the penitentiary and headed south. They were both to figure in my life at a later time.

Fight cards were held every so often. They were special events attended by the local radio station, who broadcast the fights to the surrounding community on a live feed. The first fight night I attended there were several fights I watched with interest. One was Fulstrum fighting a large native man by the name of Henry Blyne. Blyne looked like a fighter and walked like a fighter, and he was one tough prisoner. Another was a fight featuring Clifford "Bobo" Olson, a man who would go on to become Canada's most infamous serial killer. Olson was my age and we had met and talked on several occasions. The fighters would usually train for at least three months; however, Fulstrum had apparently decided that because he had his own system of fighting, he didn't need to train. I was sitting ringside when he went up against Henry and it was with more than a little satisfaction that I watched him get knocked out in the first round.

Fulstrum seemed to think he could bowl Henry over, much as he'd done to me on the range. When he charged like a bull, Henry smoked two body shots into him. I could hear—and almost feel—the wind exploding from Fulstrum's lungs, and when Fulstrum's hands dropped, a left hook and a straight right hand stretched him out on the canvas.

In the evening, we younger prisoners would spar with each other. Some of us were in excellent physical shape, and there were more than a few good trainers around. Some of the men went on to fight once they were released. One of these was Ronnie Westadt, a man who would become a long-standing friend.

While we were on the fish range, we'd been cautioned not to accept gratuities from anyone, because "accepting candy from strangers" placed young men at the mercy of the prison "beasts." Beasts were men who would manipulate younger men for sexual favours. I wasn't in the prison long when it happened to me.

I walked into my cell one afternoon to find a small bag of goodies on my desk. In the bag was gum and candy, and a package of tobacco. There was no note, and no indication who had placed it there. Initially I thought it might be

Bill, my partner, trying to play a joke on me but he denied it and he had no reason to lie. Over the next few weeks it became a regular occurrence. I felt I was being watched, I felt threatened and it puzzled and frightened me. I asked some people I knew to watch my cell, but it did no good; the goodies kept coming and I was none the wiser about the identity of my benefactor. I finally talked to one of the older convicts who suggested I set up whoever was doing it by writing a note and leaving it on my desk. I wrote a note, thanking the man for the treats and the kindness, and I added that I would like to meet him. I left the note on my desk in the same place he had placed the little brown bags. I couldn't help but think it was like being involved in a spy game of sorts.

That day I returned to find another bag of goodies. My note had been taken, and in the bag was another note. When I read it, the message chilled me to the bone. *I believe you could be my son,* it said, *but of course we would have to get your mother to confirm this. I will leave you another message behind the sink in the mop room on A range tomorrow.* The note was unsigned. I showed Bill the message and he pledged to help me deal with the problem.

The note in the mop room gave me instructions on how to meet the author the next day. The meeting was at two in the afternoon in the shop dome, an older building in the prison set apart from the cellblock building. We had to get prepared to do whatever we had to do. We made some discreet inquiries and in a matter of hours we had two very sharp knives in our hands. I didn't sleep well that night, and though some of the veterans told me that stabbing a man was like slicing through butter, the last thing I wanted to do was knife another man.

The next day Bill and I walked into the old dome and closed the door, and while Bill hung back in the hallway out of sight, I walked around the corner to confront the man who was harassing me. He stepped out from under a stairwell with a smile on his face.

He wore a brown, custom-made cap with a short brim and he was dressed in "tailored" clothes. The veteran prisoners had a buddy system whereby their clothes would not only be carefully washed and pressed, but tailored to fit as well. I had seen the guy around the main dome from time to time, but never paid much attention to him. He was a craggy-faced man in his late forties or early fifties, one of those silent men who would look away whenever another man looked at him, but the way he was dressed indicated he had at least some respect from his fellow prisoners. I stopped when I saw him—and the expression on my face brought him to a halt.

"You stay the fuck away from my cell," I said menacingly. He showed his tobacco-stained teeth in a grimace which passed for a grin, and took a step toward me.

"You stay the fuck away," I said again. I pulled my knife from under my shirt-tail, and he halted. I was conscious of the quiet in the large steel and concrete dome, and I could smell the disinfectant which I'd come to identify as the odour of prison.

"I see you brought your friend with you," he muttered. He had his hand in his jacket pocket, and the menace in his voice made me grateful for Bill's presence. I didn't have to look around, because the man had told me Bill had made his presence known.

"Yeah, I did," I acknowledged, "he's my partner and he backs me up." The note-writer just stood there, grinning, and it was one of the most frightening, disconcerting experiences I'd ever had.

"Leave him alone," said Bill. His voice was quiet, but there was an intensity and a strength in it that couldn't have been mistaken. Not even by a grinning fool.

Bill and I backed up and walked out of the dome. As we headed back into the main building, he and I discussed what we'd do if the man came after us. He never did, and I never had further problems with him, but I did learn something about him. He had more than ten years in on a life sentence for killing a young woman on a train in Saskatchewan. He'd just been released from Prince Albert penitentiary, and while he was travelling to Winnipeg, he'd raped and murdered her and thrown her body from the train. He was a very dangerous man. Bill and I were dangerous too, although not in the same way.

Many men had pictures of their families on their desks or on their tack boards, but I had none. My family considered me too much of an embarrassment. It was as if I had no family. I didn't discuss my family life with any of the men in the penitentiary. I did once get a letter from my mother and I was ashamed of it because she had signed it "sincerely," and not "with love." I ripped up the letter and flushed it down the toilet because I didn't want anybody to know that not even my own mother really cared for me.

The Christmas concert was only weeks away and I sat in the gym and watched some of the rehearsals. The only guests in the audience were the guards, their wives and their families, and even then there were restrictions on the age of the people allowed to attend, and there were dress restrictions for the women. It was believed the prisoners might not be able to control themselves if they saw a woman's knees or more than a little bare skin. Prisoners' wives and families were not allowed to attend and it struck me as strange that so many men would get so caught up in performing for their keepers. Why would they do it?

Fyodor Dostoevsky asked that question through the central character in his book, *The House of the Dead*, which was set in Siberia a hundred years earlier. Not only would the prisoners dress in rags, charcoal their faces, and perform for the men who made their lives miserable throughout the year, the prisoners would flush redly with pleasure when they were applauded. I could see the same thing in the men around me. Through literature I discovered that the reality of prisons and the people in them have changed little over the course of history. It doesn't matter what country the prison is in, or what language the prisoners speak, or how serious the punishment might be; human beings are emotionally similar and they experience their lot in life in a similar fashion. As well, the conversations taking place around me indicated further that men in prison all saw their keepers in a similar light. "He's firm but fair," and, "At least we know where we stand with him," were comments made by prisoners about particular guards in Siberia. Those same ideas were expressed in the cellblocks in the prison of Prince Albert penitentiary a hundred years later. It gave me reason to pause, but I would quickly turn my attention to my own survival during the day, and leave any superficial philosophizing to the nights when I was alone, after the cell doors slammed shut.

There were no television sets or radios in our cells, and reading was the one thing most prisoners had in common with each other. I was in the library one afternoon, borrowing a book for a late-night read, when the librarian suggested to me that he could judge a man by the quality of his reading.

"Take old Jim for example," he said.

"What about him?"

"I can take a look at his library card and tell you every book he's borrowed in the last two years, and he reads a great deal." Jim never wore a shirt or jacket, only an underwear top that he rolled up from the bottom to expose his huge, sagging belly, and the waist of his pants hung almost to his knees. We thought Jim was more than just a little bit crazy.

"So what does he read?" I asked curiously. We were standing at the counter in the small library, and we were the only two people there at the time.

"The classics," he replied. He reached into a drawer, searched through the stack of cards in a box, and pulled one out and he began to read some of the titles. I had seen those titles in other books I'd read. It gave me food for thought; Jim looked anything but intelligent. It also made me realize that the penitentiary system could have good insight into the character of a man, if they used all of the information from the different areas of the prison.

It didn't take me long to have a run-in with authority which ended with me serving my first sentence in the Prince Albert Penitentiary hole. One afternoon I was going to work when the guard with the door key gave me a bad time.

He was a young, tall, skinny man with a pot-belly who had developed a certain gait when he walked. His uniform cap was pushed back on his head, his shoulders were back as if to help make his bony chest appear more broad and full, and his unusually large belly was pushed forward. From time to time the large brass keys on his belt would jingle almost musically when he walked.

"Where are you going?" he asked me. His hand had paused so the nose of the key was poised at the chamber of the lock.

"To work," I replied.

"Where's your pass?" he asked.

"Here," I said, and I held up the small, white movement pass so he could read it.

"The pass isn't dated," he said.

"Well my shop boss told me this pass would get me back to work," I offered.

"Well, you tell your shop boss that this pass has to be dated." He held the key no closer than a quarter of an inch from the lock of the door.

"Are you going to open the door?" I asked, impatiently.

"Maybe, maybe not—I don't like your attitude."

"Well I don't like yours either," I said, "you're acting like an asshole."

"You're calling me an asshole?"

"Yeah, I'm calling you an asshole," I replied, "because you're talking like an asshole and you're acting like an asshole." The key suddenly dove into the lock and with a twist he opened the door.

"You're on charge," he said.

"What for?"

"For disrespect to an officer," he replied. He seemed quite pleased.

"I don't see any officers around here," I replied. "There's just you— an asshole in a uniform—and me." I walked through the door, knowing I would soon be in the hole.

My appearance in Warden's Court was brief. The warden read out the charge.

"How do you plead?" he asked. He was sitting at his desk with the Union Jack draped across the wall behind him, and I was flanked by two uniformed guards.

"Yes," I readily admitted, "I called him an asshole."

"Why?" he asked.

"Because he was acting like an asshole."

"My guards do not act like assholes; they're just doing their job," he said, gruffly.

"Yeah."

"If you apologize to him it'll go easier on you," he offered.

"If I apologize, it means he wasn't acting like an asshole, so I can't do it."

"Three nights hard bed in disassociation, Number One diet," he stated, rendering his judgement and handing down his sentence. I was whisked out of his office and taken directly to the hole.

There were differences between the prison hole and the hole in the provincial jail. The first thing I discovered was that there were two diets: Number One, and Number Two. Number One diet, the one I was sentenced to, consisted of four slices of bread and a cup of warm water for breakfast, a scoop of unseasoned mush for lunch, and a repeat of the bread and water for supper. There was also a stipulation that the prisoner sleep on a "hard bed." A hard bed was a plank seated in a bed of concrete, with a horse-hair blanket for a cover.

There was no smoking in the hole, but federal prisoners had a smuggling system that worked well. Library magazines were encased in a heavy cardboard binding which, when carefully hollowed out, would hold an ample amount of tobacco, rolling papers, and flints. We used a dangerous but effective method to light the cloth to make punk to light our cigarettes.

A light bulb hung from the high ceiling in each cell, and if a prisoner climbed his bars, he could remove the bulb. The tricky part was to jam his metal fork, with toilet paper wound through the tines, into the exposed light socket without electrocuting himself. The fork would short-out the wiring, creating a surge of power that would light the toilet paper. We would use a magazine rolled around the steel bar and another around the fork handle to act as insulators to protect ourselves. Once the paper caught fire, we would light the cloth and make our punk. The only drawback was that the method would blow the breaker, but the breaker would be reset the next time the guard came by on his security walk and all would be well once again. There would be times when guards would curse the electrical system, and I was never sure if the guards knew what we prisoners were doing and ignored it, or if they actually believed it was the age and natural deterioration of the electrical system that was the root of the problem.

During my first bit in the hole I learned about sharing in the prison system. The scarcity of food brought it home.

Whenever a man was sentenced to more than seven days of bread and water, it was legally and medically required that the prison feed the prisoner one day of full meals. When a man received a meal, he almost always shared his fare with the prisoners on bread and water. A lottery system was in place: each man would guess a number between one and ten, and the winner would receive a portion of the meat. The bread, and the vegetables would then be divided among the rest of the hungry prisoners. We would save our slices of bread and the man with the meal would make sandwiches from whatever happened to be on the tray. I learned how to appreciate a carrot, a potato, a pea, or just a gravy sandwich. After days of bread and water, anything at all between the slices of bread became very tasty indeed. It was through these initial experiences that I became jail-wise myself, and it was through meeting good men whom society had condemned as unfit to remain in the community, but who, though hungry, would unhesitatingly share their food, that I adapted to a life of crime.

I managed to survive my prison sentence without being stabbed, piped, beaten up, or in any other way seriously hurt. When my release date came, I had a head full of knowledge of crime and criminals, but in the free world I was just as naive as the day I was arrested. When I walked out the prison gate I was just another young criminal at the end of one sentence, looking for a way to get into the next one.

I went home to my family, to my mother and father, to my sisters and my brother—but I was different now. I saw the world and people differently, and the world as I once knew it, would never be the same again. It was May, 1962. I'd served nearly two years and I was not yet twenty years old.

My family decided that I should travel to British Columbia where relatives would assist me in landing a job, and I arrived in Quesnel in late May. The day following my arrival, I was downtown when I happened to see Kenny, a man I knew from my hometown. He'd lived at my house for a few months years before.

Kenny was with two other men and all three were job-hunting, so we hooked up immediately and later the same day we were in Williams Lake. We stopped at a supermarket to buy some food, and Kenny went with me into the store. On our way out he was stopped by the manager, searched, and a $2.05 can of ham was produced. It was not on the receipt. Ken was asked to re-enter the store where the matter could be "straightened out." I went with him, believing that I could pay for the ham, he would be released, and we would be on our way. It was not to be.

The RCMP officer questioned the store owner's wife, who explained how Ken had put the ham in his jacket, and the officer then turned his attention to me.

"Who are you?" he asked me. He was young and very focussed.

"My name is Wayne Carlson," I replied.

"Did you have anything to do with this?"

"No," I said. Then the owner's wife spoke up.

"He was with him," she said. We were all standing inside the front door of the store and I began to have a bad feeling in my stomach.

"You were with him?" the cop asked me.

"Yes, but I paid for my food."

"Do you have a receipt?"

"Yes," I replied, and I produced it. He glanced at it and turned to the woman again.

"He was with him?" he asked.

"Yes, they walked in together and they left together," she said. I didn't like the way she was looking at me.

"You're going to have to come to the police station with us," stated the cop. I began to protest but he said it would all be straightened out once we got there.

Our two friends followed us in their car. Upon our arrival Kenny was charged for the theft of the ham, and after a criminal record check on me, I was jointly charged with him. Ken assured me he would testify on my behalf, but the other prisoners in the holding cells seemed to have some insight into what was about to take place in our lives.

"Have you got a record?" one asked me.

"Yeah, I just got out of the penitentiary in Saskatchewan," I answered.

"You're fucked," he said.

"What do you mean? I didn't do anything."

He laughed, then went on to explain, "If you have a record, you're going down in this town. It's just the way it is. They have a charge, you'll be convicted."

There was a small hole chipped out of the wall. Prisoners would put their ear to the hole and listen to the conversations unfolding in the room next door, which served as both witness interview room and courtroom. When it came time for my case to be heard, my ear was pressed against the wall and I listened with bated breath.

Kenny pleaded guilty and was immediately sentenced to thirty days in jail, and though I heard Ken make an attempt to exonerate me, he was cut off in mid-sentence, removed from the courtroom, and returned to the holding cells. As he walked through the door, he told me that the woman who ran the store was in the hallway. I immediately pressed my ear to the hole and listened. I heard a man's voice.

"You know the man in the red school jacket?"

"Yes," the woman replied.

"Did he steal an item from your store?"

"He was with the man who did."

"Did he steal an item?"

"Well he must have known his friend was stealing."

"Well, he's the one we're interested in. He was just released from the penitentiary."

"Oh, I see..."

"Did he put the ham into the man's coat?"

"Yes, I think he did," she replied, tentatively.

"You have to be sure. If he did he's guilty of theft," he stated.

"Yes, he did," she said.

"You have to be sure..."

"I'm sure."

"Fine, you just have to tell the judge he did."

"Okay."

I pleaded not guilty. The woman was the only witness called by the crown, and Kenny was mine. When I tried to explain to the judge what had taken place between the crown and his star witness, I was rebuked for casting aspersions on a good woman of the community. I was sentenced to four months in Okalla prison farm in Burnaby, British Columbia.

Following an induction in Okalla, Kenny was sent to Westgate to serve his thirty-day sentence, and because I had a criminal record, I was sent to the East Wing. The East Wing was the cellblock area where seasoned criminals were held. Almost all of them were dope fiends.

I was assigned to the kitchen. Over a two-week period I became acquainted with the jail-wise prisoners. One of these was a man called Guy, whom I'd met in the penitentiary, and because he knew me, it wasn't long before word got around that I was "okay." If any prisoner heard that another prisoner was okay, it meant he could be trusted, at least with the general, everyday skullduggery that went on inside the prison. One day Guy told me about charges he had waiting for him once he was released, and he was looking to escape. I asked him how he knew he had charges waiting for him, and he explained he had a friend who could check things out in the record department. I asked him to check for me. I hadn't committed any crime—but I hadn't stolen the ham and I was in prison for it. Could they charge me with something else? It took two days for Guy to check it out.

"Wayne, you have a D&H on file," he said. A D&H was a Dress and Hold, which meant the police would arrest a prisoner the day he was to be released following completion of a sentence. We were in the kitchen, sitting at the table having a cup of coffee and a cigarette.

"Are you sure?" I asked. He became impatient with me.

"You asked me to check it out, that's what I did, and that's what I was told," he said. I believed him, and I resolved to escape.

Dope fiends on the west coast were different from the men I'd met in the penitentiary; they were more polished in language and appearance, and many of them believed that if heroin was legalized they wouldn't be in jail. The professional criminals I'd met in the penitentiary expressed their belief that west coast dope fiends were not to be trusted. They'd give up their partners and provide information to the police if they were put to the test; it was believed that an addiction to narcotics would ruin any man and bring ruin to the people around him. On one occasion I had found a syringe, or "rig" or "outfit," in the flour bin, and I mentioned it to a man named Emmet. It was my first encounter with him, and because I'd come to him first he was complimented. He told me to leave it alone, that it belonged to Alex, and if I ever came across others—and there were many more stashed around the kitchen—I was to leave them where I found them. Days later, I was having a cigarette in the kitchen with Emmet and he gave me more advice.

"See that guy over there?" he said. He didn't point or in any physical way indicate who he was talking about, and there were a dozen men working on the kitchen floor. But there was one man who worked as a baker and he was busy at one of the bread mixers. I knew his name but nothing else about him.

"You mean Pete?"

"Yeah, Coca Cola Pete—stay away from him," Emmet replied. Pete was a man in his late thirties or early forties, of average height with greying hair which gave him a distinguished appearance.

"What's he all about?"

"Did you know Joe Gordon?" he asked.

"No," I said, "I didn't. Who is he?"

"Was," he answered. "He's dead—Joe Gordon was hanged here not that long ago."

"Yeah?" When people talk in prison, the events described may sound current and present-day, but they could have happened ten or even twenty years ago; in prison men have long memories and scandal is never forgotten.

"Yeah. Joe was a nice guy—well respected. He was sentenced to death for killing a man in a fight in Vancouver. He was just a rounder and dope fiend and he should never have been hanged; it was a manslaughter beef, at best."

"Yeah?"

"Some of the guys on the street got together and decided they'd help Joe out and send him in a couple of caps of pure stuff."

"So he could top himself?"

"Yeah, so he could beat the hangman. Pete was working here in the kitchen and he ended up with the two caps. He was supposed to stash them in Joe's food."

"Supposed to?"

"Yeah, *supposed to*," he said. His voice was now full of hatred for the man working across the kitchen floor, and I could feel my revulsion for Pete begin to grow as if it were flowing from Emmet into me.

"He didn't send it to him?"

"No—he fixed it himself over a period of time, and there are men here, who were here when the trap door sprung and dropped Joe down the elevator shaft."

"Elevator shaft?"

"Yeah, the elevator shaft in the West Wing was used for the gallows. They'd haul the man up and drop the floor out from under him," he explained. I felt a chill go through me.

"Just like that?" I asked.

"Yeah, that simple. We could hear the trap door slam as he dropped," he said. Emmet's face mirrored his hatred for Coca Cola.

"But nobody does anything about it?" I asked.

"No," he replied, "nobody does anything about it." I wondered why Emmet himself didn't do something about Pete; it would be some time before I realized that most men expect someone else to do something about a problem.

The summer days were beautiful and the gorgeous weather brought home to me all that I was missing in the world. I was still looking for a way out when one was provided. It was an event that seemed unconnected to anything like escape; it sprung from a water fight in the kitchen. One minute we were having a grand old time spraying each other with water hoses, and next thing we were fired and placed on an outside work gang called Gang Two.

Gang Two was a maximum security work crew of nine prisoners, guarded by two riflemen armed with 30:30 carbines, and a gang boss with a .38 pistol on his hip. We had the responsibility of chipping out chunks of clay with pickaxes from a hillside, loading the clay into wheelbarrows and hauling it to a gully, where we would dump it in order to make a road. The gully was thirty feet deep and a couple of hundred yards wide. It would take thousands of loads of clay to fill it. Although it seemed like an insurmountable task, it could be done over a long period—we just didn't want to be the ones doing it.

There was a high fence surrounding the jail property and we worked a hundred yards from it. If we could get to the fence and over it, we had acres of woods for cover. The Burnaby community surrounded the jail so once we made it through the woods, we could lose our pursuers in a residential area. Over the next few days we laid our plans. There were five of us who wanted to take the risk.

Guy and his French Canadian partner were working on top of the hill of clay while three of us were working at the bottom. Our signal was this: Guy would ask me an innocent-sounding question, which would be his way of indicating the view from the top looked good and it was time to make the move.

"Did you hear the news last night?" he said. If I responded I hadn't, we wouldn't move. However, if I said I had, we'd all run into the tall swamp grass and make for the fence.

"Yes," I said, "I did." Five of us made a mad dash for the bottom of the gully.

The riflemen opened up and I could hear the sound of the bullets whipping through the grass around me. I threw myself headlong into a creek bed, and by using the creek's banks for cover, three of us found ourselves looking at a small fence which we would have to get through to reach the larger one. The problem was there was a six-foot opening in the grass and we would have to get across that without being shot.

"You go first," suggested Bobby. He didn't realize that as soon as I dashed across the opening, the gunmen on the hill would be moving the muzzles of their weapons to that very spot. A number of shots rang out, and I heard the Frenchman yelling.

"Arrêt! Arrêt! Ils vont tous nous tuer! Ils vont tous nous tuer!" But I ignored his warning and made my move.

Though the rocks in the creek bed were slippery, I was able to get across before the rifles opened up. When Bobby and Keith crossed the open spot it was different. The rifles were now trained on that very spot and a flurry of shots rang out, scattering pieces of rock and shale into the grass, and they stopped. I kept going but I had only gone a short distance when the flat sound of a pistol shot sent a rock flying in front of me. I paused to turn and see where it came from and found myself looking down the muzzle of the gang boss's pistol. It's one thing to run while being shot at, but quite another to run when you can see the barrel of the gun trembling in the hand of a man six feet away, whose eyes are burning with the fire of excitement and adrenalin. I stopped.

I learned later that the reason the Frenchman had yelled they were going to kill us all was that he'd been shot in the back with a 30:30 bullet. The slug had gone right through him and he was in bad shape. We were all captured and taken to the hole, while the Frenchman was later taken to the Burnaby hospital. He survived, but when I saw him months later, he'd lost fifty pounds and there was little fire left in his eyes. For a long time after our escape bid the prisoners referred to the gully and clay mound as Pork Chop Hill, the site of a battle in Korea, and they'd sing a song whenever the boss of Gang Two walked by. The guard's name was Howard, and they sang... "that dirty little coward, by the name of Mr. Howard, who laid those prisoners in their graves."

In Okalla the hole was not called the hole. It was officially called the Elementary Training Unit and its name was a joke to all prisoners, especially the ones who served time in it.

I found myself lying on the cold cement floor in a black cell under the cow barn in a part of the prison no one in authority would publicly admit existed.

The cell had no light fixtures and its only furnishings were a plastic toilet bucket and a roll of toilet paper that doubled as a pillow on the floor. The interior of the cell was almost pitch black. The human conditions were even darker, and the door was a rusting but solid steel whose only opening was a food slot at floor level. The door's construction did not allow any light to filter through the cracks, and the cell walls were painted with only the grunge and grime and odours of time.

I'd been there for ten days when I met a fellow prisoner across the hall named Bill, and I thought of him as "the fighter." He was a rectangular man with square shoulders and large square hands. He was serving a thirty-day sentence for pushing a police officer who had issued him a ticket for jaywalking in downtown Vancouver. He was in the hole because he absolutely refused to work or do anything the jail guards asked him to do.

The position of our cells allowed us to see each other. The fighter's forty-year-old face needed a shave, so he looked tough and mean. His blue eyes always looked directly into the eyes of any man he spoke to. Although many thought him taciturn, once you came to know him, he was a well-spoken man. I found myself identifying with him because he was in jail for jaywalking, and I was in jail for a wrongful conviction of stealing a two dollar can of ham.

My formal introduction to him came when two other men, one on my side of the hallway, and the other on Bill's, were fishing a lighter flint across the floor on a blanket string. The flint had become dislodged from its tie, and it was now lost somewhere in the no man's land of the hallway. Fishing was a practice and an art I'd learned while in the penitentiary. It consisted of sending a thread stripped from your clothing and weighted at one end for casting, from one cell to another. We would fish for the only two commodities we had to share: bread, which though scarce, was legal, and smoking paraphernalia, which was not only scarce, but strictly forbidden. Possession of tobacco or anything associated with smoking was a punishable offence.

The flint had been tied into a small package at the end of the fish line and it was being towed over the floor from one cell to another when disaster struck. The package had opened and the flint was lost somewhere in the desert-like expanse of floor between Bill's cell and mine. Bill was in a lighted cell: unlike mine, his had an open-barred door which allowed the light of the low-wattage light bulb hanging bare in the hallway to filter into it. When we heard of the dilemma, I stretched out on my belly and put one eye to the food slot. I could see Bill, but Bill could see only one of my eyes and a slice of my face at a time.

A flint was a precious thing in that part of the prison; it ensured a light for a smuggled cigarette when we were able to get our hands on one. Most of the men who came through that area had a nicotine habit, and a great deal of their energy was devoted to schemes to satisfy the craving they lived with each day. Searching for the flint was like a search for gold, or a diamond.

With my cheek on the floor, I looked at my neighbour through the slot. Bill was on his feet, face pressed against the bars, and eyes bright with intensity.

"Bill," I said, calling his name quietly because the guards were in their office and we didn't want to alert them.

"Yeah?" He looked across the hall and I could see Bill focus on the food slot and my one visible eye.

"Can you see anything from there?" I asked. The position I lay in made examination of the floor very difficult, but Bill had a clear view.

"I'll take the left side, my left, and you take the right," said Bill, and he got down on all fours.

"Okay."

"The terrain is rough," ventured Bill.

"Yes," I agreed, "it is." We said nothing more to each other, and simply went on an intense visual search of the floor. There were old paint chips which could trick the eye into thinking it had spied the hunted object. Finally, after more than ten minutes of careful, inch-by-inch inspection, Bill found something.

"What about that small piece of foreign-looking material to my left?" he asked. His deep voice rolled like a boulder across the floor to my ear. I twisted my body to peer in the direction he indicated, and I suddenly made out what he had found. We discussed it first, briefly, which brought some excited encouragement from the two fishermen who'd lost it. We decided we'd attempt to fish it in. We used a thread which Bill had stashed in a crack in the cement, and after he threw one end of the string to me, we tied a piece of cloth in the middle of the string and pulled it back and forth until it caught the object and held it. Bill soon had the treasure in his hand, which he held aloft between a thumb and forefinger, brandishing it triumphantly like a trophy.

"We got it!" he said with a grin. He used the thread to pass the flint to the man it was originally meant for. Everyone was pleased. The find was no small accomplishment, for the flint would ignite the punk made from a piece of cloth, which in turn would light a cigarette. A strip of cloth would be lighted—cotton proved to be the best fabric—and then blown out at the height of its flame. The result was saved to be re-lit with the spark from a scratched flint. The burnt cloth made a fine tinder, requiring only the slightest spark to ignite it. The search for the flint stone was our own small quest for fire in a dark and dismal world.

From that moment on, Bill and I spent hours talking to each other. Our conversations usually consisted of me asking questions, and Bill answering by telling an interesting story. During one such session Bill told of his prize-fighting days in British Columbia. He had fought in many small towns, answering any challenge for a price. He was from the old school of bare-knuckled fighters; his face and hands showed the scars of the bouts he'd fought, and one of his ears had been cauliflowered.

It was one of my life lessons that a man who lived such a hard, difficult life, could still have respect for life and people. Yet to others Bill was probably just a bum, albeit a tough bum, just one of the faceless flotsam that can be found in every city in any country in the world.

Addiction to nicotine created a desperate situation for all of us, and the constant search for ways to obtain tobacco could even take the form of self-mutilation with a razor blade. The cuts had to be deep and serious enough to warrant being taken from the hole to the hospital, where a man had at least the opportunity of getting his hands on some tobacco. I could always tell when a man who'd slashed his veins had found at least one cigarette for his painful efforts; he was calmer, more relaxed, and there seemed to be a sense of peace in him when he returned to the hole in a bandaged state. On one occasion a man by the name of George Gallashon cut himself so deeply his slashed arms were pumping blood all over his cell and into the hallways. He just stuck his arms out and let the blood flow so the guards could see it. A short time later he was removed to hospital. George was in the hole for chewing gum, but he claimed he hadn't been chewing gum at all. He worked as a cleaner on one of the cell ranges in the jail, and he was pretending to chew gum to irritate a guard everyone called Shaker Baker. Baker was his surname and he picked up the name Shaker because he was always shaking down the addicts, looking for needles and drugs. I had come across him briefly when I worked in the kitchen. One day I'd heard a prisoner berate Baker with a string of profanity that would have put the most foulmouthed man to shame.

"Oh yes, I am that," he said, calmly. "Oh yes, I'm every bit of that…" I wondered how any man could've withstood such a barrage of verbal abuse and still remain calm, cool, and rational.

George had been mopping the floor when he saw Baker appear on the range. He started working his jaws as if he were chewing gum. When Baker called on him to spit it out, George pretended to swallow it. Baker charged him with possession of a piece of gum, and when George went to court he tried to explain it was all just a jailhouse joke. The judge didn't believe him and sentenced him to the standard indefinite period in the Elementary Training Unit. The rule governing a prisoner's stay in the hole was a simple one: the man stayed in the hole until he asked for a pen and a piece of paper, and wrote out what the prisoners called a "crumb letter." A crumb letter was a note written by a repentant prisoner to the prison administration, asking for mercy. George was not the kind of man to write out a crumb letter; besides, he could neither read nor write.

When George was returned to the hole from the hospital, his arms were bandaged so tightly he couldn't bend them at the elbows, so they hung stiffly at his sides. He was standing in my food-slot field of vision, surrounded by four guards, while he waited for the man with the key to open his cell door. I heard one of them say something insulting to him, and when he responded to the insult with a curse, he was kicked in the groin so hard he lost consciousness. Then they opened the cell, dragged him inside, closed the door and walked away. I was horrified by their actions, but like everyone else, I never said a word. Though fear has a way of clamping down a young man's tongue, I felt guilty and ashamed for not speaking out.

The smell of blood was commonplace. It was dampened by the rank smell of feces and acrid urine from the open toilet buckets. Whenever a particularly abusive guard received the swooshing contents of toilet bucket over his body, which was often, the stench was overpowering and the foulness lingered in the air for days.

There was a guard who used to give the prisoners in the hole a bad time, but he really couldn't get to me because I was already in the black cell, and he had no occasion or reason to talk to me. One day he managed to find a way to do so. It started innocently enough with a loud bang on my door.

"Carlson!" I recognized his voice. He was an average-looking man in good shape, and he wore steel-rimed glasses. One of the prisoners in the hole had told me he was an ex-cop out of Vancouver, and he was working in the jail because he had abused his police powers.

"Yeah?" I replied.

"You're going to West Wing," said the voice.

"Okay," I answered. Excitement coursed through me like rushing water down a gully. I rose to my feet and began pacing, and I walked for hours. Each time I heard the jingle of keys my heart was in my throat, thinking they'd finally come to cut me loose. I had no way to keep track of time except for the meagre meal of bread and pea soup we were given each day. By the time it arrived, I knew the shift had changed and it was late afternoon. Long past the soup and bread I asked the guard on his punch round when I would be escorted back to the main prison. He laughed.

"Carlson, you're not going anywhere," he said before he walked away. I felt anger and hatred for the man who had put me through the emotional roller coaster ride. The next morning he was the one to open my cell door and I did the only thing I could think of at the time to express my hatred for him.

The price paid for throwing the toilet bucket was an instant, brutal beating, followed by removal to the hole in the "old jail." The old jail was a wooden structure, no longer used, but which held a cell in the bowels of its basement. The floor of the cell was bare earth and it had a damp, fetid, musty odour which I became used to over a period of time. The time of day could not be accurately told, but bread and tea spoke of lunch hour, and split-pea soup and four slices of dry bread for supper told that another day had finally passed. The Stockholm Syndrome hadn't been named at that time, but the more mean-spirited guards understood that they could treat a man horribly for days on end, and then ease the prisoner's hatred by throwing a lit cigarette into the black interior of the cell. No matter how hard I fought to hang onto my self-preserving animosity, the gratitude which flowed through my veins became a powerful force that blended with the nicotine as I inhaled my first drag. Many a prisoner hated himself for it, yet each and every time we would reach over in the darkness and pick up the small glowing torch which kept our addiction alive.

There were rats in the old hole that could not be seen because of the pitch-black interior. But a man soon learned that if he shared his bread, and did not make any sudden moves when he woke startled from sleep, the scurrying and sometimes vocal rodents would not bother him. Sleep always came easier when I rested in the knowledge that my unwanted four-legged comrades had something to snack on while I dozed fitfully. At least one of the four slices of bread at each meal paid for that simple, but necessary, psychological assurance. There was a respectful and mutual fear in our peaceful coexistence. Many a man had a haunted look in his eyes after experiencing time spent with the permanent furry residents of the pit, and I was no different I'm sure.

One week later I was back in the hole in the ETU, none the worse for wear, but still feeling emotionally cold from the experience.

Security in the Elementary Training Unit consisted of two guards with keys who could open our cells whenever the need arose. If a prisoner could get his hands on the keys, and in some way deal with the guards, escape would be a simple matter of walking out the door. However, it would take violence to get the keys and deal with the guards, something to which we were not prepared to commit ourselves. Then Murray Boyd came on the scene.

Murray had recently served a sentence in Chino, California. After being deported to Canada, he'd made his home in Prince George, British Columbia, where he picked up charges for armed robbery and assault. He appeared ready to do whatever he had to do to escape, and though many men talked a good game, he quickly proved he could walk the walk as well.

Murray fashioned a knife from the handle of a soup ladle, and once armed, he enticed one of the guards to look into a black cell next door to me. He pushed one guard into the cell, locked the door by twisting a piece of a coat hanger taken from the guard's coat rack through the hasp, then pulled the homemade shank on the other guard and locked him into another cell. He then went back to the first cell, opened the door, and demanded the keys to the front door and our cell doors. In less then five minutes, we were all out in the hallway waiting for the arrival of the tea and bread.

In most prisons, prisoners do most of the work, and often this is done without supervision. The bread and tea came to us on a three-ton truck driven by a prisoner whose helper was also a prisoner.

After half an hour the truck arrived, and when the knock came on the door, we flung it open. The two prisoners gave up the keys to the vehicle, entered the hole as our prisoners, and we commandeered the truck. Tommy, John, and I rode in the back, while Murray drove and George sat in the passenger seat. We headed for the front gate.

We were fifty yards from the gate, picking up speed, when the gate guard walked into the middle of the road and folded his arms across his chest. His rifle was propped against the side of the building and he appeared to think his presence on the road would halt the vehicle. It wasn't until we were only a few yards from him that he realized we weren't going to stop. He dove to the side and we were heading down the lane toward the streets of Burnaby. Those of us in the back began throwing the large thermal cans off the truck, which bounced in front of the vehicles behind us so they had to stop to avoid running over them. In a few short minutes we were on a residential street where we scrambled out and abandoned the truck.

Tommy and I were running across a lawn when I looked back to see Murray and George trying to stop a car to commandeer it. The two of us kept going. We hadn't run far when we heard the sound of police sirens. They seemed to be all around us.

As we were running through a huge backyard, we came across a greenhouse. We entered and discovered we were in a small room that served as an office of sorts. In the room was a large furnace, which obviously hadn't been used for months.

Like hunted animals seeking a small hole in which to hide, we crawled inside and closed the door. It was a tight squeeze, but once inside the furnace itself, there was enough room to sit comfortably.

We were there no more than two minutes when we heard the sound of running footsteps, and seconds later a mass of men with crackling walkie-talkies entered the furnace room.

"I saw them come this way," said a panting voice.

"You sure?" asked another.

"Damn right I'm sure," said the panter.

"They might have run right through this place," responded his partner. I'd noticed a door leading to the interior of the greenhouse, and there was another door that appeared to lead outside, but it was nailed shut with one-inch boards. One of our pursuers decided to take the short way out, and he kicked the door until it burst open and they all ran out that way. Within minutes another group of men entered, saw the other door with shattered pieces of wood lying beside it, and decided we were the ones who'd done the damage. Consequently, they too left that way. In a very short time, during which our breathing seemed to echo so loudly in the steel chamber it seemed we could've been heard for miles, the world outside of the furnace fell completely silent. My heart was pounding so rapidly and so hard, I could hear the rush of blood through my veins.

"Think we made it?" Tommy asked. Although he whispered, the sound of his voice seemed to reverberate like thunder.

"Yeah, unless they come back." I'd no sooner said it when I heard a strange sound that seemed to be getting closer. It sounded like a vacuum cleaner with a short-circuit. For a moment I was puzzled, but then I realized it was the sound of a dog sniffing and snuffling on our scent. There was a small hole in the furnace door, and by putting my eye to it I had a wide expanse of vision. I peered through it and was suddenly confronted with the large nose of a German shepherd inches away from my eye. I drew back in surprise and held my breath. The dog had found us, and my heart sank in my chest. I waited for the command for us to come out. There was a loud clang as someone banged the side of the furnace with a hard object, but the command never came.

"What's wrong with that dog?" said a voice.

"He seems to have lost the scent," offered another.

"Here—give him some water—maybe he needs some water..." I heard the sound of a tap being run and then the sound of the dog lapping it up and I thought I knew what had happened.

The dog had done its job, and done it well, but his handler had misread his dog's actions. When the shepherd found us, he quit, and because the game was over, he began to meander around the room, checking out this and that as dogs will do. The way the dog would see it, the water was just a reward for doing what it was asked to do, and it seemed to me that any further command to hunt would require a new scent. I believed I was proven right when, within minutes, we were again left in complete silence.

We stayed in the furnace for many hours, even dozing off from time to time. It was late evening and the sun had gone down when we finally crawled out and slipped away into the looming darkness.

We had no real idea of where we were going; we were just going to get away and live a different life somewhere off across the mountains. Blue River was a place Tommy had his eye on and it sounded good to me too.

The woods surrounding the jail were thick and extensive and we made good time, heading for the river. We would have to cross the river to get to Tommy's house, where we would eat, rest, and get some different clothes to wear. Tommy seemed to know the direction we had to travel, and we finally arrived at the banks of the Fraser River. We took the first small sailboat we came across and paddled into the current.

The Patullo Bridge loomed ahead and, though it seemed we would run our small craft into one of its pilings, the current carried us around it and we safely continued on.

Tommy's mother greeted us, but with reluctance. With her was Tommy's younger sister who appeared fascinated with us. We stayed only long enough to have something to eat and we both changed clothes, but we kept our jail-issued boots. A railway track ran close to the Fraser River, and luckily we only had to wait a few minutes for a freight train to come rolling by. We had to run to catch it, but we both managed to climb on, and we sat down on a walkway between two cars and headed east. It was cold, and as the train gathered speed, it became colder. But I felt great because I believed I had finally, successfully escaped.

The train stopped at a small town and we quickly broke the seal on one of the cars, slid the door open and climbed inside. It was a boxcar full of huge rolls of paper. We simply lay down on top of them, and soon the train was again rolling down the tracks. We rode until the train stopped. When the train didn't move for a couple of hours, we decided to get out and check our surroundings.

We walked along the tracks, between two lines of freight cars. When we looked into an open boxcar, we discovered it had an occupant. The man who stood inside the doorway looked oriental, and he was not only friendly and accommodating, but as railroad-wise as any man could be. We never learned his name and he never asked ours, but he certainly read us well.

"You both just escaped from Okalla," he said confidently.

"What do you mean?" I asked. Tommy and I were standing in front of the boxcar door and he was standing in the doorway. The door was open just enough to allow us a peek inside.

"Your boots," he answered, "they are Okalla prison farm boots."

"Yeah," Tommy reluctantly admitted, "we broke out yesterday..."

"Well, c'mon up here," he said, sliding the door and stepping back so we could join him. We hoisted ourselves into the car and I was amazed to find it laid out like a small house.

There were cardboard boxes on one side and old car seats made the other side into a living room. Everything was neat and tidy.

"Look in that box over there," he suggested, pointing to a large soapbox sitting off to one side. Tommy and I found ourselves looking at more than a dozen pairs of shoes. Some of them were boots, some were street shoes, and all appeared to be in decent shape.

"So do we just pick a pair?" I asked.

"Yeah, go ahead, but don't take those boots." The boots were in good shape, and there were two pairs of them.

"No? Why not?" asked Tommy.

"A couple of young fellas, just like you two, came by yesterday - they escaped from Walla Walla, Washington. Those are jailhouse boots and you don't want to change jailhouse boots for jailhouse boots, do you?"

"No," I replied, "we don't." I selected a different pair that appeared to be my size, and sat down to try them on. Tommy did the same. We found some that fit and placed ours into his shoe box.

"Would you like some soup?" he asked. I glanced around, but I couldn't see anything that looked like a kitchen.

"I've got a firepit across the tracks." he explained, "It'll only take a minute to get it going." When Tommy and I both thanked him he stepped to another box, opened it and pulled out a large, fire-blackened can. Inside the can were numerous other cans and they fit together, one inside the other, as if they were custom-made for travelling, which they were. He gathered up the materials he needed and left us sitting on the car seat in his living room. He was back with hot soup in no time at all. We learned we were on a siding in Boston Bar, and that he'd been there three days.

While we ate, he explained how he lived in the boxcars and travelled up and down the line to different towns, hitting on the welfare offices in each one. He would do this all summer long and he knew the train schedules as well as if he made those schedules himself. I thought of Roger Miller's song, "King of the Road", because he fit the description so perfectly.

I know every engineer on every train,
All of their children, and all of their names...

We remained in the car talking to him for some time after our lunch and we finally decided we would explore Boston Bar—but we should have stayed right where we were.

As we walked down the street, we passed a building that looked to be a town hall but was serving at the moment as a small movie theatre. When we paused for a moment to peer into the dimly lit interior, we discovered the ticket office was vacant. The cash box was within arm's reach, and in a moment Tommy had it in his hands and we were running down the street to the railway tracks and out of town. We ran and walked for a mile or so, and when the lights of the town could no longer be seen behind us, we stopped and sat down on the tracks to count our loot. There wasn't much, and I felt a strange sense of guilt and shame for stealing the cash box, but I was consoled by the fact that we now had a few dollars in our pockets.

We decided to wait for a freight train to come so we could catch a ride to the next town, and we both went to sleep alongside the tracks. It wasn't long before we were abruptly awakened by a fast-moving freight. It was travelling much too fast for us to catch so we had to wait for the next one. When it finally did come, it was going the wrong way, back into Boston Bar. We caught it just the same, thinking as we did so that we could catch one heading east if we were in the rail yard itself.

There was a passenger train hissing at the station and we boarded it, asking the conductor if we could pay for our tickets to Lytton. He readily agreed.

It was comfortable sitting in the darkened passenger car, and though there were quite a number of people there as well, they didn't pay any attention to us. At our next stop the RCMP boarded the train and arrested us both, not as escapees, but as thieves of the cash box.

We were taken back to Okalla the next day and were placed in the West Wing, where prisoners on trial were held. We now had a theft charge added to our escape charge, but, as Tommy pointed out, there was a good chance we could escape from the cells in Chilliwack when we went to court for the theft charge. We would only have to get our hands on a hacksaw blade and bring it with us the next time we appeared.

We managed to find a friend who was able to reach out to a man who worked in the maintenance shop. He supplied us with the much-needed hacksaw blade. A couple of weeks later, we cut through the bars in the RCMP cell in Chilliwack, but as we were working on the window bars, a newspaper boy out on his early-morning rounds heard the sound of the saw blade cutting through cold-rolled steel. He walked into the station and told the cop on duty he'd heard strange noises. A few minutes later we were found out.

The West Wing was a fairly secure cellblock with a high corrugated fence surrounding the exercise courtyard. There were also armed guards stationed in gun towers around that area of the prison. Escaping from the exercise yard would be very difficult. However, the cellblock was old, and the interior had been renovated to include a flat-topped storage room on the opposite side from the exercise yard.

They had built a sloping roof over the room to stop prisoners from climbing on top and getting next to the window in the wall, but we found a way to crawl under the roof and we went to work cutting the bars on the hidden window. We'd taken two meat saw blades, pilfered a broken band saw blade from the kitchen, and placed one over the other, so the teeth were reversed and the blades cut both ways.

Norm Beckman and I worked for more than a week, and we each took turns cutting while the other watched the ranges for guards on their walks.

Norm Beckman was absolutely brilliant with his hands. With a steel cup and tin cans and little else, he could make a steam engine that worked as if it had been manufactured with lathes and fine-tuned machinery. On one occasion he made a dozen handcuff keys from the tops of Zippo lighters. Each one worked perfectly.

Norm was known as one of the best can men on the west coast. It was for safecracking that he'd been arrested by the RCMP in the interior of British Columbia. The police were determined to put him away for a long time, and he was just as determined to find a way out. When the barrier of the window bars was cut, there'd be a number of other men who'd escape with us, but we were the only ones doing the cutting.

We could only work during exercise periods, which meant we had to hide under our beds until everyone was in the yard before we could go to work. The method worked well and we were well on our way to success when a guard came unexpectedly from the other side. Because it was my turn at the window, it was me he heard. I was arrested and taken to the Elementary Training Unit, where I remained in the black cell for a record-setting thirty-three days.

After all my court appearances were complete, I was transferred to New Westminster Penitentiary, and I now had a sentence of three years, eight months and six days.

The New Westminster Penitentiary was an old prison, one of the original five in the country. I was just as determined to get out of it as I had been to get out of Okalla. And like all prisons and jails, there is always more than one man who feels the same way. The fact that I had escaped, or tried to escape, so many times, meant there were prisoners who already knew who I was, and it didn't take me long to hook up with them.

There were basically two kinds of men in the penitentiary; those who were heroin addicts and those who not only didn't use it, but despised those who did. Of course the non-users had their own foibles, greed being chief among them, yet they didn't see their own as anything but natural.

Gerry, Bernie and I became involved in a plan to escape over the prison wall, and over the next few months we put the plan in motion. The success or failure of our escape bid would hinge on our timing - but most of the planning was left to Gerry and some of his contacts inside the prison. Bernie and I were similar to pawns on a chessboard; we were necessary in the initial opening moves, but once the game got underway the major pieces would play the major role.

On April 19, 1963 we slipped out of the gym window and made our way across the prison yard to the wall. Earlier that day, one of the men who worked on the yard crew had casually placed an eighteen-foot long plank beside one of the buildings adjacent to the gym. It was with this plank that we would scale the high wall. The one obstacle to deal with was the guard who made his rounds with a German shepard, but Gerry maintained he had the times of the guard's walk down to a science. Gerry had been a member of the Red Hood Gang of bank-robbers in Montreal, and an important part of their modus operandi was split-second timing. However, in case something went wrong, we had light bulbs filled with lighter fluid to keep the dog and guard at bay.

Our escape was a total fiasco. We rounded a corner and found ourselves confronted with the guard and the dog. The only thing that saved us from being shot dead was the dog's lunging at the end of the leash, which spoiled the guard's aim so he was unable to get a bead on us. Gerry pulled out one of the light bulbs from his jacket, lit it and made an attempt to throw it in the direction of the guard, but the rag came out and the burning fluid was spilled onto his arm and neck. In a hail of pistol shots, Bernie and I doused the flames from his body. We retreated to the window and crawled back into the gym, taking the guard on duty as a hostage. And so began the infamous riot in New Westminster Penitentiary.

It was a nightmarish night, full of tear gas, screams, violence and destruction. Although we didn't encourage the men in the other parts of the prison to riot, they just reacted to what was happening in the gym— however, without doubt, we were the direct cause of the damage. I have regretted my involvement in those events for the rest of my life; they were to have dire and lifelong consequences for many people.

Gerry insisted on contacting Jack Webster, a controversial radio talk show host on CKNW, because he believed that with Webster on the prison grounds, we wouldn't be shot to death by police and prison guards. When Webster showed up, the guards backed away from the outside doors and allowed him to do the negotiating. The riot and its aftermath became national and even international news.

We were finally transferred out, Gerry and I went to St. Vincent de Paul in Québec and Bernie was sent to Stony Mountain Penitentiary in Manitoba.

St. Vincent de Paul was one of the oldest prisons in the country. When we arrived it was in a state of lockdown, so we were first placed in the hole where we stayed for a couple of days until we were transferred to Cellblock Two.

Gerry insisted he had the contacts in Québec to make our time much easier for us, suggesting as well that he had influence to get me a job in Montréal once my time was done. The authorities had agreed there would be no charges for our actions in the riot, so we had at least escaped the legal ramifications. However, our actions had put ideas in the minds of other prisoners and two of them, cousins as it turned out, decided to act on them.

The Marcous took a guard hostage in Cellblock One. They placed blankets over the cell bars, stood behind the guard with a knife to his throat, and demanded a transfer to Dorchester, New Brunswick. They also insisted there be no legal repercussions for their actions. The negotiations didn't last long because the warden issued a demand of his own: if the cousins didn't immediately release their hostage, the warden would order his armed guards to open fire blindly through the blanket.

To show the warden they meant business, one of the cousins cut the guard's leg making him scream out in pain. The warden ordered his guards to open fire. A number of them pushed their pistol barrels against the blanket and began pulling their triggers. The guard and one of the prisoners were killed in a hail of bullets, and the other prisoner was badly wounded. He maintained he'd played dead and it had saved his life. The warden claimed the guard had been killed with a knife, but this was later proven to be false. One of the guards had not fired his pistol, although he did have its barrel pressed against the blanket, and he later testified to the events at the inquest.

Soon after the killings, we were brought back to New Westminster to stand trial for prison break and attempted escape, and for forcibly confining the guard in the gym. We were lodged in the hole and slept on bare planks for six months while we waited trial.

Gerry believed he had cancer, that he was dying, and that his mother was dying of cancer as well. Those were the reasons he gave for attempting to escape, but Bernie and I had known nothing of this at the time. When he finally told us his fears, I suspected his plan all along had been to force prison authorities to transfer him to Québec where he could be closer to his mother. Bernie and I continued our friendship with Gerry and supported him in his endeavours to be closer to his mother, and because he insisted he was ailing, we insisted that the prison authorities give him proper medical treatment.

One night Gerry complained he was bleeding and that he couldn't stop the flow of blood. We couldn't see him, but we believed his pleas for help and we began making noise in the hole. The next day I was ordered out of my cell by four guards. My hands were tightly cuffed behind me and my feet were shackled with heavy chains.

"Where are you taking me?" I asked.

"You're going to court," stated Gurling, a tall, huge man who weighed in at over two hundred and fifty pounds. He propelled me toward the end of the range with a push.

As I shuffled along the tunnel leading from the hole to the main cellblock, the guards seemed relaxed enough; Gurling was talking about his latest outing in the mountains and the conversation seemed innocent, but something about them made me very uneasy. When we walked out of the tunnel, I noticed there were no prisoners in sight, and only a guard or two in the dome. I was quickly taken to the lower area of the administration building and I walked into a large room where three senior prison administrators, two in civilian clothes and a third in an impressive uniform, sat behind a makeshift table. One of them was a psychologist and the Head of Classification. He wore glasses and was smoking a pipe with one hand and slowly turning pages of a document with the other, and he appeared to be studiously engrossed in reading a report in front of him.

Another, whom I recognized as the deputy warden, was wearing a suit and shuffling sheets of paper together as if he'd finished reading them and was ready to put them away. The deputy warden did not look well. Neither the psychologist nor the deputy warden looked at me as I came in. The third man was in the uniform and I recognized him as the Chief Keeper. He stared directly at me in a confrontational fashion; his eyes were a cold grey. His large hands were resting casually on the table, fingers interlaced, and though he sat militarily straight in his chair, he appeared the most relaxed of the three.

"Step to this line," Gurling told me. There was a white line on the floor and I toed it. The deputy warden read out the charges, which were creating a disturbance and destroying government property. He asked me how I pleaded to them.

"Guilty," I answered. I glanced at the psychologist who was still smoking his pipe, and I caught the wink he gave to the guard at my side.

"Due to the seriousness of the charges, I'm going to ask one of the officers to speak to them," intoned the deputy warden in a quavering voice. He never looked up from the table, and I noticed the sheet of paper he held quivered in his trembling hand.

"This prisoner destroyed a blanket, and he was fishing for tobacco," said Gurling. "We have to put a stop to the destruction of property."

"Yes—is there anything else you want to say?" said the deputy.

"This prisoner caused a major disturbance," stated Gurling, "and other prisoners in the cellblock above complained. Even they want it to stop."

"Yes," said the deputy, "it has to stop. Do you have anything to add, Carlson?" he asked, flicking a glance up at me, and it was so fleeting that I doubted if he saw me. I thought he might have a hangover; his nose was a mottled red and his eyes looked rheumy.

"Regarding the disturbance," I replied, "Gerry needs medical attention—if you give it to him, the disturbance will stop. If you need to put him in a different cell, use mine." Gerry was in a cell in an area across the hall from us, but I wouldn't have minded being totally alone. The deputy warden then asked his two colleagues if they had anything to say, and when they declined he handed down his sentence.

"You are hereby sentenced to fifteen paddles, ten to be administered forthwith, and five shall be suspended," he stated, still not looking at me. I think I went into shock at that point; I didn't say anything, and I don't believe my face reflected any emotion.

"Take the prisoner away," said the Chief Keeper. His eyes had never left mine. I glanced at the psychologist, who was nonchalantly examining the dying embers in his pipe.

Again Gurling propelled me to a door across the room, and two of the younger guards, one on each side of me, walked me through the door and indicated that I was to continue down a hallway to a door at the end.

I found myself with my two escorts in the Admitting and Discharge area of the prison and the two men who supervised that area of the prison were working behind a long counter, which had a long bench in front of it.

"Sit here," said one of my escorts, indicating the middle of the bench. I sat awkwardly on the edge of the plank.

"What's going on?" asked one of the A&D guards. He stood looking at us, a bag of personal property held in his hands. His partner was looking at us curiously as well.

"Paddles," said the guard. This brought such an immediate response it surprised me. The A&D guard tossed the bag on the floor and in two steps he was at the phone and quickly began dialing. In a moment he had someone on the line.

"Phone me back," he said, "just tell them you want to talk to me, that you have an emergency at home." Before he could hang up, his partner asked him if his wife would phone for him and say the same thing. He hung up the phone, but he didn't move; he just waited for the phone to ring. I looked at one of my escorts, and then the other. Both of them were stone-faced and very tense and they didn't acknowledge me with so much as a glance. The phone rang and the A&D officer answered it.

"Yes? Okay," he said, "I'll be right there." No sooner did he hang up when the phone rang again, and the second man answered it. He told his wife he would be right there as well, and a few seconds later both men had their jackets and caps on, and they quickly walked out the door behind them. My guards and I were left alone, each to our own thoughts.

In the early sixties there were two ways a prisoner could be officially beaten during his or her sentence: the lash and the paddle. The lash was meted out by Canadian courts for breaking into a dwelling at night and for armed robbery, as well as other crimes; the paddle was meted out in warden's court for a variety of offences. Both were liberally applied, and in each case the procedure was similar. Once a prisoner was sentenced to the lash by the sentencing judge, the warden could use his discretion as to the time he would have the punishment meted out. This would sometimes be carried out over a period of a year or more, depending on the number of lashes a man was sentenced to. In the case of the paddle, the warden had to request permission from headquarters in Ottawa, and once permission was granted, the punishment was immediately carried out. There was no such thing as appealing the sentence. In riot conditions the warden's power was absolute and he did not have to request permission to use corporal punishment; in riot conditions the permission to use the paddle was deemed granted to bring the prison under control.

The general consensus among men who'd received both was the paddle was more painful. The lash, they said, would burn and sometimes even cut, but the pain was not as great as that from being beaten with the paddle. In that time both methods were the accepted ways of inflicting the most pain without leaving any long-lasting tissue damage.

We sat there in silence on the bench, not speaking for many long minutes, and it wasn't until I heard a strange sound that the silence was broken.

It sounded like the flat report of a gunshot, then silence, then the sound came again. Before the third one I realized what the sound was: someone was getting beaten with the paddle. I glanced at one of the guards, intending on making a comment of some sort that would assuage my fear and halt my imagination from making this experience more horrible than it was. My mouth was dry and I attempted to swallow in order to speak, but the look I caught on the young guard's face took away my need to say a word.

Just as I glanced at him the sound came again, and he grimaced, as if he were feeling something only he could see. I looked straight ahead and didn't attempt to speak again.

Time seemed to stand still as the flat sound of the paddle continued. It was almost as if I were just a listener, and not a direct participant, but then the door we'd come through opened and a guard beckoned to his colleagues. We all stood up and I shuffled down the hallway to a room full of uniformed guards, and one civilian whom I recognized as the doctor. No one spoke. everyone was just standing around the paddle machine and my presence was being completely ignored.

The paddle machine was a short, padded bench, fitted with leather straps to hold a man down while he was beaten. Without a word being spoken, I was forced to shuffle forward until my groin touched the bench. I could feel hands unbuttoning my pants and pulling them down, my shorts with them. Other hands wrapped straps around my hamstrings and buckled my legs tightly to the legs of the bench, then ankle straps did the same to my feet. My handcuffs were removed, and with guards tightly gripping my arms, I was pulled forward until my belly was pressed against the padded surface. I felt a large leather strap flop across the small of my back and I was cinched tight. My arms were stretched forward to the front of the bench and wrist- straps buckled them down, and finally a canvas bag was roughly put over my head, and a string on it was drawn tight around my neck and throat.

It seemed as though I lay stretched out like for a very long time in complete and utter silence, but it was probably no more than a minute. Though there were so many men in the room, it was so silent that even through my fear I found it eerie.

"You have been sentenced to fifteen paddles, ten to be administered forthwith," intoned a loud official voice. This was followed by another long silence, and I felt the fingers of a hand touch the inside of my wrist, as if someone was taking my pulse. *That must be the doctor,* I thought.

I heard the sound of the paddle hitting me, but I felt no pain; my first reaction was to think it wouldn't be too bad. Then, a few moments later, after the shock of the second blow, I realized why there was such a long period between each one—the delay period was to allow the shock to dissipate and allow the pain to come driving up the spine to the brain; it was unbelievably excruciating. The hair on the back of my neck literally stood on end as the pain flowed upward.

At the third blow I felt as if the bench had moved, and I found myself welcoming the next one, because the shock would momentarily remove the pain. I felt as if my head were going to explode. Though I tried to count the times I was hit, I lost track after the fifth. It was at that point that I tried to break free, and when my right wrist slipped out of the strap, I literally lifted the bench off the floor with my back muscles. I felt the weight of the guards as they jumped on my body. Hands grabbed my right arm and almost pulled it from its socket, and more blows struck me.

I didn't realize it was over until I felt my wrists being released, but tightly gripped by hands, then the strap on my back fell free, and with the bag still on my head, I was forced to stand upright while my legs and ankles were released. Finally, the bag was taken from my head and I caught the strong, unmistakable odor of rubbing alcohol. As my pants were pulled up, and the cuffs and leg irons put on me again, I was able to look around.

Not a man would look at me, except the Chief Keeper. His cold grey eyes stared into mine unblinkingly, and I'm sure he could see the hatred in mine.

"There's more where this came from," he said. "Keep in mind you have five more waiting." He looked away and I glanced around at the sea of faces, trying to identify the man in the room who had beaten me. Of course they all had played a role, yet I could read in their faces that they received no pleasure in what they had to do. If I focused on a man's face, he would become disconcerted, and appeared ashamed; I felt strange solace in that.

As I shuffled through the open door, I saw Gurling sitting on a chair in the outer room, sleeves rolled up past his elbows and casually talking to another guard. But the man standing beside Gurling had a look on his face like the others, strained and tense, and because Gurling was acting much too casually and speaking about something totally unrelated to the torture at hand, I felt certain he was the man who had beaten me. I needed the image of someone I could focus on— to think they were all men who would willingly and gladly torture another human being bothered me, even then. I glanced around for the doctor but he'd apparently left the room. Later I heard from another prisoner that a doctor was always present during the administering of corporal punishment in case the prisoner undergoing the torture was physically unable to survive the pain. I never heard of a doctor halting a paddling—which is either a testimonial to the strength and overall health of the prisoners, or a statement on the professional character of the doctors in the system.

While I was shuffling back down the tunnel to my cell in the hole, I thought of how a prisoner must feel as he's going to his execution, and I also thought of what the guards in such a situation would be experiencing. It struck me that an execution would be easier than a beating for the guards, at least in some ways, because they wouldn't have to look into the accusing eyes of the man they'd just executed.

When the handcuffs and shackles were removed and I was placed in my cell again, I sat down on the plank that served as my bed and felt a crunch, as though I had just sat down on crumbs, and I believed it was the result of broken blood vessels. Gerry and Bernie, being the first to receive the punishment, were already back in their cells and the prisoners there knew what had happened to us all. Hours later a prisoner quietly called to me from the next cell.

"What was it like?" he asked.

"It was like going to my execution, but surviving it to live through another day," I answered. I'm sure my answer didn't enlighten him, but it was the best answer I could give.

When the penitentiary system built a new hole in New Westminster, it was unofficially referred to as the Penthouse, because it was built on the very top of the existing buildings of the prison. Gerry, Bernie and I were taken up there on the very day it was completed. There was a great deal of cement dust on the floor and nothing had been painted. We served our time there while we waited trial. The trial was to last for months, and we acted as our own lawyers.

Our focus was not on what we'd done but on what penitentiaries across the country were doing to prisoners inside them. Although there was little we could do to dispute the hard facts, our defense became an offense where we attacked the character of many of the guards who testified on the witness stand. I quickly learned that even an unanswered question lingered long in the minds of the observers.

I searched through the Criminal Code of Canada for loopholes that would allow us to use tactics that would, to a lawyer, be unethical and unacceptable. My rationalization was simple: the law had wrongfully convicted me of a theft, therefore, in seeking a not guilty verdict for trying to escape, I could use any means available.

We had a sympathetic jury who found Bernie and I not guilty on two of the four counts of the indictment: the charge of prison break and a charge of assault with intent to cause bodily harm, and Gerry was found not guilty of the prison break. It was a major victory for us, and when the judge dismissed the jury and they filed past us on their way out of the courtroom, many of them stopped and shook our hands. The judge remanded us for sentencing on the convictions of assault and forcible confinement, and we were taken back to the Penthouse.

The next morning my cell door flew open. Three guards stormed in and began pummelling me, but the cell was much too small for the four of us, so they were unable to do me serious damage. Gerry and Bernie received the same treatment; however, Bernie fought back.

I was wiping the blood from my face with a towel when I heard the scuffle next door in Bernie's cell. I peered out the small window and saw one guard stumble back against the security fence, and while the shotgun guard tried to get a bead on what was taking place, a guard came running out with Bernie on his back. Bernie's hands were wrapped around the guard's neck, and when the guard hit the wire, they both went down in a wild tangle of arms and legs. The guard's face was turning blue, and though his fellow guards attempted to pry Bernie's fingers from his neck, they were unable to do so. The shotgun guard behind the wire was frantic because he couldn't shoot without hitting one of his colleagues. Finally, a guard grabbed one of Bernie's legs and another guard grabbed the other, and they kicked Bernie in the groin. It took two such kicks to force Bernie to let go, then he was dragged back into his cell and the guards left the range. Although they did return in the afternoon to confiscate our legal papers, they never came back to assault us again.

We were a bit banged up, had bruises on our faces—so the authorities arranged to get our sentencing date postponed without our consent. It was a week before we were taken into court and sentenced to an additional four and a half years. Shortly after the sentencing, we were transferred out to different prisons, and I arrived back in Prince Albert Penitentiary in November, 1963. I served my sentence until my release in September of 1966.

In Prince Albert I found myself being treated differently. I was no longer a young, naive fish; I was instead a veteran, a seasoned convict and in many ways a man to be respected. It was at this time, when I was twenty-one years old, that I began to understand what it meant to be considered a professional criminal.

A prisoner who commands respect in the penitentiary is also a man to be feared, because inside, respect is synonymous with fear itself. If a man cannot, either directly or indirectly, generate fear of bodily harm, the man will not truly be respected. Therefore, a prisoner who is physically weak must have good friends capable of doing serious physical damage to those who get out of line, or be willing to use a knife or a club himself to make his point. In my case, it was understood that any man who could go through my experiences and come out the other side without breaking, had to be respected. Individual respect in a prison is everything, and without it, one doesn't survive long among his fellow prisoners.

Even the smallest slight can become a major life and death matter in a maximum security prison. A prisoner will say, "it's the principle of the thing," just before he pipes, stabs, or in some other way does another prisoner serious physical damage. This doesn't mean the action for which he's exacting revenge would, of itself, justify killing another man. It simply means that if he doesn't act, he admits ownership for the slight or accusation. I instinctively knew this when I fought with Fulstrum over his failure to repay the jar of peanut butter, and I would have carried the matter to the extent that I could have badly hurt or even killed Fulstrum, if he hadn't paid me back, because not to have done so would've shown me to be an easy victim at the whim of predators. A prisoner who chooses to act in a violent, brutal fashion, sees himself as preferring to die like a lion instead of living like a lamb. Prisoners unaware of this philosophy will misread the repercussions when attempting to make a victim out of a perceived weaker man, as Fulstrum did with me, and they could find to their great regret that they've now become involved in a life and death matter for a seemingly inconsequential act or even word. An examination of the circumstances behind a large number of deaths of prisoners by prisoners will show this to be the case.

In 1963 I became one of those men who did their time gambling, but I had an edge, a head start, on rest of the young prisoners at the time. I was just into my teens when I worked in my father's logging camp on the weekends and began playing poker in the evening with other loggers. Cat skinners, truck drivers, sawyers, tree fallers, yard men and lumber pilers: most would, at some point during winter, sit at the table and play cards. We only played for nickels and dimes, with three raises allowed, and though it seems like small potatoes, most of us were working for ninety cents an hour, so a bad night gambling at the poker table would mean we had worked in the brutal Saskatchewan winter cold for nothing.

Many of the loggers had families, and they darned their own socks and mended their own clothes. I was the boss's son and losing held less significance for me than for them. Over the period of two winters I learned a great deal about how to read cards, and just as importantly, how to read the players themselves. I was no expert card sharp, but I did have the rudimentary knowledge needed to become a good player, and in the prison for the next three years I gambled year-round and curled in the winter months.

I worked in the gymnasium and played poker all day long, in a cash game where, in order to sit down at the table, a man had to have the money in front of him. No matter how good a man's credit rating might be, if he ran out of money at the table, he had to leave and come back with the cash. Of course many deals were made outside the poker room, even among the players themselves, but no dealing at the table was allowed. If a man went "all in," if he threw all he had in front of him into the pot, and lost, he had to get up and leave. In a credit game, many players would call a bet with a bad hand because they only had to ask for more chips and go further in debt to continue playing. In the cash-only game, the psychology was different. A man could bluff another player—we called it playing the money as well as the man.

Many of the prisoners inside the penitentiary at that time were professional criminals: bank robbers, paper hangers, can men, dope dealers and boosters. There were also those men who found themselves in prison because of their inability to handle alcohol, which resulted in charges and convictions for robbery with violence. Usually these men would sit drinking in bars until they were blind drunk and broke, at which time they would follow another patron into the washroom, beat him senseless and rob him for the change in his pocket. They would invariably be caught, and sometimes, upon release from the prison, they would be back in with a new sentence before many of the prisoners knew they'd been gone.

"You must be short now?" one prisoner would ask another, while standing in the food line.

"No, I've got three to do," he would answer.

"Three? Shit, I thought you were only doing a deuce."

"Yeah, I was. I got out last month and picked up four-and-a-half." The questioner might then look at the number on the man's shirt or coat and see that it was a new one.

The good thieves were well-known, and that's how the bank robbers, the paper hangers and the can men were referred to. "He's a good thief, and good people," one man would say of another as a compliment. If a man was "good people" it meant he could be trusted even when he was using alcohol and drugs. A pair of "good thieves" who befriended me, Don Kolot and Roy Holland, had escaped during my first bit. They were arrested in Dallas, Texas and had served time in Huntsville. They were partners both inside and outside the prison, and they were can men as well as armed robbers; when it came to safecracking, Roy was an expert. One day we were talking in the gym and when the conversation came around to crime he gave me some advice on cracking safes.

"It's clean Wayne," he said. "Nobody gets hurt except insurance companies, and who gives a fuck about them."

"Yeah, right, fuckin' insurance companies," I murmured, as though I knew something about them. He told me how easy it was to get into safes and vaults, and emphasized how good the money was. I learned how different safe companies had different security methods, how some safes could be drilled and punched, and while others couldn't, he explained in detail how easy it was to make "grease." Grease was nitroglycerine and consisted of basically three chemical elements, which, when mixed together in the proper order and amounts, could blow the door clean off many of the safes on the market at the time. The key to success was to manufacture the grease and get it into the crack in the door of the safe, and then set it off with a knocker. A knocker was a blasting cap attached to a dry cell battery. I was an apt pupil.

With the technical knowledge came a philosophy, the belief that if there was blood on the money, it didn't spend well. This meant a man should never kill someone while committing a crime. It was one thing to be a romantic figure in the form of a bank robber or can man, but it was quite another to be murderer. If three men committed a crime where someone, even a police officer, lost his life, the older and wiser cons believed one of the three would turn on his partners to save himself from the death penalty.

The death penalty was still in place at the time and men often spoke of Raymond Cook who was hanged in Fort Saskatchewan, Alberta in the early sixties. It was interesting to hear them say Raymond was a good man who was never quite the same after he was badly piped in the head while serving a sentence in Prince Albert. Some men felt he was not guilty; others felt he was not completely responsible for his actions due to the head injuries he'd received. I remembered reading in the paper that the warden had said Ray Cook went to his death "like a man."

And so went the time. I read a great deal at night and I played poker, chess and bridge during the day and evening—and my time slowly passed. In September, 1966 I was released and I went home to Sturgis. In December my father died, intestate, and in March I was back inside the penitentiary for three-and-a-half years for armed robbery. In the short period of time I was on the street, neither the prison nor the people had changed. It was back to the poker table with my regular cronies.

There were credit games going all the while as well, and in one instance a man learned the hard way that one should never make casual, off-the-cuff remarks to try and save face. One day a man was bragging about his gambling expertise. The man he was talking to wasn't impressed.

"If you're so fuckin' big on the street," he said to the braggart, "why aren't you playing in the big cash game?"

"No, I won't play in that game after what I saw," he answered.

"What do you mean?"

"I saw a guy make a move with the discard pile," he answered, "and I don't want to get involved in that kind of bullshit."

It didn't take long for that conversation to get back to us, and the man was called upon to not only repeat what he said, but to name the man he'd seen cheating. We had a meeting about the matter and I suggested we all forget about it, because we all knew we were honourable men and not cheaters at cards. There was one problem with forgetting about it, and that was a man who had lost a great deal of money. There was a table rule in effect that if anyone was cheated, he'd get his money back; the loser therefore needed a cheater to exist.

One of the players in the game was Charlie, a good friend of mine, and we sat down and talked about the situation.

"Who do you think it is?" he asked.

"It's not who it is, it's who is he going to say it is," I said. We were sitting in the bleachers in the gymnasium and though I did have some concern that the whistle-blower might name me, I believed he would in fact name someone else.

"You think so?" he asked.

"All we have to do is look at who is at the table regularly, and we should be able to get an idea who he going to name," I suggested.

"What about you?" he asked.

"He might name me," I replied, "but I know a lot of people in here and he may be a little afraid of me. Let's look at the possibilities." We went through the people at the table, and finally Charlie came to realize that he himself would probably be the one the braggart laid his finger on. Later on in the day it was decided we would all gather in the gym that evening, and the cheater would be identified.

There were a dozen men gathered in the card room. We all sat or stood around a card table and the braggart walked up and made his claim, the same thing as he'd said before.

"I saw a guy go into the discard pile and pick out cards," he said.

"Show us how he did it," I said. I dealt out some five-card stud poker hands, selected a card from each hand and made a discard pile in front of the braggart.

He picked up the discard pile and began fumbling with it. It was a pathetic attempt at cheating, and as far as I was concerned he had exposed himself as a dangerous liar.

He wouldn't name the cheater outright. He said only that the cheater was present; he would name the man later, before the night was through. I made my position clear to him.

"I don't believe you," I said. I looked directly into his eyes when I said it.

"What do you mean?" he asked, aggressively. I stood to my feet and confronted him.

"I think you made a statement and it snowballed from there," I replied. I looked at Larry whose face reddened in defense. I walked away from the table and later that evening I found Larry sitting in the gym with a crony, also named Larry. They were partners and they considered themselves smarter than the average prisoner.

"Well, whose name did he drop?" I asked. I was carrying a knife in the back of my pants, because the situation warranted it.

"I don't believe him," stated Larry. I didn't say that it was about time. Instead I handed him a folded piece of paper with a name written on it. He took it from my hand and opened it.

"Well?" I asked.

"Yeah, it was Charlie," he said.

"That son of a bitch!"

"How did you know?" he asked.

"The same way I know what a man's hole card is," I replied.

"Yeah, but if it was anybody else..." his voice trailed off.

"Do you know what you just said?" I asked.

"What?"

"You would've believed it if it was *anybody* else," I answered.

"Well..."

"Nobody will believe that Charlie's a cheater," I stated. Not only did I know Charlie as a stand-up guy, the fact was that money was not that important to him. Charlie was a bank robber and he not only had money, but he gave it away to people who needed it. Of course the braggart didn't know this when he'd named him.

"No, they won't, so there's no harm done." Larry was well aware of Charlie's character.

"Charlie will feel obligated now to do something—that's the problem—and there's not a fucking thing we can do about it."

"Yeah, I guess not." I would have liked to punch him in the face, but I didn't.

"And the sad part is you might have backed up that asshole if he'd named me," I said. I looked at him in disgust, and he saw it in my face.

"No, no, not you, Wayne," he said. He now knew the onus was on him, because he'd been the one pushing the issue.

"The guys we play with are good guys, every one of them."

"Oh yeah, they are."

"I hope we all learned something from this. Charlie knew he was going to be named," I offered.

"How could he know that?"

"Process of elimination," I replied. "The fingerman looked at us all, and he picked the man he thought would do him the least damage."

"Maybe..."

"But he has a surprise coming to him," I said. I knew Charlie would feel compelled to act in order to protect his name. It didn't matter that none of us believed the accusation. I left the gym to take a walk in the outside yard with a poker-playing friend of mine, and though the matter seemed over and done, we knew it wasn't over yet.

The next day the braggart had his ear almost cut off his head and he sought protection by asking to be placed in the hole, out of the general population. A short time later he was transferred to another prison. I faulted Larry for it, because he'd pressed the issue. It wasn't much later that Larry ate some goof-balls (what we called barbiturates) and hanged himself in the hole.

Suicide was fairly prevalent and though we all briefly felt a sense of loss, we were so caught up in our day-to-day struggle to feather our own nests, that life just carried on. Suicide was seen as a weakness, and few men had any respect for those who chose that way out of their misery. However, there was one man who went to the hole for being stoned on pills and when he pretended to hang him-self in order to get more tranquilizers from the on-duty nurse, he miscalculated and ended up dead. He'd manufactured a noose from his shirt and when he heard the keys in lock of the front door of the hole, he strung himself up. The guard only made a punch on the range opposite to the one he was on, and then left the area.

The men in the cells around him repeatedly called for help, but the guards didn't hear them or, if they did, they ignored the cries as those of men simply seeking unneeded attention. It was said later that the hanged man had been badgering guards to call the nurse and when the nurse went to see him on sev-eral occasions, he didn't need medical attention. Though his death was acciden-tal, it was listed as a suicide, and in a way it was due to his crying wolf, one too many times.

The dead man had a partner and his partner was allowed out during the noon hour to go cell-to-cell to gather donations so the dead man's family could have his body shipped home for burial in Manitoba. The man's partner managed to get a large sum of money, much of it cash in hand, but he failed everyone, including himself, when he jumped into a poker game and lost everything: his reputation, his friends, and his own self respect.

Billy was a man who became my partner in a range store, where we sold can-teen items on credit for a profit. It was lucrative; the price of borrowing or buy-ing something from our store was based on the "two for one" system: borrow a bale of weed and pay two back. We became fast friends and planned on carry-ing our partnership to the street, where we would rob a bank and go on to legitimate enterprises. We weren't sure what those enterprises might be, but once we had a lot of money we knew that something would come to mind. Billy was released first and he was on the street a month before me. I was excited about our plan.

Three weeks later, Art Newman, a mutual friend of Billy's and mine, called to me from the range above.

"I've got some bad news, Wayne," he said.

"What is it?" I asked.

"Billy's pinched in Saskatoon," he answered.

"What for?"

"Breaking and entering a drug store," he replied.

"Shit," I said.

"Yeah, it's too bad, but he said he was going to have somebody meet you at the train station."

"We'll see." As far as I was concerned, Billy's arrest ended any plans I had with him. Still, by the time November, 1969 rolled around I felt I was a truly seasoned, knowledgeable criminal, with contacts throughout Canada, and I would get by. I fully intended on pursuing a life of crime.

I stepped off the train in Saskatoon. There were people everywhere and I didn't recognize anyone, but before I'd taken ten steps, I heard my name being called. I looked around, my suitcase in my hand, and saw a man looking at me.

"Wayne?" he asked.

"Yeah, I'm Wayne."

"I'm Tom. Billy asked me to pick you up," he said.

"How's Billy?"

"He's on the hill," he answered, meaning the provincial jail in Prince Albert. Tom and I walked out of the station and into a friendship which, though it had its ups and downs, managed to survive thirty years.

I checked into a hotel and Tom and I went for a ride, to the courthouse of all places. Tom began a plea bargain for a sentence on an assault charge. He was about to plead guilty then and there, but I talked him out of it, explaining as I did so that we could do well together. He thought about it for a few minutes, and off and on over the next year we partnered up and made money in variety of different ways. Tom and I remained loyal friends, both inside and outside of prison, for the rest of our lives.

I'd heard a lot about the art of boosting while I was inside, but until I met Kenny Brown I never knew what it meant to be a good booster. Kenny was the best I'd ever hoped to meet and we became partners.

One day we stopped at the home of a friend, Peg-Leg and after being invited in, we entered his house while he was making grease. I watched as he and his partners manufactured some high-quality nitroglycerine in the back yard. I learned that it was best to wear old clothes when doing so.

"Have you got an old coat in the car?" asked Peg.

"Yeah," I replied. "It's in the trunk—want me to get it?"

"We could use it," he answered. I went to the car and returned with the coat, which was an expensive, high-quality, full-length leather with a fur collar. I walked back into the house and handed it to him.

"Perfect," he said. He handed it to one of his partners who put it on. I walked with him outside and into the backyard where a large glass bowl was half-buried in the snow bank. Inside the bowl was a large thermometer which would allow him to see the temperature rise as he mixed the two main acids together. If the temperature was allowed to rise too quickly, it could be disastrous. I watched for a couple of minutes and then returned to the house. A short time later, the grease maker came in with the bowl and set it on the kitchen table, and Peg first mixed in the glycerine, then the baking soda.

"This will clarify it," he said to me, "but you have to do slowly."

"I can see why it's called grease," I said. I could see small globules of the nitro forming in the clear fluid, and it looked like small pockets of oil, or grease, floating in water.

"This is a good batch," he said, admiringly. He turned to his partner and complimented him on the mix. He had no sooner said that when there was a loud knock on the back door. Peg picked up the bowl and, as he carefully but quickly carried it into the bathroom, he told one of his partners to get the door. The bathroom door closed behind him.

I could hear the voices but I couldn't hear what was being said. We sat at in the living room and waited to see who'd arrived. Soon Peg's partner returned to tell us it was the meter man, asking to read the water meter. I heard the toilet flush. A moment later Peg stepped out of the bathroom with an empty bowl in his hands.

"It's cops," said Peg. He looked at me. "Will you check it out?" I nodded my head and walked out the front door to my car. I looked up and down the street and I could see what appeared to be a cop car parked down the block. After looking in my glove compartment, as if searching for something I'd forgotten, I returned to the house.

"Well?" asked Peg.

"I think it's cops," I replied. I told him about the car on the street, and my impression of it. Peg had rinsed out the bowl and it sat shiny and clean on the kitchen table.

We sat waiting for a sound at the doors, but none came. I left with Kenny a short time later, taking my leather coat with me, and in a minute we were headed back downtown. Five minutes later two city detectives pulled us over.

One of them approached the driver's side of our car and asked for Kenny's driver's licence and registration and, when Kenny produced both and handed them to him, he retreated to his car. Kenny gave me a report on what he saw in the rearview mirror.

"He's calling it in," he said. "Did you notice how nervous he was?"

"Yeah, I noticed," I replied. It was five minutes later that a pair of uniformed cops pulled in front of us, but they didn't get out of the car. The detective finally got out and walked to our car, handed Kenny his papers, and asked that we go to the police station. He wanted to drive Kenny's car himself.

"Nobody drives this fuckin' car but me," replied Kenny bluntly.

"Then I'll ride with you."

"Go ahead," agreed Kenny. "But you ride in the back."

"Sure, no problem." But I had other ideas.

"No, you ride in front, I'll ride in back," I said, and I opened the door and got out. The detective walked around the car and he climbed in front while I climbed in back.

I had a stolen ten thousand dollar bond in my pocket, taken from a can score, and I had to stash it or I was pinched. By the time we arrived at the police station, I'd managed to pull it out of my front pocket and stash it in the front of my pants. Not only did I save the bond, I saved myself a great deal of trouble as well.

They searched us, placed us in separate rooms and held us there for many hours. We knew they'd be ripping the car apart, searching for anything illegal, but we were clean and we knew it. They finally came in and told me that they would let us go if we gave them our permission to take our pictures. We agreed; after all, they already had all kinds of mugshots of us. What was one more?

I had just checked out of the motel room and, as I was putting my suitcases in the trunk of the car, I picked up the leather coat. I found myself holding a sleeve. I touched the collar and though it held to the coat, when I lightly tugged, it too fell away. The coat had been eaten through by the sulphuric acid used in the grease-making. When Kenny appeared I explained what had happened. We got rid of it right away.

I'd rented a house with a long narrow living room and a large kitchen. The narrow living room made it perfect for the bootlegging joint I had in mind. I could seat a large number of people on each side of the living room, and there was still room for someone to walk between the drinkers and keep the alcohol smoothly flowing. I put the word out on the street that I'd be open for business on a specific night. I also put out the word that I had a house philosophy and practice: if anyone were beaten for their money, the house would pay them in full. I wanted people to feel protected and safe, because we were all brothers and sisters in crime and punishment.

I chose a man to run the place. He'd just been released from the penitentiary and needed money. He was loyal, I was sure, and because I'd known him inside, I strongly believed in him. His name was Razz and he was half-tough, which was important when one considered the collective history and character of the patrons. They were all hookers, pimps, robbers and thieves, and we all knew each other, in one way or another.

The first night I opened I had forty-one people in the place and all were heavy drinkers. People kept coming all night long, and if someone was too drunk to drive, I paid the cab bill to get them home. The money was flowing in, Razz received forty percent of the net and I took care of everything else, including stocking the place with booze. Booze was cheap, because I simply bought and paid for it from boosters and thieves.

I decided to go to Calgary and I left the bootlegging joint in Razz's hands and though I was going to be gone for only three days, he had enough supplies to last longer than that.

On my way back I was driving down one of the main drags, on my way to the house, when I saw a string of fire trucks ahead.

"I hope they're not going where I think they're going," I said to Linda. I'd been with Linda for only a few weeks; she was good people.

"Yeah, me too," she replied.

I turned down my street and saw my fears were well-founded—there was a car burning in front of my place of business, and as I slowly drove past, I saw that every window in the place was broken. I didn't see anybody I knew and I didn't stop to enquire from the firemen as to the cause of the flames and smoke and broken glass. I kept going until I'd put a few blocks between us and the house, and I pulled over. I took the house key off the ignition key ring, and I threw it out the window. My bootlegging days were over, but I was determined to find out what had happened. It didn't take me long to get the story.

Kenny always carried a lot of cash in his pocket, and when he stopped in to see who was around, two of Peg's crew, along with one of the women, drunk and feeling mean at the time, tried to rob him, but he managed to get away. This was enough to send them into a drunken rage so they trashed the place. One woman produced a can of hair spray from her purse and they used it to torch Kenny's car. It was his car that was on fire when I drove by, and though the men were the ones doing the damage, it was the women who provided the fuel for the flames, in every way. I never forgave them for it.

Life was good for me, but I wasn't good for the community and it was only a matter of time before the police would catch up to me. It was less than two months later, in November, 1970 that I was arrested for possession of instruments of forgery, and I was placed in the remand section of Regina Gaol. There I met a very unusual man who was to become my friend, and later my enemy.

Maurice Laberge was a young thief who had been arrested for safecracking, and because he was on my range, we naturally came in contact and we spoke to each other. Maurice—or Mo as he preferred to be called—was bright and articulate and he also offered to help me, if he could, because he was making bail. I asked him to stop in and see Linda, and let her know that I would be seeing her soon. Mo told me he would gladly deliver the message.

There was an escape plan underway and, though I initially had no intention of escaping, it didn't take long before I was an integral part of the plan. It was a simple plan. Security windows had to be removed before the bars could be cut. I showed one of the escapees how to notch the blade of an ordinary butter knife and make it into a working tool which would saw through the cement holding the window blocks together. In a matter of hours, the windows lay under a bed and we were cutting through the outer steel bars. Once they were cut, there was just one fence standing between us and the open Saskatchewan fields.

I escaped a few nights later with John Dolack, an American who was wanted for some very serious charges in Kansas City, Missouri. We walked the ten miles into Regina. When I hooked up with Linda I found myself in the company of Dave, whom I'd known in the penitentiary and who was now with Linda's sister, Ramona. Mo was there as well. Once I had changed from prison clothes into my own, my next concern was John. I'd left him stashed in the attic of an empty house. Dave and Mo took him some food and some clothes, and I sent him a message that we'd get him out that evening. Later on that day, John was arrested, and though we initially believed he'd foolishly allowed himself to be seen, we later learned the truth.

Two days after my escape, Dave and I managed to take down the biggest drugstore score in the history of Regina, and we had every dope fiend for a hundred miles trying to find us. We contacted a friend of mine named Arnie, and explained that we were on our way to Boulder, Colorado. He bought a sizable piece of the narcotics from us, and we had the cash to get us there comfortably. Arnie and I sat down and picked out the good drugs from the bad, and we flushed more than ten thousand goofballs down the toilet. Goofballs were deadly on the street; the people who used them would become violent and uncontrollable. We felt quite proud of ourselves for being so civic-minded.

Dave and I never did get to Boulder. We were arrested while waiting for Mo in a parking lot in the north end of the city. I received a sentence of nine years for the B&E of the drugstore and the escape. Dave was handed five years which, when added to the sentence he was serving on parole, gave him more than seven to do. We knew Mo had set us up, as he'd set John up, but more than seven years would pass before I would see him again.

The penitentiary welcomed us once again and Dave and I began doing our time in the traditional way, by wheeling and dealing and running poker games. He and I made a good team and we had some good friends, one of whom was Bobby McKinnon. We were all half-bright, and though we were criminals, we still retained a decent value system under the circumstances. We became students in the university program and did well in our intellectual pursuits. We became prison politicians by running for election on the inmate committee, and when we were voted in, we did what we could for our fellow prisoners.

In late 1972, Dave and others had transferred to the east coast, and I applied for a day-parole to attend university in Saskatoon. I learned I had a flair for writing, demonstrated by the quality of papers I submitted in my classes. I actually believed my Criminology and English professors when they told me I could go as far as I wanted in university.

One of the strongest supporters we prisoners had was the John Howard Society. The local chapter of the society was headed by Al Hartley, a positive-thinking individual who had a belief in the good of his fellow man. He believed that prisoners could change, and he put his energy into helping those he believed in. I was one of those men.

The John Howard Society found the funding to assist me with my tuition to continue my education, and our expectations were high that the national parole board would approve my plan. After talking to one of the parole officers, who told me he was strongly recommending that I be granted a day-parole to attend university, my expectations were raised even further. It was not to be. The same parole officer wrote a report reflecting his belief that I was not a good candidate for parole, and the Head of Classification wrote in his report that the community did not owe me an opportunity to go to university. I was instead granted a day-parole to work as a bartender in the Golf and Curling Club in Prince Albert.

Although I was disappointed, I appreciated being allowed out to work for a few hours in the evenings, and Carol, my girlfriend from Edmonton, was staying in town. But I wasn't able to earn enough money to pay my cab bills to and from the penitentiary. The people who worked at the Club had had some previous negative experiences with prisoners on parole, and it showed in their relationships with me.

One very slow night I walked into the kitchen to see if I could have a snack, and I was met by a woman who obviously did not want to be near me. I could see fear and concern in her face, so I thanked her for her time and walked out. When I mentioned the incident to one of my co-workers in the bar, she explained what had happened a few months earlier.

A man from the provincial jail had been hired to work as a waiter and bartender in the curling club and, for a time it went well, but then one bright summer day things went from good to bad. The man started drinking and the alcohol gave him the idea he could be more familiar with the club members, many of whom were the city's most prominent businessmen. The man who owned the local radio and television stations, and who was on the board of directors of the club, was one of the unfortunate ones to be chosen as a recipient of his rude and overfamiliar approach, and he called the parolee on it.

"Do you know who I am?" he said.

"Yeah," the convict replied, "just another rich alcoholic, but I don't give a fuck— I'll serve you anyway." The patron left to find Les, the manager.

The parolee had a couple more drinks, which kicked-started his hunger, and he decided he would step into the kitchen and have a snack.

The head of the kitchen, a short, rotund, middle-aged woman named Rae who wore her dark hair in a severe bun, was not accustomed to anyone taking over any part of her domain.

"You can't do this!" said the woman, as he proceeded to walk into the cooler where he quickly selected a platter of cold chicken.

"No? I'm doing it aren't I?" he replied, aggressively. He brushed past her, found a loaf of bread, and proceeded to make himself a sandwich.

"I'm telling you to get out..." she began. But his actions interrupted her in mid sentence. He reached past her and picked up the meat cleaver.

"Fuck you," he responded, punctuating his sentence by chopping his sandwich in two on the chopping block with such force that it took the manager considerable effort to later remove it. The woman fled.

He took a bottle from behind the bar and wandered out to the green of the first hole, where the police found him sleeping beside one of the sand traps. I understood then why the woman had looked at me askance when I walked into her kitchen. Although I did try and assure her that not all parolees were bad men, she forever remained unconvinced. Whenever she walked into the bar, she made a point of steering away from me. It hurt, but there was nothing I could do about it.

Many penitentiary guards and their wives frequently dropped in after their curling games for drinks, or to watch a bonspiel on the ice below. Some were quick to take offence when they felt I was discriminating against them for being guards at the penitentiary. But in such instances, I could usually assuage them, and they'd seem to believe that I wasn't prejudiced against them.

One day, during a minus-forty cold snap, I was reading the local paper and I mentioned to the female bartender that the temperature in San Francisco was a balmy seventy-two degrees.

"Are you thinking of going there?" she asked. And of course I had thought about it.

"No, just making a comment," I replied. Carol left for Edmonton and it was less than a week later that I not only left Prince Albert, but impulsively left the province and headed to Montréal.

I was walking across the dome, heading for the dining room in the morning, and as I passed by one of the guards seated on a chair, he rose to his feet and signalled for the gate to be opened.

"Going to work?" he asked.

"Yeah," I said, hiding my surprise because it was my day off. We walked through the door and into the change room where my street clothes were hanging on a peg. I quickly changed and walked to the front of the prison. I asked one of the guards in the security bubble to call me a cab. It was a regular routine for me, and we'd become accustomed to it. Ten minutes later the cab arrived and I climbed into it. I wouldn't be back for three long years.

A friend of mine drove me to Saskatoon where I stayed with some friends, made a few phone calls, and a day later I caught a train for Montréal.

HOUDINI

The lights of Montréal filled the windshield of the half-ton truck, and as we headed south, I felt I could hide behind the bright lights of the city forever. Donny McKinnon and a friend of his had picked me up at the train station and, though I considered staying in the city, after talking it over, it seemed wiser to find a safe place in the small town of Bedford.

Bedford, Québec was only ten miles from the United States border, and Donny had often been back and forth from Bedford to Burlington, Vermont. It was easy to unofficially cross into the U.S. by taking one of the country roads which would allow me to completely avoid customs if I so chose, though I'd picked up some identification in Winnipeg which was good enough to withstand a spot check by police or customs.

The Maurice Hotel in Bedford was one of those small country hotels where the bartender was most accommodating, and the bar would stay open as late as we wanted. For a week we did nothing but drive around the countryside during the day, and sit drinking tall cold ones by the cherrywood fire in the evening. During one of our fireside chats, we decided we'd head to Burlington, Vermont, and check out some of the night spots. The next day we drove through the customs checkpoint without a problem, and an hour later we were in the city of Burlington.

There was a supper club called The Old Board Restaurant, where the food was great and the live entertainment was even better, and we naturally gravitated toward it. The Vietnam war had taken away many of the young men in the area, so there were unescorted women, and there was never a shortage of partners for the dance floor. Within a week, Donny and I had met many people, most of them women, and while we were living as if we were financially independent we wouldn't be able to keep up our facade much longer. Then I met Lora.

Lora was a slim, attractive blond woman barely out of her teens. She liked to dance, and there were times when she was just as mysterious as I was. Most of the people I met seemed ready to believe, with no help from me, that I was a draft dodger and not a Canadian at all. It was in my best interest not to encourage them to think otherwise. I was sitting at a table in the Old Board when Lora asked me, "What is it you do?"

"I'm working on the oil rigs," I answered. She reached across the table and took my hands in hers and casually ran her fingers across the smooth surface of my palms and smiled.

"You're not an honest man," she said. I didn't answer, choosing to remain silent and not make it worse for myself. I liked her.

Donny decided he'd go back to Edmonton, and I decided to remain in Burlington with Lora, at least until I heard from him. I truly did want to go work and live an ordinary life, but I would need the money to get me through the first month or so. I wouldn't be able to obtain assistance from anything like welfare, and I'd have to put together some strong identification. Over the next few weeks I set about putting together a plan to rob a bank. After that, I'd get a job and live happily ever after. The green mountains of Vermont were beautiful in winter, and as I traveled around the state with Lora's brother John, I could well imagine how nice the summers would be and I wanted to make Vermont my home. In March I decided I would travel to Edmonton, make some money, and return to my safe haven in the United States. I didn't have the money to travel by commercial means, and I didn't want to steal a car or steal money to get me to Alberta, so I decided I'd hitchhike.

Lora and I took the bus across the border. She would visit her father in Montréal and I began my hitchhiking trek at St. John, Québec. It was bitterly cold, and I was in for one of the most difficult trips of my life.

It took me five days to reach Edmonton, and even a day after I arrived, I still had to figure out what I was going to do. After I met Bob the decision was made for me.

Bob was a man I'd met a few years earlier, the partner of a good friend of mine who also happened to be a bank robber. I had run into Bob at a friend's home, and in a short period of time we'd renewed our acquaintance, at least to the extent that he wanted me as a partner in a safecracking score.

The safe sat on the lower floor of a business in Edmonton, and we'd have to rent a truck to haul it away. I used my false identification to do so. Later that night we drove the U-haul truck across town to pick up the small, five-hundred-pound safe. There were only the two of us so it wasn't an easy task, but we managed to get it done.

I spent most of the night hacking my way through the bottom, using only a five-pound hammer and a chisel to get to the money. When I finally had a hole big enough to get at the contents, I found myself holding a handful of one dollar bills in one hand, and a bottle of cheap wine in the other. We didn't make enough money to pay for the hammer and chisel, which we had to destroy, let alone pay for the truck. I decided I would rob a couple of banks and go back to Vermont.

The afternoon before the robberies were to occur, I received a telegram from Lora, who said she'd decided to travel to Edmonton herself, and I was to meet her at the airport on Saturday. I immediately phoned her and told her I would call her the next day, and that if she didn't get a call from me she was not to come. She agreed.

I phoned her the next afternoon while I was still counting money on the living room floor at a friend's house, and she told me she was on her way. She arrived less than twenty-four hours later.

We rented a car on Sunday and traveled to Calgary where I'd made reservations at the International Hotel. Our plane would leave for Montréal at ten in the morning, and we'd travel from Montréal to Burlington on the bus the same day. I asked Bob to travel with us so he could bring the rental back to Edmonton, and he agreed to do so when he learned it was fine with me if his girlfriend and her sister accompanied us. We were soon on our way.

At Red Deer, Alberta we decided we would stop at a restaurant and have a late seafood supper and a bottle of wine. I felt that I was with good friends and I decided to do the right thing by Bob, just in case he found himself in trouble. I had trusted him thus far, to the extent that I had placed three handguns in his care to deliver to the original owner, and I believed I could trust him even further. I wrote down Lora's phone number on a corner of dinner napkin, tore it off and folded it into a very small ball.

"Does your wallet have a change purse?" I asked Bob.

"Yeah, it does," he replied.

"Let me see," I said. He took out his wallet and handed it across the table. I opened the flap of his change purse and tucked the paper ball into a corner of it.

"What's that?" he asked.

"My phone number," I explained. "If you ever find yourself in trouble here, just call me and we'll have a place for you." He took his wallet and thanked me, and we continued with our supper.

It was close to midnight when we stopped in front of the International and began unloading our suitcases. Bob was giving me a hand by taking the suitcases from the trunk and placing them on the sidewalk. We said our goodbyes and I carried our luggage in and put it by the front desk. As I was setting the suitcases down, I noticed the absence of the attaché case which held the money, and I quickly walked back outside.

I could see the tail lights of the rental less than a block away, and at the same time I spotted a cab parked a few yards away. I ran over to it and jumped into the back seat.

"Follow that car," I said. I realized how foolish it sounded, but there was no other way to say it.

"Yeah, right," said the cabbie, who thought I was joking.

"I'm serious," I said. I threw down a handful of twenties on the seat beside him and ordered him to do what I asked. He didn't hesitate; he put the car in gear and burned rubber. We caught Bob at a light about ten blocks away from the hotel. The cab pulled up beside him and I got out. Bob rolled down his window.

"You have my case, Bob," I said.

"Ah no, I put it on the sidewalk," he said.

"Open your trunk," I said. He looked at me for a moment, and I couldn't tell if he truly believed he'd given me the case or not. I only knew he was going to open the trunk of his car.

When he opened it, the case was in plain sight. I wondered how he could have missed it, but he was very apologetic and I was very happy the cab had happened to be idle at the hotel.

The next morning Lora and I were on the plane, heading for Montréal, and as we flew over the cold landscape, I mentioned my hard experience hitchhiking a few days before.

"I'll never hitchhike again in my life," I told her. We were drinking wine and eating shish kebob. She looked very nice in the seat beside me.

"You made it, though," she said.

"Yes, I made it," I agreed, "but there were times when I didn't think I would. And I promised myself, if I did make it without freezing to death in a ditch somewhere, I'd never travel like that again." The plane made one twenty-minute stop in Toronto and we arrived in Montréal in late afternoon without incident, and caught the bus to Burlington on time. It couldn't have been better.

Lora went back to work as the Secretary of the State Board of Registration, and I lived the quiet life of a man without a care in the world. Spring had arrived, and though I had no clear idea of what my future would be in the States, it was the first time in my life I'd lived as a normal human being in the community. Every once in a while I'd think about the phone number I had put into Bob's wallet, but many weeks had passed and the phone hadn't rung so I wasn't overly concerned.

Lora and I took a short holiday to New Hampshire where I bought a Bearcat III police scanner because I had a plan to rob another bank and it would come in handy during the robbery. By this time, Lora had a fair idea who I was, and how I had made my money.

One night we were sitting at home when I asked her about the local jail, if she'd heard of anybody escaping from it.

"Yes," she replied, "they get out of there all the time."

"That's interesting," I remarked.

"Do you want to take a look at the jail?" she asked.

"Yes, I would."

"We'll go tomorrow," she said.

The jail was a surprisingly small, square brick building with ordinary steel bars on the windows, and it sat right on the corner of a busy street. Though I didn't want to think of being arrested, I knew the possibility existed and if it did, I wanted to be prepared to get out again. Lora was driving the Opel I'd picked up, and she went so far as to drive around the jail as if doing a dry run. She was getting into the outlaw image, something I didn't discourage.

"If I'm arrested, will you bring me a handgun on a visit?" I asked her. She glanced at me and gunned the motor at the lights.

"Yeah, I'll bring you a gun," she agreed. I began to feel better. I had a damned good partner, one I could trust and count on. A few nights later, the phone rang, and, because it was long past the time when the phone should ring, it frightened me. Lora answered.

"It's Bob," she said, holding the phone out to me.

"Hi Bob," I said.

"It's not Bob," said a voice, "it's Vera." Vera was a woman I knew from Edmonton, and though she and I had had a brief encounter, she had no business calling me on the phone.

"How did you get this number?" I asked.

"Bob's old lady gave it to me," she replied.

"I want you to lose this number," I said.

"Don't you love me anymore?" she asked. Her tone was mildly sarcastic, as though she was teasing me and that it was no big deal.

"I like you," I said, "I always have—but don't call me here anymore." I heard her say something to somebody else in the room, and I heard a woman's laughter in the background.

"I have to go, Vera," I said.

"Oh sure," she replied. After I hung up the phone, I suggested to Lora that she change her phone number to an unlisted one.

I called Bob and asked him how he was doing, and I told him about the phone call from Vera.

"Yeah, my old lady took the number out of my wallet and gave it to her," he said. He apologized but I told him it wasn't his fault.

"I'm getting an unlisted number."

"Great," he replied. "I think I'm coming out there to see you."

"I'll call you with my new number," I offered.

"I'll look after it," he said. The next day I called him and gave him the new one. Two days later Vera called again. I was now very worried, but there was nothing I could do about it. Less than a week later I was arrested by the FBI and Immigration Officers. I was lodged in the Burlington Correctional Centre. It was Friday morning.

The jail was an old one. I was placed on the second floor, which was used for maximum security prisoners. Sunday afternoon at two o'clock I was called for a visit from Lora. At three-thirty, armed with a .38 calibre Smith and Wesson revolver, I locked up seven sheriffs and five prisoners and made my escape. Less than two days later I was arrested by detectives from the city police and taken back to the Burlington Correctional Centre.

The next morning I was brought before the judge and charged with the escape. The State's Attorney, Mr. Patrick Leahy, was to prosecute me on more than one appearance in Vermont's system of justice, and would later go on to become a well-known and popular Democratic Senator. After court I was escorted to Windsor Prison.

Windsor State Prison was well over a hundred years old and it had a history of keeping people confined for many years. It even had an execution chamber where, years before, men had gone to their deaths in the electric chair. It also housed Vermont's long-term prisoners and it didn't take me long to get to know some of them. In a matter of a few weeks, eight of us had put together an interesting escape plan.

A locking mechanism at the end of each range lifted and dropped a locking bar across the latch of the lock of each cell. Each cell had a steel plate which protected the latches and locking bar, but if we could remove the plate, it would be a simple task to lift the bar with a screwdriver and open the door. It was Gene's job to remove the rivets from the top of the plate. He brought in a drill and a quarter-inch bit from his place of work to drill out the old sinks—we drilled out the rivets in the door plates at the same time. In less than an hour we had our cell doors set up so we could go in and out any time we wanted. However, we needed some time to get away, which meant the guard in the security bubble would have to neutralized. If we could get inside the bubble and tie up the guard, we could then climb out the fire-escape window in the bubble and be in a position to reach the high wall.

The lock of the door leading into the bubble was controlled by a guard on the inside, and it seemed the only way to get in was if the guard on the inside hit the electronic button releasing the locking mechanism. However, there'd been a serious mistake made when the door was put on— all of the nuts on the bolts holding the locking mechanism plate were on the outside. If we could remove the nuts from the bolts and remove the plate, we could trigger the locking mechanism ourselves. And that's what we did—it went just as planned. To make it easier, the guard on duty dozed off at his post. He never heard a thing until we were standing in front of him.

With the guard safely locked in a cell we all crawled out the window and, with the aid of some picnic tables in the prison yard, we quickly made our way over the wall and into a waiting jeep. It carried us across the bridge of the Connecticut River and we were suddenly in New Hampshire. We were well aware of the rule of law that "hot pursuit" meant we would be hunted in New Hampshire as well as in Vermont.

Once we stepped out of the jeep, Gene, Dick, Tony and I went one way, while the other four went off in a different direction. I now had new partners.

Gene was a grey-haired, forty-two year old man who seemed much younger. He was a veteran of the Florida work gangs, allegedly referred to by fellow prisoners in Florida as, "a state-raised, good old boy." And I was soon to learn he was a bad drunk.

Tony was a twenty-four-year-old who had served two tours of duty in a tank corps in the mountain areas of Vietnam. He returned from war with two purple hearts on his sleeve, to what he thought would be a hero's welcome at the San Francisco airport. He instead found himself spit on by a beautiful young woman with long brown hair, only because he smiled at her on the street. "Baby killer," she'd said, with hatred and contempt. He checked into the nearest hotel, put on his civilian clothes, stuffed his uniform in a suitcase, shoved it under the bed, and left the city hitchhiking an hour later. Tony planted a bomb in a state official's cottage; the bomb was discovered before it went off, his fingerprints still on it. He was sentenced to five years in Vermont's state prison.

Dick was a young car thief who was quite serious about making a name for himself, and dangerous because of it. He was a tall, lanky, stringy-haired nineteen-year old who had spent the last three years in the joint.

The four of us took to a country road and in a short time skirted the edge of a hamlet. We stopped to rest and Gene managed to find himself some whiskey in a camper, and in minutes he was drunk.

We were walking down a dark country road when car lights stabbed through the darkness ahead, and as I dove into the darkness of the ditch, my knee struck a large rock. The pain was excruciating, causing my mouth to open in a silent scream. I could only walk with a straight-legged gait after, but I was pleased I could walk.

An hour later, we came across a car beside a farmhouse and within minutes we were on our way. Gene drove, there was no talking him out of it, and he gave us a scary ride.

On the outskirts of Concord, New Hampshire, the motor began to knock from a broken rod and piston, something Gene had caused by pushing the old car too hard. A short time later the engine seized up and locked solid. We simply pushed it off the road and into the ditch and continued on foot through the woods. After walking for miles through woods and swamp, sleeping now and then, at dawn we found ourselves on the shore of a large lake.

The woods around the lake were quite thick, and they offered us the cover we needed as we slowly made our way along the shoreline. Then a summer cabin, squatting peacefully atop a knoll and overlooking the lake, came into view.

It seemed vacant even though a jeep was parked by the front door. We looked across the lake to see a rowboat with four people fishing alongside the far shore, nearly a mile away.

We needed food, a fact which necessitated at least one of us approaching the summer cottage, and because Gene and Dick were both healthy and agile, it was decided they would make the move as a team. If someone was in the house, the two were to ask for a gallon of gas and immediately leave. Tony and I would remain out of sight in the woods.

"What if there's only one person there?" asked Dick.

"What do you mean?" I asked. I knew exactly what he meant but I asked anyway.

"Well, if there's only one you never know what could happen." There was an ominous, sinister tone in his voice, suggesting something evil.

"You leave them alone," I quietly replied. "We're not going to terrorize any of these people." There was a hollow feeling in my stomach. "If the cabin is empty just take some food and then get the hell out of there without leaving a trace." I turned my gaze on Gene, looking to him for some confirmation that he understood. "We'll meet you back at the creek Gene, at the same place we crossed." I was initially relieved when Gene nodded his head.

"It'll be okay,' he stated, but he broke away from my gaze too quickly. I could feel a sense of foreboding close in and over me.

Tony and I retraced our footsteps to the creek, easier now we had some idea of where we'd been. Once back at the site we built a fire.

The small bundle of dry twigs was full of orange flames, and Tony and I were putting the last of the branches in a pile for later when there was a crash in the underbrush. Gene and Dick had returned.

Both of them carried pillowcases full of heavy objects. When dumped onto the soft floor of the forest, these turned out to be weapons and whiskey, topped off with one red can of tomato paste. *Whiskey and guns*, I thought, *one hell of a combination.*

There were six handguns, a 12 gauge pump shotgun, a .32 Special carbine and ammunition for them all. Gene and Dick quickly laid claim to their weapons, with Gene selecting the large stainless steel .357 Magnum with a six-inch barrel. Dick wanted the .45, but after a quick look told him the clip wouldn't fit in the butt of the pistol, he settled for the carbine. Tony took the shotgun and I picked up a .22 calibre, nine-shot revolver on a Buntline Special frame. It was perfect for shooting game birds, something I knew I was going to have to do if I wanted to eat. I felt weak from lack of food, and I knew I'd have to get some nourishment into my body if I wanted the healing process to take effect in my leg. I heard the clinking of the bottles of whiskey. I turned to see Gene pick up a bottle of brandy and watched as he tossed the cap over his shoulder, suggesting he was not going to stop until the bottle was empty.

Gene took three long swallows, his Adam's apple working in an effort to keep up with the liquor flowing down his throat, and he passed the bottle to Dick. Three more swallows from Dick, whose lanky arm passed it to Tony, who took a small taste and then took three paces to pass it to me. With his long hair and steel-framed glasses Tony looked completely out of place.

I leaned back in a reclining position on my left side, the bottle in my hand, my right leg held straight because my swollen knee was impossible to bend. I watched the whisky flush slowly appear on the faces of the two guzzlers. Tony did not present a problem, but the other two would soon be drunk, a fact that promised very dangerous things. Gene's .357 lay a good three feet from where he squatted, which meant it would take time, effort, and balance even for a sober man to reach the revolver, and more time to turn and fire, which made me feel more at ease. Dick was jacking the action of the carbine, asking Gene how to load it. Gene showed him. Unnoticed, I was examining the can of tomato paste, reading the label to see if there was anything in the can that I could use for energy. A glance over the label told me there was little or nothing there.

"Give us a slug," said Gene. I tossed the bottle to him and as it floated through the air I noticed that Gene was able to catch it with a minimum amount of fumbling. *The man has soft hands,* I thought.

Gene tipped back the bottle and three more swallows sent a considerable amount of alcohol into his belly. I was pleased. *Drink it up boys,* I said to myself. The .22 felt comfortable and very reassuring in my belt. Gene handed the bottle to Dick, who tried to match Gene's consumption. He started to cough on the third swallow, Gene laughed and reached for the bottle and Dick almost retched as he gave the bottle back. When he'd caught his breath, it seemed the brandy had given him an idea.

"Let's get the jeep," he said.

"Yeah, we could," agreed Gene.

"What jeep?" asked Tony.

"The jeep by the cabin—it's got a stereo and everything," Dick answered. He said that they'd seen car keys on a counter by the sink, keys which would, he ventured, fit the ignition of the jeep parked in front of the cabin.

"I'll drive," stated Gene, glancing sideways at me. It was a look that was not meant to be recognized for what it was: mean and dangerous.

"I'm not going," I said.

"What the fuck do you mean?" Gene asked, belligerently.

"It's too dangerous," I replied. The position of my body, propped on my left elbow as it was, allowed my left hand to be within inches of the butt of my gun in my belt.

"Fuck dangerous!" It was Dick. "We got the guns, it sure as fuck won't be dangerous for us." He sat upright, the carbine across his lap. The full effect of the liquor was apparent. If he tried walking, he'd stagger and stumble. Danger crackled in the air like the flames in the fire beside me.

"By now the police have found the car we left on the side of the road, and once this housebreaking is reported, it won't take much detective work to put together who stole these guns," I reasoned. "The cops will be looking for us. They'll know that we're armed and they'll blow us off the road." I looked directly at Gene, but Dick jumped in.

"I might have something to say about that." He cocked and uncocked the carbine and glanced at me malevolently.

"Well you guys can go," I stated. "As for me, I'm comfortable walking."

"What about your leg?" asked Tony. He peered at me through his steel frames.

"My leg will be fine," I answered. "Once we get some food into us we'll feel better and I'll heal up."

Tony interrupted me. "We could go for a few miles," he said. He was obviously trying to keep the peace.

"Not for one mile," I stated firmly. I knew there would be no stopping the jeep once it was on the road.

"We're going," declared Gene, the brandy bottle dangling in his hand. I noticed there was only an inch left in the bottom. Gene glanced at Dick for support.

"Yeah," Dick muttered, "we're going." Dick was clearly feeling the power of both the brandy and the carbine, yet I knew he'd most certainly miss the first shot he chose to take. I could feel the fear building in me, and with it came hatred for the two of them, but I wanted to avoid any kind of real confrontation, like a gunfight, even though I believed I could win.

"Okay," I agreed. I rose to my feet, keeping the fire between them and myself. I turned my back on them and began to walk with a stiff-legged gait along the stream. "I'm heading into the woods."

I had taken no more than ten steps when I heard the guttural murmur of Gene's voice. I couldn't make out the words but the menacing sound became cold fingers ruffling the hair on my neck. I pulled the .22 from my belt with my left hand and quickly turned to my right to face them, the gun hanging loosely at my side.

Gene was stretched out on his side, his arm outstretched and reaching for the .357. As Gene's fingers touched the checkered butt, he looked up to what he thought would be a retreating back. His hand froze when he saw me standing a few yards away, the .22 revolver at my side, calmly looking at him. For the briefest moment there was a drunken calculation on Gene's face, but even with the brandy in his veins his courage failed him, and he slowly rolled his body away from his handgun.

"What the fuck," he said, turning, "can't we talk about this Wayne?" In that instant the tension broke. There was now a petulant tone in Gene's slurred words.

"Sure we can," I said. I kept my tone neutral, as though nothing had happened, and I saw that even Dick appeared more relaxed. Tony's eyes were large, almost luminous behind his glasses. I walked back to the place I had been resting and assumed my comfortable position. The jeep idea had died.

Gene and Dick began to talk quietly while they finished the last of the brandy; Tony moved closer to me as we all felt the night close in on us.

"You really have a strong personality," murmured Tony. I looked at his bearded face only a few feet from my own. Although I knew Tony would've helped to dig the hole to bury me if Gene had put a bullet in my back, I felt no animosity toward him. On the contrary, I felt a kinship, for any man who wouldn't have pulled the trigger on me would have to be considered a friend under the circumstances.

"I like to think I'm a realist," I acknowledged. A last-minute check revealed Gene telling Dick one of his war stories from Florida. I lay back and allowed myself to relax. A short time later, after the fire had died down and the two drinkers had fallen prone into drunken snores, I took a closer look at Gene's .357 magnum.

It was a large, well-polished steel handgun, deadly in its appearance. I opened the cylinder and found it loaded with semi-wad cutter ammunition, which would mushroom on contact with flesh. The mechanical action was smooth, as if it had been well oiled recently, but when I cocked it, I found the firing pin had been sheared off at the hammer—the gun was incapable of firing. Tony had been watching my examination, but I gave no indication of what I'd found.

"Nice gun," I remarked, replacing it where I'd found it. "It would make a hell of a hole in a man." I didn't tell the others that the gun was useless, and I rested much easier. If I had trouble with either of them, I'd now only have to focus on Dick and the rifle. The thought was comforting. I put a few more branches on the embers of the bonfire, just enough to take the chill off my bones, but not enough to be noticed unless someone stumbled into our camp.

The next morning, as dawn broke, we took to the woods and travelled fast. By the time night fell we'd covered a considerable distance. We seldom stopped to rest and I'm sure the others wished they had taken the jeep.

That night, as we crossed a road which we'd been avoiding and stopped to rest on the lip of a gravel pit, Tony and Dick decided they would walk the road into the next town. They assured Gene and me they'd steal a car and return to pick us up. I didn't bother telling them I wouldn't get in the car, even if it was a Rolls Royce.

"If you leave," I said to Tony, "you're buying a ticket on a train heading straight back to the penitentiary." But he had made up his mind.

"No hard feelings?" asked Tony. He looked completely worn out and his face and hands were swollen, evidence of his suffering from insect bites over the past few days.

"No," I replied, "no hard feelings, but you leave the rifle and the shotgun here." They agreed, we all shook hands, and Dick and Tony slid down the side of the gravel pit. I watched in the moonlight as they walked away down the road.

Gene and I backed away from the lip of the gravel pit to lie in the thick grass along the edge of the woods. I needed only to lift my head and glance to the mouth of the gravel pit for a clear view of the county road. We went to sleep where we lay.

The crunch of tires on gravel woke me some time later. When I raised my head I saw a police cruiser coming to a halt fifty yards in front of me. After watching the car for a few minutes, during which time there was no other activity, I realized the cruiser had picked the spot to surprise and inspect any vehicles that might pass by. I woke Gene to let him know the car was there. After a word of caution to be careful if he rose to his feet, we both went back to sleep.

Dawn was breaking when the sound of voices brought me awake. There were now two police cruisers, parked side by side with their engines running. It appeared the two drivers were exchanging information. Perhaps they were simply passing the long hours, but when another police cruiser slowly drifted past, I knew they were searching the area. There was a good chance that Tony and Dick had been arrested, and that at full light there would be police, and their dogs, looking through the woods. I woke Gene.

"Those fuckin' idiots," muttered Gene when he was fully awake and apprised of the situation. We backed away from the gravel pit, and within minutes we'd put a considerable distance between ourselves and our makeshift beds.

Gene and I kept moving slowly through the swamps of the lowland outside Concord, sometimes walking extra miles to avoid open meadows and fields, but then the dogs were on our trail. When we first heard them they were a long way off, but soon their baying told us they were hot on our scent. We did everything to throw them off.

When the baying of the bloodhounds took on an excited, feverish pitch, we'd backtrack to throw them off. It always worked, at least for a time; the baying would dwindle away into the distant woods, but then, inexorably, it would always return.

At one point, we came upon a four-foot high stone fence which cut through the forest like something prehistoric, and though there was no reason for it in the present day, we knew it had been painstakingly made many years earlier to designate a property line. We walked on the top of it, for the stones had been well chosen and flat, which made walking on them as easy as strolling down a street. We travelled on the fence for more than half a mile. When we left it to take a diagonal course through the thick woods, we did so by leaping to a low branch and swinging our bodies as far as possible from the fence itself. It had been hours since we'd heard the dogs.

We thought we'd lost the dogs for good when we stumbled onto a cabin in the middle of a clearing. After careful investigation proved it to be empty, we simply walked in the front door.

The inside was laid out like a bunkhouse with an old radio on the table and two bunk beds in the far corners. The empty cupboards on the walls told us the place was temporarily unused. There was a gallon of apple cider on the floor by the stove, and a four-ten pump shotgun stood propped up against one wall. The shells were in a drawer. I picked up the shotgun, loaded it, and carried it outside to shoot squirrels for food. The trees were full of them, but I shot only two for our stewpot.

Gene had built a fire and as I lay the squirrels by it, I noticed Gene didn't have the 12 gauge shotgun, but that he still clung to the useless revolver.

"Where's the shotgun, Gene?" I asked.

"I dumped it in the slough," he replied. The slough was only a hundred yards away. I took a pot from inside the cabin, walked to a small creek and filled it with water, and in minutes the water was boiling.

The squirrels were almost cooked, and though they were unattractive and bounced like grotesque rubber toys in the bottom of the pot, we knew that once we'd eaten them we would find at least some of our energy restored.

I was poking at the squirrel meat in the boiling water with a willow branch, conscious of how weak I felt. There was a numbness around my nostrils and mouth that comes from hunger, and I knew I was rapidly approaching exhaustion, but the meat was done.

"Let's eat," I said, but before he could take a step, we heard the sound of an approaching vehicle. I snatched up the rifle, Gene hurriedly picked up the .410 and we both quickly went to the window. A car with two passengers was slowly making its way down the old bush road toward the cabin. In a moment, both of us were running toward the woods. I glanced back to see a blue sedan parking beside the building.

"Down," I said, and Gene sprawled beside me in the tall grass. We turned and lifted our heads to see the cabin. Only the front of the car was visible. We heard a male voice.

"Leave me here and go," said one of our visitors. This seemed to bring about a short argument, an argument which the driver obviously lost, because the car backed up, and we could hear it pulling away. A moment later an old man appeared around the corner. As he walked inside the cabin, a curse flew out the open door.

"Okay you sons of bitches! I know you're here!" A moment later he was outside and looking at the edge of the woods where we lay. "And I want my God damn gun back!" He took a few steps toward us and paused for a moment. The old man had noticed the telltale markings of our hurried flight through the tall grass. Again he moved forward, muttering that he was glad we didn't get to eat his squirrels. The way he said "my squirrels" made me think the old man felt he owned the woods.

"He's coming," I whispered, and I couldn't help thinking as I saw his age, that he probably did own it, through longevity if nothing else.

"Think so?" asked Gene.

"I know so, he's seriously pissed off." He was almost upon us when I rose to my feet. I held the rifle at my side in my hand. The old man looked at it.

"I want my shotgun," he said. His tone of voice said he wouldn't accept "no" for an answer. Gene unfolded himself from the ground, the shotgun in his hand.

"Is this your gun?" asked Gene.

"You're God damn right it is—and I want it." I was surprised to see Gene begin to walk forward with the shotgun offered at the end of his outstretched arm.

"Gene!" I said sharply. Gene paused to look back. I moved so quickly that I felt a jolt of excruciating pain shoot through my injured knee. I snatched the gun from Gene's hand and backed away. With the rifle cradled in my elbow I continuously jacked back the action of the pump shotgun until it was empty, and then walked the few feet to the old man and warily handed him his gun. The man took it, and backed away himself. I knew that Gene was ready to quit and call it a day, but I had no intention of doing so.

"There are hundreds of police heading this way," said the old man. He was in his seventies, wearing a checkered shirt and khaki pants, and from the manner in which he held the shotgun, I knew he was familiar with guns, the bush, and perhaps even danger. It was easy to visualize him at the Legion on Remembrance Day, drinking beer with a chest full of combat medals.

"Hundreds?" I asked. It was very quiet in the meadow, and even the light breeze seemed content to only sway the tall grass without a sound.

"Dogs too," he offered. "And I told my granddaughter to tell them..." But I cut him off.

"Coming from which direction?" I asked.

"That way," said the old man. He pointed west, which was the direction Gene and I had come from. "If I were you I'd go the other way."

I carefully picked up the shotgun slugs I'd ejected from the old man's gun and put them in my pocket. I could feel the old man's eyes watching me closely as I did so.

"I'm sorry about the cabin," I offered.

"No harm done," replied the old man, and almost as an afterthought he added, "and you can have the squirrels if you want them." He seemed calm now, as if his gun were his most prized possession and he was satisfied now that he had it back. He would no doubt have a story to tell his grandchildren, and I felt some affection for the brave old man.

"No, thanks just the same," I answered.

"Suit yourself then," he replied, shrugging his shoulders.

"Let's go," I said to Gene, and though it seemed it was with some reluctance that Gene accompanied me, we both began walking toward the woods. Once in the cover of the trees, I looked back to see the old man trudging his way back to his cabin.

We headed east, against the wishes of Gene, who thought the old man shouldn't be trusted. It made sense to me that he'd been telling the truth, as there was no reason for the police to be coming from the other direction. And I was right.

It was over an hour later that we heard the baying of the hounds on our back-trail. We immediately took evasive action by wading through any water we saw, and at one point we found ourselves in a swampy area that spread for a quarter of a mile. At what seemed like the edge of the marshland we came to a grid road, with a culvert running under it. After we'd crawled through the small tin tunnel and walked through the water on the other side, we heard the baying of hounds slowly recede on a wild goose chase in a different direction.

Gene was completely played out, panting with exhaustion, so we paused for a few minutes, lying down on our sides on the soft earth of the forest to rest.

"We can stay right here," suggested Gene.

"The dogs will eat us up," I replied.

"They'll never see us in all this," Gene argued, and he waved his hand to indicate the dense underbrush.

"I can't quit," I stated. My tone suggested that Gene could do so, if he chose. Gene had no time to answer because the stillness of the woods was suddenly shattered by the sound of a police car siren whooping to our right, perhaps a hundred yards away. The sound was brief, as if a clumsy hand had inadvertently hit a button. It lasted for less than a heartbeat, and once gone, it made the closing night seem even more still and silent.

I stood to my feet and looked to our back-trail, my ears tuned to any sound that might indicate pursuers. There was no sound except my breathing. I held my breath and just before I released it, I heard a twig snap. I released my breath, and heard another. I recognized the sounds as the sounds of someone, or something, moving carefully through the woods. Take a step, wait a moment, listen, then take another step—it was the sound of either a predator on the hunt, or the sound of prey trying to avoid capture. Gene heard it too.

"Let's go," I whispered. I knew Gene would hear the fierce determination in my voice.

"No!" Gene reached out his hands and grabbed me, and I found myself in a wrestling match which, though short-lived, was enough to make our presence known to the searchers. I broke free of Gene's grasp just as the woods broke out in the crashing sound of men no longer concerned with maintaining their silence.

I ran forward, the pain in my knee unnoticed, the rifle grasped in both hands and held out in front of me to break a trail through the branches clutching at my body and clothes. The sounds of bullets snapped the air around me, and though I realized the men were shooting at the sounds I was making, I knew to stop running would mean immediate capture. I ran for a full minute, stopping only to pivot with the Winchester and fire three shots in rapid succession to buy myself some time. I heard a voice shouting at the pursuers to stop, that they were ruining the trail, but the rushing men ignored both my gunfire and the instructions, and they just kept on coming.

I ran again for some minutes, and I saw a clearing directly in front of me. If I could reach it, and cross it, it would put more distance between me and the pursuit. I ran headlong toward it.

I reached the edge of the clearing but just as I tried to cross it, I found I was falling. As I lay on my face in the mud and weeds, I felt the first brush of defeat touch me. I had fallen into a marsh bed, almost dry, whose tall grass had belied its depth.

Exhaustion had taken its toll, but as I looked up, I noticed an umbrella tree four feet from where I lay. It was shaped like an open umbrella, and with its full, leafy branches and hollow interior, it would offer me perfect cover. I quickly scrambled on all fours into its hidden confines. The space it offered was so small that I had to carelessly jam the rifle into the soft earth to hide it, but then I found I could curl myself into fetal position around the trunk of the small bush; only if someone actually parted the branches and peered in would I be seen. While I lay there, I noticed I'd lost my .22 revolver in my flight.

In less than fifteen seconds, men and dogs rushed through the area in a cacophony of sound. They were all around and they passed no more than three feet from me. In the midst of the noise, a voice could be heard haranguing the men to stop. For a full minute the sounds continued unabated. It was like a stampede that slowly began to dwindle and diminish, and a few moments later the sounds of the searchers faded into the distance.

I lay without moving, conscious that my body was slowly stiffening from the exertion and the damp. I calculated that it was thirty minutes after my injured leg had turned completely numb that I heard a quiet voice break the silence.

"They ruined the trail," said the deep voice, which sounded less than a dozen feet away. There was no answer. The voice went on, "I told them they should leave me out front—I know he's here, I can damn well feel it in my bones." I understood that the voice belonged to a man-tracker, and that he'd lost the trail because the rushing, charging men and dogs had destroyed it. The man's voice was confident and self-assured. There was nothing I could do but wait until evening came; only after night had completely covered the area did I have a chance to slip away. I did the only thing I could do—I allowed exhaustion to carry me into the heart of the darkness of sleep.

I woke hours later, and by the stiffness in my body, I judged the time to be well after midnight. I listened with bated breath for any sound that might speak of danger, but I heard nothing but the beat of my heart in my ears.

As quietly as possible, I began to unfold my cramped and stiffened body from around the tree. I had to slowly move each joint, from my fingers to my toes, but I gradually managed to successfully straighten my protesting muscles until I could stand. My knee was so badly swollen that my pant leg seemed to be the only thing holding it from ballooning further.

I recalled when my grandfather's foot slipped into the grain auger in the wheat granary we were emptying one cool fall day. He gave my uncle and me instructions on how to use a stick to slip the belt from the flywheel of the heavy water-cooled engine, figure-eight the belt and replace it on the pulley so that the reverse action would free his crushed foot from the auger's painful screws. My grandfather had refused to take off his ankle-length boot, saying "It'll swell so bad

I'll never get the damn boot on again." I knew that if I took off my pants to examine my knee, it would balloon and I wouldn't be able to put them on again.

I took off my heavy, mud-caked boots, and checked the carbine. Finding the muzzle solidly plugged with wet earth, I discarded it by pushing it back under the bush. I decided I'd backtrack. I knew the area now, and I felt there was a good chance that if they were waiting in ambush, it would be in front of me, not behind. I carried my boots in my hands, using my stocking feet as sensors to feel my way over the forest floor and out of the trap, but my injured knee made smooth motion impossible.

The adrenalin pumping through my body made each small scrape of a branch on my jeans sound like chalk across a blackboard, but I slowly made my way until I'd put a hundred yards between myself and the umbrella bush. I stopped, listened, then carefully moved forward again. I snapped a twig which sounded like a small explosion to my ears in the silent night of the woods.

A moment later came the sound of pounding feet and the light of flashlights held in the hands of running men danced down the road to my left. I began to move further into the woods, away from the road and the danger.

I finally stopped beside a huge maple tree whose trunk was large enough to conceal my body. I looked to where the flashlights were now moving through the woods toward me.

There were at least three men, and I calculated the distance between the lights to be twenty yards. They were making one last sweep of the woods for me, but it seemed that if they continued on their present course they wouldn't come within ten yards of the maple tree. I felt a sense of relief flood through me, but it was short-lived.

The light closest to me suddenly veered closer, and as it continued on a collision course with me, I saw why. An old but well-used game trail passed a few feet from where I stood. The light was moving more quickly because the man had found it easy walking. In a moment the light in the man's hand flooded the tree, as if it was that particular tree itself the man had been hunting all along. I knew it was too late to move, it was too late for anything.

"Come out," said a calm, sure voice. "Step into the light." I recognized the voice as that of the man-tracker I'd heard while I was at ground in the umbrella bush.

I stepped into the light, my boots in my right hand and the other held at shoulder height. The flashlight was centered on my chest, and as my eyes grew accustomed to the brightness, I could make out a figure pointing a short-barrelled pistol at my belly.

"Jimmy!" called the gunman. The response was an instant crash of bodies moving through the underbrush. In my peripheral vision I could see two more lights rapidly moving toward us. The first man there carried what appeared to be an M-16, but at the soft-spoken command of the man with the pistol, the muzzle of the high-powered weapon was lowered.

"You did it," said the man, "good stuff." His voice was full of admiration, but if he was about to add something further, it was lost in the crashing arrival of the third man. A large figure literally leapt into view, blocking out the lights of his partners, a man in his late twenties who held the barrel of his 12 gauge shotgun four feet from my chest.

"Move, you son of a bitch, and I'll kill you," he said. The voice seemed disembodied, as if it came out of the barrel of the shotgun itself. Above it I could see a face, contorted in hate and aggression, and the man's burning eyes held the energy of the hunter who, after a long and difficult hunt, had finally closed in for the kill.

"I'm going to drop my boots," I said quietly.

"Drop those boots and you're dead," said the man. His voice was flat. In the background I could hear the placating voice of the tracker telling the man it was over. I felt the exhaustion of the last week flow through me. It seemed to drain my will, as if my life's blood were running from my body and into the earth. I seriously considered dropping the boots and allowing the man to do what he wanted, but I didn't.

The man with the shotgun suddenly spun sideways and pumped three shots in quick succession into the trees around us, and I watched as bits of branches and leaves fluttered to the ground in the dim light.

"What the fuck are you doing?" demanded one of his partners, shocked his buddy could fire his weapon as he did.

"Just giving the boys something to think about," he answered. There was still a tremor of excitement in his voice.

The segregation cellblock of Windsor State Prison held twenty-four cells, twelve on each range with two ranges situated back-to-back. On one side of the block were the men who were unmanageable—they absolutely refused to bow to any of the rules and regulations, and were constantly fighting with prison guards. To add further to the problems in the Unit, was a new supervisor who seemed to believe he had the answer to handling the unruly, disobedient and disrespectful. He'd been brought in by state authorities to solve problems and had introduced a new "program" which consisted of instant, arbitrary punishment for any type of disobedience. If a prisoner threw his food tray at a guard, he was given a sandwich on a paper plate. If he threw that, his food was withheld until he apologized for his behaviour. If he still didn't agree to behave himself, he wasn't given another meal. Of course, the prisoners understood the logic behind the "program," but what the prison administration didn't seem to understand was that the prisoners knew such a system was against state law; they'd recently filed a lawsuit against the state requesting that the new program be discontinued as unconstitutional.

On my range, opposite the unmanageables, were the men who were escape risks, or in other ways dangerous to the prison. I had been confined on the range since my arrest outside Concord and I'd badly injured my knee during the escape from Windsor. I had further aggravated the initial damage by travelling a long distance on it, and though medical staff had written reports that my knee was irrevocably damaged, it was fine. However, because I continued to use a crutch, the muscles in my leg had deteriorated and I was beginning to worry. It was in my best interest that people believe I was incapable of full physical move- ment and real exertion, but I couldn't exercise it without exposing myself as a malingerer, and my muscles were suffering the effects. The smell of feces and urine was ever-present. It drifted to us from around the corner; as a last resort for the negative attention they required, the unmanageables would throw their feces and urine on guards as they passed their cells. We all gradually grew accus- tomed to the foul air, as we did many other unpleasantries in prison. We would realize this upon returning from a half-hour exercise in the small, fenced court- yard, in which there was only a horseshoe pit for recreation facilities. The fresh air felt and smelled great, but when we returned to the cellblock, the stench would be overpowering all over again. Yet no prisoner on my side of the block complained; we had to bear whatever we had to bear in order to lend our sup- port to the men who refused to recognize the authority of the state prison administration. Sometimes even the promise of the good air in the courtyard wasn't enough to entice me outside, because walking back into the stench of the block, and having to once again grow accustomed to it, made the short-lived pleasure of the thirty minutes not worth it. In a real way, the smells were appro- priate. The cellblock was situated in the deepest recesses of Windsor Prison— we truly did live in the bowels of the prison beast. As well, we didn't think the guards who worked in the area had much character. At the best of times we viewed them with mild contempt because they were there out of personal choice, while we were held there at gunpoint. Our attitude further aggravated an already bad situation.

When I had been in Windsor prison less than a week, I got a dark glimpse into Dick's soul. I was sitting shirtless in the yard one afternoon, my back against the cellblock wall. As I allowed the sun to wash away my prison pallor, a small group of prisoners were playing cards on a blanket to my left. To my right, six feet away, sat Dick who was talking with a buddy about his early childhood. They too had chosen to sit with their backs to the wall but, unlike many other convicts in the yard, they wore their shirts. Dick's companion was no more than nineteen himself.

"I never knew women actually liked it like that," Dick said, referring to a softcover book he held in his hand. The cover was a lurid picture of a woman with large breasts in a position of bondage. Her breasts were emphasized by the ropes which bound her.

"Yeah," said the kid, "I read that— it's a good book."

"I wish I would have known they liked it like that before."

"Yeah?"

"Yeah," casually replied Dick. "I knew this girl when I was a kid..."

"Yeah?"

"Yeah, she was really pretty and she lived on an acreage next to my parents. I really liked her too. But she was two years older than me." There was the sound of crackling cellophane, followed by the softer sound of a cigarette paper being crinkled as Dick rolled himself a smoke. "Want one?" he asked his buddy.

"Sure."

"Well she had a cat," continued Dick. "One of those fluffy white ones. A purebred I think, and they cost money—but her family was rich."

"A rich bitch," murmured his buddy. Dick struck a match and the sharp smell of sulphur, and then acrid cigarette smoke, drifted through the air.

"Yeah, rich. Well me and my buddy thought we'd do something nice for her. She'd left to go somewhere for a week on summer holidays, but we knew she was coming home soon. So we caught her cat." Dick's voice had taken on a whimsical tone as he recalled his first brush with young love.

"Caught him?" The kid appeared to be listening closely.

"Yeah, we kept him in a cardboard box, we fed him and everything." I was paying attention myself, although I gave no indication of it. I sat with my legs straight out in front of me, resting my back against the wall, appearing intent on simply absorbing the sun.

"What did you feed him?"

"Sardines," replied Dick. "Then, the night before she came home, we killed it. We skinned it and we put the skin in a shoe box." He paused to take a drag of his cigarette.

"It must have been bloody." This brought a snort of disagreement from Dick.

"No, no!" he declared, seemingly incensed that anyone would think him so callous. "I smothered it, then skinned it, and I was careful not to get the fur bloody." His tone of voice indicated that to him this was a very thoughtful act.

"Oh, you *smothered* it."

"I put the fur in the shoe box, fluffed it up real nice, put a ribbon around it and took it to her house the next day." Dick seemed sad now.

"Yeah?"

"Yeah. I knocked on the door and her mother answered. I asked for her. She came out right away and I handed her the box."

"What did you say?"

"I just told her there was some nice mittens inside for her."

"She opened it?"

"Yeah."

"Did she like it?"

"No. She looked at me, picked up the skin, saw the inside of it and started screaming, then dropped the box and ran inside the house calling for her mother."

"What did you do?"

"I ran away too. I just don't understand it. I went through a lot of trouble for that bitch— but she didn't appreciate a fuckin' thing I did for her. Do you know how hard it is, and how long it takes, to skin a cat and not hurt the fur?"

"No," replied the kid. "I never did that."

"And I spent my money on sardines for that fuckin' cat too, to keep it alive and fresh for her. It would've made some real nice mittens. I thought girls liked things like that." I felt a chill go through me. Dick had no feeling at all for what he'd done. Dick's companion seemed oblivious to the horror himself.

I felt as though the sun had suddenly lost its warmth. I unfolded myself from the ground and stood. As I casually shrugged my shoulders into my denim shirt, I glanced at the two kids. They were busy looking up a scene in the book Dick held in his hands, and I thought to myself *A little learning is indeed a dangerous thing*.

On my range were the men who'd escaped with me in July, including Dick and Tony. One day we were outside sitting beside the horseshoe pit, when I saw Tony using the end of an exacto blade to carve a small wooden pipe. He was very good at it and it got me thinking, *John Dillinger used a wooden gun to break out of prison. Why couldn't I do the same?* I watched Tony as he worked, until a moment came when he and I had a few seconds of privacy.

"Could you carve me a wooden gun?" I asked him quietly.

"What kind of gun?" he asked.

"Something small, like a snub-nose .38."

"If I had a picture I could," he replied.

"I'll find it in one of the magazines."

"A Banker's Special would be good," he suggested. I noticed and appreciated that he never asked me why I wanted it.

It didn't take me long to find a picture of a short-barreled .38 revolver. During our next indoor, out-of-cell exercise, period I gave the copy of Outdoor

Life magazine to Tony suggesting that he look at page seventeen.

"Let me know what you think about it."

"Okay," he said, and immediately went to his cell. He was back in a few moments to tell me he could do it. I explained that I wanted the gun to look real from the front, and that the side view didn't matter. I asked him to concentrate his efforts on that perspective. He said he would.

"How long will it take you?" I asked.

"Give me a couple of days," he replied. I was pleased to hear it because I'd be going to court very shortly.

Tony worked alone in his cell and I never bothered him, not even to look at the progression of his work. Two days later he called me to his cell.

It was a work of art. True to my instructions, the front view was excellent. He'd placed silver paper from a cigarette package into each chamber of the cylinder, so when I looked into the front end of the revolver, it appeared to be loaded. Tony had burned the wood and then blackened it further with shoe polish, giving it a dull, gunmetal shine. But there was a small problem: the butt of the gun was true to scale and it made secreting the gun in the front of my pants impossible. I asked him if he could cut it down to make it more compact. He said he could.

Later that afternoon he called me back to look at it again. The butt was now only two inches long, just big enough to fit comfortably in my hand and still look authentic. I thought I would check it out on an unsuspecting prisoner whom I could trust not to repeat what he saw.

I called Jimmy to my cell, as if I had something important to discuss with him. I'd placed the gun under a folded blanket at the head of my bed, and as he stepped into my cell, I reached under the blanket and threw down on him. The front end of the gun was inches from his face. He staggered back in complete shock. Before he could take another breath, I quickly replaced the gun under the blanket.

"Where the fuck did you get that?" he croaked.

"Oh, c'mon buddy, you know there are ways to get anything here," I calmly replied. He had no idea he was looking at Tony's artwork. As we returned to the card table in the hallway, I knew I had the means for my next bid for freedom. I needed to get the gun through two major body searches: the "body pat" search for weapons, and the skin search when I'd have to strip off my prison clothes and put on my own to go to court. I'd have to get lucky both times.

The routine of going to court consisted of a two guard escort from the cellblock to the Admitting and Discharge area in the front of the prison. It was in the A&D area that a prisoner removed his prison denim to put on his own street clothes. Armed sheriffs would be standing by and a Banker's Special on my body, real or not, would not go unnoticed. I'd have to fool more than a few professional men several times, which sounds difficult except for one thing; prison guards, sheriffs and average police officers have little or no respect for the intelligence of the prisoners in their custody—in other words, any bizarre behaviour would be accepted as normal.

I kept the gun well hidden. Five days later I received a message from a guard to call Richard Blum, who had been my lawyer since my arrest following my first escape.

"You're scheduled to appear in front of Judge Costello on Friday afternoon," he said.

"What time?"

"One o'clock," he replied. It was Thursday afternoon and I had only hours to come up with some way to get the gun past the two searches, but I now knew when I'd be leaving the prison and I could be prepared.

As soon as I hung up the phone I returned to my cell, placed the gun in my pants and wound an elastic bandage around my lower body. This would allow for a quick pat search without any telltale bumps under my clothes—but the search would have to be quick and I still had to find a way to avoid the strip search. I dug deep into my experience with prison guards and believed I had the answer.

On Friday morning I was playing cards with three other prisoners at a table in the middle of the range. We were allowed out for exercise in a group, and while staff watched from a security bubble with a full view of the front of the cells, we would play cards or use the weight bars to exercise. I heard the jingle of keys. A moment later, the wire gate opened.

"You're going to court, Wayne." A guard stood off to the side of the table looking at me. I glanced up into his eyes, but I didn't acknowledge him. A tension filled the air. I could see it in the faces of my fellow card players who had no idea what was about to take place.

"Uh, listen Wayne," the guard said uneasily, "the Chittenden County Sheriffs are here. You have to go to court..."

"Fuck off," I said, contemptuously.

"No Wayne, it's not a joke. The sheriffs are here and..." But I didn't let him finish. I looked deep into his eyes and he stopped speaking.

"I told you to fuck off," I said with menace in my voice, "because I'm not going to court."

"You have to go—"

"Fuck off," I said again, my voice louder and more aggressive. He turned back to the front of the range where his partner waited at the gate. The door banged shut and they both turned the corner and walked away. The card players at the table were now tense, nervous and fearful. They knew I'd have to go to court, it was only a question of how I'd leave the range and the prison. If I didn't get up and walk to the gate, they would come in and literally hog-tie me and carry me out. Two minutes later I heard the keys in the gate again.

The man who walked toward me was the Lieutenant of the shift. He was a seasoned veteran with silver hair and probably the best guard in the prison, because he used intelligence, reason, and plain common sense in his dealings with prisoners and staff alike. He always gave the appearance of having a broad respect for people, including prisoners. However, he was also used to getting his way and was confident because of it. He stopped five feet from the table. As I turned to look at him, I could see two guards on point at the front gate, which was being held open. If the Lieutenant needed to make a quick getaway, it was there.

"Wayne," he said, "you do have to go to court." His body language and tone of voice told me he thought there was some sort of simple prisoner-staff misunderstanding, that reason and reassurance would bring everything back into proper focus. After all, only a madman would think he could throw a wrench into the works and stop the wheels of justice from turning, and he knew I wasn't a madman.

"Fuck off," I said, looking back at the table top. The three men at the table fidgeted in their chairs.

"Wayne..." the Lieutenant began, and that's when I exploded.

I leapt from the table, my momentum throwing my chair backward. While my fellow card players scattered like startled grouse, I hobbled rapidly to the end of the range and grabbed a weight bar. I quickly spun around and approached the table again. The Lieutenant had retreated to the front gate and was just going through it when I smashed the card table with the bar. It splintered like balsa wood. I looked into the faces of three guards who were now safely behind the wire.

"I fuckin' told you people, I'm not going anywhere." The Lieutenant murmured instructions to his guards and they quickly walked around the corner out of my sight.

The men on the range had disappeared into their cells. For effect, I wielded the bar and smashed more of the table, creating noise and adding further to the tension. The speed at which the guards returned in full black battle gear including full-face shields and body armour, told me they'd been waiting around the corner. There was now a force of four men approaching.

They stepped in unison, just as they were trained to do, and the loud smack of their combat-booted feet on the concrete was impressive. They held their batons at the ready and looked very menacing indeed. The Lieutenant was directly behind them, and as they advanced, I retreated in my hobbling gait to the relative safety of the end of the range. With my back to the wall they'd have to come at me head on. The weight bar could hurt them and they were cautious, yet determined. All the while, the Lieutenant was quietly assuring me this didn't have to happen.

There is a point when the "goon squad," as we called them, make their move on a man to rush him and take him down. I waited until that moment was upon us before I spoke.

"What happens if I put this weight bar down?" I asked. I looked directly at the Lieutenant.

"We'll forget this ever happened," he said with relief in his voice. There was a pause in the goon squad's advance.

"Okay," I said. "Do I have your word?" There was an immediate relaxing of the tension. The relief was obvious in the Lieutenant's face and apparent in the collective body language of the goon squad. In prison, giving one's word, or asking another for his, was the first step in the peace process.

"You have my word," he said, "you have my word."

"And no beating?"

"No, we won't beat you," he replied. I lay the weight bar on the floor, and in a second I was spun around and pat searched. The patting hands didn't detect anything and they quickly placed belly chains on me. My hands were now linked to my waist with six-inch chains, but I could still use my crutch to walk. With a guard on each side of me, I was hustled off the range and up the stairs to Admitting and Discharge—and the skin search.

The man who ran the A&D office and area was a veteran. With him were two sheriffs, one young and one middle-aged. The younger, Kevin, was a tall, lanky, blond-haired man, who had told me on an earlier court trip that he knew Lora. She had been convicted of bringing me the .38 calibre revolver while I was being held in The Burlington Correctional Centre. Apparently she had been a cheerleader for his basketball team a few years earlier. Steve was older, shorter, and huskier, with close-cropped grey hair that looked as if it'd been cut by a military barber. He took himself very seriously. My concern at the moment was Robert, the A&D officer; he was the man who would process me into the hands of the two sheriffs.

The sheriffs stood off to one side of the small admitting room, which functioned as Robert's office . Adjacent to us was the property room. One of my escorts removed my belly chains and both of them quickly left. Whenever a prisoner is handed over from one law officer to the next, the chains are removed from the prisoner and replaced by the next people. All material has to be accounted for, handcuffs, shackles, and belly chains included.

I could see and feel the tension in the three men in the room, which told me they were well aware that I'd been brought to them by force. They were anticipating a serious problem.

My street clothes were laid out across the back of a straight-backed chair: my expensive leather jacket was folded across my pants, shirt and socks and a pair of boots sat alongside. I didn't acknowledge Robert, even though he made a point of calling me Wayne, and mentioning that it looked like a good day for a ride. I'm sure it appeared as though I was still resentful at having to leave the prison for court.

"What's this shit?" I asked, stepping forward and pointing at the clothes and boots. The sheriffs were standing off to the side, not looking at me, as if what was happening in the office was of no concern to them.

"Those are your street clothes, Wayne," replied Robert. He stepped closer to me, but he was being cautious.

"What do you mean?" I asked menacingly. He took a step back.

"Your street clothes. You know—the clothes you came in with."

"I don't recognize them," I said. I looked at the clothes as if puzzled and confused. I even touched the jacket with my fingers.

"Yes, that's a nice jacket," Robert said. "In fact, I remember how good it looked on you when you came in with it..." I exploded again. I kicked the chair and sent the clothes across the room. Robert leapt back and the sheriffs stepped forward to stand beside him. Then two of the goon squad, still dressed in battle gear, stepped through the open doorway. I couldn't see their eyes behind the smoked glass of their face plates.

"I want my fuckin' clothes, not this hand-me-down shit," I declared. I motioned contemptuously at the clothing now scattered across the floor, and I ignored everybody in the room except Robert. He was in control and the others would follow his orders.

"I'm sure those are your clothes," Robert said soothingly. "I took them out of the bag with your name on them."

"Those are not my fuckin' clothes," I stated. I spoke as though I was speaking to a child who just didn't seem to want to get the point I was trying to make. "Don't you understand?" Robert handled it well, choosing to humour rather than antagonize me.

"Well, I'll take another look and see." He walked into the property room and pretended to look for my clothes. There was a loud crackling of heavy paper, and I could picture him in my mind's eye as he rattled an old bag, much like we used to do to make the sound of crackling flames for sound effects when we played with a tape recorder as kids. There was something about his making those sounds that made me feel everything was going well; his actions were the actions of a man convinced he was dealing with a prisoner who'd "lost it." In a moment he was back.

"Looked through everything Wayne," he said, shrugging his shoulders as if he were as puzzled as me. "Couldn't find a damn thing." The way he looked at me told me he was expecting just about anything, but he also seemed to welcome this momentary diversion from his regular, mundane routine. I narrowed my eyes, looked directly into his, and did what any paranoid, suspicious and schizophrenic prisoner would do in the circumstances—I understood.

"I know what your fuckin' game plan is," I said, with quiet menace.

"What's that Wayne?" He glanced at his colleagues as if to reassure himself that they weren't missing a word of this. I lowered my voice about ten decibels so they had to strain to hear me.

"You *know* those are not *my* clothes," I answered, conspiratorially, "and you *know* I won't wear them."

"Why would I do that?" He was now blatantly patronizing and condescending. And I gave him the reason.

"You want me to wear this state-issued shit," and I plucked at my denim jacket with my fingertips, then added triumphantly, *"because you want to humiliate me in court!"* I glared at every man in the room. They immediately reacted by shifting on their feet in anticipation of having to take me down.

"Well, you have to go to court," said Robert, shrugging his shoulders.

"We'll bring you right back. You're either going the easy way or the hard way," said Steve, and he started to move deliberately towards me. The two men in black shifted their feet to get into position to rush me, and Kevin gathered up the belly chain to lock me in once I was immobilized.

"Well maybe I'll go the hard way," I replied. I made a stance as if I were getting ready to duke it out with them, and they in turn answered the call and began to move in unison toward me. I glared at them, then I changed my mind.

"I'll tell you what Robert," I began. They stopped.

"I'll wear these clothes—this time, but never again."

"Okay, Wayne," he replied. He made a motion to the sheriffs to hook me up. The tension broke. They didn't so much as pat me down; they simply put on the belly chain and two minutes later I was hobbling out the prison door on my crutch, placed in the back of the police car and heading down the highway. I didn't say a word for an hour.

The countryside was truly beautiful and it tore at my heart to see the rich woods and meadows pass by. I knew I'd be going down for years if I didn't escape; the thought of it made me physically ill. Steve and Kevin were making small talk as if they had no concerns about anything that had happened back at the prison. They were doing it to make me feel more comfortable and relaxed, but I could tell they were tense. There was no divider between us. They relied on the chains and the fact that they believed I had a ruined kneecap. I decided

I would add more fuel to their tension and concern. I leaned forward—they were both aware of my move.

"What am I going to court for?" I asked belligerently. It was Steve who answered.

"I don't know." He turned his profile to me, then looked at Kevin who was driving. "Any idea Kevin?" Steve seemed pleased I was acknowledging them.

"Nope," replied Kevin, then added, "they don't tell us anything, except to pick you up." His voice conveyed the message that we were all in the same boat, just sailing along in the dark together.

"C'mon," I went on, "you guys know."

"No, we really don't."

"It's about that cop killing in Canada, isn't it?" I wanted them to believe I was a very desperate man, ready to kill them if it proved necessary. I saw them both stiffen in their seats— this was something new, this was something no one knew about, and I could see the wheels turning in their minds: *This guy is a cop killer and we're the first ones to know about it.*

"No," said Steve, casually, "we really don't know what's going on."

"Yeah, *right*, you think I'm stupid," I responded sarcastically, then fell back in my seat and into a morose silence. Steve and Kevin both stared studiously ahead, but after a few minutes of silence where we all seemed to sit listening to the tires humming over the pavement, I watched Kevin and Steve exchange nervous glances. It was a tense ride to the courthouse in Burlington.

Steve tried to help me out of the car in the underground parking lot, but I shook off his hand. "Leave me the fuck alone," I said. "I don't need your help."

"Okay, okay," he responded. We were now below the courthouse. There were only a few cars parked in stalls, and it was quiet in an echoing kind of way. We took the elevator to the second floor where Judge Costello would hand down the sentence previously agreed upon by my lawyer and the state. If the usual practice and routine was followed, the handcuffs would be removed from my wrists, but the belly chain would remain. I would however, have full movement of my arms.

The large anteroom on the second floor was quite crowded. People stood talking quietly in small groups along the walls, and though we attracted a few curious stares, for the most part we arrived and walked into the courtroom unnoticed.

The courtroom was empty, the judge having not yet entered, and in a moment I realized my court appearance for this courtroom was timed specifically for my case. My wrists were freed from the handcuffs, and though the wrist chains hung from the belly chain, I didn't feel them. Less than a minute later, as if the judge had been watching through a keyhole, he appeared, sat down and sentenced me to three to seven years in Windsor prison. The judge rose and left the room, and after some papers were signed, we would be back on the highway.

"I guess that's it," I said, "I won't have to do this again?"

"No Wayne, you won't have to do this again," said Steve patronizingly.

"I'm glad," I replied. "It's all finally over." I adopted a fatalistic tone of voice, and one that I hoped would communicate that I felt and believed all hope was now lost, that I was totally accepting of my fate, which meant there would be no further trouble from me. But I had one thing left to do, and when Steve asked Kevin to get the paperwork signed, I made my request.

"I have to go to the can," I said. "Bad." Using "bad" meant I had more to do than use the urinal.

"Sure," said Steve, "no problem." We walked out of the courtroom, crossed the anteroom floor and entered the hallway leading to the bathroom, which was just across the hall from the clerk's offices. When we arrived at the bathroom door, Kevin paused and looked at Steve.

"Have you got him?" he asked, as if I wasn't standing there. I'm sure I looked quite harmless with my crutch under my arm. Steve just nodded his head and pursed his lips, and the expression on his face said, *Of course I got him, nothing to it, I'm surprised you asked.*

All three stalls were unoccupied. I hobbled into the middle one, closed the door and locked it. I stood facing the door, in case Steve glanced at my feet. In a few seconds I had the elastic bandage in one hand and the wooden revolver in the other. I leaned forward and peered through the crack at Steve.

He was standing by the sinks, unconcerned, picking at some peeling wall plaster with one of his keys. I placed the bandage in the toilet and flushed it. I looked at the gun in my hand, said a silent prayer, threw back the door and leapt out to confront him. The gun was only two feet from his face. His hands went up.

"What are you doing? Where did you get that?" He was in shock. He thought the gun was real, and before he could take a good look at the weapon in my hand, I dropped my right hand with the gun to my side. He could only catch a glimpse of the barrel trained on his midsection. I made a move with my left hand to take his .357 Magnum Colt from its holster, but he wouldn't have it. He turned his hips and lower body so the butt of his gun was just out of my reach.

"Don't fuck around, Steve," I told him, quietly. I kept my eyes locked on his, and he was doing the same. I made another attempt to unsnap the strap on his holster and he twisted away again.

"What do you think you're doing?" he asked. "What do you think you're doing?" I didn't answer him. I just stepped back a foot, just far enough out of his reach that any move for my gun would be futile. I knew then that he was one of those men who'd sooner take a bullet than willingly hand over his sidearm to a criminal. But he might drop it, if he thought I was going to simply disarm him, and not use his weapon.

"Take your gun out of your holster, use your thumb and index finger, and lay the gun on the floor," I instructed. "If you don't, I'll kill you." By this time the wooden gun in my hand had become real in my mind and he felt it was real too.

I held his eyes with mine as his right hand lowered, my heart pounded as his fingers unsnapped the strap on the holster, and I never unlocked my gaze as his thumb and index finger gingerly removed the gun. He held it at his side, carefully, and as he lowered it and the barrel touched the floor, his eyes left mine to carefully lay it down. I slammed him in the left shoulder with my left hand. He staggered back trying to catch his balance, and the gun spun free in front of me. It was still spinning when I snatched it up.

The first thing I did was to point the gun at my own face—I wanted to be certain it was loaded. It would be one thing to hold Steve at bay with what he believed to be a fully loaded weapon; it would be quite another to attempt to do so with his gun if it was unloaded. As I looked into the cylinder I glimpsed semi-wad-cutter ammunition. Semi-wad-cutter bullets are indented instead of pointed, and the slugs immediately expand on impact with flesh and bone, leaving huge gaping wounds in their wake. As soon as I saw the slugs I put my gun in my pocket and used his. I pulled the hammer back and left it on full cock.

"What's going on? Steve asked. He didn't understand why I'd looked into the barrel of his revolver. I didn't answer him.

"We're walking out of the courthouse," I said, "and you're going first. Now lower your hands." He lowered his hands, turned, took three paces to the door and opened it.

Kevin was leaning his lanky frame against the wall, his Stetson tipped forward and half over his eyes. His jaws worked on a piece of gum and his thumbs were hooked in his belt. He looked exactly like what he was: a deputy sheriff on the job. When Steve appeared first, Kevin turned toward us with a puzzled expression. A heartbeat later he saw me and his puzzlement was replaced with a tense concern.

I moved a half step to the side and showed Kevin the fully-cocked weapon in my hand by pointing it at him. He stiffened.

"Don't reach for your gun. Stay just in front of Steve. If you go for your gun Steve goes down first, then you," I told him quietly. Of course I meant it. "Walk past the elevators, down the stairs, and go out the back way." The back way was down a staircase, through a hallway to the back door, and across the lawn behind the building.

We started moving, and as we did, I kept one arm half outstretched so I could touch Steve's back with the palm of my hand. With my gun hand, I reached behind me and placed the gun under my jacket, so to a cursory glance it would appear I was trying to scratch my back as I walked. The gun was hidden to onlookers, but Steve and Kevin would believe that any onlookers would be seeing what was happening to them.

In a matter of seconds we were past the elevators and heading down the staircase to the main floor. There was an office window looking into the hallway, and because the route we were using was seldom used, we attracted the attention of a young secretary. She actually half rose from her chair to look at us curiously, and when her eyes met mine I winked at her. She became flustered, turned her head and quickly sat at her desk again. Five steps later we were out the back door and walking across the lawn, past a sign proclaiming Do Not Walk On Grass. As soon as we were outside, I pulled the gun out and held it at the ready.

"Walk to the car," I said. It was only a short distance to the driveway leading to the underground parking lot, and both Steve and Kevin moved forward without argument. I stopped them when we were partway down the ramp, told Kevin to stop, then not to move or turn around, and I carefully removed his handgun. I kept a good distance between Steve and me while I did so. I put Kevin's gun in my belt and instructed them to walk to the car.

The parking lot was completely empty of people, but I kept my voice down when I told Steve to produce the keys for the car. He readily did so, but when I told him to put the key in the door of the driver's side and leave them there, he deliberately dropped them on the pavement. I think he thought I might try to catch them before they hit the ground, giving him an opportunity to jump me. I took a step back.

"Kevin," I said, "Steve is going to get you both killed."

"No he's not. It was an accident."

"It was no fucking accident," I assured him. "You exercise some control over him." I reached down and picked up the keys, opened the door, hit the power button on the locks and told them to get in. They both did so. I ordered them to sit close to each other, in the farthest corner from the driver's side, and after they obeyed, I climbed into the car myself. I didn't want a casual observer to become concerned about two sheriffs riding in the back of their own car, so I told them to remove their hats. Steve was closest to me, and I thought of having them switch places, but I was concerned about the time. I turned the rearview mirror on them both, then I lifted the .357 in my left hand and showed them it was still on full cock. I emphasized the fact that my left arm was held across my body and that the gun was placed against the front seat, pointing directly at them.

"You both know what this handgun is capable of, especially when loaded with semi-wad cutters. This seat won't even slow the slugs down, so don't fucking move back there." I kept my gaze locked on Steve, who now had a resentful expression around his eyes.

I made every light leading out of town, except one, and there was no problem leaving the city. In less than five minutes I was heading south, down Interstate 89, and I kept the speedometer at a steady ninety miles an hour. With the gun pointed at them, I knew they would hesitate to make a move on me; however, the speed of the vehicle would make them hesitate further. We were only a few miles out of Burlington when Steve made some suggestions.

"Do you know how you can get away, Wayne?" he asked. I glanced at him in the mirror.

"Tell me," I said.

"We'll help you stop a car on the highway," he said.

"Yeah?"

"Yeah."

"What will that do?"

"You can take them hostage," he said helpfully.

"Yeah?"

"Yeah."

"That sounds like a good idea," I offered.

"Then you can take the bullets out of our guns, throw them in the ditch, and take my car keys with you and off you go. You have your gun," suggested Steve. In the mirror his eyes registered sincerity, but I knew then that he knew *my* gun was fake. I could see the wheels of his mind grinding on where the gun in the restroom had come from, and he would realize I wasn't body searched before they put me in the car at the prison. But he wasn't sure if there was any real method in my madness.

"That is a good idea," I said. "I think I'll do that." We sped along for several minutes in silence, then I began to slow.

"Are you going to do it?" asked Steve.

"Yes," I replied, "I am." I pulled over on the shoulder and opened the back door and told them to get out. Once they were out I motioned with the gun, directing them to stand behind the car on the shoulder. Steve looked at me, hopefully. I could see a car coming at a rapid speed, and I could hear the engine slow as the driver saw the uniforms.

"Should we stop this one?" asked Steve.

"No." The approaching car began to pick up speed before it reached us, and I could imagine the relief of the driver as he realized he wasn't being pulled over. In a moment it was rushing past us and on down the highway. There was another car approaching, but it was a distance away.

"What about this one?" asked Steve.

"No," I said, and as I looked down the highway it appeared as if the car now approaching was the only one on the highway. I stepped to the open driver's door and climbed in.

"What are you doing?" Steve asked.

"Listen," I said. "You can stop any car you want, but don't stop this one." I put the car in gear and started moving forward slowly. The approaching vehicle was only seconds away, and because I was moving forward, Steve started walking into the center of the highway. I slammed on the brakes, there was a squeal of tires, and Steve quickly darted back to the side of the road.

In my side mirror I could see that the driver of the other car appeared curious, and he too had slowed down at the sight of the uniformed men, but like most drivers, if he wasn't ordered to stop by the police, he was going to just fly on by. And that's what he did. As he picked up speed, I did the same, staying just in front of him in the inside lane, and in seconds we had left the sheriffs behind.

I was a free man, relatively speaking. I still had to "get away," but for this moment, I'd just accomplished what only a few men had, and I felt exhilarated. A few seconds later I was doing a hundred and fifty miles an hour, heading south on Interstate 89.

I was still accelerating when I saw the sign for the exit I needed to take to get me where I wanted to be. Before my arrest by the FBI, I'd lived a block from the shore of Lake Champlain and I'd travelled throughout the state of Vermont. I knew where I was going.

There was a wooded area on the side of a small mountain where I wanted to leave the car and walk to a small village. It only had a few houses and a small corner store, from which I would phone a friend I knew in Johnson, Vermont. I'd been to Johnson and to the farm just outside it on a number of occasions. The farm was situated on the lip of a valley not far from the town, and the people who lived there were special, for a variety of reasons. They believed a revolution, evidenced by the random acts of violence that were becoming more prevalent and widely reported in the United States, would soon take place in the country.

We'd sit in the backyard in the evening, discussing life. On one such occasion the subject of the aftermath of the revolution was brought up.

"They'll have to come to us," said one young woman.

"Who will?" I asked.

"The revolutionaries," replied John, a teacher at Johnson State College.

"What for?" I asked. I took a hit off the offered joint and passed it on.

"To put society back together," said the young, pretty woman.

There were ten of us sitting around a late evening fire. Earlier in the day, I'd been target shooting with a .38 Special, and I had three other pistols in a case beside me. I was accepted as an unusual character, and they all seemed to view me as an interesting man, not a dangerous one. The fact that I lived with Mary's sister in Burlington seemed to give me further credibility in their eyes.

"Well, my unlearned opinion, based on reading the history of revolutions, would be that the intellectuals of society would be in the most danger once the power structure changed," I offered.

"What do you mean?" asked the young woman.

"The country is run by the intellectuals—revolutionaries believe the teachers in universities and colleges perpetuate *the status quo*. Why would revolutionaries turn to the people who grease the wheels of the social machine the radicals have just destroyed?" I asked. It was John who answered.

"The violent radicals don't think like that," he said. "They simply tear it all down and they'll need us to rebuild it into something new."

"I'll bow to someone who knows more than I do," I replied, not wanting to carry the conversation further. "But I'll give Mary something, just in case." I reached into the case and produced a nine-shot handgun. I handed it to John, who passed it to Mary.

"What will I do with this?" she asked, looking curiously at the weapon now held gingerly in her hand.

"It's not loaded," I said.

"What do I do with this?" she asked again.

"Keep it in a safe place," I replied, "because when the revolution does come, you just might need it."

"I will," she responded.

I knew I'd have some assistance from the Johnson State College people, if only I could get there.

Just as I slowed to make the exit, the car radio came alive with static. A disembodied voice spoke clearly.

"Car Seven, what is your position?" Of course there was no answer, because I was in Car Seven. In seconds the voice returned.

"All cars switch to emergency channels—maintain radio silence on regular frequencies—Carlson has their car and their guns." I was shocked. I was supposed to have had at least six minutes lead time, but I obviously didn't have that at all. As I turned onto the county road the radio fell silent. I made my way slowly, so as to not draw undue attention to the car. Within five minutes I'd skirted the town and was at the picnic area at which I'd chosen to leave the car. I drove the car into the underbrush, and after covering it with large ferns and branches to hide it from the air, I walked off into the woods, heading east. My knee held up very well and I hardly noticed the weakened muscles in my right leg.

My plan was to make the village less than five miles away, and though the terrain was rough, with valleys and streams and small Vermont mountains in my path, I believed I could do it by eight o'clock in the evening. If I made it, I knew a phone call to the farm in Johnson would bring someone in a car to carry me to a safe place.

I stayed away from buildings, kept to the woods, and walked around clearings, not through them. At times it was difficult to see more than a few feet in front of me, the underbrush was so thick, yet I enjoyed the struggle. The air was clean and fresh, the sun was shining in a clear sky, and I was a free man.

I travelled slowly, not only to conserve energy—I was concerned with making noise. Once I'd put a few miles between myself and the car, I took a break.

I sat on the edge of a canyon, my feet hanging over the ledge while I rested for a few moments. I knew there was a good chance that I'd soon be chased by armed men and bloodhounds and as the creek rushed through the bottom of the canyon I contemplated the easiest route down its side.

The rock and shale would make it difficult, but the far side of the canyon seemed to have a trail worn into it by many years of travel. I noticed too short pieces of rotted rope hanging over the lip in tatters, the only remnants of what once was a bridge spanning the thirty-foot gap. The canyon had been grooved into the mountainside by many thousands of years of erosion, and the area seemed timeless. I glanced down to the stream and saw that flat rocks had been placed in strategic positions in the creek itself, indicating that the people who'd used this route in the forgotten past, had built a stepping-stone pathway on which to cross the rushing water below.

I listened for any sound that would indicate that my trackers had found the car and were on my trail. My senses were acutely tuned to the woods around me, to the quiet sigh of the afternoon breeze, the hum of insects, the liquid rush of water below, and the sunlight streaming through the tree branches overhead speckling the rich green foliage in surrealistic patterns. I felt if I died at that moment I would not have any distance to travel to get to heaven, because I was already there.

The steep side of the canyon offered only a minimal amount of footing and I began to feel the cumbersome weight of the handguns I carried, but I had to keep them—they might be helpful in getting me out of a tight spot. It probably seemed to take me longer than it actually did to get to the bottom, and once I was there the stepping stones made a near-perfect path through the rushing water. The climb up the other side was difficult as well, but once I reached the top and began walking through the woods, it was fairly easy going. No matter how tired I might be, the thought of the angry man-hunters armed to the teeth, still smarting from the sting of my escape with their guns and car, was a great motivator.

The last thing I wanted was a direct confrontation with anyone— it made a shootout a possibility. Man-hunters are like hunters of any animal: there's always a great deal of adrenalin flowing, and the thrill of the hunt is something that almost all police officers enjoy. Of course it's frightening, but that too was part of the thrill. I'd felt some of that myself when I used to hunt in northern Saskatchewan, and I could well imagine the young sheriffs, armed with high-powered hunting rifles, scouring the countryside for me, an armed and danger-ous fugitive. Adding to the excitement was something I'd learned from the Vermont boys inside the prison: the state had an old law stating that if a man were designated an outlaw by state authorities, he could be hunted down and killed like an animal by any citizen of the state. Whether Vermont would actu-ally call this law into play was another matter, but the possibility existed.

A few miles on I came across an area that had been stripped of trees, to make a ski run down a small mountain. Along the edge of the clearing was an old, tangled and frayed piece of tow rope. Much of it had unravelled and could easily be separated. I used a piece to make a pair of shoulder slings for the hand-guns, and at the same time I removed the bullets from under the hammer of each weapon. With the guns now slung beneath my armpits and under my jack-et, their weight was much easier to handle, and they were well hidden should anyone happen to see me.

I always took the hardest, most difficult route, which meant slower travel-ling, but it was safest. Most of my pursuers would stick to the game trails, no doubt walking slowly and carefully, listening all the while for any sound which would indicate my whereabouts. I seldom paused to rest. I had to put the most distance between myself and the pursuit, and it would be difficult travelling through the woods at night. As well, I had to arrive at the small store in the vil-lage before late evening. Once I phoned friends and received their help getting a ride out of Vermont, I'd be on my way to a new life.

The woods were thick—heavy underbrush impeded my progress, and every so often I'd hear people talking as they walked down the trails. I would always stop and wait until they'd passed— sometimes it took more than a few minutes for them to be out of earshot—and almost before I knew it, dusk began to fall, and then it was dark.

I came across a road that seemed to head toward the village, and I could smell the river. It was a beautiful calm evening, no breeze to speak of, no traffic at all, and I felt in my belly that I was going to make it. Suddenly, car lights appeared ahead but the vehicle was moving so slowly that I had ample time to lie down in the grass along the road.

The car stopped no more than six feet from where I lay and the engine shut down. It was very quiet. I didn't dare turn my head to see whether it was police or civilian. In a few minutes I heard a squeaking of the glass on the rubber frame as the window was rolled down.

"Don't..." a woman's voice.

"Honey..." a man's voice.

"No, not now."

"We don't have to do anything I just want..."

"No," she said, her voice more adamant.

"What's wrong?" he asked.

"He's here," she said.

"He's miles away by now. Even the news said he's probably out of the state by now."

"I can feel him," she said. She sounded sure and she sounded scared.

"I can feel you."

"Stop it. I want to go now," she insisted.

"Okay, we'll go," he said. I smelled cigarette smoke, the car started, and I heard the window squeak as it was rolled up again. A moment later the lights came on and the car slowly drove off. *The intuition of a woman is not to be underes -timated,* I thought. The smell of the cigarette smoke still lingered in the air, bringing home the realization that I truly needed a cigarette, but I lay prone, not moving in the ditch for minutes before I continued on my way.

The village was very quiet, and though lights were on in the houses, there was no movement on the streets. I saw five vehicles in a small parking lot, but I had the sense they were parked there long-term. The store was around the corner and as I turned to enter the block, I saw a small truck with Pennsylvania plates parked beside a house just beyond the store. The truck was laden with household furnishings and personal belongings tied in bags. The store was dimly lit and it appeared to be closed. The sign on the door said it closed at eight each evening, and my heart sank. As I turned away to retreat to the darkness, a female voice broke the silence.

"Can we help you?" she asked. I glanced to my right and saw a young woman, accompanied by a young man, standing beside the back of the truck.

"I really need to use a phone," I answered. We stood looking at each other.

"We're just moving in and our phone isn't hooked up yet," she said.

"I thought this store was open," I explained. "My car broke down on the interstate and I do need to phone some friends." They walked closer to me.

"There are phones in the houses. That house over there," she said, "will always let you use their phone. They let us use it." They both laughed, indicating they'd done so on more than a couple of occasions.

"Thanks," I replied, "I'll ask." I walked away, heading in the general direction of the house, but I couldn't be knocking on doors in the area and I had no intention of following their helpful suggestion. As soon as I was around the corner, I slipped into the shadows.

It was so quiet that I could hear the cars and trucks travelling on Interstate 89, and I could see any vehicle on the county road heading my way long before the occupants of the vehicle saw me. I decided I'd use the woods and follow the interstate to Johnson. In a matter of minutes, I realized it would be impossible to make any headway—the night was too dark and the going was too rough. I went back to the town, thinking I might be able to steal a car. It was risky, but my choices were limited.

I was retracing my steps down the side of the street toward the parking lot when a beautiful Irish Setter came bounding around the corner. She ran in circles around me, and when I reached down, she stopped long enough to smell my hand and I petted her. When I glanced up I saw the same young couple walking toward me, and again the woman spoke.

"Did you make your call?" she asked. She was a slender, fairly tall woman, and her slim companion had his hair tied in a ponytail.

"Yes, I'm waiting for some friends," I answered.

"Oh, good," she said. We walked past each other, and I commented on their dog.

"She's young," said the man, speaking directly to me for the first time.

"That explains her energy," I replied. We kept walking.

"You should be careful," the woman said.

"Careful?" I asked.

"Yes, there's an armed escapee in this area."

"Escapee?"

"Yes—there's police all over this area too."

"Well, they should have him soon then," I offered.

"The man's escaped a lot of times," she said.

"I'll be careful."

"Good luck," said the woman, and her man seconded her comment. I thanked them and continued on.

We hadn't walked another twenty yards when I saw the lights of a car coming from the south, and it was moving quickly. I had to make a decision on my next move; if I was alone I'd just take the ditch, but with two people watching, it made that just as dangerous. What would they do?

I chose the ditch, and a few seconds later a car went whizzing by. It didn't slow on its way to the highway, but I now would have to explain why I did what I did, and any explanation at that point would be hardly believable. The woman herself brought the matter to a head.

"You're Wayne Carlson, aren't you?" she asked. I started walking back toward them, but they didn't retreat or show any undue concern.

"Yes," I answered, "I am."

"I know Lora," she said calmly. "We worked in the same company for awhile."

"Lora's a good person," I replied.

"What do you want to do?" she asked. I didn't feel comfortable telling them my true destination, so I lied.

"Burlington," I said. "I have friends there."

"We'll take you," she offered. I looked at the man for confirmation.

"Yes, we'll take you there."

"There's bound to be roadblocks," I suggested.

"We'll take the dog too," he said. It was a good idea and it just might work.

"Okay," I agreed, "let's do it."

The three of us walked back to their truck and climbed in. I sat in the middle, and with the dog hanging her face out the window, it might mislead police into believing it was a vehicle carrying normal, everyday, good people.

We travelled toward Burlington and passed one minor roadblock set up on the other side of the highway, indicating that the Vermont authorities didn't believe I'd be travelling into the city. I thought I'd ask what they'd heard on the news.

"We heard you disarmed two sheriffs and took their car," she said with a note of admiration in her voice.

"We know you didn't hurt anybody," offered James, suggesting that if I had, they wouldn't be doing this.

"Was there anything said concerning the direction I might be travelling?"

"Only that you were believed to be headed out of the state," she answered.

"In the sheriffs' car?"

"No, they found the car. They thought you had an accomplice, somebody who left you the pistol in the washroom of the courthouse," John replied.

"As you can see, there was no accomplice."

"Well, we are now," said the woman.

"We're the only ones who know it," I said.

The press had been relatively kind to me, treating me in print as an exciting man and not especially dangerous to the public at large. But Americans are different from Canadians—they respect and idolize men and women who demonstrate a fierceness of spirit. America has given birth to many anti-heroes, from Jesse James and the Daltons in the 1800s, to John Dillinger in the 1930s and Willy Sutton in the 1950s.

"Is there anything more we can do for you, Wayne?" asked James. We were now entering the city. I hated to ask, but it had been a long time between cigarettes for me.

"Would you mind buying me a pack of cigarettes?" I asked.

"We'll buy you a couple of packs. What kind?" she asked.

"Winston, thanks. And one more thing."

"Name it."

"Four quarters."

"Okay," he said, and he pulled over at a Quick Stop, got out of the truck and went inside. I was amazed at how trusting they were. He seemed unconcerned with my being alone with his wife, and she appeared completely comfortable. I'm sure I was more insecure in the situation than they were.

"How long have you known Lora?" I asked her.

"About a year," she replied, "in fact, I saw you with her one morning." She petted the dog who appeared happy to be able to see the city lights.

"You did?"

"Yes, you dropped her off at work and we saw you kissing her goodbye." She was interrupted by James, who climbed back in the truck. He handed me two packs of cigarettes, four quarters and a couple of packs of matches.

"I'm very grateful for this," I said.

"We know," he acknowledged, and then added, "where would you like us to drop you off?" I gave him directions on where to take me, which was just a few blocks away. In a minute we were there.

I said goodbye to them, and I watched as they drove away and headed home.

The city was now dark, and it was quiet on the residential street I chose, but I knew Burlington well. There was a pay phone I could use a couple of blocks away, but first I discarded the rope bandolier which held the handguns, and I placed one in my waistband and the other in my jacket pocket. I wondered if the couple had even considered I was armed.

I used the change to call the operator and made a collect call to my friends in Johnson, but there was no answer. I would have to keep trying, but it couldn't be from a public phone—my photo would be on television and in the newspaper. I made a decision to break the law again, and break and enter a business where I would have private, unlimited access to a phone. I would make a call, I thought, and once I had my party on the line, I would ask them to call me back. A business would hardly pay attention to a short long-distance call on the bill. The last thing I wanted to do was cause problems for my friends. Yet the system that would protect my friends would also put my location in jeopardy—trust was important in the situation. There was one thing I had to do before I entered a business place.

I had placed two thousand dollars in a small tin box and buried it at the back of the house Lora and I had lived in. Not even Lora knew it was there. I was less than four blocks from where it was. I walked down the street, took the alley, and a minute later I had the box and the money in my hand. The money was in hundreds, fifties and twentiess and I felt rich.

The business I chose was on a residential street ten minutes away, in a house secluded from its neighbours by a small stand of maple trees. There was also a small wooded area behind it, so I could break a window and withdraw to the woods to await any response from the noise.

I used the sleeve of my jacket to dull the sound of the rock shattering the glass, and I quickly cleared the broken shards from the pane. Anyone glancing at the window wouldn't readily see the damage because it would appear intact. I retreated and lay down in the woods facing the building and watched; for half an hour the street remained quiet and peaceful.

The first thing I did inside was make a pot of coffee. While that was brewing, I began making phone calls. Again, the phone on the farm in Johnson rang six times. I decided to call some friends in Canada, but I knew I'd have to get lucky—the people I knew were sometimes out of their homes for days at a time. I was about to hang up when Carol answered.

"Hi, Carol," I said. She was one of the few people I knew who always recognized my voice, even after years of not hearing it. "Got a pen?"

"Yes," she said. I gave her the number.

"Call me right back."

"Okay." In less than a minute the phone rang.

"Hi Carol," I opened.

"Where are you?" she asked. She knew I should be in prison.

"In a place of business in Vermont where I shouldn't be," I replied.

"Are you coming to Edmonton?" She understood that I would have had to escape to be calling her from a business place.

"If I can find my way home."

"You're in trouble?"

"Serious trouble."

"Can you make it across the border?"

"It's going to take some doing," I said, "but if I can reach some people here, they'll pick me up and drive me to the border."

"If you can get to Montréal I'll pick you up."

"Are you going to be home for the next few days?"

"Yes, I'll be here."

"If you're not, I'll leave a message and a phone number and we can hook up through it."

"Okay."

"See you," she said. I could hear the concern in her voice. We'd been together for seven years and knew each other well.

"Yes, I'll see you," I said, and we both hung up. I put the phone back in its cradle and poured myself a cup of coffee. It was now getting late and I'd have to get some sleep. I had a phone number in reserve given to me by my friend Jimmy Polidor inside the Vermont state prison, but I didn't want to use it except as a last resort. The number belonged to Becky, Jimmy's girlfriend. He assured me she'd help me if she was in a position to do so. He'd suggested that if I called her it would be best for her if I did so in the morning. I lay down on the floor and within minutes I was asleep.

When I woke the lunchroom clock told me it was just after seven a.m.. I'd wait for another hour before I used my ace in the hole and phoned Becky. I made another pot of coffee, confident that nobody would be working on the weekend and that my Saturday morning would remain uninterrupted. I was mistaken.

I heard the crunch of tires on gravel outside the office window, and I glanced into the parking lot to see that a red GTO had pulled in. I ran to the back door, which I'd left ajar. I waited until I heard the sound of someone at the front door before sliding the back door open, and as quietly as possible I left the building. There was a short distance between the back door and the wooded area, but I walked, not ran, toward it. I was halfway to the woods when I heard the back door open, and a man's voice yelled at me.

"What are you doing?" he demanded. I looked back and saw a tall, lanky man in his thirties standing in the doorway. I said the first thing that came to mind.

"I'm just looking around," I answered. I continued to walk toward the small stand of trees, but I also kept looking at him over my shoulder. He didn't look like a police officer, but he decided to act like one.

In four long strides he was at the passenger door of his car, which he quickly opened, and he bent forward to reach under the front seat. Before he'd fully straightened, I saw a Luger-type handgun in his hand. As he turned with his weapon, I pulled out and cocked the .357, and pointed it at him. Without looking at me, he began walking toward the corner of the building—if he made it to the building, he'd have some cover. But when he was only a step away, he turned toward me and saw the gun in my hand.

He panicked and threw his hands up. His weapon flew fifteen feet into the air, and before it reached the top of its arc he was yelling, "It's a toy gun, it's only a toy gun."

"Don't move," I told him. I kept my gun pointed at him, and walked over to where his had landed. As I picked it up I noticed how light it was, but it looked like the real thing. It was a perfect replica of a German Luger and it would fool anyone.

"What the hell are you doing with this?" I asked.

"It's not mine. It belongs to my son."

"Let's go inside," I said. He walked into the building without argument and I closed the door behind us. I told him to sit down at the table, and as I sat across from him, I told him he could put his hands down.

"I won't tell anybody you were here," he said.

"You just tried to arrest me with a toy gun," I replied, "so please don't expect me to believe you won't phone police."

"I won't."

"Let's stop this, and let's concentrate instead on what we can do to ensure both of us come out of this okay," I said. I kept the gun on my lap, pointed at him, but I'd uncocked it.

"Okay," he said. He seemed somewhat relieved at my calm attitude and rational approach.

"What's your name?"

"Richard."

"Do you work here?" I asked.

"Yes," he answered.

"Is there anyone else coming to work today?"

"Yes, my boss should be here soon."

"Are you sure about that?"

"Well, yes," he replied, hesitantly.

"Is he, or isn't he?"

"No, I don't think anyone else will be here," he admitted. He was afraid, but he was handling himself well. The last thing I wanted was for him to feel immediate fear for his life and do something desperate.

"Do you know who I am?" I asked.

"I do now," he answered.

"Who am I?"

"You're Wayne Carlson." I nodded my head. "You escaped yesterday." I nodded again. "The police think you're out of the city."

"When did you last hear the news broadcast?"

"This morning, on my way here."

"And?"

"It said they believed you might have left the state." This was good news for me, but I had to deal with my unwanted prisoner.

"I only want one thing," I said, "and that's my freedom. I'm not going to hurt you, Richard—not unless you try to get me arrested."

"I won't do anything to cause that to happen," he assured me. I believed him. I explained to him what we were going to do.

There were two hard hats on a filing cabinet. I instructed Richard to put on the white one and I put on the yellow one. We left the building, got into his car, and drove to a park not far away where there was a pay phone on the side of the street. I had Richard park with the driver's door next to the phone. I took the key from his ignition and told him to stay in his seat. He agreed. A woman answered on the first ring and when I asked for Becky, I was asked to wait a minute. A minute later Becky came on the line.

"Hello," she said.

"Hello Becky," I responded, "this is Wayne Carlson. Jimmy gave me your number and suggested I call you."

"Yes?"

"I'm in a car near Ethan Allan Park and I'd like to see you." She began to give me her address, but I interrupted her.

"I can't drive to you—the man who owns the car doesn't want to be with me."

"Oh, I see."

"Can you meet me?"

"I can take a cab."

"All right, we can meet at the Bank of Montreal in the mall."

"I can be there in half an hour."

"Okay, wait in the cab in front of the bank and I'll come to you."

"I'll be there," she said. When I climbed back in the vehicle, I explained to Richard that a man would be meeting me in the parking lot in the mall, and when he arrived I'd allow Richard to leave.

As we drove down the street I turned the rear-view mirror to afford me the view behind us, and I had Richard park where I could see the whole of the lot in front of me while the Bank of Montreal was in the rear-view mirror. We sat there quietly, and to a casual observer we would appear to be couple of normal men going about our business. I smoked two cigarettes before Becky's cab stopped in front of the bank. I leaned forward, making it appear that I was focusing my attention on the other side of the parking lot.

"Drive straight ahead, Richard," I instructed.

"Okay," he replied. He started the car and when he'd driven fifty yards, I told him to stop. He did so. I took off my hard hat, laid it on the back seat, got out of the car and leaned in through my window to give him my last instructions.

"I want you to leave, drive past that service station, and head straight down that street. Don't stop for anything and don't look back."

"I'm going to drive slowly, Wayne," he said. "I will drive very slowly to the police station, which will give you about fifteen minutes to get away from this area."

"Thanks," I replied gratefully, but with disbelief. I took a step back and Richard drove away, slowly. I stood watching him and even after he left the parking lot and reached the street, he didn't reach up to adjust his mirror. I walked toward the taxicab and Becky got out and walked toward me. She was a dark-haired, brown-eyed, beautiful young woman.

"Hi, Wayne," she said.

"Hi, Becky," I replied.

"Let's get the fuck out of here," she said, and she took my arm as if she'd known me for years.

We climbed in the back and I was somewhat dismayed to find another young woman in the cab. She simply said "hi," as if we knew each other too, and the cab driver didn't seem to pay any undue attention to us. Obviously Becky had already given him an address, because without a word, he drove down a residential street toward Lake Champlain. When we drove past a park, Becky told him to stop. I paid the fare.

We sat in the grass on a small hill overlooking the lake, and I learned who the other woman was. He name was Sue, she was seven months pregnant, and she was a friend of Becky's. I learned then too that both of them were in an open-custody facility. This was getting complicated, but now that it was in motion, it had to play out.

"I'm going to stay with you until you're okay," said Becky. I sat between the two women, looking at my options. I had expected Becky to have a place of her own, somewhere where I could hide out for a day or two.

"I need to get off the street, and I need to have a shave." I told them.

"My aunt has a cabin she hardly uses," Becky offered, "and I can go a store and buy you a razor." She was strikingly attractive, and I doubt if anyone meeting her would believe she had a criminal history. She was Jimmy's girlfriend and I had no intention of trying to make her mine.

"How far away?" I asked. She named a lake not far from the city.

"We can take a cab there," she said, "and we can bring some food with us."

"I'd sooner just wait until tonight and steal a car," I started to say, but Becky interrupted me.

"People take cabs out there all the time," she suggested. "It wouldn't be out of the ordinary."

"It would make it a lot easier to just take a cab," I replied hesitantly. Sue didn't say much, except that she'd like to come along. Sue and I waited on the hillside while Becky went to the store for the shaving gear. I shaved in Lake Champlain. Becky called a cab from a phone a block away and a few minutes later we were on our way.

I thought the women would give me some cover, but to be on the safe side, I talked about make-believe, mundane activities we three had been involved in over the past few days, giving the cab driver the impression we three were old friends and living a normal life—at one point I mentioned our car breaking down. Both women responded well to my comments and I believed we had established ourselves in the cab driver's mind as ordinary. Close to the outskirts of Burlington we stopped at a small store to buy some supplies. I waited in the cab while Becky and Sue did the shopping. The cab driver got out of the car to buy some gum, and I watched closely to see if he did anything else while at the counter. He didn't.

We had left the city and were travelling down a gravel country road when a city police car showed up behind us. He didn't turn on his lights or make any suspicious moves—he just followed the cab. I asked the cabbie to pull in for a moment at a farm house situated a short distance off the main road. The cabbie pulled in; the police car kept going and disappeared over the rise of a small hill. I walked up to the farmhouse and knocked on the door. A woman answered.

"Is this the Johnson home?" I asked

"No, this is the Derksens," she replied.

"Do you know if the Johnsons live close by?"

"I don't think so," she said.

"Have you lived here long?"

"Fourteen years," she replied.

"Then you'd know them if they did live close by?"

"Most certainly." I thanked her, and as the door closed, I turned toward the cab. The cop was slowly driving past, heading into the city. I felt relieved.

We drove over the hill ourselves and hadn't travelled a mile when the cop was behind us again. We were in a small valley on a curved road with woods on each side. I asked the cab driver to pull over again. He did so. The cop kept going.

"How much do I owe you?" I asked the driver.

"Seven dollars," he answered. He didn't turn to look at me, and he didn't look in his mirror. I handed him a twenty dollar bill and when he fumbled for change I told him to keep it. As we got out of the cab I told him we were going to walk the rest of the way.

"That's the best thing I've heard all day," he said. I shut the door and the cab took off with a roar, spewing gravel.

Twenty feet into the woods we came to a barbed wire fence. I was holding the top wire down for the women to climb over when the cop car came back and stopped a short distance away. I could see the cop trying to pick us out along the edge of the woods and Becky let me know that I shouldn't wait for them.

"Go like a motherfucker, Wayne," she said, quietly. And so I did.

As I ran through the woods I headed east, which was the direction w'd been travelling in the cab. I'd made good ground when I came to the edge of the woods which overlooked a huge meadow. The main road was to my left, a fence-line with tall grasses alongside it ran to my right, and further to my right I could see a truck, a tractor and a bailer, and two men on foot with pitchforks. Half a mile away there was a road running north and south, on the other side of it was one of the small green mountains for which Vermont is famous. If I could get to that road, cross it, and make it into the woods on the mountain, I'd have a good chance at escaping the immediate search area. I also noticed bulrushes and cat-tails along the north-south road in the distance ahead of me, indicating I would have to cross a slough before crossing the road. If I could make that slough, I could rest.

There was a small stand of trees fifty yards in front me. In the trees I'd have some cover from the main road, and I just might be able to use that cover to crawl down the fenceline to the mountain wood. So I ran and I made it. I watched the main road, but I could see no sign of the cop car—he was stopped far enough away down the road that the corner of the woods blocked his view.

I made it to the fenceline, threw myself flat on the ground, and with the tall grass on either side of me, I began to combat-crawl toward the sanctuary of the mountain. I didn't stop for a moment, not even when it felt as though my heart was going to explode in my chest.

The water of the slough was cold, but it wasn't more than a foot deep. The swamp grass and cattails were so abundant that I couldn't see in front of me—and if I couldn't see, they couldn't see me. I used the roots of a strong, tall cat-tail to prop my head on my arm, and concentrated on bringing my heartbeat back to normal.

I either went to sleep or simply passed out for a time, because I woke to hear a tractor idling loudly no more than twenty feet from where I lay.

"Have you seen a man running through this meadow?" asked a voice. The tractor shut down and the driver asked the voice to repeat what it had said.

"Have you seen anyone cross this meadow?"

"No," replied the driver. I heard another voice say he didn't think anyone had.

"We are searching for a prison escapee—he's armed and dangerous. When we find him there's going to be some shooting," said the voice, which I now identified as a cop. My body was trembling and my heart was pounding, and though I tried to control my breathing, I felt like my breath rattled the rushes so loudly they could hear me.

"Maybe we should quit for the day then?" said the hay farmer.

"That would be a good idea," said yet another voice, which I took to be the cop's partner.

"Okay guys," said the farmer, "let's pack it in." I heard the roar of the cop car as it took off, and I could hear the voices of the hay farmers receding as they talked to each other on their way to the truck. The truck pulled away and the slough fell silent.

I dozed again, but only for a short time, or so I believed. Upon waking, I began crawling to the far edge of the bulrushes, toward the mountain road. I believed the police would be focussing their search on the interior of the woods now, especially after confirmation that I hadn't crossed the meadow. The next half hour would be crucial.

I lay in the rushes looking at the twenty yards between me and the road. I was lying in a lowland, and the road itself dipped between two small rises. If I could crawl to the ditch at the edge of the road, I could cross it without being seen, unless a car was right on top of me. I decided to use an old Indian trick. In many of the westerns I'd seen as a kid, the Indians would use brush, branches and leaves to camouflage themselves as they crawled up close to the white man's camp. There was a hay bale no more than four feet away. I rolled it close to me and I used the barrel of the gun to break the twine and open the bale. It was just damp enough to stay together in flat clumps, which I placed on my back, legs and head. Carrying my miniature haystack with me, I crawled across the thirty feet of open meadow and reached the ditch without being seen. Once there I shook off the hay, ran across the road, and threw myself into the woods. There was no time for rest; I had a mountain to climb.

As I moved up the side of the mountain, my leg was beginning to tire. The unused muscles had atrophied to the point where my right leg was considerably weaker than my left, yet I was able to make good time just the same.

The view from the top afforded me a clear picture of the search area. There were at least thirty police vehicles on the roads surrounding the woods from which I'd just escaped. I could see cars stopped along the north-south road, cars along the east-west road, and men armed with shotguns and rifles standing beside their cars. I had a feeling of exhilaration, because I knew that I had just accomplished a feat I would never be able to duplicate. I had grown up reading about the courageous escapes of Canadians and Americans from German prisoner of war camps in the 1940s, and though I was not a prisoner of war, nor even a man deemed worthy of respect by the average, law-abiding person, I felt I'd proved something to myself.

It would take the police many hours to completely search the woods, and even when they believed they'd covered it thoroughly, it would be hours more before they actually believed I was not within their cordon. I was going to try to make Burlington by nightfall. I was still wet from the slough, my cigarettes had been turned into a disgusting yellow mush, and as I briefly rested, I thought of the women who were now in police custody. I felt pangs of guilt, yet I knew they'd come out of it relatively unscathed. As I got to my feet to continue, I knew if I could get to the north side of the city, I still might be able to make the border, with or without help from friends.

Dusk was rapidly falling and it was cloudy and beginning to drizzle as I made my way through the woods and the underbrush. Even though it was tempting to take the well-travelled pathways, I simply crossed them as if they weren't there. I felt comfortable in the knowledge that the sheriffs and state police would still be milling around the original search area, but I had to cover as much distance as I could.

Night was almost upon me when I came to a small cabin, situated at what appeared to be a bush road. The cabin was almost surrounded by the woods, so it was easy to walk close to it without fear of being seen by anyone inside. I circled the place; I was cold and hungry and very tired, and I seriously considered entering, but only if there was no one home.

I stood beside a half-open window and listened for occupancy. I could clearly hear a television at low volume, but I had the impression the place was unoccupied.

In both Canada and the United States breaking into a dwelling by night is one of the most serious crimes. In Canada the maximum penalty is life in prison. But I wasn't worried about the penalty, I was worried about the people that might be inside. Right then I wouldn't have hesitated to frighten someone into giving me some dry clothes, some food, and perhaps even some tobacco to get that nagging, growling, nicotine wolf from that very needful door in my mind. However, not everyone is a willing victim, not everyone is easy prey; there are people who will fight to the death to preserve their fortunes, no matter how small those fortunes might be. It would be foolish to put others at risk, not to mention myself, and I wanted to be absolutely convinced there was no one home. So I positioned my body in the Vietnamese squat, leaned back against the cabin wall, and waited for a sound from inside.

The news came on and the first item on the agenda was me. Upon hearing my name I stood to my feet, moved my head closer to the window and listened.

"Wayne Carlson eluded a massive police search in the Burlington area earlier today and police have now expanded their search to include most of the State of Vermont. Police are asking residents to keep their homes and vehicles locked, and to immediately report any suspicious persons to their local police."

I listened for any sound that would indicate movement in the cabin, but there was none. Again I was tempted to try the front door, and again I hesitated. While I debated the pros and cons, I imagined a scenario where I entered to find someone home—the person there panicked and struggled, and I hurt them. That overrode any thought of momentary comfort I might find inside, and I turned away and continued walking through the woods. The farther I went, the better I felt.

The woods were getting dark and an overcast sky made it difficult to make any real progress. I knew that I would have to lie down soon for the night. I wasn't concerned about police walking up on me unannounced—they'd have to use lights and make a considerable amount of noise. Yet the last thing I wanted to do was give any indication as to my whereabouts. I picked up a long, straight stick, and used it like a blind man's cane to feel my way.

A grey fog had begun to form, it was cold and damp, and I was nearly exhausted. Whether I wanted to or not, I would have to stop and rest. I was past the point of being hungry. I knew I would have to get some food into my body, but I had no idea how to satisfy that need.

Whenever I came to a place where the ground sloped down, I'd use the stick to feel the earth in front of me. I would grasp a small tree or a shrub in one hand, and feel my way forward with my feet. At one such point I found the woods thinning, but in the fog I couldn't tell whether it was a meadow I was crossing, or if it was just a clearing I had happened upon. I heard ducks ahead, clucking as they sat socializing in a body of water ahead of me. I could smell, as well as feel, a large body of water. Perhaps it was a lake and a shore on which I could continue, but I would have to maintain my sense of direction, otherwise I'd wander around the lake until I was right back where I started.

The stick in my hand was suddenly no longer tapping the ground, it was tapping nothing but air. I stopped. The area in front of me was completely black. I felt my way by sliding one foot forward, bringing the other beside it, then sliding the other forward in the same way. I did this twice. As I went to do it again I felt a bush beside me, so I grabbed a handful of branches, turned sideways to lower one foot down the slope when the hair on the back of my neck literally stood up. I pulled my foot back and tried to peer into the dark but to no avail. Once again I tried to continue, but again the chill ran up my spine and raised the hair on my neck. I stopped and backed away slowly, until I was twenty feet from the danger point.

I decided to make a small fire and try to get some sleep. The fog would cover the firelight from any distant observation. I could hear the ducks quietly and gently squabbling with each other as I made an effort to gather sticks and twigs to make a fire. The stick in my hand would serve as firewood too. The wood was damp and only by using matchstick-sized twigs was I able to get a blaze going.

Once I had one going I quickly made another, but even in the light of both I was unable to see what lay ahead. In order to get maximum warmth and dryness, I lay down between the two blazes and quickly fell into an exhausted sleep.

When I woke up dawn was breaking, the fog was just lifting, the fires had long since burnt themselves out and I was cold, stiff, and, for a moment, disoriented. I quickly gained my senses, got to my feet and stretched my aching muscles. As I walked toward the spot I'd retreated from earlier, the sense of being in the open was strong. I immediately saw why the hair on my neck had stood up.

I was on the tip of a peninsula of land that was part of a rock quarry, and it ran into a narrowing, cliff-like point. Along the edge were shrubs and small trees, and forty feet straight down lay a sea of huge boulders which rested on the shore of a slough-like lake. I couldn't see the water, only rushes and swamp grasses, but I could feel the chilly breeze flowing from across the body of water. It had a smell to it; I knew it was there.

I backtracked at least seventy-five yards before I was able to find a way down, and once at the base, I looked up the sheer side of the cliff. I looked at the huge boulders surrounding me and I knew I would never have been able to survive such a devastating fall. My imagination gave me the image of my body, twisted and bloody and broken on the rocks, and I knew it might have been months or even years before someone discovered me. I would be identified, of course, if by no other means than the clothes I was wearing and the guns I was carrying. My previous night's experience gave me a new respect, and a new awareness, for the sixth sense. Perhaps not everyone has it, or pays attention to it when it comes alive, but I knew without a doubt I had it, and I was grateful for it.

The fog was lifting as I quickly made my way north, always sticking to the cover and sanctuary of the trees. When I encountered fields and meadows, I skirted them, preferring to take the longer but safer route.

When I encountered berries I ate them, but there was nothing else to feed on. I crossed roads quickly, and only after ensuring the area was void of people. There were farms, but I always stayed behind cover. I was in no hurry—I didn't mind if it took me months to get to safety. I was determined to make the border and disappear into the lights of Montreal, or Toronto, or even Vancouver.

Years before, when I was serving my time in Prince Albert Penitentiary, two men had escaped from the minimum security farm annex situated outside the wall of the main prison. One of the men had been recaptured quickly; the other, a man by the name of Don Larson, had disappeared, and for years he was on the RCMP's Most Wanted list. There were rumours that his partner had killed him, because both escapees had been drinking immediately prior to the escape. There were also rumours that he had died trying to swim the North

Saskatchewan River, and had simply floated away, never to be found. But this was not the case.

It was close to Christmas when an off-duty police officer thought he recognized Larson in a Toronto department store, so he followed the man to his home. He then called for backup and they went in. It was Don Larson, married and living under an assumed name, and he and his wife had just had their first child. Larson was transported back to Saskatchewan, tried, convicted of escape, and sentenced to two years more imprisonment. He appealed, and because Saskatchewan had one of the best jurists in its history sitting on the bench as Chief Justice at the time, his appeal was heard.

The judge asked him how he'd managed to get to Toronto, over a thousand miles from Prince Albert, without resorting to crime. Larson explained he had walked on the railway tracks to Winnipeg; it had taken him the better part of three months to make the trek. From Winnipeg he caught a freight train to Toronto, got himself a job, fell in love with a woman and married her. His wife and his employer were in the courtroom, having flown from Toronto to Regina to appear with him in court. Chief Justice Culliton ruled the two year sentence was excessive, reduced it to time served, and strongly recommended Larson's immediate release to return to his wife and his job. "This is a classic example of a man rehabilitating himself," he said. The other two Justices concurred. Within two weeks Larson was released by the penitentiary service. This kind of legal ruling gave hope to many of us that the courts, and the officers of those courts, were indeed sometimes kind and humane.

As I walked, I began to limp—not a good sign for a man who had many miles ahead of him. I still felt quite strong, but I could feel a numbness in my body which extended to my jaw and lips. I would have to find food, and fairly soon.

I crossed sloughs, crouching to stay below the tops of the bulrushes, and in the evening dusk I could see the lights of the city of Burlington. I was walking down a ditch alongside a country road when I came across a small field of tall standing corn, so I slipped into the centre of it, sat down, and selected the ripest ears I could find. It was deliciously sweet and I could actually feel the energy it gave me flowing through my body. I ate a half a dozen ears and filled my pockets with many more, and as I walked away I felt rejuvenated and optimistic.

The road I'd been travelling on ran toward the eastern part of the city, and it was dark when I came to its bridge running across Intestate 89. I recognized the area now—I was only a few short miles from the suburbs and residential areas surrounding the city itself. The interstate posed a problem; the traffic was far too heavy to be able to run across the four lanes and the wide distance between them without being seen by at least two vehicles.

I backtracked a few hundred yards, then took to the woods leading to the interstate and using the cover of the trees and bushes, I watched the traffic of the county road. I'd be better off crossing the bridge than the highway below it. Carefully I made my way to the edge of the road, sat by the bridge, and ate my sweet corn while watching for signs of traffic coming from either direction.

The bridge traffic appeared to be infrequent, with more than five minutes between cars. As each car passed I watched intently as it reached the far side of the bridge, but there didn't appear to be anyone on the other side. The sound of the cars was uninterrupted, telling me there were no roadblocks in the immediate vicinity. It looked reasonably safe. I calculated the distance I'd have to run as about a hundred and fifty yards—even on a bad leg I believed I'd be able to manage it. I stuffed both handguns into my hip pockets, and made ready to make my crossing.

Right after the next car passed, I scrambled up the incline and ran as hard as I could across the bridge. I kept as low a profile to the horizon as possible because there were cars and trucks barrelling down the Interstate below. When I'd arrived at the retaining cables, and only had another twenty feet to go, I caught a movement to my left—it was the barely discernable shadow of a man. Just as I threw my body upward to roll over the cable, the explosion of a shotgun blast came at me. I could hear the pellets snapping past my ears, and then I was rolling down the steep decline. As I hit bottom in a tangle of small bushes and shrubs, I heard an excited voice yelling.

"I got him! I got him!" The wind had momentarily been knocked out of me, and as I regained my breathing, I realized it was pitch black. I could see nothing, and it would be suicide to try and move without sight. I heard the sound of cars gunning their engines down the road and I knew then that I'd happened onto a police trap at this end of the bridge. It would be impossible to run into the woods. I had nowhere to go. And then I heard it.

There was the gurgling sound of running water to my right and I knew immediately what it was. There had to be a culvert running under the road from one side to the other. I blindly crawled toward it and immediately fell into three feet of water. I half-crawled and half-floated through the large pipe, and when I came out the other end, I just kept going.

The creek flowed west to east and I tried to keep most of my body submerged, with only my head showing. *I hope I look like a muskrat,* I thought. When I reached deeper water, I slowly rolled over and looked back.

There had to be a dozen men and their cars, with lights and armed to the teeth. They were standing on the bridge with their backs to me, looking into the woods on the other side. I could hear one man emphatically proclaiming he'd hit me with the shotgun blast, and I'm sure it had appeared to him that he had. When I flew through the air it just might have appeared to him that the shotgun blast had blown me off the road. I could hear the sound of sirens in the distance, rapidly approaching.

There was a darkened farm to my right and I continued floating until I was far enough away that even the most powerful searchlight would have difficulty picking me out of the night. As I climbed out of the creek, I found myself behind one of the farm buildings. I used the buildings for cover until I passed a small camper trailer. I'd actually walked past it, when it occurred to me it might make a hiding place. *Probably not open,* I thought, but when I tried the door, it readily and quietly opened. I climbed in and locked the door behind me.

I knew I had nowhere to go, so after I caught my breath, I looked out the windows. The blinds had been drawn and some of the windows were of opaque glass, but it appeared everything was quiet and peaceful in the farmyard. I immediately explored my sanctuary and found two bunk beds and two rolled up sleeping bags behind a curtain, and there were four cans of food in the cupboard.

After stripping off some of my clothes and my boots, I wrung out most of the water and I began to warm up. I quietly fumbled through the drawers until I found a can opener and a spoon, and I opened all four cans. They were filled with peaches. I would have preferred them to be protein-rich beans, but I wasn't complaining. The peaches were delicious, sweeter than the corn. I rinsed out the cans, put them back upside down on the shelf and decided I'd crawl into bed and go to sleep. I laid out my socks, shirt, jacket and boots, and hoped the morning would find them drier. I climbed into the lower bunk and wrapped myself in the sleeping bag, taking the guns with me.

I'd just closed my eyes when lights began flashing in the windows. I was so tired I simply ignored them—the bed was comfortable and the sleeping bag warm...

The sound of a voice woke me. I could tell it wasn't the police, but I was instantly alert.

"This shouldn't be locked," said a mature man's voice. The door rattled. "You go to the house and get the key from mom," said the same voice. "Wait, I'll go with you."

I scrambled into my still-wet clothes, stuffed one gun into my pants, put on my boots, and with my socks in one hand and a handgun in the other, I opened the door. There was a corn field dead ahead of me, and with the camper as cover, I made my way into it. I stopped inside the green stalks, and sat down to take off my boots and put on my socks; I needed socks inside my boots to save my feet from being rubbed raw. I'd no sooner laced them up when I saw the farmer walk up to the door of his camper. When the door now readily opened, his body stiffened in surprise. He quickly glanced inside and when he saw nothing, he stood tall and looked at the corn field. The fact that his child was no longer with him indicated he was suspicious.

Moving as quickly as I could, I managed to get through the field and into a small wood behind it. Without hesitation I made off in the general direction of the city.

There were tree-lined fences surrounding the fields throughout the area, but it was now becoming much more open farmland, and dangerous for me. But I had no choice. I'd been walking and jogging for close to an hour when I heard the baying of bloodhounds, but almost immediately the sound seemed to veer away from me, and began to recede, as if the dogs were now going in the opposite direction to the one I was travelling.

I made good time, seldom resting, and by afternoon I'd put a considerable distance behind me. I was walking through woods, thick enough that I couldn't see open spaces in front or on either side of me. It was quite beautiful there, and though it was cool, it was not uncomfortably so. My clothes had dried on my back and again I felt I would make the border.

The woods became thinner, I could see fields both to my left and right, and I knew I was rapidly running out of cover. There were farms on either side of me. At one point I saw a woman working on something in her yard, so I squatted down until she'd walked around to the other side of the house. When she disappeared from view I continued to travel forward.

Suddenly the sound of sirens seemed to come from all around me, and I knew they were coming for me. I made a quick decision to try and hide. I picked an area close to the edge of the woods, beside a field, believing the edge of the wood would be the safest. When the searchers walked through the area they'd be inclined to walk ten or fifteen feet inside the woods, and if I could find a hole deep enough they just might miss me.

I scooped enough of a depression out of the leaves and soft loam to lay in, and once in it, I covered my legs and torso with maple leaves, grass and earth, and after throwing leaves over my chest and face, I burrowed my arms and hands into the ground. I lay there without moving, but I could feel my breath rattling the leaves. I didn't have long to wait.

There was the sound of many vehicles racing across the open fields, and in moments I could hear the slamming of car doors and someone giving curt commands to search the area.

I could only see what was directly in front of me—the leaves on my face obscured my peripheral vision. I saw a state trooper walk toward me, but he was looking straight ahead, as if trying to catch a glimpse of me walking or running. He passed no more than six feet from where I lay. I could hear many people, and in seconds they'd passed by and were walking away. The adrenalin of fear was coursing through my veins, making it difficult to control my breathing, and it making it difficult to hear clearly what was being said. The only thing I knew for sure was that they knew I was in that area. Then I heard a male voice, clearly.

"How big is he?" he asked. The sound came from in front of me.

"A hundred and sixty pounds, bushy brown hair," answered another man, behind me, a considerable distance away.

"Well, at a hundred and sixty pounds he'd have left tracks if he came through here," said the man in front. Then I saw him.

He was a fifty-year-old civilian wearing a floppy hat, and he could have come out of a scene from Deliverance. He was moving forward, taking slow steps, looking at the ground for tracks. He was on a direct path toward me. He would look at the ground, take a step, look some more, and repeat the process. He was standing right at my feet, but he missed them, and I could see his eyes scan the ground, over my legs and chest, and then he looked directly into my eyes.

His eyes widened in disbelief, and when the full realization struck him, I saw his amazement. His mouth moved to say something, but he couldn't speak. Shock and bone-deep fear, those two emotional cousins, momentarily robbed him of the capacity for speech. He tried to whistle, but that too was gone, so he could only make a harsh, rasping, hissing sound. He stumbled backwards out of my view, and an instant later I could hear him running through the leaves away from me. Suddenly, he found his voice again.

"He's there!" he cried. "He's right there: my God! There he is!" I didn't move, I just lay there. A second later a trooper ran past me looking away from me, his gun held in both hands. He held his combat stance until he followed my discoverer's pointing finger. He turned his body and his gun toward me, and finally our eyes met. His eyes were blue. He was the older trooper who'd obliviously walked past me on his first pass.

"Come up out of there," he said. His voice and his eyes were surprisingly calm. I slowly raised my hands.

"You don't have to shoot," I said. "I'm coming out." I slowly sat up, keeping my eyes on him all the while. I rose and stood to my feet. I was ringed by more than a dozen armed men. My captor gave someone instructions to handcuff me, and in a moment my hands were behind my back and I was being led out of the woods. There were reporters snapping pictures and men milling all around me. One young deputy sheriff came running up to grab my right hand, and he began twist my thumb and fingers until they were reaching the breaking point.

"You don't have to do that," I said, quietly. He twisted even harder and I looked at his face to see hatred, and a desire to seriously hurt me. I had to stop him or he'd break the bones in my hand. I kicked the side of his leg with a karate-type kick. It hurt him enough that he let go. A deep voice gave a command to lighten up, and I looked over to see a tall, silver-haired man in an expensive suit walking toward us. He looked like a senator, and he appeared to be in complete control. The hate-filled deputy sheriff slunk resentfully away and I was relieved. Had he been the one to first see me, the men would be ringed around my corpse in the ground back in the woods.

"You take him," said the senator look-alike, "and put him in the car." He pointed to the calm, older trooper who'd first pointed his gun at me. The troop-er came over and took my arm and we walked to a state police cruiser. He put me in the back seat, and as he did so, the senator climbed in next to me on the opposite side. As we began driving away he gave the trooper route instructions in order to avoid further contact with the press. We were travelling down a country road when he turned his attention to me.

"Do you know the names of the deputy sheriffs you escaped from?" he asked.

"Yes," I replied, "Steve and Kevin."

"Do you know what Kevin's last name is?"

"No."

"It's McLaughlin," he said.

"Oh," I answered.

"Do you know what my name is?"

"No."

"It's McLaughlin too. Sheriff McLaughlin. Kevin is my son," he stated, mat-ter-of-factly.

"Oh," I lamely responded. I thought I was probably in for the beating of my life down this back country road somewhere.

"Why didn't you rob them? You don't have to answer if you don't want to." But I did answer.

"It never crossed my mind," I replied. "I just wanted to get away."

"Makes sense to me," he offered. Then, "Would you like a cigarette?"

"I would love a cigarette," I said. He put one in my mouth and lit it for me. I took a drag and felt the welcome relief familiar to all nicotine addicts.

"You know that crutch you left in the bathroom?" he asked.

"Yes," I answered around the cigarette in my mouth.

"I nailed it to Kevin's wall, right above his bed." I laughed. I couldn't help it. There was no further conversation, and I'd just finished the last drag on the cig-arette when we arrived at the Burlington Correctional Centre. Reporters were there sticking cameras in our faces, and a few seconds later I was in a holding room. Sheriff McLaughlin ordered me a meal, but I was able to eat only a cou-ple of bites. I was heartsick, completely exhausted, and all I had to look forward to was the unappetizing atmosphere of the segregation unit of Windsor State Prison.

I was escorted back to state prison by Kevin and Steve, sitting on either side of me in the back seat of the police car. Sheriff McLaughlin rode in the front passenger seat, and our driver was a young state trooper. A car full of state troopers led the way, and we were followed by another car, again full of troopers. The Sheriff turned to look at me.

"Kevin figures he could've taken you at the court house," he said. I looked at Kevin for confirmation. He blushed.

"I could've taken you," he said, confirming what his father had stated.

"At what point?" I asked.

"When we were walking down the stairs to the car."

"No," I replied, "you can tell your father that, but don't tell me that. I know different."

"I could have..." he began, but I interrupted him.

"Kevin," I said kindly, "you did the right thing by doing exactly what you did." He seemed to lighten up. The Sheriff then turned his attention to Steve.

"Steve hopes you try to escape from him again," he said. I turned my gaze on Steve.

"Is that right Steve?" He too turned red. They both knew they could be dead men, and I felt no guilt or shame for the way I'd treated them.

The boys back in the segregation unit greeted me with congratulations, as if somehow my escape had been a great accomplishment. Perhaps it was. But I was only able to feel the agony and deep disappointment of being back with them. It took me weeks to shake off the depression that followed, and I found myself not wanting to go to sleep at night because of the dreams of being free, and the pain of waking in a cell again.

The cells were one hundred and fifty-seven years old, and they looked it. The thing that set these cells apart from other cells was the window. Most cells have bars in the front, but these had small barred doors *and* barred windows which had a small slot in the bottom to slide food through to the occupant. The cells could have come out of the dungeon inhabited by the Count of Monte Cristo.

The bars had a lot of iron in them, making them soft; it wouldn't take much of a hacksaw blade to cut them. When cutting more modern cold-rolled steel bars there's a great deal of noise, and the filings are fine; in cutting the softer metal, the filings are larger and the sound of the burrowing saw is much quieter. If I could get my freedom-hungry hands on a blade, I'd be able to cut through the window bars without difficulty—but because of the spacing, I would have to cut at least four of the bars to squeeze through. Once they were cut, I would have to deal with one night-shift prison guard and after tying up the guard, I'd have to hit a button on the inside of the new maximum security bubble which would open the door leading to the main prison yard. Once in the main yard of the prison, I'd have to scale the fifteen-foot high wall and escape into the woods which surrounded that side of the prison.

It would take time, and most of the work would have to be done at night when there were only one or two guards on duty. It would also necessitate taking on a partner because I wouldn't be able to open the outside door without help—I couldn't be standing at the outside door and be in the bubble pushing the button at the same time.

Most of the men on my range had long sentences to serve, but because the risk of discovery was so great, they'd be hesitant to get involved. As well as a partner, I'd need, at the very least, the passive participation of all of my fellow prisoners; there was no way such an escape as this one could be effectively carried out without every man on the range being aware it was in progress. Over the course of the next few days I felt out each man on the range, and though some of them would have made good partners, the only one who showed any real enthusiasm was Dick. Because of my previous experience with him on the earlier escape, he was last on my list, but for what he had to do, he was acceptable.

The first step of the plan was to obtain some blades capable of cutting through at least seven bars—the bars on my window would have to be completely cut, and the bars on Dick's window would have to be at least partially cut. Once I was out of my cell I'd be able to use one of the heavy weight bars of the range gym to break him out. It was risky, but it was doable.

The men in the general population knew who I was, and they knew I was serious when it came to carrying out a plan. It was easy to find someone who'd steal some blades from one of the shops and slip them under the exercise fence which separated the main prison yard from the segregation yard. One day while we were out in the yard a prisoner hollered that the message had been delivered and posted at the right place and time. This meant the hacksaw blades were in the prearranged hiding place. We needed to only distract the guards on duty for a moment, which we did, and I picked them up.

The men on the range gave their cooperation by increasing the volume of their television sets, and by taking turns keeping six—watching for guards— while I made my cuts. I'd made a practice of placing books and magazines between the bars; this served the purpose of disguising the cuts, and at the same time holding the bars in place once they were cut through.

Many of the guards were friendly, without an axe to grind, and one of them used to stop in front of my cell to talk to me. We always got along well, but one day he reached over to pick up one of the books between the bars and I exploded.

"Get your fuckin' hands off my property!" I shouted at him. He immediately withdrew his hand in surprise and stepped back. The prisoners in the cells exploded as well, shouting obscenities at him.

"Keep your fuckin' hands to yourself!"

"Yeah, fuck off motherfucker!"

"Hit the fuckin' road!"

The young guard was mortified, because only moments before he'd believed he was an accepted member of our little range community. For the next few days he was quite subdued. He was a good man and I felt sorry for him.

My plan was a simple one: after the bars were cut and I was out of my cell, I'd duck into the darkened, recessed doorway leading to the main yard. On his way down the range, the guard would pass my cell and walk past me hiding in the doorway. Once he'd passed, I'd step out behind him and make him my prisoner.

Pork Chops Hunter lived in the last cell at the end of our range. I would tie up the guard in his cell. I trusted Chops not to untie the man once he was tied, but I would have to pretend to threaten him with serious bodily harm to get him to do what I needed him to do. It was not unheard of for the state to charge someone with aiding and abetting a fellow prisoner in an escape attempt; however, if the aider and abettor were coerced into assisting, there was a good chance no charges would be laid, or if they were, that they wouldn't result in a conviction.

It was after eleven o'clock at night when I carefully removed the books from between the bars. Richardson, the graveyard shift guard, had just made his second round down our range, and he'd just turned the corner to go to the range on the other side, when I got the green light.

"Go," whispered Jimmy from the cell next to mine.

I squeezed out the window. Seconds later I was standing in the recessed doorway, my back flat against the wall. I had one of the bars and a makeshift knife in my hands, and my heart was pounding. One of the men on my range began to holler for a guard. I could hear the key in the wire gate at the front of the range, and I watched as his shadow approached.

"Who called?" Richardson asked.

"Down here!" declared a voice near the end of the range.

"I'm coming," he said. I tried to melt into the wall. If he saw me, he might be able to run to the bulletproof bubble, slam the door and raise the alarm. He walked right past me. As he walked by, he again asked who'd called for him. I stepped into the hallway and took an aggressive stance in the middle of it.

"Stop right there," I ordered. I saw his back stiffen in shock, and as he turned around to face me, he put his hands out in a placating gesture.

"What are you doing?" he asked without aggression.

"I'm tying you up," I said. "Don't fight it and you won't get hurt."

"No, I won't fight you," he answered.

"Walk to the end cell and sit down with your back to the bars and your hands behind you," I ordered.

"Okay," he replied, and he did exactly what I told him to do.

"Chops, tie him up," I ordered, and I placed two long shoelaces on the bars of his cell.

"I can't get involved in this..." Chops began. I interrupted him before he could protest further.

"You tie him or I'll break into your cell and kill you," I told him.

"You'll kill me?" he asked.

"In a New York second."

"I'd better do what you say. I don't want to die," said Chops.

Then the guard spoke up. "Do what he says," he told him. "Just do what he says." I was surprised at his instruction, and pleased. Chops would be covered, and he knew it. He tied up Richardson, and I immediately broke out the bars of Dick's cell.

It wasn't an easy task because Dick hadn't been working on his bars as he was supposed to. They'd been cut, but I had to break them out, and there was a considerable amount of noise. It would have been great if the keys to the cells were in the bubble, however, the keys were kept in the main security bubble on the floor above us. Finally the last bar snapped off with a crack that resounded like a rifle shot on the range. Then it was strangely quiet.

I helped Dick through the new slot in the window, and as soon as he was standing beside me, we walked to the security bubble. I pointed out the button which would snap the electronic lock on the outside door.

The door opened and I propped it with a chair so it wouldn't close behind us. After gathering up a long, coax television cable and a chair whose legs I'd use for a hook to straddle the wall, we walked out into the yard. I double-checked to make certain we had everything we needed to get over the wall before I allowed the door to shut behind us.

There were no guards in the gun towers after the eleven o'clock count. To have the towers manned in the night, when no prisoners were out of their cells, was seen as a waste of money.

The fences in the segregation exercise yard abutted against the prison wall, and one of the fences ran against the wall itself. From the top of the fence to the top of the wall was only seven feet—but it was a long seven feet. I quickly tied two long broom handles together with shoelaces and tied the chair to the broomsticks. It didn't take long to push the chair up the wall until its legs straddled the top.

I put Dick on top first, and once he was there he held the chair in place while I made the climb. In minutes we were standing side by side on the six-inch ledge, four feet below the top, on the outside of the wall.

"I'll hold the chair while you go down," I told Dick, "but don't drop your weight on the cable all at once. Hold the cable with one hand and support your weight with the other hand on the ledge."

"Okay," he replied excitedly.

"Do you understand?"

"Yeah, yeah," he assured me, "I understand."

"Okay," I instructed, "go." And go he did.

He just stepped off the ledge, both hands on the cable. His full weight hit the chair. I was flung sideways and left hanging on the wall by one hand while he dropped like a stone. I heard the crash of the chair on the cement below, and I didn't want to look down, because I didn't want to look at his broken body.

"I'm okay," I heard him say. "I'm okay..." I looked then, and saw him hobbling around in a small, tight circle. I was amazed. It was a long way down.

Without the chair and cable, it'd be difficult for me to make the drop to the ground below, but it had to be done. Then I noticed the ledge I was standing on ran down the wall, and right past the tower.

I quickly shuffled my feet until I was standing between the wall and the tower, reached out my hand, grabbed the railing of the tower stairs, and swung myself to the stairs. I was on the ground and we were moving to the small woods behind the prison when the escape siren went off.

It soon became apparent that Dick had injured both feet in his fall. Once the numbness had eased, pain made his injuries known to him. The toes of his left foot and the heel of his right were causing him problems. I helped support him as best I could, at times almost carrying his full weight across my shoulders.

We had traveled for more than two hours when we decided we'd stop and rest in a wooded area for the night. Dick's feet had become very painful, and though he didn't complain much, he did need to rest. We lay on the ground, and within minutes I was fast asleep.

The next morning we woke to find ourselves on a small hillside, safely surrounded by the woods, and I knew we'd have to be extremely cautious and avoid being seen by anyone. The blaring siren in the middle of the night would've woken people for miles around the prison, and it was loud enough, and howled long enough, to wake the dead. We'd only be able to move through wooded areas, and if we encountered open spaces or residential areas, we'd have to wait until nightfall to continue.

If we could live with our hunger and avoid being seen for three days, I felt confident the authorities would believe we'd successfully escaped the area, and the roadblocks would be lifted. Once the highways and byways were clear of police, we'd be able to drive ourselves out, but it would take willpower and determination to go without food and live with the discomfort of sleeping on the ground. I felt I could do it. I just hoped Dick would be able to.

On the second night we came across a large warehouse on the northwestern outskirts of Windsor. We'd been shuffling along the fields behind the houses for about two hours when the building came into view in front of us. There were houses scattered along the road, but we were at least a hundred and fifty yards from them and they didn't pose a problem for us.

The warehouse had old-style, slide-up windows which made entry easy. The building was used to store dry goods as well as a horse-hauling van and a camper trailer. I used my lighter to check out the camper, and found it held sleeping bags and a flashlight complete with good batteries, but no food or water. Still, we had some reliable light. The horse van was open and a quick glance into the interior with the flashlight told me its engine could be started by crossing the ignition wires, however, it was too soon to try to drive down the highway.

Immediately outside the camper there was box upon box of every kind of junk food imaginable; corn chips, potato chips, popcorn, and more, in a wide variety of flavours. To give in to temptation would lead to an experience of the torture of the damned—the craving for water would be so great that we'd have to go looking for it, no matter the consequences, and I refused to place myself in such a predicament.

"We're going to stay here for tonight and tomorrow. Tomorrow night we'll seriously consider taking the van and heading north," I told Dick. I knew he was in pain, and I did feel sorry for him, yet I was not going to risk apprehension by jumping the gun.

"We could eat some chips," he said.

"Don't eat any of that stuff," I told him. "Not until we find some water."

"But I'm hungry."

"Dick, don't eat them. If you do, you'll go crazy for water, and I'm not taking the risk of leaving this building to find water for you." I could see the resentment in his face, but he'd have to live with my decision.

"Yeah."

"You have to dig deep to get yourself through this." I looked into his eyes. "Do you understand?"

"Yeah, yeah, yeah," he muttered. I told him to stay in the camper while I went exploring, and I instructed him to not take off his boots.

"If you do," I said, "you'll never get them back on."

"Yeah, okay. See if you can find some water, will you?" There was a pleading note in his voice. I told him I would and I went exploring the interior of our sanctuary.

There was an upper level and I explored that as well, but in all the variety of the stored material, there was not one drop of water to be found. We'd have to live without it for the next twenty-four hours. I checked out the area surrounding the building, and found we were in a residential area situated almost outside of town. There was a house across the street, but it was a considerable distance away and didn't pose a threat. When it came time to leave, I'd cross the wires of the ignition in the truck, open the large double doors, and just drive down the highway to freedom. I returned to the camper and found, to my utter dismay, that Dick had completely ignored my instructions.

I cast the light around to see bags of junk food, crumpled and empty, scattered around Dick's bootless feet. He had a look of resentful defiance on his face and all I could do was shake my head.

"For Christ's sake, Dick, don't you know what's going to happen?" But he cut me off.

"I'll be okay."

"No, you won't be okay—and don't ask me to leave to find water for you."

"I won't ask for a fuckin' thing," he replied. I knew he probably believed it, but I knew better.

"I'm going to sleep," I said. "Wake me if anything comes up."

"Yeah," he answered petulantly. I rolled myself into the sleeping bag and quickly fell asleep. I estimated it was no more than two hours later when he woke me up.

"What is it?" I asked. I sat up thinking someone was entering the building.

"There was a house we passed before we got here, and I think it had a water hose on the side," he said.

"I told you, I'm not leaving this building until tomorrow night."

"Fuck!"

"I told you, Dick."

"You could do it if you wanted to."

"Of course I could."

"Please?" Now he was begging me. I angrily threw off my sleeping bag, took a handful of the plastic junk food bags, stuffed them in my pocket and left him lying there.

I climbed through the window, walked around the corner of the building and looked at the house across the street. The windows were dark, it was very quiet in the night, and against my better judgement I slipped across the road, walked to the back of the house and found an outside tap. I should have checked for a better container for water, but the bags would do. I quietly turned the tap handle until a small trickle of water flowed. I bent down and took a long drink, rinsed out four of the bags, filled them with water, and just as quietly slipped away to return to the warehouse.

"Don't drink them all at once," I told him. "Save some for later—I'm not going back. And keep one for me." It appeared he'd learned something because he drank one slowly. I opened the cupboards, found a plastic container to hold the rest of the water, and we carefully poured the water into it.

"Thanks Wayne," he said. There was gratitude in his voice so I didn't belabour the issue. We rolled ourselves into our sleeping bags, but I found myself unable to let it rest.

"Did you ever read about the two men who escaped from an Australian prison?" I asked him.

"No," he replied.

"It seemed they both got so hungry in the outback that one of them killed the other and ate him."

"No shit?"

"No shit," I replied. "And the man who ate his partner acquired such a taste for human flesh that after he was recaptured, he escaped again, and took a partner with him, just for food."

"You're bullshitting me," he said half-heartedly.

"Nope—straight goods. And I think he did it more than twice."

"Jesus."

"Yes, life is strange." I let him stew on that thought behind his closed eyelids before he went to sleep. I'd read that story, but whether or it was true was another thing.

The next morning I was the first one awake, and I immediately looked over to the plastic jug. He'd actually drunk very little of the water. I didn't bother getting up. There was nowhere to go and nothing to do but wait patiently for nightfall. Until then, I'd get all the rest I could.

Later, the sound of voices inside the warehouse brought me fully awake. I feared the place was being searched, though the tone of the voices quickly dispelled that notion. I rose quietly, woke Dick and told him to stay where he was.

Through the curtain on the window I could see two men busy loading boxes of junk food into a small white van. As they worked they said little, and in a short time their work was complete. They shut the door behind them and I heard the vehicle drive away, heading toward town. It was the only interruption we had to contend with, and the day passed uneventfully. Dick did not eat any more of the goodies.

When it was dark, I tore the wires from under the dash of the van, and though it took a few trials and errors to extricate the starter wire, in a short time I had the radio going and the gas gauge told me the tank was more than half full. I crawled through the window, walked to the large front doors and examined the lock. It was a padlock, and the hasp was attached to the old wood of the door with standard screws. I needed a small pry bar or screwdriver to pull out the screws and I found a tire iron behind the front seat of the truck. I went back out through the window and in seconds the double doors were ready to open. I cracked one of them, walked back to the truck, put the tire iron back in place, and climbed in. We sat in the truck, had a cigarette, and waited for the news to come on.

"Do you think we'll make it?" asked Dick. I could see the strain on his face in the dim light. He was just an inexperienced kid. I felt sorry for him, yet he had an attitude I didn't like and attitude is everything.

"Of course I think we'll make it," I replied. "If I didn't think so I wouldn't have started this whole thing."

"Yeah, but this truck will be slow."

"Do you think speed will get us through, where this truck won't?"

"Well a Trans Am would be better."

"Maybe," I replied, "but it's the not the size of the vehicle that will get us safely through this—speed won't do it. We have to look legitimate and drive right by police cars, not outrun them."

"Yeah, I guess so." But he didn't sound convinced. I'm sure he wished he hadn't gotten involved. I knew too that he was experiencing a considerable amount of pain in his feet. He'd carried his boots in his hand and he had to literally heel and toe his way to the truck.

"We'll be able to get some codeine or morphine for my feet, won't we?"

"No problem," I assured him. "We'll get you fixed up as soon as we get to Boston."

"Boston?" he asked surprised. I turned to look at him.

"Didn't I tell you? We're going to Boston first, Canada second."

"I thought we were going straight across the border."

"Nope—not broke and hungry we're not."

"We'll pull a score in Boston?"

"We'll make some money," I replied.

"I'd like to get a good car..." he began, but I held up my hand and he fell silent as the news came on.

The newscast suggested the escape had been well planned in advance, and that authorities believed we'd had outside help and were probably out of the area. The rest consisted of a history of previous escapes and the fact that I was wanted in Canada.

"I like the sound of that," I said.

"What?" asked Dick.

"The outside help, being out of the area."

"Yeah?"

"Yeah—it suggests the roadblocks might be lifted."

"Oh yeah, it does, doesn't it?"

"Indeed it does, Dick, indeed it does."

There was no reason to wait any longer; it was dark, it was late enough, and the truck would make good cover traveling down the highway. We'd have to siphon gas on the way to Massachusetts but that was a minor problem.

I touched the starter wire to the bare wire mess I'd created, and the engine immediately turned and came to life. I had the feeling the truck had been well cared for and I resolved to leave it in good condition when I finally parked it.

I was opening the double doors when a car pulled into the long narrow driveway leading from the roadway to the warehouse. It stopped dead in the middle of it and I was half blinded as the brights of the headlights were turned on and the engine of the car stopped. I shielded my eyes with my hand and saw a man leap from the car and run to the house across the street. Not only was I made, the panicking driver knew I was taking the truck and had blocked me in.

I could've tried to move his car, but I knew the police would be there within minutes. If I chose to take the truck, I'd be lumbering down the highway with local and state police in hot pursuit. It was not the way to go; I preferred to take to the woods.

I ran back and told Dick what was happening, and as I helped him get out of the truck I told him we had to hit the woods.

"We can take the truck," he said.

"The road's blocked," I replied.

"We can push the car off the road with the truck."

"No we can't, and even if we do we'll have dozens of cops on our ass right away. We only have minutes to get out of here." As we moved out through the doors, Dick could see the other car blocking our path.

"We can take the truck..."

"No, we can't. You can try it if you want. I'm going to hit the woods," I said firmly.

"I can't drive," he said. I was shocked.

"You can't drive?"

"No."

"Then I'll help you into the woods."

"No, you go. I'll tell them I was the only one here," he offered.

"Are you sure?"

"Yes, I'm sure," he replied. He seemed relieved, not disappointed. I accepted his offer.

"Thanks Dick," I said, "and I'm out of here." I left him standing in the headlights, and as I ran from the lights into the darkness, I couldn't help but wonder if there were eyes watching us from across the street. If there were, the police would know there'd been more than one man in the warehouse.

Moonlight lit up the woods and I found a pathway, which appeared to be a hiking trail, so I was able to make very good time. I headed back the way we'd come and within minutes I was standing at the door of what appeared to be a large shed. I could hear chickens clucking from inside, but the size of the two storey building told me there had to be more than chickens inside. The sirens were beginning to howl when I opened the door and walked in. The chickens didn't like the intrusion and scolded me for it—I hoped they'd settle down before the searchers came by.

There was a car in one side of the large shed, chickens in the other, and on the ceiling there was a pull-down ladder with a rope attached. I pulled down the ladder, climbed it, and found myself in a hayloft filled with hay. The ladder came up behind me and I scrambled to the farthest corner of the loft, selecting the area I thought would be safest. I burrowed myself deep into the hay and lay there.

It didn't take long for the sound of men searching the area to reach me. I could hear them long before they reached the building and the sudden cackle of the chickens below told me when they entered the chicken house. The sound of the ladder being pulled told me they were now coming up to the loft.

Even from beneath the pile of hay I could see the harsh white light of their flashlights, and though they were initially quiet and stealthy, their frustration brought their voices to life.

"I hope that cocksucker's running when I see him," said one.

"Yeah, I'll blow a hole in him so fucking big..."

"We should poke every inch of this hay with pitchforks," one said.

"I'll get the forks," said his partner. I couldn't remember seeing any forks, but there probably was more than one in the building. I heard the ladder descend and I could hear his partner tramping into the hay while he waited for the fork. I was in a spot where the roof sloped downward; he'd never be able to touch me with his boots. Only by crawling into the narrow confines offered by the roof, or by jabbing with a long-handled pitchfork, would they discover me. I heard the ladder descending again, and a moment later the man's voice told me he'd been successful.

"There was only one," he said, "but it's all we'll need." I could hear the fork digging into the hay, and I gritted my teeth to steel myself from the pain.

"That mo-th-er-fuck-er—that cock-sucker—that-piece-of-shit-scum-bag," said the voice, his cursing keeping time with his jabs of the fork. This went on for five long minutes at least, and at one point I felt the hay move around me.

"Fuck this," said his partner, whom I took to be holding the light.

"Yeah, he ain't here." There was suddenly a new voice added to the mix.

"What's up there?" asked a man from down below.

"Not a motherfucking thing," said the cursing man as he continued to jab with the fork.

"No, we jabbed every inch of this loft with a fuckin' fork - he ain't here."

"Then let's get out here," said the man from below.

"Yeah," said the man with the light, "the smell of this chicken shit is more than I can take."

"Let's go," said the jabber. I heard the ladder being lowered, and though I listened carefully to hear if both had left, or if one had elected to stay behind and wait for any movement from me, it was impossible to tell. The ladder rose again, and in a surprisingly short period of time, the chickens and the rest of the building fell into complete silence. I didn't move for hours.

It had to have been long past midnight when I finally crawled out of my hiding place and quietly made my way to the ladder. I sat there for ten minutes, straining my ears for any sound that might indicate my pursuers were still in the vicinity. It was as silent and as still as still could be.

The lowering of the ladder brought the chickens to a ripple of clucking life, but it seemed minor to the clamour they raised when I first entered. *Maybe they recognize me,* I thought, smiling to myself as I thought it.

The car in front of me was an older Pontiac. It looked to be in good shape. In short order the ignition wires were hanging from under the dash, and I hoped it would start without too much noise. The fact that the house of the owner was a distance away from me made it reasonably safe.

I stepped outside and waited for a car or a truck to come by, but it was some time before I heard a car leaving town and heading for the interstate. It was a beautiful night, the stars were shining in a clear sky, and the coolness made the air crisp and clean and I could hear the car continuing down the road for many miles. I heard the car slow, then stop, and then roar to life again as it headed north. I opened the double doors, climbed into the Pontiac, pumped the gas pedal a couple of times and tried the starter.

The car came to life after only turning over a couple of cranks. I drove it out of the garage and immediately shut it off. I quickly closed the doors, and found the chickens were aroused again. Above their clatter I listened for any sound from the house that would indicate I'd woken people as well, but the house remained dark and undisturbed. As I was driving away I thought it might've been nice to take one of the hens with me. I was hungry enough to eat it raw.

In the light of the dashboard I could see I had half a tank of gas, enough to get me a long way from Windsor. I headed for the northern part of Vermont and arrived there before dawn.

John answered the door and directed me to the stairway in the garage. I'd been there before so I knew my way. Mary lived on the top floor.

"You made it," she said. She was standing in the doorway in a nightie, and even though I'd roused her from sleep, she looked beautiful.

"Yeah, just barely," I said.

"Come in," she said, and as I followed her she asked if I was staying. I appreciated her offer, but I couldn't jeopardize her or her friends.

"The devil himself couldn't keep me out of Boston tonight," I replied. "But I need some gas."

"Your car still has gas in it," she suggested.

"My car?"

"Yes, the Opel."

"It's here?" I'd wondered what had become of it.

"It's here. We picked it up after Lora was arrested."

"Oh," I said. I still felt guilty about Lora. "I'll siphon the tank before I go."

"Okay," she said. Then she made a good suggestion. "I'll give you a haircut and you can have a shave."

"That sounds good."

"When did you last eat?"

"A couple of days ago."

"I'll make some sandwiches and coffee."

"That would be great."

"You have some clothes here," she said.

"Yes?" I was surprised and glad to hear it.

"I'll get rid of your prison clothes," she offered.

"Okay—don't leave them lying around. Into the garbage, right away," I suggested.

"They'll be gone," she stated, and I had no doubt they would.

"Thanks Mary," I said. I sat in her kitchen, she made coffee and three roast beef sandwiches, and we talked.

An hour later I was back on the road, after receiving instructions and directions from John on how to get to Boston on county roads. I could avoid the main highways and still be in Boston by mid-morning. My belly was full, and though the taste of gasoline lingered on my tongue, I was dressed in some decent clothes and I felt I was going to make it.

The sun had been up for hours when I pulled into a service station a few miles from Boston. I counted my change and found I could put only two dollars worth of gas into the car, but two dollars would get me into the city limits. Once I was away from the vehicle I'd feel much safer.

"How far to Boston?" I asked the gas station attendant.

"Thirty minutes away," he replied. He seemed surprised when I asked for just a couple dollars worth of gas.

"Which is the best way to get there from here?" I asked.

"The fastest way is the interstate and the freeway," he answered. "But there's a tollbooth just ahead."

"How do I avoid the tollbooth?" I asked. I only had nickels and dimes in my pocket. I couldn't afford to pay a toll.

"Stay on this road and you'll be okay," he answered, pointing down the county road on which I'd been traveling.

"What part of Boston will I be in?" I asked. I had two addresses, one for the Backbay area and the other for Cambridge. The Backbay area was an old part of Boston; Cambridge was situated outside of the city. I had the addresses of bar owners in each area.

"You'll be in the Backbay area."

"Great. Thanks."

"No problem."

The city traffic was very heavy and there was a traffic cop standing at the intersection when I stopped. As he waved me on, the car stalled. I was out of gas. I considered getting out and running, but common sense told me to brazen it through. I got out of the car, lifted my hands and shrugged my shoulders, telling the cop with body language that my car had died in the middle of the street.

The traffic backed up behind me, and I could see frustration on the cop's face as he looked around. There were two men walking down the street toward the intersection and the cop waved them over.

"Push that car off the street—down there," he demanded, pointing to a side street. The men obeyed him and together we pushed the car until I could steer it into a parking spot. I thanked the men and started walking.

I had no idea where I was in the city, but I walked for thirty minutes as if I knew where I was going. A woman was walking toward me so I excused myself and asked for directions. I mentioned the bar.

"I never heard of it," she said. She was very friendly. "What's the address?" I gave her the address of the Backbay bar.

"That's just a block over, and a block down," she said.

"Thank you," I said, and I continued walking, a block over and a block down. I had arrived in Boston safely. I was free and well on my way to wealth and happiness.

A MAN AMONG MEN

He was a miserable old man—there was no other way to describe him. Even his hair was a miserable grey, and he was as grizzled as a grumpy old bear in the last stage of its life. Any sounds he made while hunkered in the doorway were grunts and grumbles, and though he thought they passed for speech, anyone within hearing distance who might pause for a moment in the mistaken belief he'd said something to them, would quickly put it down to crazy, old-man noises before they hurriedly continued on their way. George and I didn't pass by like the others. We were hunters and the old man seemed like easy prey in the mean streets of Boston a few blocks away from Fenway Park.

The doorway afforded the old man a small shelter from the cold fall night, and even if the old man's crutches weren't in full view at his side, George could smell helplessness a block away. The smell of cheap whiskey was a cloak around the old man's head and shoulders. He sat hunched over his knees as if keeping them warm, and his hands were tucked inside the sleeves of his jacket. The sight of him made me want to dig in my own pockets for a few bucks to give him, but George had a heart harder than the cold sidewalk.

"He's ripe," George murmured. George was a thief who made a living doing anything that would bring him a dollar. He also wanted to prove his independence to the regular crew at Clancy's Pub down on Chaucer and Weslyn.

"Jesus Christ," I said. Ever since I'd met George after escaping from the state prison in Vermont two weeks earlier, my life had turned to shit. I fancied myself an outlaw, a bank robber and an escape artist. George was a man who thought robbing the blind was a good thing; for as long as you didn't speak when you did it, there would be no eyewitness identification.

"Let's sit down beside him," George said. There was a quickening in his voice and movements that I noticed in him whenever he became excited. He immediately stepped into the doorway, and with a hurried hello, he picked up one of the crutches. After leaning it against the wall, he sat down on the old man's left side.

"Hey fellas," muttered the old man. I stepped into the doorway, moved his other crutch to the side and sat on his right. There was now just enough room for all three of us to sit shoulder to shoulder in the small, dim shelter. The building was under construction and the shelter was more like a porch than a regular doorway. Though the street had lights, they were almost a block away.

"What's up old man?" asked George. The sound of his voice was friendly, almost helpful, as if he was looking for a way to do something good for our victim.

"Just resting," said the old man. He turned his face towards me. It was only inches away. I could see his whiskey-soaked eyeballs peering at me in the dim light. They looked like bad boiled eggs in a milky jar.

"Got anything to drink?" George asked. George was tugging at the side of the old man's coat and the old man turned his head to look at George.

"Sure," he said, "for a man among men I do." The old man turned his face to me and pointed to the corner beside my foot. I saw a bottle of cheap whiskey half-hidden by a wooden brace. I leaned forward, picked up the bottle and handed it to him. He unscrewed the cap and handed it to me. I took it in my right hand.

"Igday his acketjay ocketpay," George said. He'd leaned forward to look at me. He then leaned back to keep the old man busy while I dipped into the side pocket of his jacket. I had a small handful of bills out in a moment, but at the last second I inadvertently dragged them over the edge of his pocket and there was the small sound of rustling paper. The old man turned back to me. His eyes were full of hopelessness, fear, and puzzlement.

"I know you," he said.

"No," I replied, "I don't think you do."

"Have a drink," he said.

"I don't think I want one," I replied.

"You're a man among men," he said into my face.

"What?" I asked. *Was that contempt in his tone?*

"I can see you're a man among men," he said again. I knew George had his hand in the other pocket of the old man's jacket. I handed the bottle back to the old man. I stood to my feet and stepped into the street where I could no longer see the old man's eyes. George was but a moment behind me. As we walked away, I heard the old man muttering to himself.

"Yes sir, a man among men," he said. Then I heard him laugh. It was a harsh, whiskey-soaked laughter, fathered by cynicism and so full of mocking that it was darkly haunting. I was relieved when I could no longer hear the sound, yet the echo stayed with me. We counted the money. I had seven one dollar bills, George had three. I gave the seven in my hand to George and told him he could have it all.

The next day in Clancy's, the bartender, Dave, mentioned that he'd heard we'd made a good score.

"George told you that?" I asked. I kept my voice neutral. I wanted none of my disgust to come dripping off my tongue.

"Yeah, he even bought Kelly a drink." Kelly was a local drag queen who stopped into the street bar every day. Only those of us who were regulars knew she was actually a man, and she looked so much like a willowy blonde female, that even Kelly herself believed she was a woman.

"Yeah," I said, "sometimes a man just gets lucky."

"We all need luck," agreed Dave.

"And when a man is a man among men he deserves the best there is," I added. "Yeah," he said, "ain't *that* the truth," said Dave, who was one of the two men whose names Chops had given me.

The woman had been right—the bar was only two blocks away. I walked in and asked the man behind the bar for Dave.

"Dave don't come in for a couple of hours," he said, "I'm George." George was a slight man with quick, ferret-like movements. The way he shifted his eyes and chewed his lips suggested that he might be a bit of a speed freak.

"Do you mind if I wait?" I asked. The bar was small. It had two entrances, one from the main street and the other from the side street. Booths lined one wall and the bar ran down the other. I sat at the end of the bar by the door on to the side street. It was shortly after twelve noon. I had fifty-five cents in my pocket, and cigarettes cost sixty cents. Though I really needed a smoke, I knew now was not the time to be bumming nickels.

"Wanna beer?" asked George. There were no more than six people in the place, and I was the only one sitting at the bar. I would've loved a beer, but paying for it was out of the question.

"No, thanks anyway," I said.

"Do you know Dave?" he asked. George stood peering at me, and I could see he was trying to get a handle on who I was. Perhaps it was my Canadian accent that aroused his concern.

"No," I replied, "I don't, but Freddy, or Chops as we call him in Vermont, wanted me to give him an important message."

"Yeah? You know Chops?"

"Yeah, I know Chops."

"Wanna beer?" he asked again. Then quickly added, "on the house?"

"I'd love a beer," I said.

"What kind?"

"How about a Miller?" George turned away and walked the few feet to the cooler and returned with a bottle. He set it down in front of me.

"Thanks," I said as I picked it up and took a grateful swallow.

"Are you in some kind of trouble?" George asked. He chewed his lips as if the mere thought of it made him feel sorry for me.

"Yeah, kind of."

"Wanna burger?" he asked.

"I'd love a burger," I answered.

"How about two?"

"Two is perfect."

George walked to the other end of the bar and quickly inserted two burgers into a microwave on the shelf, and I watched as he talked over the bar to a couple of blue-collar guys sitting in one of the booths. There was a familiarity between the three of them that spoke of a history. There was no indication that I was the subject of the conversation. I felt vulnerable and exposed, and like a good hunting dog, my instincts were alive and I was on point. The fact I sat by the door was little comfort.

George returned to place a plate of two steaming burgers in front of me, and without a word, he went back to the conversation with the men in the booths. I ate slowly, savouring each bite, and as I swallowed I could feel the energy returning to my body. The beer and burgers were a celebration dinner for me; I was no longer inside a small, dingy, dimly lit cell, along with many other men who individually sat in a long line of dingy, dimly lit cells in a prison that was at least a hundred and fifty years old and smelled of urine and feces.

George stayed away from me, seemingly respecting my privacy at the bar, only making his presence known when I set an empty bottle of Miller on the counter. At one point I found I had some company in the form of a pretty girl who decided to sit beside me.

"You're new," she said. Her voice was close to my ear, which startled and surprised me, for I'd thought I was still being vigilant. I realized my lack of attention was due to the effect of the alcohol.

"Yeah," I replied, "I am." I took her comment to mean that she was a regular in the bar and would know who was, and who wasn't, around at any given time.

"It's going to be a cold winter," she said. I looked at her more closely. She was young, no more than twenty, but her face seemed too heavily made up. *A hook - er,* I thought.

"You think so?" I asked. Was she looking for companionship? Did she have a safe place for me? There's an old saying that a mature man needs only three things in life to make him happy: loose shoes, tight pussy, and a warm place to shit. I didn't think of myself as mature at the time, but those same three things would've made me a very happy man indeed.

"Are you going to be in town long?" she asked.

"A few days at least," I replied. I wanted to keep my options open. She wasn't drinking, and I noticed George at the other end of the bar didn't seem in any hurry to wait on her. I cursed my empty pockets—for I'd have liked to buy her a drink.

"Maybe I'll see you around?" she said. She got up from the stool and I noticed her long, slim legs.

"I look forward to it," I replied. I watched as she moved down the bar toward George, and she paused for a moment to speak to him. They seemed to know each other well. A moment later she walked out the far door without looking back. I felt disappointed. I took a swallow from my bottle, and George glanced over at me. He slowly made his way past the other patrons who now sat on the bar stools, pausing to talk to a couple of them who, though they were alone, seemed familiar with each other.

"How was the beer?" asked George. His eyes seemed even brighter, and his nervous chewing of his own lips was even more pronounced.

"I'm okay," I said.

"Sure?" he asked. He eyed the bottle to see if I needed another.

"I'm fine," I replied. I knew I was on the verge of being drunk, and this was not the time to be in a drunken state. "Do you know the girl who sat beside me?" I asked.

"Yeah," he said, "that was a guy." He seemed surprised at my question. He even quit chewing his lips and his eyes stayed focused on me.

"What?" I asked. I was shocked, and perhaps even a bit mortified.

"That was a guy—you know— a drag queen," he said.

"You're kidding!" I didn't know what else to say. I felt my face flush red.

"No, she's a he," he replied. George reached in his pocket and pulled out a pack of Parliament cigarettes. I eyed them hungrily. George caught my look, offered me one, and then held the lighter for me.

"I'll be damned," I said as I blew out the smoke. It made me dizzy in a very pleasant, nicotine-high kind of way.

"She goes to the Playboy Club all the time," he told me. "It's hard to tell."

"Yeah," I said, "it's *really* hard to tell."

"She *likes* you," he told me.

"I'm flattered," I said, sarcastically.

"I'll get you another beer. Dave'll be here soon," he said. Before I could refuse, he'd opened another bottle and placed it in front of me. He walked down the bar to talk to the two guys who sat a dozen stools away from me. Five minutes later Dave came in.

I knew it was Dave before he introduced himself. One second he wasn't there, and the next second there was this guy who came through the door, breezed past me and down the bar. Placing the palm of his hand on the counter top, he effortlessly leaped over it to stand on the other side beside George.

Again there was that familiarity between them which seemed to permeate the place. As George leaned close to the newcomer and spoke with a new intensity, he appeared to be conspiring. When he surreptitiously glanced in my direction, I quickly looked away to study the label on the bottle in my hand. I knew I was the subject of his conversation. A minute later, the high-energy newcomer was in front me.

"I'm Dave," he said.

"Hello Dave," I responded.

"So you know Chops, from Vermont?" he asked pleasantly. I looked up from my beer to see a brown-haired, blue-eyed man of average height, who looked to be in good physical condition. He appeared to be no more than thirty years old.

"Yeah, I know Chops," I replied.

"What's he doing these days?" he asked. His tone of voice was neutral, and if someone had been sitting within hearing, they would've thought it was just a normal conversation between a bartender and a patron.

"Eight to twelve in Vermont," I answered. I was being guarded, but not to the degree that I discouraged further enquiries.

"How's he doing?"

"Last week, when I saw him on the max range, he was doing well."

"He gave you my name?"

"Yes, he gave me your name and the address of this bar, and he suggested if you weren't here to get in touch with Vincent at a bar called Vincent's Spa in Cambridge," I said. At hearing this Dave laughed.

"Vincent's no longer with us," he said. "It's Rod's Bar now."

"Oh."

"So what does Freddy want?"

"Freddy said you might be able to help me."

"Who are you?" he asked. Then, as if this kind of encounter was not something entirely new to him, he added, "And I mean your real name." I hesitated as I looked at him. Of course it's always best to be frank and forthcoming, but I was wanted by the police in two countries, and if caught and captured, I had long federal prison sentences to serve in both. My trust in Chops dictated that I be open with Dave. I told him my name.

"I'll be right back," he said. He walked down the bar to where the draft pump and bottles were situated, reached under the counter and pulled out a telephone. I felt my stomach tighten, my instincts came alive and I suddenly felt quite sober. He dialed a number. A moment after he began speaking into the phone he turned away, but not before I saw him mouth my name. In prison one becomes a lip reader out of necessity; one can learn much about other people's attitudes and intentions when one can "hear" them with his eyes from long distances. I looked down at the bar in front of me, and made myself a promise that the first thing I'd do when I had some money was buy myself a carton of cigarettes. The stress, the alcohol, and now the waiting for the verdict to come in, was the food upon which my addiction to nicotine thrived. It was no longer a quiet nagging at the back of my mind—it had turned into a full-blown voice inside my head shouting to be satisfied. It was with relief that I found Dave standing in front of me once again.

"Step into the back," he said. He pointed to the far end of the bar where a swinging door allowed a conventional entrance to the back of the counter. In the wall beside the bottles on the shelves, there was a closed door. I stood and Dave accompanied me by walking on the other side. A few moments later he was closing the door behind us.

"Okay," he said, indicating a chair in front of the small desk. I sat. He walked around to the chair behind the desk and sat down, then asked, "How did you get here?"

"Stolen car," I answered.

"Where is it?"

"About five or six blocks from here."

"You just parked it and left it?"

"I ran out of gas," I said. Dave laughed. The room we sat in was almost bare. There were only a few cardboard boxes stacked in one corner, and except for the desk and three chairs, there were no other furnishings. No pictures on the walls. Nothing on the desk but Dave's resting hands. They looked capable.

"So it's on the street?"

"Yeah, and I got lucky."

"Yeah?"

"Yeah, I did," I said and told him about my encounter with the traffic cop.

"Could you find it again?" Dave asked. I wasn't sure if his interest was in recovering the car, or if he just wanted to check out my story.

"Yeah, I can find it."

"Let's go," he said, and he rose to his feet.

The bar was slowly beginning to fill with people, yet as we walked past the barstools and booths, nobody seemed to notice us. It was as if everyone knew Dave was on a mission and had no time for interruptions. We got into Dave's blue Lincoln which was parked out front, and I gave him directions. We found the car and slowly cruised past. Dave pulled in to park ten feet in front of it, got out and walked back to give it a cursory once-over. I knew the ignition wires were hanging below the steering column, a telltale sign that the last person to drive the vehicle had done so without the benefit of keys. A moment later, he was back with me and we were driving away.

"Yeah, we can use that car," Dave said as we headed back to the bar.

"And my prints?"

"We'll clean it up."

"Okay," I replied. I noticed that Dave always referred to himself as "we," as if he operated with others. Finding the car seemed to confirm that I was who I claimed to be.

"What do you want?" he asked. The Lincoln was new and fully loaded, and the peace and quiet it provided added an air of complete privacy. To me there's nothing in the world more reassuring than cruising along in a clean, powerful luxury car when one is running from the baying of the hounds. I was beginning to feel comfortable.

"A gun, some ID, and a place to stay for a couple of days," I answered. Ordinarily they would seem like unusual requests, but in the world of the rounder, they're commonplace.

"A gun and ID are no problem," he said, "but we need a few hours on the place to stay." Then he added, "got any cash?"

"I'm completely tapped out," I said. I didn't think the fifty-five cents in my pocket qualified.

"Don't worry about that," he said. He leaned back in his seat to reach in his pocket and pulled out a flat of folded money held together in a silver dollar clip. He let go of the steering wheel for a moment, and with a flick of his fingers, I was a hundred dollars richer.

"Thanks," I said gratefully. I stashed the bill in my shirt.

"We have a rule," he said.

"Yeah?"

"Yeah, no violence."

"Like, no robbing people in the can?" I said.

"Yeah, no robbing people in the can," he laughed. "No robbing people on the street either," he said. He pulled into his original parking spot in front of the bar and shut the engine off.

"When we go in, just sit at the bar, you drink and eat compt here, and we'll see if I can find you a place to hang your hat," he said. "Compt" meant compliments of the house.

"Thanks Dave," I replied. I put out my hand and he took it. His handshake was dry and firm.

Back in the bar as I was finishing my second beer, the place was filling to capacity. I found myself talking to a man who'd sat down beside me a few minutes earlier. He appeared to be in his late forties, needed a shave and was slightly drunk. Before I knew it, he was telling me he was in a federal halfway house around the corner, for interstate transportation of stolen goods. I gave him no indication that this information was new, or surprised me. He seemed to think I belonged, which made me feel even more comfortable. My drinking partner was telling me he had a problem with his halfway house curfew, when Dave stopped in front of us. He knew the man beside me by name, and he acknowledged him before turning his attention to me.

"See those three broads sitting at the other end of bar?" he asked me. I looked to where he indicated and I saw three women in their twenties looking our way.

"Yeah, I see them," I answered. All three were quite pretty in polish and paint.

"The one on your right, by the wall," he directed.

"Yes, I have her," I replied. The buzz from the crowded bar forced me to lean forward to hear his voice.

"Last week her old man took a serious pinch—armed robbery. She went down too, but she's out on bail. He's back in Walpole for at least a sawbuck," he explained. As Dave spoke, I kept my eyes on her, and it appeared she was watching us at the same time.

"I gotta go," said the man beside me. Both Dave and I bid him goodnight and, as he made his way to the side door and disappeared into the evening, Dave continued.

"What do you think?" he asked.

"She looks fine," I assured him. "Besides, any port in a storm." He laughed.

"I'll talk to her," he said. I knew by the way she was checking us out he had already done so, but I just nodded my head. I watched as he approached the three women, and a moment later I saw them all laugh, and then glance over at me. I casually looked away. *Life is getting good,* I thought.

I smelled her perfume before I saw her, and I felt her presence even before she sat down on the empty stool beside me. I glanced to her hands as she set her highball glass on the bar in front of her, and the sight of her long, polished nails brought an ache to my belly. *She can scratch me anywhere she likes,* I thought.

"I'm Miranda," she said.

"I'm pleased to meet you," I responded.

"So you're from Canada?" she asked. I turned my head to look full into her grey eyes. She had long, wavy brown hair, she wore a blouse that hinted of full breasts, and she was in her twenties.

"Yeah, Canada," I said.

"Dave explained you need to crash somewhere for a few days," she said. She was soft-spoken, which I used as an excuse to lean closer to her. The beer was buzzing in my ears, and the rate of my heartbeat had considerably increased with her presence. I noticed a small, moon-shaped scar on her cheekbone, but it didn't detract from her good looks. I thought it added character to her face.

"He mentioned you to me too," I told her.

"Did he tell you I'm out on bail for robbery?" she asked. Her question was matter-of-fact, and I could detect no remorse.

"Yeah, he did," I answered.

"That's cool?"

"Sure, that's cool," I said, "I won't hold the pinch against you, everybody makes mistakes, and I believe in second chances." She laughed. She had nice teeth and she was pretty. She was an escaped convict's dream.

"I'm glad," she said, and at hearing her breathe those two words, my heart began to beat in a slow, steady, powerful rhythm. It brought a rich flood of anticipation into my bloodstream. I noticed her glance to her two companions who'd been watching our exchange. When I saw them leave a few moments later, I knew she'd let them know that she was going to be busy, at least for the rest of the night.

"All I need is a pair of loose shoes," I told her.

"What do you mean?" she asked.

"Well, I think a loose pair of shoes would make my life perfect right now," I answered. I didn't elaborate.

"Oh," she replied, as if she understood. It wasn't until the next day, while we sat at her kitchen table, that I mentioned the three criteria which made a mature man happy. I told her I was going to buy myself a pair of loose shoes and make myself a completely happy man. She quietly laughed. She had a very nice laugh for an armed robber.

I spent the next three weeks running credit cards for fifty percent of all that I purchased, and it was almost risk-free work. The real danger for those of us who were active in the credit card business lay further down the road. Once the unpaid bills started rolling in, and the people refused to pay, the secret service became involved. We'd always carefully select the cards we used, and Jimmy, the man who ran our crew, made certain the hot list was up to date. The hot list was a list of stolen credit card numbers; any card whose numbers were on the list meant the card had to be immediately discarded. In a week I was making a decent living, and Miranda herself jumped in by using the cards to buy items, and then enlisted the aid of her friends for the rehash. Rehashing was the term for returning the items purchased on cards for cash. Life was very good for both Miranda and me, but I had one small problem. His name was George.

It was a week after we'd robbed the old man in the doorway, an event which I'd kept to myself, not even telling Miranda about it. *This is it,* I'd say to myself each time I worked with George, *this is the last time.* But no matter how many times I felt disgusted, no matter how many times I said it to myself, I always found myself walking down the street with George. He'd helped me out on my first day in the bar, and in the criminal world as well as the straight, old loyalties take a long time to die. In fact, sometimes death is the only thing that kills it.

Late one afternoon I was having drinks in the bar with Miranda and a couple of other regulars when George and Sherry walked in. Sherry was a healthy-looking blond woman who worked behind the bar occasionally, and she was George's old lady. She was also known to turn a trick or two whenever times were tough. Though I never suggested it openly, I figured times were tough almost all the time with George as a partner. George stopped to tell me he had to talk to me. I got up from the table and walked outside with him.

"I got something good," he said when we were on the sidewalk. I looked at him and saw his excitement, and though I felt a sense of foreboding, I was unable to say "no."

"What is it?" I asked. He looked around as if somebody might have been watching, then reached into his pocket and pulled out a key. It had a tag indicating it had originally come from a hotel or motel room. He put it back in his pocket.

"It belongs to a trick," he explained. "He's loaded and leaves his shit in the room." It sounded like it might be worth a few dollars, and tricks were always fair game. A trick was a man who bought and paid for sex, and we held them in contempt.

"Where?" I asked.

"Holiday Inn," he answered, "in Cambridge."

"When?" I asked

"Tonight," he stated. "We'll phone first." I turned the idea over in my mind, and I could see nothing to concern me. If the trick wasn't there, there'd be little that could go wrong.

"Okay George," I said, "we'll do it." As we walked back into the bar George carried a new excitement with him.

Just after ten o'clock that night, George slid the key into the lock of the hotel room door, and a moment later we were inside. I'd phoned the room from the lobby myself, letting the phone ring ten times before going to the second floor. I could see a topcoat and two suits hanging in the open closet, and while George checked the drawers in the night tables, I checked out the two suitcases. The first was empty. The second one was empty as well, except for one item: a nickel-plated 9mm pistol with a loaded clip beside it. *Strange*, I thought, *this guy's not our usual trick.* I picked up the gun and clip and put them in my pocket. George came up empty. As George and I left the room I thought of slamming the clip into the butt of the pistol and unloading it into George. *Never again*, I said to myself for the tenth time, *this is the last time I'm working with this guy.*

I stashed the pistol behind the motor plate in the back of the fridge at Miranda's. Although she never asked me where I got it, she did tell me she was glad it was there.

"You never know when you might need it," she said later that night as I was putting the screws back into the plate. It wasn't difficult for me to imagine the nickel-plated pistol in Miranda's hand, with her slender finger curled around the trigger, and her grey eyes squinting down the barrel as she lined up the sights on the centre of a man's chest. The thought of the gun in Miranda's hand was enough to cause me to give each screw an extra twist to lock the plate more firmly in place.

Two nights later, at around three in the morning, the phone in Miranda's apartment rang. Miranda shook me awake.

"It's George," she said. I rolled out of bed, walked to the living room and picked up the phone.

"Yeah George," I asked, "what's up?"

"I just got a phone call from Lucky," he said.

"And who's Lucky?" I asked. *Definitely not me,* I wanted to say.

"The guy who owns the gun," he answered. I felt that same feeling of foreboding I'd felt when George had first told me he had something good.

"And?"

"He said if he doesn't get the gun back we're both dead."

"Jesus Christ, George," I replied. Miranda must have heard the tone of my voice, steeped in disgust, for she came out of the bedroom to stand beside me. It was suddenly very quiet in the room. I'd never noticed how quiet it really was in that apartment late at night until that moment.

"What are you going to do?" he asked. I knew by the way he said it that I was taking the weight for stealing the pistol. In the criminal world, nicknames are important; they speak of a history, and anyone called Lucky was a man who'd been around. There was only one thing to do.

"I'm giving him his gun back," I said.

"Okay," said George.

"Where is he?"

"The same place."

"Alright George," I said. I hung up the phone before he could add anything. I was thankful I hadn't thrown out the ill-gotten key, but had tossed it in one of the drawers in the bathroom. Miranda seemed worried. She called me a cab while I dressed. I took the screws out of the plate on the back of the fridge, cursing myself each time the screwdriver slipped. Just when I thought I'd actually stripped the head of a screw and would have to rip the plate away because of it, the screw head turned. Miranda watched from the kitchen table, her eyes wide. She didn't speak until I had the pistol in my hand and had put the plate back in place.

"Will you be coming back?" she asked. Her hands were clutched together in her lap, and her shoulders were slumped in resignation. *I wonder how many men haven't?* I thought.

"Of course I'll be back," I replied. She rose to her feet and her silk dressing gown fell open. She had a great body. I wondered how many men had been stopped at the door by this sight.

"I'll go with you," she offered. I knew she would.

"No, you stay, I'll be back before four-thirty." She walked into the bedroom and closed the door. I called Lucky's hotel room and let it ring ten times. There was no answer. I didn't have a handkerchief, so I selected a thin cloth napkin from the drawer by the kitchen sink and put it in my pocket. I placed the clip in the butt of the pistol, jacked back the slide to put one in the chamber, and flicked on the safety. I put the gun in my jacket pocket and left the apartment to wait in front of the building for the cab.

I didn't relax until the cab was cruising at the speed limit down the empty street, away from Lucky's hotel. By the time we were rolling over the Charles Street Bridge, I was visited by a sense of deep relief. *This is the last time,* I said to myself, *never again.* Miranda was sitting at the kitchen table when I walked back into the apartment. A few minutes later we made love like it was the first time.

I spent most of the next day looking for George, first at Clancy's, then at his apartment above the bar. I left a message with his girlfriend Sherry for him to get in touch with me as soon as he got in. Just as I was about to descend the staircase from his apartment, I heard the front door open, then slam, and the sound of hard shoes on the wooden stairs reverberated upwards. They sounded ominous, intent on a serious purpose. I paused on the top step and looked down the stairwell. I could see two men, both wearing short leather jackets, moving up the stairs, one behind the other. *Detectives,* I thought. I pulled my head back out of sight thinking I'd wait where I stood until I heard them knock on the door of one of the apartments below. *People need the key to get in here,* I thought, *and I don't recognize these guys. Sure as hell they're coppers.* The ID I had in my pocket would get me through a cursory police examination, but if at all possible, I wanted to avoid any kind of confrontation with them.

The footsteps got louder, and when they arrived at the third floor, and turned to continue up to where I was standing, I thought of ducking into the bathroom. Instead I casually began to descend the stairs.

As we met on the stairs the man in front paused and put out his hand.

"I'm Robert," he said. He was in his early thirties, and he was clean-shaven with dark brown, curly hair. I automatically returned his friendly gesture and put out my own hand to take his.

"Lorne," I replied. He took my hand in a firm grip and, just as I attempted to pull away, the man behind him moved to the side and showed me a pistol. It was a small calibre revolver, a Saturday Night Special, the kind a man throws away right after he uses it.

"Let's go upstairs," said Robert. I turned and walked back to the landing. The man with the gun said nothing. As we reached the top, I took a few steps to stand in the center, and the man with the gun used it to motion me toward Sherry's door. I had no idea who these guys were, but I knew dicks didn't carry throwaway guns, at least not out in the open when they're making a pinch.

"Give me the gun," said Robert. His partner, who was also in his thirties and my height, but slender in a greyhound kind of way, handed the revolver to Robert who then casually held it at his side. He was very confident. *These guys are very bad news,* I thought.

"Do I know you?" I asked Robert.

"They call me Lucky," he replied.

"Oh," was all I said. He smiled and kept his eyes on me, while he used the butt of the gun to rap sharply on Sherry's door. She opened it as if she was expecting us, which she wasn't. Her face went white.

"Hi Sherry," said Lucky. He walked through the doorway as if he'd just arrived home.

"Hi," replied Sherry meekly. I followed Lucky into the apartment, and he turned to me in the living room. A moment later, I was falling toward the floor from the sucker punch the man behind me had landed at the base of my neck, and as I struck the carpet the two men began kicking me. I felt my nose break, and then an excruciating, lightning-like jolt of pain slammed into my left kidney area and I was completely paralyzed. I couldn't catch my breath. I was conscious of being kicked, but there was no corresponding pain. I was only semi-conscious as I watched the heel of a heavy shoe stamp twice on my right hand. Suddenly, I was lifted as easily as if I weighed nothing, and thrown into a seated position on the couch.

"Do you know who we are?" asked Lucky. I looked into a pair of calm, clear brown eyes, that appeared unconcerned with what was taking place. This wasn't new to him.

"I do now," I replied. He smiled. I saw him hand the gun to his partner, and a moment later I felt the blunt end of the barrel jam painfully into the bone behind my left ear.

"If you're going to shoot him, use the pillow," he calmly told his partner. A pillow from the couch covered the left side of my face, and I could feel it cushion the barrel of the revolver as it was placed at my head again. I felt only contempt for the man with the gun; he meant nothing to me. I kept my eyes on Lucky. He was the gun. He was the trigger. It would be he who sent the bullet into my brain.

"You did get your pistol back," I said. I was having trouble breathing through the pain in my left kidney.

"Yeah," said Lucky, "I got it back." The tone of his voice implied it wasn't because I was a good guy that he had, and then he continued, "I'm going to ask you a question," he said.

"Okay," I answered.

"Your life depends on the answer you give," he added.

"Okay," I said. The pillow and the gun didn't move.

"Did Sherry and George have anything to do with the key?" he asked. Lucky was one of Sherry's tricks, and because Lucky was connected, George held a great deal of resentment toward the man in front of me. He had used the key, and me, in an attempt to get his balls back. I was going down for taking the gun. *I wonder what George or Sherry would do?* I asked myself. I felt a cynical smile in my belly. I knew the answer to that question.

"No," I said, "they didn't."

"Where did you get the key?"

"I found it in the bathroom."

"No you didn't," he said. "You stole it off this table." He pointed to where Sherry sat out of my sight. The pillow at my head blocked my view of the table and Sherry.

"Yes," I answered. "I stole it off the table." Lucky waved his hand and instantly the gun and the pillow were gone. I turned my head slightly to see Sherry sitting at the table. Both hands held to her terror-stricken face and her dark, blood-red fingernails were spread across her cheeks. I felt a strange flow of pity for her.

"Okay," said Lucky, "let's get you cleaned up." He motioned his hand toward the closed door, indicating the bathroom across the hall.

As the running water washed my blood down the sink, I looked at my face in the mirror. Both my eyes were going to be black and swollen closed in a matter of hours, but if I held the trunk of my body rigid and straight, I'd be able to walk without too much difficulty. The bones in my right hand appeared to be only painfully bruised and not broken.

"You're not from around here," said Lucky. He stood leaning on the wall by the open doorway, watching me as I washed.

"No," I replied, "Canada."

"Canadians are good people," he said. I knew then that he was well aware that George and Sherry were involved in giving me the key to his room. My refusing to implicate them had not only saved me, it had saved them, and saved Lucky from carting my body down four flights of stairs and into the trunk of his car. I suddenly felt much better.

"Thanks," I said. I meant it.

"If there's anything you want, just ask," he said, "Dave knows where to find me."

"Okay," I replied. We both knew I wouldn't be asking for anything. I dried my face and hands on the blue towel, and when I saw the blood on it, I put it in the sink, but Lucky stopped me.

"Let Sherry get that," he said.

"Right," I said. I left the towel in the bowl and we returned to the apartment. Sherry had composed herself, at least to a degree, and when Lucky motioned his partner to leave, his partner nodded his head at me. I nodded back, and then he left the room. Lucky was the last one out, but before he closed the door he looked directly at Sherry.

"Next time, don't leave my key on the table," he said.

"I won't," she replied, her voice completely subdued. The door closed, their footsteps descended the stairs, and in a few moments Sherry and I were left in silence. I stood looking at her. She leaned forward, put her face in her hands and muttered something.

"What's that?" I asked. I stood beside the table. She lifted her head, took her hands from her face to look into my eyes.

"I saw death," she said.

"Yes," I replied, "death was here, but now he's gone."

"But George?" she whispered, almost as if to herself.

"George will be fine," I assured her, "it's over now."

"Is it?"

"Yes." I knew it was. "I have to go," I told her, "and you'll be okay." I walked to the door and opened it.

"What were you thinking?" she asked.

"The pillow?" I asked.

"Yeah."

"The question?"

"Yeah."

"I was thinking, what would George and Sherry do?" I replied.

"Oh," she said. She was on the verge of crying. That wasn't a bad thing.

"We both know the answer to that, don't we?" I said, but kindly.

"I'm sorry," she murmured, and as she put her face back into her hands, I saw her shoulders begin to shake as she wept. I closed the door and walked down the stairs.

The street in front of the bar was quiet, and just when I thought I'd have to phone for a cab, I saw a Checker cruising slowly toward me. I asked the driver if I could sit in front with him. The pain in my kidney was so severe, I was afraid I'd never be able to get out of the back of the cab once I got in.

"Sure," he said, "climb in." As we pulled away, I couldn't help thinking of the old man in the doorway. I wondered if he would have forgiven me if I just gave him back his ten dollars? *Yes*, I thought, *after today perhaps he'd count me as a man among men.* I knew Lucky had. It was the reason I was alive. *Miranda will be pleased it's over*, I thought. *And she can help me get in and out of bed for the next week. But George, now... well George has just got to go... yes, this is the last time...*

I lived on Weslyn Avenue and when I'd been living there for some time my land-lady, a middle-aged black woman called Mrs. Potter, told me ninety percent of the property stolen in the city of Boston showed up on the avenue just a block from where we lived.

I had a small apartment in a brownstone building. The steps were wide and high, and the corner posts at the top of the stairs were wide enough to sit on. I'd open a can of beer, sit on the top of a post, and talk to some of the girls walk-ing by. One day I was coming home when Mrs. Potter stopped to talk to me.

"Do you know the man in the old Cadillac across the street?" she asked. We were standing in the front foyer of her building, in the area between the outside security door and the inside door. I was coming in and she was going out.

"I think I know who you mean—the man with the girls ringed around him," I answered.

"That's him—he's a pimp," she declared.

"Oh." Actually, he dressed like a pimp.

"He also deals in drugs," she said.

"Oh."

"I don't want any drugs in here," she said, looking into my eyes, "I don't want the drug police coming in here."

"No, we don't need that," I agreed.

"They'll rip my building apart."

"They will?"

"They'll tear down the walls until they find drugs," she stated.

"What if they don't find any?"

"When they come looking, they always find them," she said. There was a cer-tainty in her voice and I was not about to doubt her on her home turf.

"I don't use drugs," I said.

"Jimmy does, and so does Charles."

"Oh."

"I see you talking to them. They're bad news."

"I'll keep it in mind," I replied.

"Could you help make my building safer for me?"

"Safer?"

"Yes, I'd like to be able to see who's at my door at night," she explained. She didn't have to explain, because after living there for more than a month I knew it was a tough neighbourhood. Not that the local people would harass Mrs. Potter because they knew she had important friends in Boston. Her concern was for the people she didn't know because they didn't know who "we" were.

"What's behind this hallway wall?" I asked her.

"My living room."

"Let's take a look."

"Okay," she agreed, and she took me into her apartment. I'd been there once before when I'd helped her hook up her new stereo system.

Two paintings hung at eye level on the inside wall, and I suggested we take one down and drill a hole through to the other side. She could move the painting and see who was knocking at the door without making an appearance. She liked the idea.

Boston wasn't a violent city, at least I never thought so. I often walked at night and I was never concerned about being stopped by police. But I never took a cab directly to my apartment building, choosing instead to walk two blocks to my front door. But there were places I wouldn't go, and bars I stayed away from. One Friday evening I learned how important it was to always use my instincts.

One of the new tenants in Mrs. Potter's building, a man in his early twenties named Jerry, asked me if I wanted to go to a bar for a few drinks. He was wearing a white, very expensive leather coat, and he was dressed to go out on the town.

"Where are you going?" I asked.

"Not far," he replied, "the bar's only a few blocks away."

"Which way?"

"In Roxbury," he said. I knew he was heading in the wrong direction. Roxbury is a black neighbourhood—a dangerous place for a white man at night.

"I wouldn't go there."

"Why? Nobody's going to bother me. I just want to smoke a few joints and have a good time." From his pocket he pulled out a bag of pot.

"I wouldn't..."

"I'll be all right," he said. There wasn't much more I could say. He left a few minutes later.

An hour later I was sitting on the staircase when I saw a police car turn onto our street, and I immediately walked into the building to stand behind the locked security door. The police car stopped out front, and I thought I could see someone in the back seat. When the cop got out and headed toward the front step, I knocked on Mrs. Potter's door. She answered immediately.

"It's the cops," I said. She walked to the front and opened it.

"What is it?" she asked.

"Does that man live here?" the cop asked.

"Yes," she said, "he's a tenant here."

"Bring him in," said the cop to his partner. Moments later Jerry stood in the hall with a blanket wrapped around him. I could see one bare foot and the other with a sock.

"They took everything," he said to Mrs. Potter, and he threw open the blanket to show her. He caught himself and quickly wrapped himself in the blanket again. Mrs. Potter stood looking at him, but she didn't say anything.

"Can you identify your personal belongings?" asked one of the cops.

"My white leather coat was made in California," he said. He was shivering, more from shock than the cold. The cop wrote it down.

"Anything else?" asked the cop.

"My money clip," Jerry answered. "It had the Lord's Prayer on it."

"The Lord's Prayer?"

"Yeah."

"And that didn't slow them down?"

"No." It was funny and I decided I'd get into it.

"Did they get your keys?" I asked.

"Yeah, they got everything," he replied.

"No, not everything, but they have your keys so they just might come back for the sock they missed," I said.

Every so often a hooker who worked off one of the corners would call out to me, usually very late at night or in the early hours of the morning.

"Hey!"

"Yeah?" I'd answer.

"Wanna go out?"

"Only if you're giving something away," I'd reply, and she'd laugh. On one such night I walked past her having returned home via her side of the street, and she gave me a tip which told me she knew I was a rounder of some sort.

"There's police all around these two blocks," she said.

"There is?" I answered.

"Yeah, behind us and behind your building across the street," she replied. I thanked her. I walked to the end of the block, called a cab from the payphone and didn't return home for two days. When I did, Miranda was gone.

It was very close to Christmas and I began feeling guilty for causing Lora to end up with a five year sentence. I decided to call her to see if there was anything I could do for her.

The next day I was arrested in my apartment by the FBI Fugitive Squad and taken to the notorious Charles Street Jail. I was extradited to Vermont and placed back inside Windsor Prison. It was like re-entering hell after a short respite, and I was determined to get out again.

My feelings about prison in general found an outlet through a poem I wrote when they were talking about shutting down the prison because of operational costs. One of the guards whose brother worked at a New Hampshire radio station, came across a copy of it and asked me if I'd read it into a tape recorder. I agreed, and a couple of days later we listened to it being played over the airwaves. It was basically an open letter to the people of Vermont. I called it the Ballad of Windsor Prison. I'd written it one night by the light of a homemade lamp made by using a small can, a wick made from a shoelace, and oil from rendered margarine. Ever since the state had begun turning the power off, including the lights in our cells, at ten o'clock at night, each of us had one of these makeshift lamps in our cells.

My name is Windsor Prison and you say I'm far too old,
That I'm too damn hot in summer and in winter it's the cold,
Well let me tell you people, though you say I've had my day,
and though I'm steel and concrete, I want to have my say.

Now I have seen the cycles of the faces through your law,
I've held your poor for ages and by God it rubs me raw;
I'd say, *"The devil take you! The devil take you all!"*
But he can't leave to take you 'cause he's trapped inside my wall.

I can hear the jingling and the jangling of the keys,
Causing some to curse me, while others cry out, "Please,
Please give me the freedom to breath that clean fresh air—"
Why I've caused men to hang themselves and I've given some men the chair.

Yes, I hear the moaning from the men here in the night,
I take their years, I age them—you know I do what's right;
I make them beg for mercy, down on bended knee,
I've done everything you wanted and now you're closing me.

I have stood one hundred years, through blizzards, wars, and rain,
And I will stand one hundred more, if you can stand the pain;
So come on all you people, keep the faces going 'round,
Place them in me for fifteen years, then, we'll just place them in the ground.

Tony, who'd made the wooden gun for me, and other men I knew, were still in the segregation block and things were looking very dim for all of us. One day I discovered a blind spot between the segregation block and the kitchen, which was the building next to us. If a couple of men wanted to climb the bars of the cellblock, and use a makeshift ladder to climb from the top window to the roof, they could do so unseen—the kitchen building blocked the tower's view. I decided I'd scale the wall, climb over the rooftop, and rappel down the other side which overlooked the street. Tony was interested. Together we laid our plans and set about gathering the materials we'd need.

Two guards were always with us when we exercised in the small corner of the prison yard; however, if we could isolate the guards from each other, we could take care of them one at a time. There was a stairway against the cellblock wall, which led to a door on the second floor. If we could tie them up and leave them under the stairs, they'd be out of our way. We would then be able to climb the wall unhindered, and if we were fast enough, we'd be able to rappel down the other side to the street and be into the town of Windsor before anybody realized we were gone. The tools we needed were simple ones, and quite easy to manufacture. Tony and I made a list and talked about it before we made a move.

"We need a hook and some rope to get to the roof, two knives to control the guards, and a couple of shoelaces to tie them up, and we need some rags to blindfold them," I said. Tony was writing it all down in some sort of shorthand only he understood.

"What kind of hook?" he asked. We were sitting in the small courtyard while other prisoners played horseshoes.

"Something with a sharp edge," I suggested. "We need the hook to embed itself into the edge of the roof, otherwise it'll slip off and down we'll go to the cement below."

"This is dangerous," he said.

"Yeah, it's dangerous, but if we plan it well we can eliminate most of the pitfalls." I knew it could be done, in theory, but it had to be perfectly executed or we were going to be in serious trouble.

"I can get the hook made," Tony suggested, "but the knives are going to be a problem."

"Not really," I replied, "we can use butter knives—and a lot of bass in our voices."

"Yeah, well, you do the talking," he laughed. We set about designing a hook that would fit into a block of wood, which would have a hole that we could insert a broomstick into as a holder. When we were in position at the top window, we could raise the hook above rooftop level, and by pulling downward sharply, embed the hook in the edge of the copper-covered roof. The rope would have to be made of coax cable. I'd have to help Tony get on the rooftop. There was a six-foot gap and an overhang between the top of the window and the roof itself, but if he used my shoulders as a stepladder, hanging onto the rope for balance, he'd be able to do it. Once he was up, he could hold the rope while I climbed up. It was obvious to us both that if one of us slipped or failed in any way to hold up our end, we'd both plummet fifty feet to the concrete below.

The day we were prepared to make our bid for freedom, the two guards on yard duty were a small thin man named Jesse, and a huge ex-policeman by the name of Bill. I called Jesse around the corner pretending to look at the ground, and when he walked to me, I showed him the butter knife which, with the black tape wrapped around the haft, looked like a standard prison shank.

"Stand under the stairs Jesse," I said. He blanched, then took the few steps to Tony who was under the stairs waiting to tie him up. When Tony had Jesse's hands behind his back, I walked around the corner to talk to Bill.

There were four other men in the yard that day, all playing horseshoes and trying to act normal. Their voices were a little too loud and their faces a little too animated because of the excitement in the air—but they were doing a good job of it just the same. Bill was standing against the fence in plain sight of the gun tower, and I would have to get him to walk around the corner.

"Bill, can you take a look at this and tell me what you think?" I asked. I then walked just around the corner and out of sight. When he'd taken the needed steps to put him out of sight of the tower, I stepped close to him. He still hadn't seen Jesse who was standing under the stairway with his hands tied behind his back.

"What do you want me to see?" he asked. He was looking at me curiously.

"This, Bill," I said, and I pulled my knife and held it in front of me. "I want you to go under the stairs with Jesse." He was only two feet away, and towered over me, a bear of a man. He looked to the stairs and saw Jesse's predicament.

"Ho!" he said, guffawing loudly. He reached out, grabbed the blade of my knife in his dinner-plate sized hand, and held onto it. My heart sank into my belly, and I knew the game was up. With his hand tightly grasping the blade, Bill had to now know the deadly-looking shank was a butter knife in disguise. I was sure he was going to swat me on the side of my head and send me spinning across the yard, but then Jesse saved the day.

"Bill, you get over here!" demanded Jesse. There was a note of authority in his voice, and I saw a look of consternation on Bill's face, but he didn't let go of the knife.

"Do what he says Bill," I said. My heart was racing and my mouth was so dry my voice sounded more like the croaking of a frog than the voice of a man. Bill looked at me, then looked over at Jesse again.

"Bill," Jesse said, his voice now taking on the tone of a parent who's had enough of a child's nonsense. "You get over here right now." I saw the look of consternation replaced by resentment, and Bill let go of the knife. He slowly lumbered to the stairs to stand by Jesse who was being watched by Tony.

Bill was such a large man I had a problem tying his hands behind his back; no matter how hard I pulled, his wrists would not meet. I finally tied his hands together with the long shoelace, but even with a couple of good tugs I couldn't bring them closer than a foot apart. We blindfolded them both and told them to behave because there was a riot going on. We kept up a running dialogue of how the licence plate factory was burning, the dining room was being destroyed, and there were guards being held hostage in every area of the prison.

I asked one of the prisoners who was at the horseshoe pit if he'd lend us a hand, and he agreed to do so. I walked over to him.

"Stand behind them. They can't see you, and if either of them tries to untie himself, just lightly tap his hands. Don't say anything, and don't make their lives miserable. Just let them know they aren't alone," I said. He nodded his head in agreement.

"How long should I stay here?" he asked.

"For as long as it takes, but you'll hear the key in the door when the shift supervisor comes into the yard," I said, "and then you disappear around the corner."

"Okay," he said, "I'll do it." Tony and I assembled our wall-climbing gear and a few moments later we began our ascent of the building.

Everything went according to plan, and though there was a difficult moment at the top of the windows, Tony managed to use my shoulders as a stepping stone and he reached the rooftop. He held the rope for me and I crawled over the lip to lie beside him.

Our descent was well underway, and we were hanging onto the window bars thirty feet in the air on the street side of the cellblock, when a woman in a brown coat walked out the front door of the prison's main entrance. Tony and I saw her before she saw us. We froze where we were, but she looked up and stopped in her tracks. While we hung suspended, and the woman froze, I heard a man quietly whistling as he approached from around the corner. A step later he was under us. It was a guard on his way to the front door with a file folder in his hand.

I could only hope the woman was a visitor and wouldn't say a word to the guard, but she did.

"Are those guys supposed to be there?" she asked. I recognized the guard as Jacobs who often brought my mail to me when I was in the hole. He would sit in front of my cell, open my letters, and read them before he gave them to me. When he read the private thoughts of my friends, he'd smile and chuckle at things they said. At one point he laughed and said, "Oh, yes, I know exactly what she means—but you'll be reading this yourself so I don't have to tell you now." It made me angry but there wasn't a thing I could do about it.

Jacobs stopped and looked around, and said, "Are they supposed to be where?" The woman pointed up. When he saw us he threw his hands in the air, sending the file folder flying. Papers fluttered all around him.

"It's Carlson and Tanzi!" he shouted to her. "Tell them inside it's Carlson and Tanzi!" The woman turned and made for the door. Tony and I scrambled down the window bars. We jumped the last twelve feet and landed hard on the cement sidewalk. Jacobs scampered away and stood looking at us. As we ran across the grass to the street, the woman was entering the front door.

Jacobs followed us and we didn't have time to chase him away. We ran down the street heading for downtown, ignoring everyone we passed. One man we flew past was a guard named Joe. He nodded his head to us in recognition, with a look of confusion on his face.

"Stop them, Joe!" yelled Jacobs. I glanced back and saw Joe was now in pursuit, and he was getting too close for comfort. Joe was a guard we'd see in the hole or segregation area from time to time. He had a bad attitude which showed itself during his security walks and time clock punches. I used to watch him walk past the front of our cells, and every so often he'd explode with a yell, then kick the wall in a karate-like move. It was an impressive display; he was a large man in his late twenties in good shape. He did look tough and I had the impression he could hurt a man if he cut loose.

Tony and I ran side by side, turning off the sidewalk of the main avenue and into a residential area. Joe was very close now. Tony stopped dead and threatened with the butter knife.

"If you take one more step," Tony said, "I'll throw this knife right through your heart." Joe went into his fighting stance, and I then saw a weakness in him. He was posturing, just as he did inside, and as we ran again, I knew Joe was not going to be a problem.

We ran down an alley heading for the woods which surrounded the town. At the backyard of a house I saw a parked car. A man was behind the wheel and another man stood beside it, talking to the driver. We ran right to them and in a moment, without fuss, the driver stepped out from behind the wheel and gave me the keys. Both men left the car to stand a dozen feet away.

While I maneuvered the car out of the yard and into the alley, Joe picked up a piece of wood and advanced on us holding the wood like a club. In a moment we were roaring down the alley in an old Ford Falcon, heading over the bridge and out of town. Suddenly, the sound of sirens seemed to come from all around us. At the same moment, something banged into the back of our car and we were flung almost completely sideways.

I brought the car under control, and when I looked in my mirror I saw a white Cadillac with a guard behind the wheel. He gunned his engine and slammed into us again, pushing us forward, and then spun his wheel to throw the back end of our car sideways and out of control. I looked ahead and saw a string of police cars, blue lights flashing, coming right at us. But they were headed for the prison, and they had no idea they were flying right by us. Soon they were gone—but not the Cadillac.

We were travelling at a high speed when I saw a car stopped in the middle of the street. A man in a fur hat was standing in front of the open passenger door, his hand held palm toward us in the universal sign of halt. I recognized him as the head of the task force on security in the state prison; he was from New Jersey and had been brought in as an expert by the state to improve security. It was too late to stop even if I'd wanted to—and I didn't. I veered toward the curb and made it through the space between it and the open car door. It was a matter of inches. The man in the open doorway was very fortunate. He could've been killed.

A block later we were approaching an intersection when the Cadillac slammed into me again. I threw the car into second and floored it, and as the tires grabbed the pavement, we careened down a side street. When I looked in the mirror the Caddy had returned, and right behind it were two police cars, blue lights flashing and sirens wailing. Less than a minute later I ran out of road and crashed.

Four police officers handcuffed Tony and me and took us back to the prison. There a mass of men waited for us. One of them was the warden.

As soon as we were removed from the back of the police car, the mob rushed at us. They came rolling across the front lawn led by the warden himself. As they reached me, they grabbed my clothes and hoisted me off my feet. I could feel hands grabbing and twisting my flesh as I was passed along over their heads to the front door. The men weren't yelling—instead a low, angry, rumbling sound came from them, which continued until I was inside.

I was taken to the infirmary to check for injuries from the car crash, and I was dropped flat on the floor. I had the wind knocked out of me and I was still trying to get my breath back when I looked up and saw the man in the fur hat standing over me. He pointed a trembling finger at me, shaking it angrily.

"You tried to kill me!" he said. I looked at him in disbelief.

"Kill you? Kill you?" I answered, now angry myself.

"Yes, you tried to kill me! I could have you shot!" he shouted. I struggled to my feet and stood in front of him. My anger slowly dissipated.

"I did everything I could not to hit your car door," I said, "and I did everything I could to save you from being hurt. What man stands in front of an open car door with his hand up during a high-speed chase? Are you fucking nuts?" He looked at me in shock and I saw a flood of realization cross his face. He turned and shouldered his way through the angry crowd of men. I never saw him again.

The medic found I was undamaged and I was taken to the hole. Tony was already in a cell and as soon as we were alone, we started talking.

"We did it," said Tony. I could hear the pride and even some surprise in his voice.

"Yeah, we did it," I replied, "but we're still here."

"Well at least we tried," he said.

"We tried," I agreed.

The next day a con hollered through the window that he'd heard on the news that the state was going to send me to the federal system. The day after that, Tony was taken to court and charged with escape. When he returned, I learned what had taken place after the woman had seen us hanging on the windows on the outside of the cellblock.

There's a barred steel gate in the front of the prison through which visitors are first screened by sight and by monitor, before being allowed inside. The woman pressed the button and stood at the gate, waiting for it to open. The guards in the security bubble at the top of the stairs heard her cries, but when she hollered out that Carlson and Tanzi were escaping, the guards believed she was teasing them. They didn't open the door, choosing instead to wave the woman away. Finally, after some minutes of the woman's persistent yells, they phoned down to the segregation block and asked the guard who answered if Carlson and Tanzi were there. The guard said we were.

"Can you see them?"

"No, they're in the yard exercising."

"Go outside and take a look," he was told. The guard in the bubble told the Lieutenant, who took his key, opened the door and walked into the yard to find Jesse and Bill tied and blindfolded under the stairs. The prisoners were playing horseshoes around the corner and there was nobody else in sight.

"What's going on?" asked the Lieutenant.

"There's a riot going on and there's hostages all over the prison," they said. The Lieutenant angrily stripped off their blindfolds, untied their hands, and ordered them to bring in the prisoners.

The next time Tony was taken to court, he returned to tell me that Bill and

Jesse were his escorts to the courthouse. They were still fighting over whose fault it was that we had escaped.

I was taken to a boardroom upstairs and given a "fair and impartial hearing" to determine whether I'd be transferred into the care and control of the federal prison system. The hearing was brief and I was notified of the outcome a day later.

Four guards came for me at midnight. I was handcuffed and shackled, placed in the back of a state vehicle, and driven the six hours to the federal prison at Lewisburg, Pennsylvania. Little did I know that only a few months later I would be dubbed Wayne "Houdini" Carlson by the *Burlington Free Press*.

Two of the guards had to get out of the car and check their weapons at the front gate, and as we drove through, I looked out the car window at the high grey walls and thought Lewisburg prison looked impressive. I guessed it should have; it was the state of Pennsylvania that had first introduced the prison system concept hundreds of years earlier.

I was processed, my clothes were replaced with federal prison issue—cast-off khaki army fatigues on which X's and O's were randomly stamped. I was placed in the hole on "hold over" status, which meant I could be sent to a federal prison anywhere in the United States. I spent the weekend in my cell, and first thing Monday morning I was taken in front of the Segregation Review Board.

The board, five men in business suits, sat at a large table in the middle of the room. As I walked through the door, the man in the middle said, "Good morning Norman."

"My name's Wayne," I corrected, and they all laughed.

"What are you doing here?" asked the man in the middle.

"I have no idea," I replied. They all chuckled. A few days later I learned that Norman Carlson was head of Federal Corrections of The United States, and the man's comment was an inside joke based on my last name.

"Well, from what I have here, it appears Vermont lacks the security means to hold you in their system," he said. He lifted a single piece of paper from the desk, casually waved it in my direction and gazed at me with inquiring eyes. I gazed back at him.

"Yes, but you can't believe everything you read," I replied. He smiled at this and went on to tell me the United States believed in treating all prisoners fairly, even foreign nationals, and that if I worked and obeyed all rules and regulations, I'd find my stay in Lewisburg humane and comfortable. He went on at length about how I could look after my personal needs through the commissary, and how I could stay healthy through eating good food and by using the prison's large exercise yard, if I just behaved myself.

As I was being escorted back to my cell in the hole, one of the guards told me I'd just received the seventy-five dollar psychological treatment from the Chairman of the Seg Board.

Later that day a guard opened my cell door, and told me I was being cut loose into the general population. I was given my blankets and a few loose toilet articles and lodged on a range of a maximum security block. I was to learn that the United States federal system did not supply tobacco, toothpaste, and other necessities out of hand to their prisoners—prisoners had to work or go without.

In late afternoon I was sitting in front of the television set at the far end of the range, wearing the X's and O's of a holdover prisoner, and hating life because the times were so tough. I didn't have money for cigarettes, and I wasn't in the mood to go begging for a smoke. I thought I heard my name being called. I turned around to see a small group of men surrounding the front of the range. Because I didn't know anyone in Lewisburg, I turned away thinking I'd been mistaken for someone else. A moment later, a prisoner gently tapped me on the shoulder, and asked if I was Carlson.

"Yes," I said.

"Some guys down there want to talk to you," he said. I glanced to where he pointed and saw the five men were still at the front gate. I rose to my feet and walked down the range to talk to them. They were Canadians.

"I'm Paul, from Montréal," said the French Canadian, "and this is my partner Danny."

"I'm Wayne, from Saskatchewan and Alberta," I replied shaking hands. He then introduced me to three other men. Belle, Clem, and the third man were from Ontario.

Paul was a pleasant, dark-haired man of average build, and his accent and complexion spoke of his French ancestry. He appeared to be the spokesman of the group.

"We like to welcome Canadians when they come in," he explained, "and we heard from the admission clerk that you came in from Vermont." We were standing at the side of the range's front entrance, and Paul suggested we walk to the other end of the prison and see the "Old Man."

As we walked down the long corridor, Paul explained the inner workings of the prison culture. As we came to a large foyer with a red tile floor, he told me we were now walking on the "red top"—the common area where prisoners socialized and wheeled and dealed. I could see small groups of men of different cultures and backgrounds loosely gathered together. Paul told me that over fourteen hundred men lived out their federal sentences in Lewisburg.

Along the corridor were a number of checkpoints where guards sat at desks in front of each area where prisoners lived. Along the way, Danny and the man from Niagara Falls fell off, one by one. Paul, Clem and I would be visiting the Old Man together.

Paul stopped to talk to the guard at the entrance to where he lived, and I heard him explain that he'd like to take us into the area to meet the old man. The guard gave Clem and me an up-and-down cursory glance, and nodded his head.

"You got fifteen minutes," he said. We nodded our acknowledgement and followed Paul into the cellblock.

It wasn't a cellblock like any cellblock I'd known. In place of cells were large rooms with large oak doors on them. Paul rapped on a door, waited briefly before opening it, and we stepped inside.

An older man with a crewcut sat at a desk reading a Montréal newspaper. He paused in his reading to acknowledge us, and Paul immediately introduced me.

"This is Lucien Rivard—Lou, this is Wayne Carlson," Paul said. I walked forward to shake his hand, and found myself meeting a legend in the annals of Canadian crime. Lou was a big-time mover and shaker in Montréal in the fifties and sixties, and he still had his hand in a variety of enterprises in Québec and Ontario.

"Good to meet you, Lou," I said.

"Same here," he replied. Paul was pulling a box into the middle of the floor when Clem stepped closer to Lou and shook his hand.

"Hello Mr. Rivard," Clem said. I was surprised at the formality, and when I looked at Paul he was smiling.

"I've heard a lot about you," I said to Lou.

"Oh don't believe everything Paul tells you," he replied. He was half-reading the paper, but I could see he was open to conversation if it was required.

"No, it wasn't Paul who told me about you, it was the western Canadian newspapers."

"Yes, newspapers—look at this," he said, "it's another article about me in the Montréal Star." I took the paper from his outstretched hand and glanced at an article proclaiming that Lucien Rivard would soon be back in Montréal. I handed the paper back to him.

"I remember the articles on you in the paper when you escaped from Bordeaux jail in Québec," I said. He smiled and waved his hand, as to wave it all away, as if it meant nothing. But I knew it did. Lou had almost brought the Canadian government to a standstill.

"This is all your stuff," Paul said. He was off to the side standing beside the huge box.

"That's mine?" I was surprised. I examined the contents. There were cartons of cigarettes, sweatshirts, T-shirts, sweatpants, coffee, creamer, sugar, potato chips, canned food, and two watches, one a pocket watch and the other a wristwatch. One minute I was broke and hungry, craving a cigarette, and the next minute, I was overwhelmed to have so much just handed to me.

"This is embarrassing," I said to Paul, and he immediately became concerned.

"No, this is nothing," he replied, "when you're here for three or four years, you'll do the same for a Canadian when he comes in." I had no intention of being in any prison for three or four years, but I didn't say it.

"Do you want some Cokes?" asked Lou. He was pulling out a case from under his bed, but I had more than enough in the box.

"No thanks," I answered.

"Well thank you," he said.

"You're thanking me?" I asked.

"Yes, for the Cokes—when you said 'no,' you gave me back my Cokes," he said. I laughed, but it did make sense.

I carried my booty to my cell. It felt good to have some new friends, not to mention the clothes and cigarettes, and the watch would come in handy too.

The next day Paul took me around to the different areas of the prison, stopping here and there to show me items of interest, introducing me to "our barber" and others who were friendly to the Canadians. Paul spoke Spanish as well as English and French, so he spoke to a wide variety of people, introducing me to them as we walked along. He also pointed out the water fountain where Jimmy Hoffa had been waiting for a drink when a man in front of him was stabbed. After that Hoffa had hired a man to walk the yard with him, and Paul pointed out a blond-haired weight-lifter as the man whom Hoffa had hired.

A territory was associated with each and every area of the prison. The kitchen was part of the New York and Boston mob, the hallways were looked after by the Philly people, and the yard was a combination of Boston, New York, and Montréal. I learned that the connection between Boston and Montréal was a very close one, and whenever I met people from New York they always asked me if I knew the Corsican, referring to Lou Rivard. Knowing Lou always served me well because he was well respected by so many people.

Lou had been involved with the large-scale importing of narcotics to the United States. His number came up when an imported car had been involved in a fender-bender at the docks in Corpus Christi, Texas, and white powder began pouring from the crack in the car's fender. The driver was arrested and charged.

The total amount of heroin was sixty kilos. The driver pleaded guilty, and was sentenced to thirty years on an A-2 number, which meant he could be free before one-third of his sentence was served, if he cooperated with authorities.

After sentencing, the head of the drug squad had handed his card to the driver and told him to call him if he ever got tired of doing his thirty years. It took three years for him to get tired. When he did, he claimed Lou along with some other men, had hired him to carry one kilo from France to the United States. He was surprised at the amount the car actually held, and he felt ripped off. On the strength of his testimony many men were convicted for importing narcotics, and Lou was one of them. He had eleven years in on his twenty year sentence when I met him.

I found it interesting to be meeting and hearing of so many men who were always in the news for one reason or another. Lewisburg held many men from a number of New York, Boston, Philadelphia and Chicago families, and they all worked and played well together there. Paul explained it wasn't always like that—it wasn't until Vito Genovese, the head of a New York family, had come through Lewisburg on hold-over status on his way to the federal prison at Leavenworth, Kansas, that everything had mellowed out.

Vito held a meeting in the chapel where it was decided that street beefs were to be left to the street, and there should be peace between families in the federal joints. As far as I could see, the rule was followed.

Paul introduced me to a Lieutenant in charge of hiring men for different areas of the prison, and suggested that I be allowed to work with the Canadians on the yard crew. The Lieutenant said he didn't have a problem with it, but he'd have to get clearance from security before it became official. As we walked away, Paul told me the Lieutenant's brother, a Captain, was in charge of the security department, so the possibility of a job in the yard looked good.

Signs said a chess tournament was underway and anyone interested should go to the chess clubroom for more details. I asked Paul to take me there. The chess club was a quiet room full of tables set up with chessboards. A coffee pot and cups sat on a cupboard across the room, and a man sat at a desk at the front entrance.

"Is this where the chess tournament's taking place?" I asked him.

"Yes, but it's over," he replied. I noticed he had a board set up in front of him.

"Who won?" I asked.

"I did," he replied.

"How does the chess club work?" I asked.

"There are two classes of player—A class players and B players," he replied.

"How do you determine if someone is an A or B class player?"

"The rule is the President of the Club plays the man," he answered.

"Who's the President?" I asked.

"I am," he said.

"Can you play now?" I asked.

"Sure, sit down and we'll do it," he said. I glanced at Paul who gave me a nod, so I sat down.

"How many games do we play?" I asked.

"We'll play two games. Toss for white pieces and then switch for the next game." He won the toss.

I found myself in trouble in the first game. He won, but not handily. White pieces were always my strongest game, and I was determined to walk away with a split. I played the King's Gambit and was well on my way to winning when a half-dozen men walked into the room and gathered around the table.

A few moves later, I was able to announce and execute a mate in three. After the last move, my opponent was red-faced and uncomfortable. He leaned back in his chair and told me I'd be given A class player status if I joined the club.

A man beaten in a game of chess walks away feeling he's intellectually inferior to the winner. It was even worse for him because it appeared to his friends, who hadn't seen him beat me in the first game, that I'd just soundly beaten him, not drawn in the two-game match with him. As Paul and I walked down the red-top he chuckled about the chess room incident; he thought it was great that I'd won a split.

A couple of days later Paul came to see me to tell me the Lieutenant in charge of hiring had told him not to expect me to be working in the yard. He explained that I was a prisoner on the Super Seven hot list, a list of seven men seen as the highest threat to security. Once a week, the guards attended a picture presentation in the prison theatre, where a picture of each man on the list was flashed on the movie screen, and the man's history and where he was housed in the prison was broadcast over the speaker system. The movie theatre was a regular, street-sized theatre complete with seats and sloped floors, and I could well imagine how impressive such a presentation would be. The staff watching wouldn't easily forget the faces of the seven men so well displayed. I'd noticed that the checkpoint guards would call me over to ask my name, number and cell location, then they'd indicate I should carry on with what I was doing, but I'd thought it was only routine. Now I knew differently.

Instead of the sunshine of the exercise yard, I was designated to work in the kitchen. I was placed in the dish room where I worked with Jimmy, a black man from New York City who always held up his end and who was pleasant to work with. He was doing five years for bank robbery with a note.

We wore rubber boots and rubber aprons, and we processed over fourteen hundred steel food trays per meal. It was a wet sloppy job, but we only had to work about three hours a day, and because we were busy, the time went quickly.

I'd come to know a number of men through Paul, and when I was released from the hole and placed on the orientation range, I met a few interesting people there as well. One of them was Sonny Brocco, an Italian from New York, and another was Mike, an Englishman from London. The three of us walked the yard with each other on a number of occasions. There was also Tom Mullins, an Irish bookmaker from New Jersey who was doing ten years for arson, and though he talked long and sincerely of his loyalty to a crime boss in New Jersey, I felt little affection for him and I didn't trust him.

Sonny was a large, white-haired, distinguished-looking man in his fifties who could have passed for a senator. He seemed to have the respect of many men from New York and Boston. One day Sonny came to see me in the dish room, and amid the steam and rattling of steel trays, he asked me what I was doing working there.

"I'm doing what I was told to do," I replied.

"This is no place for a bank robber to be working," he stated.

"No?" I said.

"No, it's not," he said, "so when you're done, you come and see me in the kitchen." I told him I would when my shift was over.

Sonny was standing by the mixer, talking with one of the clerks whom I'd been introduced to earlier, and as I walked toward them, Sonny waved me over. The clerk and I said brief "hellos" and he walked away to return to his office.

"I'm going to introduce you to Mr. West," Sonny said, "and you just go along with me."

"Okay," I agreed.

We walked across the large kitchen to where a man in whites stood looking at a sheet of paper with a large list of names on it. As we approached, he glanced at Sonny and smiled.

"How's it going, Sonny?" he asked.

"Just fine," he answered, "and I want to introduce a friend of ours. This is Wayne from Canada—and this is Mr. West who runs the kitchen," he said. West and I shook hands.

"Wayne has worked in kitchens in the logging camps in northern Canada," Sonny said, "and he makes great flapjacks."

"We'll put him on the A.M. shift then," said West. He was about to make a notation on the sheet of paper in his hand, but Sonny disagreed.

"No, no, he should work with us on the P.M. shift," he said.

"Oh, okay," agreed West, and he made that notation on his sheet.

After we walked away, Sonny explained that the A.M. shift was almost entirely black, and none of their friends worked that shift. In fact, there was competition between the A.M. and P.M. shifts; the A.M. people hustled food for money in the general population, and they'd destroy any of the P.M. shifts stashes of food they found, particularly eggs. An egg sandwich went for a pack of cigarettes, and the A.M. shift was protecting its share of the market. We used to take the food we stashed and give it away to our friends. Some of the Boston people knew some of the men I'd met in that city, so there was a kinship and a history between us, and the men were always grateful to receive the food we gave them.

Lewisburg was a hustling, bustling prison where a man could get almost anything he wanted, particularly drugs and alcohol. In the evenings, on the red top there were men who touted for other men. When I first arrived, they'd ask me if I was looking for anything. After a week or so they understood I wasn't interested.

One of the men touting was called Red. He'd been touting for years to look after his heroin habit, but one evening he came down the stairs from making a buy, and as he left the cellblock, he crossed the hallway and walked directly to the Captain's door. The door opened and he stepped inside. A moment later, the door opened again and two FBI agents in business suits walked into the cellblock, up the stairs, and stopped in front of a man's cell. They handcuffed him, searched his cell, and when they opened up his cigarette packs and stripped the tobacco out of his cigarettes, they found packages of heroin ready for sale. The man would now be serving at least twenty more years for trafficking in narcotics on a federal reserve.

The stool pigeon disappeared, and all of his records disappeared with him. He'd be given a new identity and a new life under the witness protection plan. However, the protection was only as secure as the people with the information.

A few days after the drug bust, Bill, a man I knew who worked in the mail room, was approached by a couple of men from New York who wanted him to see if there was a forwarding address for the pigeon. One of the staff members in the mail room gave his forwarding address, which turned out to be an obscure halfway house on a little-known side street in New York. The people who asked for the address were very serious about many things in life, and dealing with a stool pigeon was very serious indeed.

Over the next few months I began putting together an escape plan. Paul introduced me to a man by the name of Thompson, who'd worked in the tunnels which ran beneath the prison. Paul and others called him "the Spy" because he was serving a thirty year sentence for spying for the East Germans and the Russians. He'd been a Sergeant in the Quarter Master Corps in the American army, stationed in West Germany.

Thompson knew the underground tunnel system very well, and though I initially thought I could use the knowledge to find a quiet way out, it soon became apparent that I would need some real tools to break through the barred barriers at the ends of the tunnels. I considered using the blanket of fog as a cover for an escape over the wall; however, whenever fog rolled in, the prison had an automatic lockdown policy. Sometimes all prisoners would be held back from the yard and other areas until the fog lifted, which meant I'd have to somehow manage to get into the yard without being seen, and then make it over the wall. Whenever the fog was thick, the guards would stand in long lines beside the wall and watch for prisoners who might make an escape attempt. It wasn't going to be easy, but I was certain it could be done.

Tom Mullins, the New Jersey bookmaker, was very interested in escaping and he'd regularly cut into me to ask if I had any plans. I always told him "no," that I was going to do my time, but he insisted that I take him with me when I did go.

Bill lived in cellblock A and I was moved across the hall to A block as well. Tom Mullins lived on the bottom range, while Bill and I lived on the upper ranges. Tom was under the impression that he ran the cellblock because he was a clerk in the Captain's office and made coffee for him in the morning. One day Tom took exception to the fact Bill was trying to avoid being locked in his cell by staying a step ahead of the guard making his rounds.

"You're drawing heat," Tom said.

"How so?" asked Bill.

"You have to lock up when they tell you to," Tom explained.

"Fuck them," Bill replied, "I've got things to do."

"I'm telling you to lock up when the guards come around," insisted Tom.

"Well, fuck you too," responded Bill, walking away. A day later, Sonny and Butch took me for a walk in the big yard. They were walking on either side of me. After a few minutes of casual conversation, the argument between Tom and Bill was brought up.

"Tom came to us, asking us to talk to you about Bill," Sonny said. I was beginning to feel an intense dislike for Tom.

"He has no business telling Bill or anybody else how to do their time," I said.

"He's a friend of the American-Italian club," said Butch. Now that pissed me off.

"Oh, I see," I said. "If a man is friendly with you guys, it doesn't matter if he's wrong, you support him no matter what."

"No, not if he's wrong," said Sonny.

"Well he's wrong, Sonny," I said. "He makes coffee for the Captain and he thinks this gives him a licence to do whatever he wants—it doesn't sit well with me. And he's a man with a head full of escape questions."

"Yeah, he's looking for a way out," said Sonny.

"He's not the kind of guy who escapes—it's not in guys like him. But he could be looking for another way out," I said.

"Yeah, there are other ways," said Butch. We walked around the yard for another half hour, and I believed the Tom issue was finished, as far as the heavyweights were concerned.

Part of my routine was eating breakfast with Mike, the Englishman. Tom began dropping his tray on our table in the mornings. One morning I simply picked up my tray and moved to another table. Mike followed suit.

One evening when the bus came in, there was a black man left over. The rule was that a black man and a white man couldn't be held in the same cell. Mike came to me and asked if I'd share a cell with him so the black man wouldn't have to be placed in the hole. I agreed.

We shared the same cell together for two weeks, and in that time we came to know each other. He was serving five years for a hash smuggling operation, and his story was an interesting one.

He had served a four-year sentence in Wormwood Scrubs in England. I recognized the name of the prison because that was where Sherlock Holmes sent the men he caught for their crimes. After serving his sentence, Mike had hooked up with his brother, and stolen a yacht in a South London port. After crossing the English Channel, they'd chartered out the boat for three months and pocketed the gains. They finally scuttled the yacht and went to work with forged papers for an eccentric English boat owner; Mike was the Master Mariner and his brother was the Engineer.

One day they were out on the water when the Englishman decided his dog was making too much noise, so he tied a rope on him and threw him overboard. Mike's brother became so upset, he couldn't restrain himself. He punched out the old man. When he regained consciousness, he fired Mike's brother, and Mike left the boat too.

They only had five thousand dollars American, just enough to buy a thirty-one foot Norwegian craft. The boat had been commandeered by the German High Command during the war. It needed work on the outside to make it seaworthy, but the teak interior was in perfect shape.

Mike had noticed a man stopping to watch him and his brother working on the hull. After a few days the man approached them. They invited him on board. He turned out to be a German entrepreneur, and after some small talk, the man asked them to do some smuggling. Part of the deal was that he'd front the money to fix up the boat. It wasn't much longer before they made their first run—and realized a huge profit on their load of hash. After the first trip, they had their connections. They bought one yacht, then another, and they made a great deal of money which they kept in Swiss banks. Mike had bought a directorship for a fee of twenty-five thousand dollars, which allowed him to move large sums of money in and out of the bank with no questions asked. At one point Mike showed me the paperwork compiled by Interpol, which mentioned a Lamborghini, a Maserati and a restaurant in Spain—and Mike's arrest at the Paris International Airport with two hundred and ninety-seven thousand dollars in an attaché case. The money was confiscated by the French police. Since Mike's arrest for importing hash, American lawyers were in the process of getting his money back from the French. He must have had a good case because his lawyer was sending him five hundred a month to the prison out of his own pocket.

I asked Mike what he wanted. It seemed to me had enough money to realize many dreams, but he told me he wanted a million American dollars in a Swiss bank account. The deal he was arrested for would've seen him pocket a million, and he and the other man even bought a farm for ninety thousand dollars, just to stash hash. It puzzled me why he would choose to deal in such large weights of hash when he could pick up ten kilos of heroin and make much more.

"When you deal in smoke dope, you're dealing with a certain type," he said. "They aren't likely to kill you for the dope and money. Heroin's different. The first thing heroin dealers think about is how to kill you and take it all—if that proves difficult they'll probably pay you for it, but only after they've fully explored the 'take it all' scenario." Mike and I discussed our futures, and my lack of one, and he told me he'd never again run hash to the United States. However, he claimed he wouldn't hesitate to make a run to Canada. He asked me if I knew anyone who'd be interested in doing a large deal.

"I know lots of men, and women too, who'd be very interested, but they don't have the money to do it now, and it's doubtful they ever would," I told him.

"If you ever want to get into it, get in touch with me," he said. I would have liked to get into something as lucrative and as exciting as international smuggling, especially with yachts on the high seas. It sounded very romantic. I could easily imagine myself as a Captain of a yacht with a hold full of money in the form of weed or hash, beautiful women waiting for me in different ports around the world, and money to burn. Yes, it would be a very good life indeed.

A couple of months later a clerk came to tell me I was slated for the bus to Marion, Illinois. Marion was the highest security prison in North America. I needed a writ prohibiting the feds from moving me further afield, especially to a super max prison. I called on my acquaintances to help me, and I found myself waiting in the hallway while the Spy typed me up a writ which would serve as an injunction prohibiting the transfer. Every five minutes or so there would be an announcement for Carlson to report to the cellblock, but I ignored the page and hung in there until the document was done. Finally the Spy walked over and handed it to me.

The writ read like an announcement of war against the state and federal political system, with words like "cohorts," "capitalists," "police states," and "regime" scattered across the pages. I knew it was going to be a hard sell in court, but I managed to get the document notarized and filed before they caught up with me in the hallway.

My property was already packed when I appeared at the cellblock. I was immediately informed I was being transferred by bus to an unknown destination, and I was taken away to spend the night in the hole.

The next morning I was given a cup of coffee and two pieces of toast with jam on the side. Minutes later I was dressed in hold-over clothes, cast-off khaki army fatigues with the large black X's and O's stamped over them, and then loaded on the transfer bus.

The bus was the size of an ordinary Greyhound, and it had wheels, a roof, and windows, but there the similarities ended. There were six armed guards riding with us. Two of them were drivers who sat in the regular seats in front, and two others were in front behind the wire with shotguns and automatic weapons. The last two were armed the same and seated in back.

The toilet sat in the middle of the van, in plain view of everyone. Food consisted of sandwiches made in the prison we'd just left. We rode the bus from sun-up until sundown and didn't stop for anything except gas, and even then the service stations were notified and well checked out in advance. I examined the windows, looking for an out. It would take special tools and more than a little time to make a hole.

We could only get out of our seats to use the toilet, and before we rose to our feet to do that we had to notify the marshals. When one of them nodded his approval, he also notified the other guards, so everyone was aware of what the prisoner was doing. There were prisoners who weren't handcuffed and shackled; they were the food, water, and cigarette boys who were allowed to walk up and down the aisle and hand out what we asked for. There was little camaraderie between any of us, but there was none between the water boys and ourselves. They were not spoken to unless someone wanted something.

"Water boy—I need some water down here," a prisoner in chains would say. The water boy would walk to the man, give him a Styrofoam cup of water, and never meet the gaze of the man he was serving. I couldn't help but think the men who walked the aisle looked beaten and used up. They presented a sad and pitiful sight. One of the men sitting across the aisle from me explained that the water boys were usually finishing a long sentence and would probably be gone in a month.

I met some Irish Republican Army supporters whom the press dubbed The Baltimore Four. They'd been convicted of buying and possessing automatic weapons destined for the IRA. They were being transferred to Terre Haute, Indiana. Jimmy and Harry were sentenced to four years, and their two partners who'd worked in a bank had been handed sentences of six years.

Belfast Harry was a small dark man with a moustache. He'd been a bartender at the Red Rooster in New York. He was on a hunger strike. They'd all gone on a hunger strike and had been on one for a couple of weeks. Harry told me he'd been taken aboard a plane by the marshals, and asked by his escorts to take a pill for airsickness, which he did, and though he didn't remember doing it, he'd eaten a hamburger while on the flight. When he stepped off the plane, the press already had the news that the hunger strike had been broken. He hadn't eaten since, and it showed in the trembling weakness of his body. Even his dark eyes seemed to have difficulty focusing.

Jimmy was the grunt man hauling the guns from one point to the other, and he'd been arrested with hundreds of automatic weapons in the back of his truck. When they learned I was a Canadian, Jimmy told me as we rode along that the FBI had offered him a hundred thousand dollars and a new identity in Canada if he'd explain how they'd smuggled the arms to Ireland. I asked Jimmy if he'd been tempted to take the deal. I knew many men who'd given up their partners, even their families, for a lot less.

"No," he said, "I wasn't tempted. There's no escape and there's no place to hide. They always find informers, and informers get a bullet in the head." Jimmy had a haunted look about him, which I imagined came from his trying to adjust to the fact that he had to do the next three years in prison, and probably wouldn't see his family for a long time.

"Jimmy has eight kids," Harry had said at one point.

The bus had tinted windows covered with heavy wire mesh, yet it seemed that neither the other drivers nor those people on the streets in the different towns we passed through paid any attention to us. We were invisible men riding an invisible bus, and even to our guards we existed only as numbers. We rode all day, and if it wasn't for the noon meal, we would've had no idea of time.

Though several of the men seemed to be acquainted, they seldom spoke, each wrapped in his private thoughts. We were all going to places we didn't want to go, and there was nothing we could do about it. I never saw a man use the toilet except to urinate, and it was inconceivable to me that I'd actually use the toilet in the middle of the bus for anything but that myself.

When the sun touched the horizon, we knew we'd soon be stopping for the night. It was July, and the weather was beautiful when they unloaded us. We stepped off in single file, military procedure at its best. The six well-armed marshals strategically positioned themselves around the bus and prison gate to block any escape route.

"Last name?" demanded the marshal with the clipboard.

"Carlson," I said.

"Given names—first name first," he said.

"Lorne Wayne," I answered.

"Number?" I gave him my eight-digit federal prison number, the last three numbers of which designated the prison in which a prisoner had first been processed. Mine was 133, Lewisburg.

Once unloaded, we were taken to a small holding room, our chains were removed and we were stripped naked to wait forty-five minutes or more before we were called out and handed coveralls. To stand naked in a small room with thirty other men for close to an hour was uncomfortable, and some of the men attempted to make small talk about meaningless things. I could smell the nervousness, as acrid and strong as fear. One by one we were called out and dressed and taken to the hold-over cells in the hole.

I had no idea where we were—this prison looked much like any other. I'd noticed the reaction of men when they learned some of us were destined for Marion; it seemed we were going to the land of no return.

The next morning we went through the same name and number routine, which was as much a part of the transfer procedure as the guns the marshals carried. The sun was dawning on another truly beautiful morning, and though I wouldn't have admitted it under torture, I was feeling heartsick and hopeless. Yet beneath the despair, I understood I was much better off than most of my fellow riders. I had a sentence that could be served, and many of them were doing more time than they had left in their bodies. I found comfort too in the fact I was a Canadian. We rode all day again, and someone said that Terre Haute, Indiana was our next stop.

The cells in the hole of Terre Haute were the same as other cells, but because the doors were solid, there was no communication from one cell to the next. There was no such thing as personal property; each time we left the bus we left our cigarettes there as well. Any unsmoked cigarettes were thrown away and new packages were handed out the next time we boarded. Packages of tobacco were handed to us through the food slot in our doors, along with a corncob pipe. The tobacco was coarse, similar to pipe tobacco. It came in a light-blue package, and it was called George Washington rolling tobacco. It was impossible to roll it in a cigarette paper, so I tried the corncob pipe. That night, by around three in the morning, I'd developed such a headache I thought my head would explode.

I heard a guard on his walk so I rapped on my door as he passed by and he opened my foot slot to check me out.

"Is there any way I can get some Aspirins?" I asked.

"What's wrong with you?" he asked.

"I've got a serious headache."

"Y'all been smoking that George Washington?" he asked.

"Yeah, I have."

"Don't smoke too much of that shit," he said, "it'll kill you." The food slot closed and he walked away. I didn't think he'd come back, but he did. The food slot opened and he placed two Aspirins on the open flap.

"Thanks," I said.

"Don't smoke that shit," he said again, and he closed the slot and walked away.

I listened to the radio through the duct.

The next day my door opened and I was asked if I wanted to exercise in the courtyard. I jumped at the chance to get some fresh air, and a few minutes later I was standing outside, looking at the gun towers and main prison yard. I walked out of the shadow cast by the building and stepped into the sunlight. It was a beautiful day in Indiana, and I felt such a longing for normal life that the pain bordered on agony. I turned and asked a prisoner standing a few feet away from me where he was going.

"I don't know," he replied. Then he asked, "What month is it?"

"It's July," I answered. He looked normal enough, but he had a way of staring, unblinking when he looked at me.

"What year?"

"1974," I answered.

"I should be getting out," he said. He walked over to the wire fence, sat down with his back to it, and looked at me with uncomprehending eyes. As I walked over and sat beside him I saw a black man pull out a pack of Camels and light one up. I briefly felt envious.

"How long have you been here?" I asked the man sitting beside me. He turned to look at me. Again I was struck by the look on his face.

"I'm not sure," he replied, "I've been in so many places the last four years."

"Where are you coming from?" I asked.

"I started in Florida four years ago, and I've been in float ever since."

"Float?"

"Yeah, they put you on a transfer bus and send you to another fuckin' prison, and when you get there, the fuckin' Seg. Review Board tells you they can't fuckin' take you because the paperwork's all fucked up, and they send you another prison," he said. He seemed to ramble, but he was making sense.

"So you've been travelling like this for four years?"

"Yeah, but I know my time must be finished."

"What about a lawyer—can't a lawyer help you?" I asked.

"A lawyer can't do anything—not until I'm in an assigned prison. And I can't write because of the security," he said. A prisoner in hold-over status was not allowed to send a letter, or make a phone call; it was a security measure to prohibit escape attempts. I sat there beside him feeling powerless to say anything, let alone do anything to help him.

The black man with the Camels sat on the ground with his back against the far fence, and when the yard door opened and a white man walked into the yard, he called him over. The black man had a jacket beside him, and as the man walked over to him, he picked it up and placed it over his lap. The white man immediately went to his knees and began giving the black man a blow job.

The other four of us in the yard didn't let on we noticed anything unusual, but it didn't take long for the door to fly open. Two guards rushed out to confront the two men.

"Stop it right now!" demanded one. The other guard stood beside him, as backup. But the two on the ground didn't move, not for another minute, and when the white man's head came up from under the coat, he kissed the other and stood to his feet. They were both ordered inside, and as they walked through the doorway, one guard asked the other who in hell had let the two of them into the yard at the same time.

The rest of us sat in the sun not saying anything for the rest of the exercise period, and it seemed like only seconds later that we too were ordered back to our cells.

That night a Lieutenant opened my door and asked me to step out of my cell.

"Do you know Carol from Canada?" he asked. He had a small piece of paper in his hand with what appeared to be notes scribbled on it.

"Yes I do," I replied, surprised.

"She phoned here," he said, "and she wants you to call her in a half an hour. Do you want the call?" he asked. I couldn't believe I was going to get a phone call because I was a long, long way from anybody I knew.

"Yes, I'd like to call," I assured him.

"The number's here," he said, holding up the piece of paper in his hand.

"Okay," I said, and I walked back into my cell. A half hour later I was taken out and the call was placed. Carol and I had been through many things together, and she was very resourceful and very dedicated to the people in her life. She called to tell me they were all thinking of me, and after the call I returned to my cell rejuvenated by a feeling of renewed hope. It doesn't take much to rebuild, and the sincere love and affection of friends and family is the cornerstone of any prisoner's hope for the future.

I stayed in the hole in Terre Haute for close to two weeks, and by this time I'd learned there was only one more bus ride to get to Marion. On the day we left it was raining, which added something to my feelings. We arrived at the front gates of Marion before sunset.

When I stepped off the bus, two other men, one black and one white, stepped off with me. Together we were escorted through the entrance of the prison, down a red carpet and highly polished floors to a series of hallways, one of which led to the hole. Marion seemed to be a new prison; the floors and walls of the hole were unmarked. I was placed on a range of eighteen cells, most of which seemed to be occupied.

I wasn't there more than ten minutes when one of neighbours called out to me.

"Cell four," said a low voice. It took a couple of calls and a knock on my wall for me to realize he was talking to me.

"Yeah?" I answered.

"Do you play chess?" he asked. The man's voice was deep, and I couldn't detect an accent. He could have been from anywhere.

"Yeah, I do."

"Want to play?"

"Sure, I'll play," I agreed. He slid a chess board from his cell to mine and I noticed it already had the move codes marked on it. We played for an hour and I beat him, which meant he would expect another game, so we continued. He won the second game and we took a break.

"I'm Joe," he said. "People call me Joe Doc."

"I'm Wayne from Canada. Good to meet you," I answered.

"Oh, a Canadian. We've got a couple of Canadians here," he said.

"Yeah? Where from?"

"One from the west coast and one from the east coast," he answered, "and one of them is French—that's all I know."

"Where are you from?" I asked.

"Philadelphia," he answered.

"How long've you been here?" I asked.

"Six years," he replied.

"Are you doing hole time?"

"No, I'm here for thirty days. I just got out of the Control Unit, but before I go back into the population, I have do thirty days here."

"Oh," I replied.

"We're locked down so tight in the Control Unit that it takes a while to get used to any kind of freedom, so we do thirty days in the hole because it's more open," he explained.

"How long will I be here?" I asked him.

"A couple of days, then they'll cut you loose into the general population," he said.

"That's not bad," I offered.

"No, you'll meet some Canadians too, and you can tell them I sent you to them." I felt good about that. There's nothing in prison like an introduction to other people to help a man become assimilated.

"How long until they release you?" I asked.

"I'll be out in a week," he answered.

"Good," I replied, "I'll be seeing you out there."

"Yeah, we'll see each other." When the meal wagon arrived, we stopped talking for the moment.

I appeared before the Seg. Review Board the next morning, and an hour later I was walking down a highly-polished hallway to Cellblock C. A couple of minutes after that, I was walking the yard, checking out the countryside through the wire fences.

Marion squatted on acres of land on a federal reserve, situated miles from any city. It was countryside quiet, and as I walked, I could hear the distant sound of trucks and cars travelling on the interstate a few miles away. It felt peaceful, but there was nothing anyone could have told me, and nothing I could have read, that could've prepared me for the next two years.

BREAKFAST WITH THE DEVIL

Marion was a relatively new prison, built specifically to house maximum security prisoners from Alcatraz and other super maximum prisoners from across the United States. Unofficially it was known as a special handling unit for prisoners deemed too dangerous or too high a security risk to live in the regular federal prisons. Then too, there were also prisoners like myself who were boarded out by a state to the federal authorities. The prisoner population, I learned over the next few days, stood at around five hundred men, half of whom were black and half white, and over a hundred men were locked up in the hole and Control Unit at any given time.

The prison yard was big enough to hold a baseball diamond and two tennis courts, but the tennis courts were in bad shape, and in the time I was there I never saw a game of tennis played— I never even saw a prisoner carry a tennis racquet. However, baseball was big and there were some good players.

Marion was laid out on the telephone pole system—the cellblocks ran off a main hallway like the arms of a telephone pole. The cellblocks were from A to G, with G Block being the hole. The Control Unit was at the far end of a hallway and a man only walked down it when he was under escort. When a prisoner did walk down the hallway, he wouldn't be walking back for at least one full year.

There were many reasons a prisoner could be sent to the Control Unit, ranging from having a contraband tool to committing an act of unjustified violence. The penalty for attempting to escape was a further ten years added to the man's sentence, and at least a year in the Control Unit. If a prisoner murdered another prisoner, the sentence was the same—ten years added to his sentence. If a prisoner murdered a federal prison guard in prison, he'd be sentenced to life imprisonment, and he'd spend his life in the Control Unit. Such men were mentally unbalanced because of the time they'd spent in solitary confinement.

I went hunting for the Canadians and in a matter of an hour I'd met them both—Bill and Maurice. Neither wanted to talk much about their Canadian past.

Bill seemed more American than Canadian because he spoke with a southern accent. He'd been in prison in the States for two decades but he still retained his sense of being a Canadian. He put me on his newspaper line, which meant I'd receive his paper along with a number of others. He had subscriptions to a Toronto paper as well as the *Vancouver Sun*.

Maurice was a French Canadian with a tattoo on his shoulder which proclaimed he was Stony Mountain Champ. He told me he'd always be there if I found myself in trouble.

One day Maurice explained to me why he was in Marion. He'd been arrested in Florida and was being transported by marshals to another state. During an overnight stop, he'd managed to slip a metal coat hanger into his belt, and when he and his escorts stopped for lunch the next day, Maurice stuck one of the marshals in the belly with the wire and ran out of the restaurant. He commandeered the first car he came across, which was driven by a woman with a couple of kids, and he took off.

He managed to get fifty miles before the state police and federal marshals ran him off the road into a ditch. When he emerged from the wreck, he was shot three times in the chest and belly with a .357 Magnum, but he survived. Maurice was serving a twenty-year sentence and he believed that he'd be serving it all in Marion.

For the next two years Maurice would step forward whenever he believed someone was about to give me a bad time, and on many occasions I had to explain it was not serious. Maurice was on a medication so powerful that only a few drops would disable a normal man. He'd take a medicine cup of the stuff, then run five miles with no problem. But it also meant his judgment was usually impaired, something I always had to keep in mind.

The prison was a showplace of prisons, hence the red carpet in the front hallway, but it could also be locked down in less than a minute. When someone was killed, which was often, every phone in the prison would ring steadily, alerting every cellblock, every workplace, and every office throughout the prison. The death of a prisoner was not seen as a major event and when it did happen, the prison wasn't shut down like Canadian federal penitentiaries. When all the phones rang, every gate in the prison would close, and prisoners were to stand still wherever they happened to be. Trying to beat the closing of the gates meant instant transfer to the Control Unit. Once the body had been picked up and carried off, the FBI would use a rope or a water hose as a cordon to identify the area, and place a sign in the centre of the circle stating no one was to step into it. Then the barriers would open and the regular routine would resume.

The weight pit was outside in the main yard and many of the men worked out. I started my own workout routine and I started running as well. Some of the men could run ten miles without taking a break, and they ran every day, rain or shine. Adjacent to the weight pit was a large fish pond which contained a huge catfish and many smaller fish. We'd stand beside the water with handfuls of grasshoppers and slowly feed them to the catfish, who lazily circled the bottom and came up quickly for the snack.

Every prisoner worked at a job assigned by the work board, but a prisoner's input was not a part of the process. One day a man could be working in the kitchen, and the next day he could find himself working as a cellblock orderly, sweeping and mopping floors and handing out sheets and towels. It seemed the practice was to switch prisoners' positions every ninety days. Guards switched stations every ninety days as well.

Guards didn't meet the eyes of the prisoners; they seemed to check everything out through their peripheral vision. At each guard post was a tack board with the photo of every prisoner associated with that cellblock or workplace, and it was obvious the guards were familiar with all the faces throughout the prison. Although it seemed it would be a difficult task to remember every prisoner's photo, the majority of prisoners had been there for years, so the guards knew them by sight as well as by their prison record.

By the time Joe Doc was released from the hole, I was reasonably familiar with the prison routine. The cell doors opened at 6:30 in the morning, and except for the lunch and supper counts of ten minutes each, the doors stayed open all day until they were locked at 10:30 each night. Through Joe I learned a great deal more about Marion and the people in it.

Joe Doc was an Irish-looking man in his late thirties. He weighed in at two hundred forty pounds, and at six feet four inches, he was an impressive figure. To further add to his physical presence, he always wore a green Irish tam, cocked to one side. He was part of a crew of bank robbers that had robbed banks in cities across the United States. Joe not only robbed banks, he moved the money through the airports dressed as a priest. He looked the part, and it was easy to imagine him walking past airport security and being smiled at and nodded to. They were headline news, and when Joe was finally arrested and convicted, he was sentenced to thirty years and sent directly to Marion from a courthouse in Pennsylvania.

With very few exceptions, all Marion prisoners had begun serving their sentences in another state or federal prison, and had either killed someone inside, or had escaped, or attempted to escape. The basic criterion for transfer to Marion was the prisoner's degree of dangerousness. It could be that he was dangerous to security, he was a killer who would in all likelihood kill again, or he was a high-profile national news prisoner seen as an enemy of the government— organized criminals fit into this category. Prisoners who carried P numbers had killed and been found mentally unfit to stand trial.

A rule of law decrees that a federal sentence takes precedent over a state sentence. For prisoners in Marion this held a special significance, especially for those men who were under sentence of death by a state. A man could not be sent back to his state death sentence if he still had federal time to serve, which meant it was in the best interest of a man under sentence of death to pick up more federal time. When one of these prisoners reached the end of his federal sentence, he'd search out a prisoner to kill for the ten-year respite from the death sentence the federal sentence would give him.

One hot summer day, I was sitting at one of the tables in the yard when Joe walked over and sat down.

"Do you want a good job?" he asked.

"Doing what?"

"Working with Junior in the vegetable room," he said. Junior was a slim, small-boned, blond-haired man in his twenties who was serving ten years.

"Why does he want to work with me?" I asked.

"He wants somebody he trusts with all the knives," he answered, chuckling as he did so.

"All the knives?"

"The guys on the vegetable crew work behind two solid doors, locked tight, and they're frisked every time they come out," he said. "The vegetable knives are honed to a razor-sharp edge, and they could slice a man in half with no effort."

"And he thinks he can trust me behind his back with a knife?"

"Yeah, he's had some bad luck with people," he replied.

"Tell me about the guy," I said.

"He's doing ten years."

"For what?"

"For killing a black faggot in Terre Haute, Indiana," he replied.

"Oh."

"Yeah, Junior had just came in. He's from California and he ran a hot car across a state line and the feds charged him with interstate transportation of stolen goods. He got a deuce for it."

"Oh yeah?"

"A big black faggot motherfucker walked into his cell one day and told him he was on his way to do a workout, and he told Junior to have his pants off when he got back."

"And it started with stealing a car," I said.

"Yeah, stealing a car. Anyway, Junior gets himself a shank, a big shank, and when the faggot was doing a three-hundred-pound bench press, Junior slipped up behind him and used both hands to drive a knife through him," he said.

"And killed him?"

"Killed him dead, right through the heart, pinned him to the bench like a butterfly and the three hundred pounds on the weight bar didn't help the faggot either."

"No, if the knife didn't do it, the weight would've slowed him down," I said.

"Yeah, that's the way he lay there, plunged through the heart with a weight bar across his chest. They gave Junior ten years and sent him here," said Joe. I didn't have to think long on this one.

"I like the job I have now," I said.

"Yeah, well, suit yourself. I'll tell him you're not interested."

"Thanks Joe."

"Yeah."

Not long after that Junior got himself in trouble. Joe and Rick and I were sitting at a table in the yard one hot, humid afternoon. We were all wearing shorts and sandals. It must've been a hundred degrees Fahrenheit. We were no sooner at the table when another man walked up and sat down. I didn't know him well, just enough to say "hello." His name was Billy.

"Well, he wants to go," Billy said, speaking to Joe.

"Did you talk to him?" asked Rick. Billy glanced at Rick, and I noticed he looked nervous and helpless and even though his voice didn't betray his feelings, his eyes did.

"Yeah, I walked the yard with him and told him to come to our block, but he's too embarrassed to listen," Billy said, "and now Peter's having a talk with him too." When he said that, I glanced around the yard and saw Junior walking with Peter, a man I did know. At that point I had an idea of what they were talking about, but I didn't comment. I thought about the childhood ditty we used to say with the encouragement of our parents and teachers, *Sticks and stones will break my bones, but names will never harm me.* But the adage didn't apply to Marion. In Marion, as in other prisons, words and names usually create swordplay.

"I'll talk to him," said Joe. He got to his feet and began walking the running track counter- clockwise, which would allow him to intercept Peter and Junior. When Joe walked off, Billy excused himself and walked into the cellblock. Rick and I just sat there and waited. On the surface it appears I could have gotten up and walked into the cellblock, out of the action and out of harm's way—but beneath the surface of choices, the only one that counted was to stay.

"So what's happening?" I asked, and Rick explained it to me.

"Junior went into a cell with Greg—alone. Didn't come out for fifteen minutes, and when they did, it wasn't good," he said.

"No?"

"No. Greg told the six man at the end of the range that it was the best head he ever got," said Rick, "and when Junior called him on it, Greg told him to move out of the block."

"And he won't move?"

"No, he won't move. He says he's right. He claims he's not the faggot and Greg is."

"And Greg won't lighten up?"

"No." There was a finality in Rick's answer.

Greg and his partner were standing at the corner of the cellblock, Junior was walking diagonally across the yard, and we watched as he walked past us to stand in front of Greg.

"Okay, how do you want to go?" Greg asked. He was dressed in a white T-shirt and army fatigues, and he had his boots on. Junior wore a shirt, running shoes and pants.

"Knives," declared Junior. He was small in stature, and he appeared much smaller beside Greg. Greg was muscular, inches taller, and many pounds heavier than Junior.

"You got your shit?" asked Greg. "Shit" meant shank.

"Yeah," said Junior, "I've got it."

"Jeff will keep six, and keep the hack off our backs," said Greg, indicating a man who stood a few feet away.

"Yeah, okay," said Junior.

"Okay—we go into the shack," said Greg, "you first." Junior started walking to the tool shack beside the weight pit with Greg a couple of steps behind. Greg quickly bent down and picked up a two foot piece of two by two and carried it with him inside.

There was the sound of a loud struggle as if the shovels and rakes and other yard equipment was being flung around the room. The guard on yard duty heard it too because he wasn't far away.

There was a rule that no guard was allowed to walk out of the sight of his fellow guards. No matter where a guard was on duty, he must be able to be seen by at least one other guard. When he stepped forward to investigate the noise, Jeff stepped up behind him and sucker punched him, but he wasn't knocked out and he managed to hit the panic button on his belt. I could hear the ringing of the telephones when Greg walked out. The guard was quickly, but cautiously, getting to his feet and I could hear the hard sound of many feet with leather soles rushing down the inner hallway to the yard.

"You can have him now," Greg cooly said. I noticed a small fleck of fresh blood on his T-shirt. Just then Junior walked out of the shack. His hands were clamped around the haft of a knife that'd been driven straight through his body. The rushing guards were out of the cellblock and coming at us when Junior pulled the knife from his chest. From the look on his face, I could see he was dead before he fell.

Soon the FBI came to conduct their investigation. As they carried Junior past, laid out on the stretcher with his hands across his chest, I made a point of looking at his face. He looked very young. His face reflected a sleep-like vulnerability, and I felt sorry for him. Rick and I didn't look at each other, but I believed he felt the same. As soon as the area was cordoned off, and everybody involved had been dealt with, movement was restored. There was a strange sense of relief in me, and as I glanced at some of the faces, I knew it was a collective relief. When somebody dies violently in prison it has an effect on everyone.

"I'm going home," said Rick, rising to his feet as he did so.

"I'll see you later," I replied, and Rick walked into the cellblock. I sat there for a while, thinking of what I'd just experienced, and I looked at the security around me.

When there was a disturbance, every gun tower would be on full alert. Some of the guys believed the towers were armed with weapons with light sights, saying wherever the light touches the bullets do too. The tactical squad would come running down the hallway in response to the distress signal, along with every available supervisor and guard in the prison. Any violent incident in the yard would be seen by four gun towers, and the area between the fences of the prison and the cellblock doors was well covered by automatic weapons.

Joe had pointed out the bullet chips on the cement around the main door, and explained how he and his partners had tried to break out by driving a commandeered cement truck through the double fences under a clear shot from two towers. They'd gone less than twenty yards when his partner, who was driving, was shot through the head and killed instantly by a tower guard. Joe and his other partner managed to roll out of the truck under a hail of bullets, the marks of which were still there. I glanced at the bullet chips, then to the towers, and I couldn't imagine trying to make that kind of desperation run at the fences.

Rick was a bank robber from Chicago, and he'd been to Canada, in a manner of speaking. He was usually quiet, but one day in the yard he mentioned he'd been in Canada.

"What part?" I asked.

"Saskatchewan," he replied.

"I was born in Saskatchewan. What part were you in?"

"Estevan," he said.

"I know Estevan," I said. "So what were you doing there?" And he told me his story.

"I was in North Dakota. I had a bank cased and I had a good van. I was in and out of the bank with no problem," he said.

"Later?"

"I was pulled over by a highway patrolman, and when he walked toward the van he saw my gun in the mirror, so I fired through the body of the van and hit him," he said. He dug through his pockets and pulled out a carrot. Rick didn't smoke—he ate vegetables instead, and he took a bite before he continued.

"As I pulled away I could see him in the mirror, firing at the van, and I knew I'd been shot. I took a secondary road and stopped to look after the wound," he said, pausing to take another bite. He chewed, then went on. "The bullet went straight through me, and I used some towels I had to try and stop the bleeding, but it wouldn't. I could slow the bleeding but I couldn't stop it. I got into the van and kept going, but I lost control on a curve of a country road and rolled it.

"I started walking with a backpack across the hills of North Dakota, and when I finally came out of the hills, I started hitchhiking on a road. When the RCMP pulled up, one kid in a car, I knew I must've crossed the border some- where along the line. The cop got out of his car and walked toward me, and I couldn't believe he didn't have his gun in his hand—it was in a flap holster, so I just stood there. He asked me where I was from, and I gave him an American address, which was a mistake because there were more questions.

"Finally he noticed some blood on my jacket and told me he was looking for a man believed to be shot following a robbery in North Dakota. I don't know why I didn't shoot him, but I didn't. He searched me and found my gun. He looked at it, then asked if it was real. He was pointing the gun into the ditch when he asked, and I didn't have to answer because it went off.

"When two other police cars showed up they drove me to the hospital in Estevan, Saskatchewan. The next day I had visitors from Regina. They were RCMP with braided patches and they all shook my hand, thanking me for not killing the young cop."

The area we lived in at Marion held thirty-six cells, eighteen on the lower floor and eighteen on the upper, and all of the men who lived in them were interest- ing. Carmine "Junior" Persico, Angelo Ruggiero, Mario Garrelli and Willie "Potatoes" Dadanno. I think my relationships with the mobsters was good because I treated them as ordinary men. We had ordinary conversations about ordinary things, but also, I didn't know their histories and I really didn't care.

Carmine had a garden, as did some other prisoners, between two of the cell- blocks. He had a green thumb and he grew huge watermelons, healthy tomatoes, lettuce, and hot peppers. He invited me into his garden one day, and he must have seen how much I appreciated his invitation because he offered me a pep- per off the vine. I accepted and ate it there, not without my eyes running, and not without feeling the inside of my mouth might melt from the heat, but I han- dled it well. Carmine was in his early forties, was from New York and serving eight years. Later on he was to become the head of a New York family, but even at the time he was a very powerful man in the free world, particularly New York.

Willie "Potatoes" Dadanno was a small slim man of sixty-two from Chicago, and he too was a powerful man. He lived two cells down the range from me, and though it was difficult for me to see Willie as anything but a frail old man, every once in a while he'd get upset at the card table playing canasta. During those brief moments when he was angry, it was easy to picture him with a gun in his hand.

On one such occasion it became clear that he was not just a run-of-the-mill old man. A guard had given Willie a hassle over a humidifier he had in his cell. I stepped in to support him. I knew he was allowed to have it.

"You know what we do with guys like that in my neighbourhood?" Willie asked me, after the guard had left.

"No, not really," I answered.

"The first time we give him a slap, and if he does it again, we kill him," he said. I could see a mean form of fire flashing in his eyes as he spoke. I just nodded my head.

Willie would get up in the morning and begin coughing at his sink. I'd hear him gasping for breath between coughs, and I'd always stop and check on him. He was becoming quite frail and he didn't look well.

"Are you okay Willie?" I'd ask. My concern was genuine because I liked him.

"Yeah, I'm okay," he'd answer, then go into another coughing fit.

Late one afternoon I walked into my cell to find two large coffee jars of hot peppers sitting on my desk. I thought someone had put them there by mistake; they were treasured by the Spanish prisoners and by the Southerners. When I inquired about them, Willie told me he'd put them there for me.

"Thanks Willie," I said. He was sitting at a card table with Angelo, Carmine, and Mario.

"You're welcome," he said, waving his hand as if it were nothing. He went on to tell me he'd given his garden away to Mario, which surprised me.

A couple of weeks later Willie died in the hallway from a heart attack, and it was then I learned considerably more about him. My first bit of enlightenment came on the radio.

"*The most vicious hoodlum per pound in the history of Cook County, Chicago died today in Marion, apparently from a heart attack,*" one newscaster said. "*Dadanno was arrested thirty-five times for murder, but never convicted.*" Mario, who'd grown up with Willie in Chicago, gave me more of Willie's history.

"Willie had a partner who grew potatoes in a garden in his own backyard, and when his partner went out of town for a week, Willie took a couple of guys with him and picked every potato he had," Mario said.

"Wasn't there hell to pay?" I asked. I couldn't imagine stealing a mobster's potatoes.

"He looked for the culprits for a long time, but it was a joke so nobody told him the truth," explained Mario. "We called Willie "Potatoes" ever since."

"What did he get his eight years for?" I asked.

"There was a five-man crew robbing banks in Cook County, and they did good for themselves, but one day they all got pinched," he said. "There was a meeting after they made bail and it looked to us like a rat had brought them down, so Willie went looking for him. He had the Cook County investigator sign out the polygraph machine, had some guys pick up the five robbers and take them to a warehouse. Two men failed the test," said Mario.

"So what happened?" I asked.

"We left those two in the warehouse, and the other three guys beat the beef," he replied.

"And Willie?"

"There was an investigation by the feds, and Willie ended up charged with Conspiracy to Conceal a Federal Offence, which were the bank robberies. The Cook County investigator got four years and Willie got eight," he explained.

"That's an interesting story," I said.

"A few months ago Willie did some checking. He wanted to know who gave the information that led to his conviction, and somebody managed to get the old files. There were two men involved. One was the Cook County investigator and the other was Willie's nephew. Shortly after that, Willie's nephew had his throat cut in a sleazy porno movie theatre, and the investigator was killed outside of his home with shotguns," said Mario.

Just before Willie's death, John Roselli, a big name in organized crime, was found shot to death in a welded barrel floating off the coast of Florida. He'd been one of Willie's partners since childhood, and Willie had taken the news hard. The rumour in the press was that John was about to testify at a grand jury hearing on the assassination of John Kennedy. There was speculation that mobsters had worked with the CIA to try to assassinate Fidel Castro and many people were being called to testify. During that same period, Sam Giancana was found murdered in his home. He was cooking for two people, and he no doubt felt safe and secure because the Chicago police were outside the door watching his place. Perhaps it was just coincidental that when the cops took a ten minute coffee break, Sam was shot to death with a .22 calibre pistol. Many believed the .22 was a weapon of choice for the CIA, while mobsters preferred to use heavier weapons, but everybody agreed that nobody would ever know for certain.

Garden plots in the prison yard were scarce—most were already in somebody's hands, but I lucked out. There were two plots of land in the yard facing the parking lot, which couldn't be used to grow vegetables, only flowers. Peter asked me if I wanted one of them; he had the other. I told him I'd give it a try.

It was big enough to be a collective bed for a variety of hardy flowers. The hot and humid weather was perfect for them.

I found it difficult to handle the humid heat my first summer in Marion. There was no respite from it. As I walked down the range, rainbows from the humidity arced from the window to the floor. Though I had an appreciation for the colours, it was only for a short time. I needed to focus on survival. Things could get serious in such a short period of time; staying in tune with the atmosphere was important.

One evening I walked onto my range, stopped and looked out the window to see a beautiful sunset.

"It's going to be a beautiful day tomorrow," I said.

"Why?" asked a voice. I turned to look at a slim serious man in his early thirties. He had asked me once if I thought he could go to Canada and rob banks with M-16's and fully automatic pistols. Even though I suggested that would be overkill, he felt he might need the firepower.

"Well, it's a nice evening, great sky, which tells me it's going to be a nice day," I said. It was an awkward moment; most of the men around me would probably die in prison, and I was talking about a sunset. The social rules in Marion were different from anywhere else: freely expressing a positive feeling was rude.

Every once in a while I'd run into a situation I couldn't avoid. A black man called Texas Shorty was walking behind me as I walked down the hallway to the yard. As he passed by, he reached over and touched my elbow. I asked him not to do it again and we parted company.

Not long after that, Rick stopped at my cell to ask if I'd hang onto a knife he had in his portfolio case. He explained he'd had a beef with Texas Shorty that day in the kitchen, and he thought his cell might be searched. We placed it on the highest crossbar of the front of my cell and there it stayed for two days.

Rick had been working in the kitchen when Texas Shorty patted him on the ass. He reacted by grabbing Shorty by the throat, and was well on his way to throttling him, when it was broken up by guards.

"Is it over?" asked the guard.

"Yeah, it's over," Rick said.

"It's over," said Texas Shorty. But of course it wasn't.

Every so often I'd hear prisoners tell Rick what Shorty was doing. We were sitting at a table in the yard when two men stopped, and one said, "He's wearing magazines." Magazines were worn like armour around the waist by men who feared an encounter with a knife.

"Yeah, but in a couple of days he'll be ripe," said the other.

The next day Joe suggested I work on my shift in the kitchen as long as I could. Something was going to happen.

Supper was just over and I was standing by the coffee machine when I heard the running footsteps of a number of men. In a moment a bleeding Texas Shorty came around the corner, running as hard as he could, and blood was flying everywhere.

The guard at the inner kitchen gate saw Shorty and opened the door to let him in, but Rick was right behind him. Shorty managed to squirm through a crack and the guard slammed the gate. Rick grabbed the gate and gave a heave. The door flew wide and he was after Shorty again. Shorty tried to hide behind the bread wagon, but it was on wheels so it didn't offer any shelter. The wagon went careening across the kitchen floor and Shorty made a dash for the door again. For the second time, he made it. The door slammed shut behind him and he collapsed over a steam table.

I could see he was badly hurt, but I felt no inclination to help him. Within minutes a crowd of guards took Shorty out on a stretcher and then took Rick to the hole.

The next day the story came out that Texas Shorty attacked Rick with a knife, Rick got the knife away from him and stabbed Shorty to protect himself. A dozen eyewitnesses agreed with that version, so we waited to see if Rick was going to be charged.

The day after the incident I heard a couple of guards talking, "Goddamn," said one, "that little nigger should've known better than to tap a white man on the ass and then attack him with a knife."

"Yeah, what did he expect?" said the other.

Three months later I walked onto my range, and there stood Rick in front his door as if he'd never left. I expressed surprise that he was out of the hole.

"Did they charge you?" I asked.

"No— it was ruled self-defense."

"What about you chasing him into the kitchen?" I asked. He laughed.

"They're racist here, Wayne," he said. "This is the Bible belt of the United States—and the Klan is strong here too."

I could clearly see the racism in both the black and the white prisoners, and it was obvious the prison administrators encouraged the split. The dining room was an example—an invisible line ran straight down the centre of the dining room. During meals whites sat on one side of the room and blacks sat on the other. If a man was Indian or Spanish he could choose to eat on either side. If a white man sat on the black side, there'd be hell to pay, and the same applied to a black man who sat down on the white side. Once while I was there, a white man who had lunch with a black man almost lost his life, as did the black man who invited him. The two men worked in industries together. Both were new arrivals in Marion and they chose to eat together. The white man was Albert, a French

Canadian from Montréal, and he said that in Montréal it didn't matter if a white man's friend was black or not. If he was a friend they ate lunch together.

White and black men could walk the yard together, work together, or run together, but to have lunch together implied the relationship was too close. If Albert and the black man had insisted on continuing to eat together, they both would've been killed; the black crew would have killed the black man, while the whites dealt with their man. Albert's decision to eat with a black man in the dining room had consequences in every area of his life, including reading the two Canadian newspapers.

"You tell that sorry old thing he's not reading my papers," said Bill. He came to my cell to tell me. I gave the papers to Albert after I read them, and it was now my responsibility to inform him of Bill's decision. Though I felt sorry for Albert, there was nothing I could do.

The movie theatre too had white and black sides, split down the middle. There were also two movies each week. One would be a regular movie, while the other would be a movie people referred to as "a black exploitation film." During the movies, especially the exploitation films, the blacks would yell and clap when a white man was killed or murdered on the screen, shouting, "Shoot that white motherfucker again!" The whites would do the same when the black man was a victim; it didn't matter to the whites if it was a cop doing the killing. I never saw a black guard on duty in the prison.

There were many high-profile prisoners. One of these was Raphael, a Puerto Rican who had stormed the senate in Puerto Rico with two other men, shooting a number of people. His name would come up in the news whenever the Puerto Rican Freedom Fighters blew up a building, or exploded a bomb in an airport. Raphael was a man committed to his cause, and though the United States government tried to buy him off every year by offering him clemency and a tidy sum of money, he maintained his commitment to his beliefs. He had nineteen years in when I met him. He always gave a casual leftist salute as a form of hello, and he was always a pleasant conversationalist.

The riot in Attica, which I'd read about, was still talked about in some circles. One afternoon, in a small room crowded with more than thirty men, we watched an educational film on the Attica riot which gave a different, perhaps radical, perspective on the events. It was a very dramatic and well put together film. In some instances, the viewer was standing on top of a cellblock looking into the prison through the crosshairs of a gun scope. So many men died and they didn't have to. There was a piece in it on a prisoner reputed to be one the leaders in the riot. He initially survived the barrage of bullets and was taken to a cellblock and locked up. A few minutes later they came in and took him out, and hours later his body was found amidst others during the cleanup. After the film I went for a long walk in the big yard, just thinking about life in general.

In the mornings I'd go for a walk, sometimes with other men, but often alone. I listened to the sounds of vehicles—some fast, some slow, some big, some small—but all of them with one thing in common: somebody was behind the wheel, going somewhere. I imagined what their lives were like, whether they knew there was a prison just over the horizon. If they were from this area, they'd know, and I'm sure they'd be afraid of the men inside the fences.

There was a fatalistic mood in Marion, as if everybody had given up hope of freedom and were now turning their attention to more important matters. Some of them had been in prison so long, with such long, undoable sentences, they couldn't picture themselves living as free men. On the other hand, some of them were very serious about finding a way out.

Joe Doc had tried twice to escape from Marion. Besides the truck attempt, there was the night he was one of a dozen prisoners who stormed the fence. Joe and others suffered bullet wounds, but one man got away.

The reason the successful man escaped was he had greater motivation than just his sentence. He believed he had a machine that could remove salt from water, and that the government was screwing him out of the patent, so he escaped to protect his invention. After a couple of weeks, he patented his work though a lawyer, who later came with him when he turned himself in. He was told later by independent professionals that his device didn't work.

I held three jobs in Marion: cellblock orderly, kitchen worker, and working on one of two Linotype machines in the print shop. I think the best time I did was while on the machine. It was time consuming, but it was interesting as well. I would type out and proofread articles for the Federal Prison Bureau's monthly magazine.

Some days there was no violence, and other days it was literally murder. Donny Smith was probably thirty years old, but he looked younger. He was slim, blond-haired, and well-spoken. I'd first met him when his daughter needed an expensive medical treatment and he was canvassing for money to help him pay his bill.

Then he was killed. He was at work in the print shop when he had a visitor.

"Hey, Donny," said a Spanish-speaking P number.

"Yeah?" he answered. He was taking packages of paper off a conveyor belt and he couldn't stop right then. The other man saw it and responded accordingly.

"Come over here when you have a minute to spare," he said. The man stood casually with his hands in front of him, one fist cupped in the hand of the other while he patiently waited.

"Okay," Donny answered. He continued to unload the belt and stack the bundles of federal document papers on a pallet. The machine stopped, Donny walked over to where the man stood, and he never walked away.

When he saw the knife he said, "Oh God, no," and the man began to stab him. Within seconds there were guards grabbing the man's arms and holding him up. Donny's body kicked. The man shook off the hands, leapt on Donny and stabbed him repeatedly until the guards pulled him off again. Donny was dead many times over.

A piece of carbon paper taken from the garbage can by an inquiring mind and carefully read, put Donny as the author of a triplicate document sent to the FBI of conversations he'd overheard. It seemed that Donny had been instrumental in directing police where to focus their attention in a number of cases.

There was an unwritten, but well-understood rule, that any man who informed on an escape plan would get a ticket to freedom. This meant I could be used as a patch. A patch was something one man traded to authorities for special favours. I didn't want to be a sacrificial pawn in somebody else's freedom bid, so I was cautious.

The smallest thing could become serious trouble. When I was the cellblock orderly I developed a small problem over nothing. It was noon on sheet day and I'd just handed out the bed sheets, placing them on the bars of every cell on my side of the block. I was in my cell, and Rick was standing along the wall in front of his cell, when we heard a loud voice complaining from upstairs. I walked out to take a look.

A huge black man who looked like a football lineman was looking down at me.

"Every week I get a sheet with a hole in it," he said. He held a sheet in his hand and shook it at me.

"I don't even look at the sheets when they come in," I said. "I don't know who's getting good and who's getting bad." I figured I could reason with the man; he was acting like a resentful kid. But he didn't sound mean. Rick had his own solution.

"Get yourself eighteen inches of steel, Wayne," he said. "That'll solve this fuckin' problem." I looked to see him standing with his arms crossed over his chest. Rick's face had a fierce look, and he was staring up at the black man. I glanced up in time to catch a look of concern on the lineman's face.

"I'll come up there and we'll talk about it," I said. He nodded his head, turned and walked into his cell. I would have liked to take a knife with me, just in case he had one stashed, but I also had to trust my instincts. However, I did bring a wrapped jar of boiling water with me. It would help me if I needed it, but I didn't because we resolved the problem by talking about it. I saw him many times after that, and on every occasion he was sensible.

One man came to me with some poetry, stating he'd like my opinion on his work. It wasn't much, just a few poems on a few sheets of paper, so I agreed. The words on the page didn't seem to have a pattern; they were jumbled and they didn't make sense to me. When he came back to see me, I tried to be as kind as I could. I told him I was no judge of poetry. He told me about himself.

"I'm a psychiatrist," he said. I looked at him, measuring whether or not he was telling me the truth. It would explain his poetry.

"Are you?" I asked.

"Yes," he said. "I've studied in many hospitals." He looked as if he could be a doctor. There were so many different men in Marion, a psychiatrist wouldn't have surprised me. However, a man in Marion who believes he's a psychiatrist and isn't, is a dangerous man. He was even more dangerous to me because I didn't have insight into how he thought or felt from understanding his poetry. There was a darkness about him, I could feel it each time I talked to him, and whenever I could, I avoided the man.

Four of us were sitting in the dining room after lunch on a hot sultry day, when a man we called Casper walked by. We all said our "hellos."

"Do you know Casper?" Joe asked, as Casper left the room.

"I've met him," I answered.

"Why do you think we call him Casper?" he asked.

"Probably because he's so pale, and he's friendly," I said. They all laughed.

"No," said Joe, "we call him that because he's killed many men in the federal system. When he goes to kill somebody, he cuts eye-holes out of a white pillowcase, puts it over his head, and does what he came to do."

Every so often I'd get visits from friends from Canada and from Vermont, and though I was glad to have the company, we lived in different worlds. One day though, our worlds almost joined. I was standing by the flower gardens, waving goodbye to my visitor in the parking lot, when a man I knew well walked over. He stood looking at the woman, then looked at me. After the car disappeared, he asked if I wanted to go for a walk around the yard.

We were halfway around the track before my companion got to the point.

"Can your visitor rent a car?" he asked.

"Why?" I asked.

"You can have a seat on a bus out of Marion, only if she can rent a car," he answered.

"I have to know more than that. I can't see any way out of here without violence," I said.

"No violence," he said. "All I can tell you is it has something to do with a black box."

"Black box?"

"Yeah, that's it. That's all I know, but these guys are serious. If we say there's a car there, and there's not one when we get there, they'll just leave us behind," he said.

The next day I asked my visitor if she could rent a car. She said she'd check it out. She was back in an hour to tell me she wouldn't be able to because the last car she'd rented had damage done to the back seats and they were still after her to pay for the damages.

After my visit, I explained to my friend that I wouldn't be able to get a car, which meant
I'd lost my seat on the bus. Before long we all knew the secret of the black box.

Carmine, John, Mario and I were watching television when we heard the sound of rapid gunfire from the front tower guard. We looked out the window, but it was dark and we couldn't see anyhing. Then came the sound of spaced shots from a high-powered rifle, which gave me the impression a guard was taking deliberate aim and squeezing off shots at his targets.

"What do you think, Junior?" I asked.

"Somebody made a break," he replied. He was standing at the window, looking toward the front of the prison. Less than a minute later, a lockdown was called. We knew we wouldn't know until the next day what exactly had happened.

A year before I arrived there'd been a Canadian serving his time in Marion. He was a journeyman electronic technician, he worked in the electronics shop, and he was given the task of rewiring some of the control panels. His supervisor apparently underestimated his ability—consequently he was able to add a couple of extra circuits in the master control panel. His work set up a brilliant escape.

The gates were all electronic. Some were operated by a control centre in the main hallway. Even if the security bubble was overrun and prisoners managed to get inside at the control panels, they wouldn't be able to open the last three gates which led to freedom through the front.

What the Canadian had done was plant a small, compact receiver in the wiring of the master control panel, which meant the last three gates could be opened by remote control. Not only did the Canadian build and insert the receiver, he'd also built a transmitter to trigger the gates when the time was right. Rumour had it that he'd insisted Ed Roach, the man with whom he'd left the plan, give his word he wouldn't use the device until one full year after his release. Ed gave his word and he kept it. A year after the Canadian was released, the "black box" was brought out of mothballs.

There was an Historical Society meeting in the visiting room that night, which put the members of the society directly in front of the last three gates. The men involved tied up the guard in the room, and while the teacher stood teaching at the front of the class, they stepped out of the room and into the hallway. Ed hit the button on the transmitter.

The gates began to slowly open and the guard in the master control room saw it on his monitors. He immediately hit the close button on the panel, which triggered an electronic field, and another of the extra circuit boards cut in and threw out the vertical sync on the control panel's monitors. The guard couldn't see what was happening, so he released the close button. The electronic field that had been building, suddenly collapsed, generating such a surge of power that the last three gates opened so violently it took a couple of men with crowbars to close them.

Ed Roach, Mike "Mad Dog" Garganno, Tim, Maurice, and Chops were running across the field in front of the prison. The shots we'd heard were fired at them by the guard as he stood atop the front tower. By the time the guards understood what had happened, it was too late. The men had run off and slipped away into the woods.

I doubt if there ever was a manhunt quite like the one that followed. Ed was serving thirty years for bank robberies and he was a member of a socialist group who didn't believe in the American way. Mike "Mad Dog" Garganno got his nick name from the Chicago Tribune, because he and his partners had used so much firepower in robbing a bank that the police had to retreat. Men were killed and Mike was shot many times, but he managed to get away, only to be found slowly bleeding to death in a bedroom in a small rooming house two days later. He was sentenced to ninety-nine years. Maurice escaped because he happened to be at the meeting. Tim was doing a double life sentence for killing two FBI agents, and Chops had a hold on him from a northern state.

This was probably the most sophisticated escape ever to have taken place in federal prison history, and the feds reacted accordingly. They sped up the freight trains running through the area to make it more difficult for the hunted men to catch a ride. There were marksmen on every overpass on the highways peering through their scopes into the moving cars, hoping for a glimpse of the fugitives. As an extra precautionary measure, all the families for a twenty-five mile radius were evacuated from their homes until further notice.

We were watching television when the station cut away from regular programming to show a freight train surrounded by armed men backed by helicopters. They believed one of the escapees was in one of the empty boxcars. When they dug the man out, he turned out to be a Mexican who'd crossed the border illegally and was on his way to Chicago. I couldn't help but wonder what he thought as he saw all of the firepower pointed at him.

Within days four of them were captured. Chops was the only man who managed to make it into Chicago, and finally into Canada, where he was arrested in

Winnipeg for an armed robbery. The other men didn't really know how to survive. At one point in a newscast a man-tracker suggested the water in the creeks running through the area was as clean as one could possibly find anywhere, and he found it strange that both Ed and Maurice were arrested after knocking on farmer's doors, asking for water. Tim was arrested after he crashed a stolen car into a ditch. Mike was arrested walking down the railway track in Indiana, over a hundred miles away. I never knew what happened to Chops until I ran into him in Prince Albert Penitentiary some time later.

Joe Doc had come up with an escape plan of his own. It wasn't a sophisticated plan, it was one of desperation. There were three men involved and I was asked if I wanted to go, but I said "no." There was a letter writing campaign underway to have me sent back to Canada, and I believed it would work. I felt sorry for Joe and the other two men; I knew they weren't going to make it, yet I knew they had to try.

They were arrested in the laundry room, where they were trapped when they couldn't make a large enough hole in the window to get into the yard. If they'd managed to do that, they were going to use a homemade rope to lasso the light fixture on the other side of the fence, which was curved to hang over and illuminate the area between the two perimeter fences. Once the rope was attached to the top of the light pole, they figured they could use it not only to climb the first fence, but to swing across the distance between the two fences, make it over the second one, and run into the woods a hundred yards away. After the press learned of the attempt, the warden publicly stated the prison had foiled another escape, and that the prisoners had planned to use "a Rube Goldberg type of device." I never saw Joe again.

On January 27, 1976 I was called to Admitting and Discharge and told to have my property packed in an hour. I was being transferred to the New York Metropolitan Correctional Centre. When I asked what was up, they said they didn't know. But I did. They were dumping me across the border into the hands of the Canadian authorities. I made a point of saying "goodbye" to the people I knew, one of whom was Carmine. He asked me to give Angelo a message—Angelo had been sent to New York weeks earlier to stand trial for conspiracy to traffic in heroin. Carmine told me he was worried he hadn't heard from his brother for some time, and he wanted Angelo to phone him. I told him I would.

The bus trip out was similar to the one in, but one of the prisons I was held over in was Lewisburg. I was placed on the yard side of the hole, which meant my window overlooked the cellblock where Bill lived. It didn't take me long to get someone's attention and in a few minutes Bill was at the cellblock window. He brought me up to date with what had been happening to people we knew. Tom Mullins was "living in a hotel," which was the mobsters' way of saying he'd turned over and was now living with the feds.

The Metropolitan Correctional Centre in New York was at least nine floors high and I was placed on a floor where one of the first men I saw was Angelo. I gave him his message and he immediately went to the phone and made his call.

Angelo took me around and introduced me to his friends. He also introduced me to one of the guards who couldn't do enough for me in regard to supplies. Angelo pointed out that the guard used to be a real asshole, giving everyone a very bad time. But that had changed after four men met him in the parking lot and beat him so badly he was hospitalized for weeks. Following his stay in the hospital, he was a different man. I later learned that Angelo was one of John Gotti's very close friends.

On January 30, I was picked up by Vermont prison guards and driven to the border, where I was handed over to a couple of Edmonton City Detectives. They arrested me for a bank robbery, drove me to the airport in Montréal and we all boarded a flight for Edmonton. It felt great to be home, and even though I had a couple of bank robberies to answer for, I knew I was going to be all right.

Fort Saskatchewan, the provincial jail just outside of Edmonton, was undergoing renovations to security. I was placed in the hole on a range with other high-security risks, one of whom was Ronnie Westadt. I'd first met Ronnie in Prince Albert penitentiary in 1960, and we were always friends. He was being held for transfer back to Wilkinson Road in British Columbia, to stand trial for safecracking and escape charges. Also in the hole was Sammy Wood, another Ronnie, and Merle. We were all looking for a way to break out; however, nothing seemed workable until the lower range of B Block had been made secure.

Ronnie Westadt and Ronnie and I were placed on a range where a great deal of money had been spent on high-security windows. The windows would be difficult to cut; they were made of cement and steel. Even if I managed to cut through the steel, I'd still have to somehow remove the cement inside the steel casing. It looked rather hopeless. Then I noticed the cell on the far end of the range had no occupant, and a closer look told me why. It appeared to have an extra door leading somewhere else.

There was a tunnel running from the main jail to the women's jail, or Cat House as we called it, and the extra door in the unoccupied cell led to the tunnel. I'd noticed that the construction workers left the courtyard gates open all night, which told me there were other gates out of our sight which were left open as well. It made sense that they felt security wouldn't be compromised, because all prisoners were kept out of the construction area. Besides, if they had had to wait for keys to go through gates and doors, it would've taken the work crew much longer to do their job. The women had been moved out of the jail next door, so if we could get into the tunnel, there was a very good chance we could find our way out through an open door on the other side.

Ronnie Westadt was all for the plan. Though the other Ronnie was on a first-degree murder charge, as well as possession of stolen property, he was more hesitant. I think most men have a hard time believing an escape could be so simple and effortless. But I had some secret information which would unlock the first door leading to the tunnel, and it would only take a hacksaw blade to cut through the bars of the second door leading into the tunnel itself.

We put the word out to our friends that we needed a hacksaw blade. As good luck would have it, there was a blade kicking around on an upper floor of Cellblock B. Within hours it was in our hands.

I used the saw to cut off a flat piece of steel from one of the bunk beds, and used it to make a holder for the blade. Without the holder there was a real chance the blade would break while cutting the steel bars. The tool to open the second door was in place and I went about making a key to open the first door.

Folger Adams keys and locks are built on a set of mathematical principles and, once a man knows the system, it's a simple matter to first read the keys and then make one. I cut a piece of plastic off the rim of a plastic garbage can, which was the perfect thickness for the key. It took me an hour to make the first one, but it didn't work. There was a glitch in the numbers. I was missing something.

Donny was in the Fort, living on an upper range while he served some remand time, and when he came to the front of our range to cut a man's hair, I read off seven numbers and asked him if he knew if that phone number was still good.

"Who's number is that?" he asked.

"It's a number of an old friend of ours," I replied. "I think her name is Adams."

"Adams?" he asked. He looked over at me and I winked.

"Yeah, Folger something-or-other-Adams," I answered.

"Oh! Yeah, let me think," he said.

"424-1-424," I said.

"No, I remember that number now," he said, "it's 424-0-424." I knew he was right. The way the locking mechanism turned, there was only one small sticking point.

I thanked him and walked into my cell and cut out a sixteenth of an inch of plastic. A few minutes later I placed my homemade key in the lock and the mechanism turned over with a loud clunk.

I'd been checking out the key for a couple of days and the men on the range would shake their heads and suggest a key couldn't be made. There were too many combinations, they said. When they heard the locking mechanism turn over, some prisoners became nervous—especially those men charged with sex crimes, or those identified as stool pigeons. A door key in the hands of a prisoner meant they no longer had a haven from their enemies. I knew we'd have to make our move quickly before one of them acted on their fear and informed.

We decided we'd make our getaway during the late movie on Saturday night. The soundtrack would cover the sound of a hacksaw sawing through the cold-rolled steel of the bars of the second door.

Carol had returned from up north on Friday evening and she came to see me during visiting hours Saturday afternoon. After we said our "hellos" I came right to the point.

"Tonight," I said.

"Tonight?" she replied, with some surprise.

"Yes, tonight," I said. Carol had been in touch with a high-priced, well-known lawyer from Calgary who'd agreed to take my case, but I had other plans. She cupped her face in her hands for a moment, but when she looked up at me I could see she understood and accepted that this escape was going to happen.

"What can I do?" she asked. I told her to check into a specific hotel in Edmonton as soon as she left the visiting room, and to wait for my call after midnight.

"I'll phone you around two in the morning," I said.

"Okay Wayne," she agreed. We discussed placing a car on a street beside the jail, but she wasn't certain if she could rent one. However, I knew Carol had kept some very good pieces of identification, including Alberta driver's licences, which we could use as soon as we could put pictures on them. Everything was in place. Now we only needed to get through the doors and into the tunnel.

That night we were released from our cells to watch the movie, and as soon as the doors opened I was at the end of the range, standing by the cell door with the key in my hand. It worked perfectly. The mechanism in the door turned over with a loud clunk, I pulled, and the door came open.

I wouldn't allow anyone else to use the hacksaw. I'd seen too many men break blades through carelessness or inexperience. By the time I'd sawn my way through two bars my arms were tired, but the hole was there.

At the far end of the tunnel was another door just like the one we'd come through, so I began sawing through those bars as well. Suddenly there was noise in the tunnel behind us which seemed to continue for some time. Finally I decided I'd walk back and see what the sound was.

A kid named Frank was trying to get through the first hole, and he was having considerable trouble doing so. I was angry with the man who was supposed to have closed the first door behind us. I questioned the kid's unwanted participation angrily.

"What the fuck are you doing?" I asked. He looked at me, sheepishly.

"Trying to break out," he said. So I helped him through the hole and into the tunnel, and together we ran to where both Ronnies were waiting for us.

I continued to cut through the bars and soon we had our hole. Westadt and I pushed Ronnie through the opening, and he ran around the corner to check out the inside of the building. Moments later, by the light of a bare light bulb in the ceiling, we saw him come running back.

"We're out!" he said. It was tough for Ron and I to get through the hole. We were bigger and heavier than Ronnie, but we managed, then we helped Frank get through.

One whole wall of the Cat House had been torn out and was only covered with a tarpaulin. As I drew it aside, it opened like a curtain. Before me was the snow-covered yard, and the street beyond.

We would have to quickly get a car and disappear into the city of Edmonton, but every car we tried was locked. We ran down an alley and we watched as a car turned into its far end, then pulled into a parking lot behind a small walk-up apartment building. Seconds later I was close enough to be seen and heard by the driver.

He looked young, and he carried an armful of clothes on hangers, as if he'd just picked up his dry cleaning. He had a bundle of keys in his hand and he was about to open the back door of the building.

"Hey you!" I yelled. I kept moving toward him.

"Who? Me?" he asked. He stopped fumbling with his keys and stood there, watching me as I walked up to him.

"Is that your car?" I asked, pointing at it.

"Yeah, why?" I was standing in front of him now. I could hear the Ronnies and Frank behind me.

"Are those your car keys too?" I asked.

"Yeah," he said.

"You'll have to come with us," I said. I reached out my hand and took the keys from him.

"Okay," he said. We all walked to the car. I gave the keys to Ronnie, because he knew the area, and I told him to drive.

I rode in front and our new companion was squeezed between Westadt and Frank, his dry cleaning on his lap. We were on our way to Edmonton and in minutes we'd be in the heart of downtown.

As Ronnie drove, he kept suggesting we "dump" the owner of the car, but the man in the back seat didn't understand him because he was using a form of pig Latin. The last thing I wanted to do was hurt the man, let alone kill him and dump him in the ditch or the trunk of his own car.

"You guys just escaped didn't you?" he asked. I looked over my shoulder at a man no more than twenty, and he seemed very naive.

"Yeah, we did," I said.

"You don't have to worry. You'll only get a couple of months for it," he said.

"That's all?" I asked.

"Yeah. I was in court a couple of weeks ago for a ticket and two guys got two months for escaping, that's all," he said. His voice was full of sincerity and I liked him. He had no idea of how much danger he was in at that moment.

"That's good to know," I replied.

"How long are you going to have my car? I just bought this car three weeks ago."

"Do you have somewhere to go in Edmonton?" I asked.

"Sure, a friend of mine lives there," he answered.

"Do you know his phone number?"

"Yeah," he said, and he gave it.

"Ronnie, you remember the number. I will too," I said. Ronnie nodded his head.

"When will you call me?" asked our friend.

"An hour after we drop you off," I said.

"No, that's too early. My friend's wife will be pissed off if it wakes the baby," he said.

"How about tomorrow then?"

"Tomorrow morning?" he asked.

"Tomorrow morning it is," I assured him.

We drove through downtown, stopping once so I could make a phone call. I suggested to the kid in the back that he phone his friend to give him the address where we were going to drop him off, which he did, and in a minute we were both back in the car.

We dropped the kid off and we went to a pre-arranged address that Carol had set up. An hour later I was sitting on the floor, my back to a table, getting my picture taken for my driver's licence. We didn't know what to do with Frank.

"Have you got somewhere you can go?" I asked him.

"Vancouver," he answered. "I have a buddy in Vancouver."

"Why don't you give him a call?" I suggested. He called and talked to his friend who agreed to put him up at his place, if he could get out there.

We gave him a hundred dollars and a change of clothes, and when Ronnie Westadt left us to go to a friend's, he took Frank with him and dropped him off close to the bus depot. We never saw him again.

We stayed where we were for the rest of the night, and early next morning Carol rented a motel room for herself. She wore a blond wig in case police knew she was associated with me. After the three of us made ourselves at home, I phoned Ronnie to give him our phone number.

"What about the car?" he asked.

"What about the car?"

"Should I phone the kid?"

"Sure, phone him. Are you a long way from it?"

"Yeah, a long way," he replied.

"Remember the number?"

"Oh yes."

"Then do it. He may not've called the police," I said.

"Could be," replied Ron.

We stayed in the motel for less than a day, and that evening we caught a ride with a friend with a van. Carol rented an expensive apartment for a week. I phoned Ron to tell him where we were, and when he arrived, we sat back letting the heat die down.

The newspapers and television news were full of our pictures and histories, and there was much speculation by police on what we were going to do. Some suggested we were going to hit a gun store, then a bank, before we left town. Others suggested we had serious underworld ties and would undoubtedly hook up with them.

One night I was watching the late news when the newscaster said there would be a special on the jailbreak right after the news. We were all sitting there when it came on. The special was an editorial, and an interview with the kid we'd hijacked. The camera was set up so we had a full view of him.

"Tell us what happened to you," said the female interviewer. He relayed the event very well, and he spoke of it matter-of-factly.

"Weren't you afraid?" she asked.

"No, not really. But the Ronnie guy—well I didn't like him," he said.

"Was there a leader?"

"Yeah, the Wayne guy—he was okay."

"But they took your car," she reminded him.

"Yeah, they also told me they'd tell me where it was, and they did."

"They called you?"

"Yeah, they said they'd call me, and they did. I told the police where it was and they won't give it back," he said, with frustration and anger in his voice.

Soon after the interview we watched another newscast on the Edmonton news, which indicated we were now believed to be in British Columbia. This was based on the fact that they'd found Frank's body propped up in an underground parking lot in Vancouver. I knew the anger I'd expressed at Frank when he was trying to get through the first door during our escape would have been relayed to the police. Some would believe we had motive to kill him and dump his body. I made a point of keeping receipts which would put us in Edmonton at the time of his death. Years later I learned that Frank had made it to his friend's place in Vancouver, and had overdosed on methadone. Frank's friend, a man named Doug Martin, was profiled years later on CBC's investigative news program called *The Fifth Estate*, as the man responsible for perjuring many men into life sentences. He had dumped Frank's body in a parking lot.

The two Ronnies decided they would leave Carol and me and hook up with us later. But the next day they were arrested in Calgary when Ronnie tried to meet with his wife. Carol and I rented a small walk-up apartment and we stayed there for a month.

We had a choice of going east or going west. I chose west because Bobby was already in Vancouver and I believed we'd have some support from him and his wife. We took the bus, catching a cab to the outskirts of Edmonton, and buying our ticket to New Westminster from there.

After we met with Bobby and Nora, the four of us were arrested by the RCMP at Bobby's apartment building and flown back to Edmonton. I was taken to Fort Saskatchewan jail and placed in the hole. I'd always believed I could run off into the night, make a life for myself like Jean Valjean or the Count of Monte Cristo, and never be heard from again. At this moment I had doubts whether I would ever be able to do it.

A few days after returning to Edmonton I was taken to court and faced a variety of charges stemming from the escape. I was also charged with an old bank robbery.

My lawyer sent me a letter stating the Crown had offered a deal where I would receive no more than six years for all charges, if I would plead guilty. Part of the agreement was that the charge of aiding and abetting against Carol would be dropped. I decided to take it. The Crown reneged.

I was sentenced to ten-and-a-half years for the old bank robbery charge and the charges stemming from the escape, which was four years more than agreed upon. However, the charges against Carol were dismissed.

My sister Jane came to visit me. It was the first time I'd seen her for years, and she brought her two sons, Jeff and Cory with her. We talked for hours about our family, and from that point on she visited regularly. I was always grateful to her for allowing me to have a relationship with my nephews. If not for her ongoing support I doubt whether I would've been able to reconcile with my family.

Sammy Wood was a man already in the hole for a previous escape from Fort Saskatchewan and we become instant friends.

Sammy and I lay on our backs in our individual tombs, separated by eight inches of cinder block wall, staring through the bars to the images inside our own heads. Though the distance between us was only eight inches, the cinder block wall made that distance wide indeed.

The hard concrete floor was our bed and our pillows were a roll of toilet paper, which, when the roll was properly placed, kept the cold of the floor from penetrating into the muscles of our necks.

"Are you awake?" Sammy asked. His voice was hushed, and quiet enough to ensure that if I was sleeping he wouldn't have disturbed me.

"Yeah, I'm awake," I said.

"I was just thinking of Christmas," Sammy said. His voice was pensive, as if he was thinking of better places to be. It was eleven o'clock at night.

"What about it?" I asked.

"Some people celebrate Christmas on the 24th, but to me Christmas is when you open your presents," Sammy declared.

"When I was a kid Christmas Eve was when we opened our presents, so I feel Christmas is then," I replied. We fell into a comfortable silence; we weren't going anywhere and we had all night and more to finish our conversation. Minutes passed. There was a sound from the floor above, a thump on the ceiling muted by a foot of rebarred concrete, but loud enough to be heard.

"Maybe that's Santa Claus coming early," said Sammy.

"Santa Claus?"

"Yeah, Santa. Santa's a good guy." The tone of his voice suggested there were not many good guys.

"My mother didn't believe in lying to us kids. She told us there was no such person as Santa Claus," I said. Even to me, my voice sounded cold, distant, and rational.

"*What?*" There was a jolt of shock, of incredulous disbelief in the question. It brought forth an image of Sammy sitting bolt upright on his floor.

"Yeah, she believed it spoiled the kids to lie to them."

"Oh no," said Sammy, calmer now. "That's not true."

"No?"

"Hell no! The story of Santa is really the beautiful story of Christmas."

"How so?"

"Well, here's this kind, friendly, jolly old man who travels in a sleigh pulled by reindeer, and he knows the hearts of kids. And if they've been good—and what kid can be really bad— they can ask for those things that they've always wished for in their hearts." Sammy's voice had become that of a soft-spoken storyteller. "Was your mother a cruel woman?"

"No," I declared defensively, "she wasn't cruel. She just didn't believe that Santa should get the credit for something the parents did."

"There's no credit to be given," declared Sammy. "Christmas presents for kids are for the kids, they're not to be given so that someone gets credit for giving them. Santa just gives with no thought to getting credit."

"It was kind of funny, now that I think about it," I said.

"Funny?"

"Yeah. Funny. There was this kid, Danny, who thought he saw Santa Claus flying over the skating rink. We were the same age—he was a believer but I wasn't. He told me he'd actually seen him land on the roof of the rink. He said he thought Santa was resting his reindeer."

"Oh yeah, kids want to believe."

"Well I guess I did too, and he was very, very convincing, and his excitement was contagious. We both went outside to look. I believed if Santa had paused to rest on the roof for a moment, we'd be able to see the tracks."

"And?"

"No tracks." We laughed quietly. The conversation was put on hold for a moment while the guard jingled and jangled past our cells on his rounds. A moment later Sammy broke the silence and summed up our situation in a heartbeat.

"Know what would make my next Christmas perfect for me?" he asked.

"What?" I asked.

"If I could just get up from this floor, walk outside, and look for the tracks of Santa's sleigh on the roof of a skating rink."

"Yes," I said, "that would be a good Christmas for me too. Maybe we can do that next year."

"Yeah, next year..." We both fell silent, and a fitful sleep soon followed.

At one time Sammy had been a ski bum living in Banff and enjoying the mountains, but that changed when he was handed a two-year penitentiary sentence for trafficking in marijuana. He'd been sitting in a bar when a good looking woman sat at a table next to his. One thing led to another and he spent two days with her, enjoying every minute of it. Then she asked him if he could find her some weed to take back home to Edmonton with her. Sammy bought her an ounce of BC bud and hours later he was arrested for trafficking in narcotics. She was an undercover cop.

Sammy served his sentence in Drumheller and when he was released, he worked in Calgary for a time. However, when the police kicked his doors in, he decided he'd enough. He bought himself ten pounds of salt and a carton of .22 rifle bullets and packed a few pounds of tobacco in a backpack and headed into the mountains.

He lived off the land, stopping at abandoned cabins for a few days at a time, and three months later he'd walked through the mountains to Jasper. He robbed a bank in Edmonton and when people followed him to an apartment, it all ended in a shootout and an eight hour standoff with police. He received a sentence of fifteen years on a plea bargain, but after making the deal the Crown reneged and his sentence was increased to life imprisonment.

Sammy and I tried to escape from the hole on two occasions, both of which involved cutting the window bars in the hallway in front of our cells. We had a system set up where we could work right under the range camera without being discovered.

I'd cut out one of the bars from my cell door, which allowed me to come and go as I pleased. We were allowed out, one at a time, to exercise in the hallway, and when Sammy was out of his cell, he'd stand in front of his cell and shake a blanket. This would block the camera and allow me to come out of my cell and help him cut the window bars—it was too much work for one man—it required another set of hands to pull out and hold the heavy wire screen covering the windows from the inside. We'd almost made it when we were discovered. When our cells were searched, one of the guards slammed my door so hard that the cut bar fell out and hit the floor with a resounding clang. I'd jammed the bar into place using toothpaste and bits of tape we'd scrounged up—it wasn't enough to hold it for long, but it looked good.

They moved us over to the other side of the hole, and into the death cells. The next day we were charged with prison break, which carries a penalty of ten years imprisonment. But we weren't done yet.

I made a key which would open our doors whenever we wanted them open. One of us would stand in front of the camera lens reading a newspaper, while the other worked on the window bars of the death cell side. It worked well, but again we were discovered and we now had two charges of prison break.

The security people in Fort Saskatchewan were so concerned about us that they took us to court, stayed the charges and sent me to Prince Albert Penitentiary.

Prince Albert had changed a great deal, and there were a number of reasons for it. The most important of which was the idea that protective custody prisoners—that is, informers and sex criminals—needed a separate prison in which to serve their sentences. This meant more prisons would have to built. What's more, it appeared to many of us that the prison administration was encouraging men to request protection status, and not deal with their problems. Adding to the problem was the new policy of not having guards in the gym during night exercise. For over four hours each night, seven days a week, we prisoners were allowed to do as we pleased.

We had dice games, poker games, roulette wheels, and even a mouse game where a mouse ran on a roulette-like wheel with a number of different coloured holes drilled in it, and a prisoner could bet on what hole the mouse would run into. The mouse had to be frequently replaced because it would be run into exhaustion.

There were prisoners who could not meet their gambling debts so they just "checked in," which is what prisoners called the act of turning to the administrators for help. Within months the prison was split down the middle, with a population side and the protective custody side, which we called PC. Over a period of a year the numbers of prisoners in protective custody grew to far outnumber those of us in the regular population. In a short time there was indeed a reason for another prison to be built. While this was taking place around me, I began to take a serious look at my lack of a future.

I enrolled in a new electronics program. At the same time, I was taking university classes and the professors were quite impressed with my writing. But I looked at a trade as something that would provide employment, whereas writing was just something I did to pass the time. One of the effects of taking programs in prison is that it took me out of the daily action. And the action in Prince Albert was deadly.

Along with the new, general internal security changes, came frequent transfers in and out of the penitentiary. This meant there were always new faces and new attitudes, and there were determined men who settled old scores by stabbing, piping, and murder.

I studied regularly, played tennis almost daily, and of course there was poker to add some excitement to my life. The time slowly passed and in 1978 I became eligible for parole again. This time I was granted day parole to attend Saskatchewan Technical Institute. Not only did I attempt to live a straight life, I attempted to put my experiences so far behind me that I'd forget they ever happened. It was an impossible task. I learned if one doesn't talk about his experiences, they weigh heavily on his mind. Strangely, trying to live such a life was like trying to live as if I was still on the run, still without any real emotional attachments, and still without a life. Yes, I went camping and I skied, and I socialized with people who had no idea of my history, but it was an empty life, devoid of any lasting meaning.

On one occasion I went camping up north, and we were almost out of the city when I decided to pull into a store to buy a fishing licence. I'd left it to the last minute because the store was on route. I searched for a parking place, found one, and was maneuvering the car into position when Christy interrupted.

"What are you doing?"

"I'm going to pick up our licence," I answered.

"We don't have to do that here," she stated. "Patricia told me not to worry about them. There's a licence store right on the lake."

I could have simply parked the car, walked the short distance to the store and paid the ten dollars according to law, but I didn't.

"Okay," I said, "we'll buy them up north." I pulled into the through-lane and left the city.

When we arrived on the shore of a lake situated in the heart of the north, two hours north of Prince Albert, it was an hour from dusk.

I decided I'd drive over to the small supply store and pick up the fishing licences, so while Christy caught up on family news with Pat, and because John appeared occupied with the camper's plumbing, I drove over alone.

I pulled to a stop in front of the cabin-like storefront, got out of the car and walked to the door. It was locked. Then I noticed a piece of brown paper bag taped to the inside of the window. It was a hand-written sign proclaiming the store closed until seven next morning. I quickly shrugged off my disappointment and slowly drove back to the campsite.

When I returned, a fire had been lit and my friends were sitting around the open flames quietly talking. They looked at me as I approached and I saw the question on their faces.

"Closed," I said, "until tomorrow morning at seven." I saw the look on Patricia's face and I anticipated her response before she voiced it.

"Are you paranoid?" she asked.

"Not really," I replied. "I just like to cover my ass when it comes to the law." Patricia poked at the fire with a twig and watched a flurry of sparks rise like orange fireflies in the still evening air.

"Never in the history of this lake have we seen a game warden up here," she stated, confidently, with a hint of rebuke in her tone. I felt somewhat mollified by her outward display of confidence.

"Never in the history of the lake?"

"Never," all three of them chorused.

"Okay," I said, "I'm in the boat at the crack of dawn." I didn't tell them I felt one could never count on history, nor did I say my experience was that when one was in for a penny, one was in for a pound, and sometimes a penny's worth of trouble could escalate into a pound or more worth of pain.

The next morning we manoeuvred into the center of the inlet and began to cast our hooks in different directions. In a matter of thirty minutes we'd caught a dozen pike and pickerel which we hung over the side of the boat on a chain to keep them fresh. I leaned back in the canoe, and as I felt more than heard the light slap of the waves against the side of the boat, I experienced a sense of peace I had not felt in many years. But then came two things, one behind the other, but so close together they almost simultaneously broke my reverie.

The first was a strike of a fish on my line, and the second was the sound of a powerboat coming to life with an authoritarian growl across the lake, a growl which quickly rose into the high-pitched whine of a speed boat racing across the water at full throttle. The aggressive sound brought a rush of adrenalin to my body. I glanced up to see a boat spearheading through the water like a torpedo on a direct path toward our helpless canoe. *If that's not the law,* I thought, *there's not a steer in Texas.* History's about to be changed. I felt the cold chill of the past once again come to visit me, like an unwelcome guest that shows up at the most inopportune time and cannot be turned away. I felt the warmth of the day, along with my quiet and peaceful feeling, run like a school of fish from the shadow of a shark. I unceremoniously netted my fish and pulled it into the canoe.

As the boat continued its direct course toward us, John's assurance seemed to lessen, and almost as an afterthought, he turned to Christy and said, "My licence is in the tackle box, along with Pat's." Christy reached for the box, opened it, and began to carefully sort through the hooks and paraphernalia for the papers.

"I guess that makes me the dead man," I said.

"It'll only be a small fine," murmured John with what I'm sure he thought was a consoling tone. I bit my tongue. For a moment I actually thought of going over the side in a splash, swimming the scant hundred yards to the shore, and simply disappearing into the protection and safety of the forest which covered three provinces like a green blanket. Such an act would not be in keeping with good common sense, but then I was a man with the acquired gift of uncommon sense, taught by harsh experience. I reached to my shirt pocket for a cigarette.

The green powerboat was only yards away and I could see the brown-uni-formed figure looking directly at me. I glanced at John, and though I wanted to say something about his history of the lake, I bit the proverbial bullet along with my tongue.

The young game warden expertly manoeuvred his craft until he was along-side our red canoe, and when he was close enough he reached out and pulled it snugly alongside his.

"Do you have a fishing licence?" he asked. He directed his question to me. The man had a healthy tan and was no more than twenty-two years old. John and Christy both were quick to interrupt with assurances that *they* did, and each held up their paperwork in their hands. The game warden gave them a cursory glance then once again turned his gaze on me.

"No," I replied, "I don't." I was aware of the pike and pickerel on the chain in the water, evidence directly linking me to the fish. On hearing my admittance of guilt the warden snatched the rod and reel from my hand.

"I'll have to confiscate this," he said. It surprised me.

"It's not mine," I protested, "I just borrowed it." Which I had.

"I'll have to hold it for evidence."

"I'll plead guilty to the charge," I assured him, and I went on to explain that I'd tried unsuccessfully to buy a licence at the store the night before. I further assured the game warden that I would buy one as soon as we went ashore. The warden hesitated for a moment.

"You'll plead guilty?" he asked.

"Guaranteed," I answered, then added, "How much is the fine?"

"Forty dollars."

"I'll pay it, no question. You have my word."

The warden handed me the rod and reel, then took down my name and address and handed me the ticket. Christy and John were studiously ignoring both the law and the lawbreaker, and I had the impression if the warden asked them if they knew me, they would express surprise that I was even in their canoe, as if an eagle had just dropped me from the sky into their boat.

Later that evening we were sitting around the campfire talking. "What scares you?" asked Patricia. I was a little surprised by her question, but I attempted to answer her as best I could. She was sitting with her back against a tall pine, her legs stretched in front of her. John was at her side.

"I would have to say the law scares me."

"Like game wardens?" asked Christy. They laughed.

"Yes," I agreed seriously, "game wardens too."

"How does a small fine hurt you?" asked Pat.

"It's not the money, it's the possibility that something can escalate."

"Escalate?" asked John. I decided to tell them something I'd once read.

"Well Alfred Hitchcock was asked that question, and though he was involved as a producer in many scary movies, he said he was afraid of the law," I replied.

"Did he say why?" asked Christy, turning her head now to look at me curiously.

"Yes, he did," I replied, "Hitchcock said he knew a man who had left his car parked on the street and the meter had run out. Just as he returned, he discovered a policeman writing him a ticket. The man thought he didn't deserve one and protested, but the traffic cop was deaf to his pleas. When the cop handed him the ticket, which was for two dollars, the man punched him in the mouth. More cops came. The man was arrested and charged with assault, and he was sentenced to six months in jail.

"While he was in jail doing his time, a prisoner came at him with a knife. He managed to get the knife away from his attacker, but stabbed him in the process. The attacker died and the man was charged with murder, convicted, and sentenced to death.

"As the man was being taken to the execution chamber one of the escorting guards asked him a question. 'If you could live your life over, what would you do differently?' he asked. 'I'd pay that two dollar parking ticket,' the man said." I told them that I felt the same way; the smallest things can escalate into horrific things.

"It was the man's own fault," declared Patricia, and the other two agreed. I'd heard many prison guards voice something similar: "You should've thought of that before." I didn't add anything further and just let the story stand.

I was having trouble adjusting to my new life, particularly when my past was kept as a closely watched secret. To add to the general stress and strain, I'd often spot someone tailing me. At first I thought it was just my imagination playing tricks on me, but Christy became frightened when she realized she was being followed when she drove my Cordoba from her school. It was very disconcerting, particularly when I couldn't freely discuss my past. Was it an old enemy ? I later learned I was being watched by police.

Colin Thatcher was in the news, and after his wife was shot through the window of her home, the police were looking for a hired gun. An eyewitness put the gunman in a green Cordoba. I drove a white Cordoba, which, because eyewitness evidence is notoriously unreliable, was close enough to make me a suspect.

In 1982 I was arrested for an impaired driving charge, my parole was revoked, and I was sent to Stony Mountain Penitentiary in Manitoba.

Stony Mountain sits atop a hill, just off the highway, twenty miles west of the heart of downtown Winnipeg. It has the appearance of an old, battle-scarred castle. I was processed and placed in a cell on a range in the recidivist block.

The recidivist block consisted of two ranges holding approximately thirty men who'd already served a sentence in the penitentiary system and were now back in it; it was Correctional Services of Canada's way of handling seasoned veterans. It was also the way it chose to keep men in a semi-lockdown situation while it decided where it was going to send them to serve their sentences. The men the administration didn't want in the institution were usually written up for placement in a higher security facility.

The man I walked through the gates with that day was destined for Québec. He'd just received twenty-five years to life for killing a woman with a shotgun in the back of a car in Regina; he was considered dangerous, a risk to escape, and he was Native. There's always some degree of racial tension in the pen, and a high-profile Native generates more than a little concern. However, in this case it was overkill to send him off to Québec, as he'd never caused any problems in the system, and he was not really an escape risk. However, the police and prison system were all concerned about how a man would handle the psychological reality of a twenty-five to life bit, and in the RCMP bucket I saw the strain on the faces of authority as they put the shackles on his feet. It was as though he'd just been sentenced to death, and in way that was the sentence he was under. Life as he'd once known it was over.

I knew at least half of the men in the recidivist block, where more than a few were Natives, and because I was not a racist and had maintained good relationships with all of them through the years, I was quickly assimilated into their midst. But unlike them, the thought of escaping was always in the back of my mind. I was still in shock at being back inside and I was feeling a horrible sense of guilt for failing. Life as I'd known it was over too.

The recidivist range was a maximum security cellblock within a maximum security institution. The cellblock itself had once been a regular cellblock but it had since been blocked off from the rest of Stony Mountain. Although it loosely followed the daily routine of the prison, it had a different routine when it came to exercise, meals, and socializing. There was no night exercise, and the outdoor exercise took place when the general population was locked up, or at least inside the walls. Those of us in the max block ate in our cells, played cards in the hallway in front our cells for a few hours each day and evening, walked the yard together. We were all held in the "no man's land" of Correctional Services. Some of the men were parole violators and had charges to go up on, including murder.

One day, while I was picking up my meal at the wagon at the front of the cellblock, one of the Inmate Committee members happened to see me.

"Hey Wayne," he called. He was behind a barrier a few feet from the meal wagon.

"Hello Steve," I replied. Steve was a lifer from Winnipeg who'd served part of his sentence in Prince Albert. He and I were familiar with each other, and he was aware that I was an electronic technician.

"When did you get here?" he asked. I picked up my tray, then paused at the juice table to answer.

"About a week ago."

"I'm going to see if I can't get you into pop," he said, meaning the general population.

"Sounds good to me," I said. Two days later I was moved to a cell on a range in the general population, and the day after that I was handed a job working with the staff electronic technician. A new satellite dish was to be installed, with more than a thousand yards of coax cable to the cells. My working with the technician would most certainly save everybody money.

I hadn't completely made up my mind to escape, as psychologically and emotionally I was still digging and scratching for something real to hang on to. It's one thing to deliberately commit a criminal act, knowing that you could be arrested and returned to prison; it's quite another to be living free and unexpectedly be returned to prison. I was still very much in a state of disillusionment and downright shock.

My new boss put me through a technician's test to find out if I knew my stuff. The cons had a two-channel amp on which only one channel worked, and nobody seemed to know why.

"What's wrong with it?" he asked me. We were standing in a room reserved for the band and in front of us was an old but usable amp. A couple of cons were standing around watching us.

"It's usually the outputs that go," I answered.

"Can you prove it?" he asked.

"If I had a gun and an Volt-Ohm meter I could."

"I'll get you one." He left for his office on the other side of the prison. Jamie, whom I'd met a few years earlier, offered me a cup of coffee and we talked briefly about some of the Winnipeg mob who were now on the street. I hadn't completely drained my cup before my boss returned, Volt-Ohm meter and soldering gun in hand. In a matter of a few minutes I had both output transistors disconnected, and the meter showed the right one was blown. I put the right into the left side and the left into the right, thereby reversing the fault. He checked it out and readily agreed that I'd found the problem.

The next few days passed slowly as I renewed old acquaintances with people I'd known for a long time, but had lost touch with over the years, one of whom I'd met in prison and then later in a bar in Regina.

Dino was young, wild, and so full of energy that any man with a smattering of insight knew he was destined for the front pages of the newspapers, or even the national news. He was looking for a way out as he was facing a couple of armed robbery trials, with the probability of a serious sentence lurking in the wings. He stopped me one day to ask what I thought about an escape plan he had devised.

"We cut through the fences between the wall and the yard," he said, "and we go over the east-side wall." We were standing in the area leading to the yard, and I had a good idea of what he was talking about.

"What about outside? It's not just the wall; it's what you do and where you go afterwards."

"We can steal a car and be gone before they even miss us," he replied. Although he was talking in the plural, he didn't mean me. He had a partner lined up.

"How do you get through the fence?" I asked. He dug into his waist band and produced a small wire cutter—what we used to call a side cutter. It was made to cut and strip small wire.

"We'll use this," he answered. It was a new cutter, in good condition, but I knew it was no match for the galvanized retaining wire he would need to cut.

"The jaws of the plier will break," I suggested.

"No, we tried them. They'll work."

"What did you try them on?" I asked.

"The wire on the ball diamond."

"Different wire," I said, "Galvanized wire is very hard, brittle, and I don't think they're strong enough."

"They'll work," he repeated. He was quite insistent.

"Okay," I replied. Maybe they would, but I doubted it. Dino was a Cree from Saskatchewan, and though we all called him Dino, his mother had named him James Dean Agecoutay. He was a classically good looking man, and with his dark skin and eyes he could've passed for a man of any number of different nationalities. His natural intelligence always came through in conversation, he had good self-esteem, and an excellent sense of humour. He wasn't dangerous, at least not in the conventional meaning of the word, but he could well be dangerous if someone crossed him. It was easy to imagine him showing no mercy to right a wrong.

There was another man I met named Keith, whom I'd known in Prince Albert before the penitentiary had changed over to a protective custody prison. Keith had given me some tokens— canteen money—and some tokes, the first night I was in the population, and he'd made it known to me that he was looking for a way out as well. But Keith had over ten years in on his sentence, and the fact that he hadn't made a move in all that time told me he was probably more full of want and words than action. However, my rather hopeless looking situation needed only something to pull the trigger to send me down the barrel of the gun. I was loaded, primed, and ready to spiral into an escape run. The trigger was pulled the very next day.

I was walking down one of the many hallways of the prison with my boss, who seemed unusually effusive. He was a large, heavy-set, big-bellied, blustery man with a loud voice, who greeted people long before they were close to him. We were walking beside each other when another staff member approached us from down a fifty-foot stretch of hallway.

"Hey John! How's it going." His booming voice seemed to carry on forever. The staff member appeared to wish he'd taken the south fork back down the line, but was now trapped. He smiled well enough, and continued to walk towards us, waiting until he was within a reasonable distance before replying.

"Not bad," he answered, "and you?" He was now ten feet away.

"Good, good," rumbled my new boss. The approaching man glanced at me, and my boss caught it, and at that moment seemed to decide to introduce me. "This is my new nigger," he said, "we call him Wayne."

I simply nodded my head and we kept going on our way. I was conscious of his big belly bouncing along beside me in the hallway, and I felt each little irritating scratch of the ill-fitting inmate clothing on my back. *I'm fucking outta here*, I said to myself.

Later that evening I walked over to Keith's cell, which was situated on another range. He and a kid were playing video games and I stood in the doorway watching for a minute. The interior of the cell was dim, and the two of them—one old, one very young—hunched over the video paddles presented a strange picture. During the kid's turn at the controls, Keith looked up at me.

"I'd like to talk to you for a minute," I said.

"Sure, go ahead." He meant it was okay to talk in front of the kid, but it wasn't okay by me. I made a motion to step outside, but he pushed the pause button on the game. The kid looked at him.

"Step outside a minute," he said kindly. The kid wasn't happy, but he left, brushing past me with a look of resentment on his face.

"I'm catching the next bus," I said.

"Yeah? Are you?"

"Yes, and there's a seat on it for you." I saw a look of consternation briefly ripple across his face, and he dropped his eyes. His hands began to make busy with tobacco, tube, and roller.

"I've been thinking."

"Yeah?"

"I've been thinking—I've been in so long I wouldn't know what to do out there." His voice was weak and subdued and I had to strain to hear him. A man quickly learns in prison not to expect men to do what they're incapable of doing. Keith was content where he was, and far from being disappointed in him, I felt sorry for him. He looked like a badass biker, with his bald head and tatoos, but he was not a strong man and his countenance as he sat before me completely belied the physical picture he presented. Some men outgrow their tatoos; strangely, I felt Keith's tatoos had outgrown him.

"I understand," I said. Then, to make him feel better, I added, "You'll have to wait for the ten dollars." I smiled conspiratorially when I said it. I'd borrowed the ten when I first arrived— Keith was a loan shark, among other things. He immediately brightened.

"Forget it man, I got lots."

"Well, who knows, we may see each other again and I can return the favour."

"You bet!" he said, and I could see he felt better about himself. I excused myself and left his cell. Just before I walked completely off the range, I turned my head and looked back to see the kid darting back into the dim recesses of Keith's cell. I went looking for Art and Dino.

Art told me he had to talk to his woman, and when he did, she told him to give his head a shake and do his time. Dino and I would be the only ones leaving.

One of the many things I'd learned in prison was how to make a dummy in a short period of time. There was another man who helped me. He was my namesake from Ontario and we'd heard about each other for years, but had never met until we ran into each other in Stony Mountain. He made Dino's dummy, and he made it well, and he also checked on the man who made mine.

On a Friday night in May, Dino and I buried ourselves under piles of dirt in the big yard and the dummies were good enough to beat the count. By midnight we were walking across farm fields into Winnipeg, a good twenty miles away, and by morning, just as the sun was coming up, we made it into a residential area. Dino had a place for us to stay and we caught a cab to get there.

It was a small basement suite with a telephone so we could make some phone calls. I especially wanted to get in touch with a couple of guys who were hiding out in Edmonton. I phoned a friend and she assured me she'd send me money, which she did in an interbank transfer. If I called her later, she'd put me in touch with the people I needed to see. We decided we would sit back for the rest of the night and go to work on making a life for ourselves first thing in the morning. That night Dino and I sat talking about the people we knew and what we were going to do once we were out of Manitoba.

The next day Dino left with the young woman whose apartment we were in, and I sat back thinking and made a few phone calls. When Dino returned, he suggested we could buy a pistol and bullets for three hundred cash from the woman's father. Dino wanted to do a quick robbery with a knife, and with the cash from the holdup, buy the gun.

When we walked into the drugstore he wanted to rob, I had no intention of robbing the place. I thought I'd buy a pack of cigarettes, he would slow down a bit, and we'd both return to the apartment and wait for the next morning. It was not to be.

As events would later prove, some of the people in the drugstore recognized us as escapees, but I had caught their looks when we walked in, and I motioned to Dino to get out. After we left and were walking down the alley, I looked back and saw the people from the drugstore standing at the back door watching us. We decided we'd return to the apartment, but I still needed cigarettes.

There was a little corner grocery a block-and-a-half from the apartment, so I stopped in to buy a package of cigarettes. Dino came with me.

We robbed the store. Though there was no violence, I was haunted for a long time afterwards by the fact that it was a family's small business, and both the owner and his wife were there. Out in the street we ran straight into detectives who were looking for us because the druggist had called some minutes before. We ran, but I slipped and I was arrested. I was taken first to the safety building in Winnipeg and then to the hole in Stony Mountain. Dino went on to become involved in a shootout in Saskatoon, after which he was across the hall from me in the hole.

The cells in the hole in most prisons are the same. The cell doors are solid with a food slot at belly level which is always locked, except at meal times. There's also a viewer slot at face level, where the guards can look into each cell while on their security rounds. Each viewing slot has a sliding metal cover which the guards can close when they don't want prisoners to see what they're doing in the hallway. There's also a locked fire exit door leading to the main yard.

If I could make a key to fit the food slot and open it, I'd be able to reach the locking mechanism of the door and, with a key, open it and escape into the hallway. If I had a key for the fire exit door, I could escape from the prison itself. I was willing to put my energy into making it all happen.

While I worked, I couldn't help imagining what would happen if we were successful in breaking out of the hole, scaling the wall, and making our way to freedom again. I had the food slot key, the door key and the fire exit door key made, and I had a hole cut out of the thick plexiglass viewing slot. It was now only a matter of waiting until that evening to make the move. However, plans made by mice, men, and prisoners often go awry.

That afternoon I was called to see my lawyer, and was taken from my cell to a holding room where he was waiting. We had a brief conversation, but it was long enough for the guards to search my cell and find the hole in the viewing slot. A prisoner across the hall told me they'd missed the hole in the plexiglass until the last minute.

I was immediately moved into one of three cells around the corner, by the hospital door. I couldn't cut through the plexiglass again because my cell was too close to the office of the guards—they'd hear the sound. But there was another way of escape—by cutting out the window, sawing through the bars, and then going over the wall. I set about doing it.

It's almost impossible to escape successfully when a considerable amount of noise has to be made. At the very least, the man in the neighboring cell would hear the sounds of metal on metal, and that sound scares a lot people, particularly when they don't know what's being made or done. Many men have sharpened their shanks by scraping a piece of metal on the cement floor; the fear of knives is ever-present, and many of the men in the holes are held there for their own protection. But I had to take that chance.

It took me the whole of one day to braid forty feet of wet sheets to use as my rope, and I had the window ready to come out. I pried open the window again, and I was busy cutting the last of the bars when the door flew open. The RCMP were called and I was charged with prison break with intent to escape, and placed in the "oriental cell," which has only a hole in the floor for bodily functions and an old plastic gallon jug that serves as a water fountain. Eventually I was sentenced to ten years and transferred to Edmonton Maximum Security Institution.

Edmonton Institution is a modern, high-tech prison which was run by a team of psychologists. A small, hand-picked group of prisoners assisted in the development of institutional programs and some of those prisoners became indispensable in the prison's operation.

I noticed that Edmonton had units with designated letters like Marion did. Later on I was to become aware that the newer maximum security prisons throughout the western world had similar practices and philosophies, but at the time I only noticed, and thought little else about it.

There were many high-profile prisoners serving sentences in the eight units. The Colin Thatcher trial was in the news and I knew the people from Regina instrumental in convicting him quite well. I'd sat down with them in the bars or run into them on the street. Three of them were the most unsavoury lot and I wondered how a jury could believe a word they said. Not only did they beat other people, they beat each other whenever the opportunity presented itself. I had no idea whether Thatcher killed his wife or not, and to me that wasn't the point—I knew only that the evidence used to convict him was tainted.

When Thatcher was convicted, he showed up in Edmonton Max. He was reputed to be a millionaire and some men searched for ways to get at his money, but Thatcher didn't seem interested in wheeling and dealing. He was interested in surviving and I believe the manner in which he handled himself, and the manner in which he handled the slings and arrows of his outrageous fortune, showed he had a great deal of character. He lived in my unit and I came to know him reasonably well.

Throughout the prison there were gunslingers who would have dearly loved to be able to put a Thatcher notch on the butt of their pistols. One of them was Daniel Gingras, who went on to become infamous for his birthday pass, escape, and murder of innocent people. Gingras wanted to kill Thatcher, not for any reason but that he was a square-john politician. Another Québecer who spoke out against such an idea found himself nursing a broken jaw because of his rational, sensible attitude. Reynold and I played tennis against each other, and we became friends over the period we were there. He was serving a ten-year sentence for a bank robbery out of Calgary.

There was nothing I could do for Reynold, except of course to arm up and take out the man who'd broken his jaw, but Reynold managed to find the strength to function without resorting to violence. There were other prisoners in the population who supported Thatcher, but they were quiet and unobtrusive men who'd speak to him as he walked past. It was a dangerous time for all of us, and for Colin in particular. Sometimes I thought he was oblivious to it, not because he was a stupid man, but because he was blinded by his own arrogance. He'd always been in a position of privilege; when he was a young man he had enjoyed the power of being a premier's son. But none of that applied now.

It was always a pleasure to watch the growth of powerful men inside a penitentiary, and I found humour in Colin's arrogance. I wasn't intimidated by him, I just found him interesting. Here was a man who came from a well-respected Saskatchewan family, a man used to money, power and control, and here we were equals, at least socially.

One day Colin and I were playing chess in one of the small anterooms, and after the third game, the frustration got the better of him.

"Mindless barbarian," he muttered. Except for the fish in the large tank on one side of the room, we were alone. When I first heard his statement, I thought I'd heard wrong.

"I beg your pardon?"

"Mindless barbarian," he said again. I had to laugh.

"Why do you say that?" I asked.

"Well, you traded a piece just to trade a piece," he said. "You had no reason for it."

"Oh, well maybe there's method in my madness," I replied. I could see what he was trying to do on the board, and by trading my bishop for his knight, his plan was completely foiled. A few moves later, I checkmated him.

"I'm going to beat you," Colin said. I looked at him, and I understood how difficult his sentence was going to be.

"No you won't, Colin," I responded.

"I'll use another opening," he stated.

"I'll use another defense," I said.

It was weeks later when Colin stopped by my cell to tell me he'd just had a visit from a friend of his.

"He's a chess master, and I told him what you said—about the opening moves," he said.

"Oh yeah?"

"He said, 'He's right.'" I considered it a compliment.

The guards gave Thatcher dirty looks behind his back when they thought nobody was looking at them. Whenever Colin walked passed prisoners in a hallway, or passed them in the outside yard, there would be men who'd mutter, "Bang, bang," to show him they would kill him if they had a gun. Still, he handled it all well.

It must have been trying for him. One afternoon I walked into the small unit servery where he was reading the paper. I was pouring a cup of coffee when

Colin spoke up.

"Somebody should drive a knife right through my heart," he said.

"Oh, come on Colin," I said, "it can't be as bad as all that."

"Well, they should," he replied.

"Do you know why people react to you the way they do?" I asked.

"Yeah," he said. "Because I'm me."

"You're right," I said. I knew by his answer that he had a good grasp of his surroundings. I believed too, that he was going to survive.

Most high-profile men are held in maximum security prisons, but in my opinion it's overkill. Colin wasn't a dangerous man. Even if he was guilty, he wouldn't have hurt anyone else. Prisoners as well as staff knew this was true; administrators were concerned about the press.

Edmonton Max was full of men who had killed, none of them as high-profile as Colin. This bothers most killers, especially those with an ego as big as their cell. The fact that Colin was so capable, and so knowledgeable in so many areas, meant they were intimidated when they were in his company.

A job as a clerk had come open in the chapel, and three of us applied for it. Colin was one, another lifer by the name of Kenny was the second, and I was the third. When it appeared I might get the job, Kenny came to me with a proposition. He would give me his job, in programs, and he would take the chapel job. In a matter of hours it was done. It wasn't because Colin wasn't capable; he was much more capable than anyone else when it came to paperwork, but prison politics dictated that a regular prisoner fill the position. Colin had his own feelings about the chapel job which he expressed to me in the unit.

"I don't get the job, and I'm the only Christian in the bunch," he said. I had to laugh at his assumption, even though I wasn't a Christian.

"Well, I'm from Saskatchewan too, Colin," I said. "We have churches in the northern part of the province as well as the south." He didn't look up from his newspaper but I'm sure he got my point.

Colin and I were bridge partners, and though we played often, we didn't win that many games. Bridge is a great way to pass the time; it requires focus and concentration on the cards, and this helps men get their minds off their situations. Consequently, men who've served a lot of time are usually good players. Bridge, like chess, is an intellectual game and those who win find their egos are given a boost. Most prisoners respect intelligence, and a man's ability to perform well in intellectual games is added to his measure. Colin had clearly said he played kitchen-table bridge, so when he sat at the table he wasn't expecting much of himself. However, a man can only lose so many games to lesser men before it begins to hurt.

Peter was a lifer who'd played bridge for years, and he was also a good hustler. Colin and I had played Peter and his partner Reynold on many occasions. One day Peter picked up another partner and talked Colin into playing in the gym. I'm sure they were going to hustle him for a few bucks. During the game Peter mentioned one of the cards in the deck was crimped.

"Oh, buy another deck," said Colin contemptuously.

"I just bought these cards," stated Peter.

"Then get a couple of new decks and put it on my tab," said Colin arrogantly. Peter took exception to Colin's tone, and he sucker punched him on the side of his face. Colin didn't fight back. He was probably too much in shock to even think about retaliation. One side of his face was swollen, and he had a black eye for a week. But again he seemed to handle it very well.

I never knew if Colin was guilty or not, and I wasn't basing my judgement of him by the judgement of the high court of Saskatchewan. For years I'd associated with men who'd done terrible things to people in their lives, and Colin was just another man sent inside by the law. But there's more to a man than shows in an act of killing or robbery.

There were a number of men who wanted out, and one of them came to me to discuss a plan. My key-making ability brought me into the picture.

There were men who'd previously beaten the security fences in Edmonton, but on one of those escapes, shots were fired and one of the men was hit. If I was to make an escape, I wanted it to be a quiet one with lead time, which would allow me to be at least ten miles away before they knew I was gone.

Our way out was to get into the hallway of industries, enter the laundry, knock out the lights by taking out the power plant which included the auxiliary power unit, and escape over the fence in the darkness. It would work, if we had the key for the hallway leading into industries, and I proceeded to make one.

There were too many men involved in the plan. Everyone seemed to know what we were doing, which brought us under the scrutiny of the Inmate Committee.

I was standing outside one of the units when the Chairman walked up to talk to me. "What's happening?" asked the chairman.

"What's happening where?" I asked.

"Last night when you were all gathered by that door," he explained. "What's up?"

"Nothing violent, and not anything anyone has to be concerned about," I answered.

"No? Well I saw some pretty heavy-duty people there," he said.

"Yeah, there was that," I acknowledged, "but it wasn't a meeting of insurrection." He laughed at the mention of insurrection because he liked to think of himself as the man in control. In fact, he often called himself "Vito," after the mobster Vito Genovese. The chairman was a good man, but I knew there was too much talk for the plan to now be workable. But the die was cast, so we continued.

Then a surprise transfer took place and the next day at noon hour I was taken to the hole for "planning and plotting an escape." I knew it was going to be another tough summer in the hole.

Maurice Laberge, whom I'd first met in Regina Gaol, then on the street and years later in Prince Albert Penitentiary, showed up as a cleaner in the hole. He was doing twenty-five years for a robbery, but the fact he had raped a teenage boy on the home invasion, made the crime a "skin beef." My problem with him was more personal: he'd fingered my partner and I following a drugstore break-in. I'd agreed to meet Maurice in the city's north end, but when we arrived we were met by a large number of police officers. It's difficult to prove that Maurice had set us up, but I felt it in my gut and I told him so. It took more than two years for the truth of his character to surface: he had worked for the police for two decades.

Maurice was bona fide Mensa member and most prisoners had never seen the likes of a man like him. He wasn't just a run-of-the-mill stool pigeon and tattle-tale. He was brilliant. When he chose to manipulate men, as he often did, he could do it like no man I'd ever seen.

There was a rumour there was a handgun with a box of .22 bullets somewhere in the prison. A gun would make a good patch for somebody looking for a favour from the administration, and on many occasions someone would ask me if I needed any .22 bullets. As soon as I was asked that question, I knew I was talking to a representative of the security department.

There was a gun, and though I never did see it, I knew it existed. I was offered it if I wanted or needed to kill Maurice Laberge. Laberge was becoming a problem for me because I'd labeled him a rat, and he was in touch with many hard, dangerous men. If a friend hadn't intervened, I would probably have been stabbed and killed over Laberge. I was picking up a cup of coffee in the unit servery when John, a man many called The Duke, asked me if I knew a kid who'd just hanged himself in the hole.

"His name isn't familiar," I replied. There were two other men with John, both of them were John's guys, and one of them had just come out of the hole after doing thirty days of punishment.

"Get the picture of the kid," John instructed one of the men. He immediately dashed upstairs and returned with a photograph. The photo showed a young man, perhaps in his early twenties, sitting on another man's lap. It was a joke photo, impulsively taken at a light moment.

"Do you know him?" asked John.

"He looks familiar but I..." John quickly interrupted.

"No Wayne, I'm asking if you know him?" I understood then that it was not just small talk, this was serious business.

"No, I don't know him."

"Are you sure?" All three men were looking at me now.

"Yeah, I'm sure. I never saw him before," I said. John turned his attention to the other two men.

"Okay, he doesn't know him," he said.

"Yeah okay, John," said one, and the other nodded that he too understood.

"I want to talk to him, alone," instructed John. Both men left, taking the photograph with them.

"You know Mo?" John asked me.

"Yeah, I know him," I replied.

"And Chico?"

"Yeah?"

"Chico told the boys in the hole that you checked the kid in," John said.

"I don't know him," I replied. Then I had a thought. "When did he check in?"

"Well, you're in his cell now," John stated.

"How could I have checked him in, if I'm in his cell now?"

"Yeah," responded John, "you weren't even in the population when he checked in."

"Yeah, it's bullshit," I said.

"Let me handle this," John offered.

"Okay, you got it," I replied. I heard no more about the allegation, but it was a shock to have found out that I was being set up to be stabbed. I also learned it was Maurice who'd approached John and told him of the plot to discredit me. Not only had Chico started the rumour, he'd also seen that Maurice was given a shank to take care of me. I never let on that I knew what they were about; I let it go and watched my back.

Tim Collins, an American who'd entered Canada illegally, was also on Maurice Laberge's case. One evening he called Roly Paton and me aside in the yard to show us an article in the Alberta Report which stated that Maurice had committed a sex crime during his robbery. Roly and me were only two of many that Tim had talked with, and within hours the news got back to Maurice. Maurice hired a Québecer named Pepe to kill Tim for an ounce of hash.

Tim was stabbed with a knife in the big yard, and though he tried to get away, he was no match for Pepe. He died in the hallway leading to the hospital, and for a long time Maurice wasn't charged with the crime. When charges were finally filed against Maurice, a number of men were charged with him—only Pepe was convicted. He later committed suicide in the Special Handling Unit, and Pepe died without getting high on any of Maurice's dope.

I managed to get myself in trouble with some of the unit staff, and following a shouting match, I was placed in the hole. The hole was great. I could've stayed right there for the whole of my sentence.

Many men there were caught up in treachery and double-dealing, mainly because of their addictions to drugs. Medication from the hospital was also readily available, and the evening and nighttime lineups at the medication wicket were very long. Serax and chloral hydrate were the drugs most liked, and many a deal was made over a month's supply of both. Some men were on both drugs throughout the whole of the day, and they would receive medication three times daily. How they managed to function as well as they did was amazing; however, when they were cut off they became mean, violent, and impossible to deal with in a normal fashion. I discovered the best way was to remain as aloof as possible.

There were men who lost their lives for no good reason at all; even in prison terms it didn't make sense. Spencer Briltz was one of them, and Rick Roach was another. In an ironic twist, Roach killed Briltz, and then Roach himself was killed by Robbie Pelletier a few years later. Spencer was a good man who minded his own business and he didn't deserve to die—but many of the men killed in prison didn't deserve to die a violent death.

On October 18, 1985 I was married in the chapel to Judy, a woman who lived in Edmonton. I'd met her six months earlier through my sister Jane.

Rick Carlson, Colin Thatcher, Joe Wapash, Ray Yoemans, Mike Toy, Dino Agecoutay, Jim Ramsay, Mackie Cox—a Grim Reaper whom everyone of us liked and respected—and many others were there. I rented the clothes and the shoes, and the boys in the kitchen pitched in to make an excellent snack bar. Gerry "Blue" Hubbert and Dennis Lyons were my best men. My mother, my two sisters and a niece were there, and my aging grandmother traveled from Sturgis, Saskatchewan to attend. It was a great wedding. Three days later, on October 22, I was transferred to Drumheller Penitentiary.

I served close to a year in Drumheller, working in the kitchen and writing in my spare time. I felt I had to keep a very low profile because of concerns the security department had about my presence. I finally transferred to Bowden in November, 1986. Bowden, in my opinion, was one of the most abusive prisons imaginable. It wasn't a dangerous place, but the guards were unfair, rude, obnoxious and mean.

In January 1987 I failed to return to Bowden on a pass. My run ended when I was charged for a robbery in Edmonton, my security level was raised, and I was sent to the hole to wait trial. While there I met old friends and old enemies, and

I made new acquaintances as well.

I was in bad shape, but I lucked out and was given a job as a cleaner in the hole, which meant I was able to workout and get myself in better condition. I punched the heavy bag, did free squats, and used some plastic jugs filled with sand weights for a lifting routine. Within sixty days I was in much better physical condition.

Edmonton Max was a dangerous prison, and it wasn't only the prisoners who were dangerous—the staff members were too. When administrators make bad decisions based on what they perceived as their administrative needs, the consequences to the community could be deadly. Daniel Gingras is a good example.

There was a plan to involve the prisoners in the Edmonton community through day passes and long-term release programs, and one of the prisoners they reached out to was Daniel. He was a man who'd escaped from a police van after receiving a ten-year sentence. While on the run he killed a night janitor, and then drove off in the janitor's car with the body stuffed in the trunk. Daniel drove the car around Montréal for weeks and the body was only discovered when police stopped him on a routine check. Daniel was sentenced to life ten, meaning he'd be eligible for parole in ten years. He was eventually sent from Québec to Edmonton Max. Soon after he arrived in Edmonton he joined the French Group, a powerful organization within the penitentiary system. Rumour had it that Daniel had been sent to Edmonton as a reward for turning in a homemade handgun in a Québec maximum security prison. For this reason, he was selected and groomed for an escorted pass to the city of Edmonton. To take a man from a prison down east, and try to integrate him into the Edmonton community, when there are many eligible prisoners with good families and friends in the Edmonton area to choose from, seems ludicrous—but it was done.

There were staff members who wouldn't take part in the exercise, and the escort duty was handed to Willard, a new staff member who had no idea of what was happening behind the scenes. When Daniel grabbed him, tied him up and left him in the back of the van, he was very lucky he wasn't killed. Gingras went on to kill at least two people, a man and a woman, and he bragged that he had killed two more in Montréal on a contract for five hundred dollars a month, to be paid to him for the rest of his life.

I was in the hole when Gingras was arrested in Edmonton, and I was there when he was brought to the hole to appear in court for his escape charge. I watched as he received cartons of cigarettes, cases of drinks, and many boxes of junk food from the Inmate Committee and French Group on the day he was returned. Gingras settled in well, believing he'd soon be in the general population doing business as usual. He was completely out of touch with the way people felt about him. Maurice Laberge befriended him immediately, and I just smiled.

Hearing Daniel's laughter on a daily basis may have struck the funny bone of many men who heard him—he did have infectious laughter. However, if one knew what it was that was tickling him, the chuckles would've caught in their throats.

Crime Stoppers asked for help in identifying a man who was found murdered beside a telephone booth very close to the prison. The man had been shot in the head and body six times with a .357 revolver. Daniel found the photo presentation strangely funny, and after it became public knowledge that he was the killer, it seemed even more bizzare to me. Many of us questioned the decision which gave him the opportunity to run loose in the community - it wasn't because he was seen as a good candidate for release.

Charles Ng was also present, and the first time I met him in the yard I found the hair on my neck standing up. There was something about him so dangerous that it defied description. The guards would send the tough guys, the shit disturbers, and the men they didn't like into the yard with him. Charlie would workout on his martial arts routine on the heavy bag, and he could make that bag jump and dance all day long. Charlie intimidated everyone just by his presence, and the more familiar one became with him, the scarier he was. I was afforded a view of the crimes he was accused of in the United States because they were all outlined in the personal diary of Leonard Lake, Charlie's partner.

The diary was a window into a real-life nightmare. It was a protected court document that Charlie allowed some of us to read and it discussed murder and torture in a matter-of-fact way. Leonard Lake and Charlie had initially met in the special forces, and they quickly began an association which would eventually see dozens of men, women, and children tortured and murdered in bizzare ways.

While in the army, Lake and Ng were charged with stealing weapons from an army base. Lake made bail, Charlie didn't. Charlie served his sentence in federal prison while Lake went on the run. Lake regularly changed identities, robbing his victims for their property as well as their personal identification. Operation Fish is what he called his hunt for his next victim.

He would read the classified ads on vehicles, and when he went to look at the cars and trucks, he measured the salesman, not the car. If the man was his size, or reasonably close, he'd return a few days later armed with a handgun and take the people in the house hostage.

Lake would take the people into the countryside of California, and once he had them at his mercy he'd torture them for their credit card pin numbers, and force them to write letters to their employers indicating any money they had coming from work should be sent to a post office box. Then he'd kill everyone and dispose of the bodies in pits in the hills and mountains. When

Charlie was released from his federal sentence, he became Lake's willing and enthusiastic helper.

Soon Lake and Charlie began kidnapping women, and taking them to a cabin in the mountains where they would physically, sexually, and psychologically torture them, before they killed and buried them. Charlie sang a little ditty—"Pappa die, baby fry, mama cry"—to a woman whose husband he'd just killed with his martial arts. He barbecued the baby and then showed the woman the video tape of both horrific murders. And there was considerably more horror. On the jacket of the diary was a formula for making cyanide, as well as a warning in Leonard Lake's handwriting of what waited between the pages of the book in hand.

Maurice was able to manipulate Charlie like a man manipulating an impressionable boy. Charlie was a very good cartoonist and Maurice had him drawing cartoons of his victims, and some of Charlie himself riding a bicycle selling pantyhose in a San Francisco neighbourhood. If one understood the crimes Charlie committed, the cartoons were easy to decipher—Charlie truly enjoyed killing and torturing people, and strangling women with pantyhose. Maurice thoroughly enjoyed hearing the gory details.

When my court appearances were finally over, I had another eight years added to my sentence and I was once again sent to Drumheller.

I stepped off the bus and walked down the breezeway to the courtyard where a couple of hundred men were sitting around the units waiting for their pay to be posted in the canteen. Gary, a man I'd known in the Max, cut me off as I headed to my designated unit. With him was a man we called Jake the Snake. Gary had no reason to pick a fight, but no reason is needed when someone just wants to rebuild their ego. Gary and his brother had been stabbed in the Max by two very tough men when a power-move the two brothers made went wrong. Gary was in the hole in the Max after he was arrested in Calgary for a robbery. He'd been transferred to Drumheller from Edmonton a few months before me.

I knew a great deal about Gary and he knew I had this knowledge; knowledge is power and he feared I might publicly embarrass him, which I wouldn't have done. I knew this and I was ready to fight if need be. I'd seen Gary punch the heavy bag on a number of occasions, and though he weighed two hundred and thirty pounds, his moves on the bag were slow, ponderous, and very sluggish. Even if he did beat me, I could bruise him a little bit myself.

"I didn't like the way you treated me in the hole," Gary said. He had his heavy parka on, which on a warm day meant he might be packing a knife. I held my light jacket in my hand, because I'd need it to block the blade.

"What was it Gary? The pancakes weren't hot enough?" I replied. His right arm was held against his chest, his hand loosely open, but I knew he was trying to get into position to sucker punch me.

"I don't think you gave me enough support," he said. There was almost a resentful tone in his voice. Suddenly Jake cut in.

"I saw him knock a guy out right there," said Jake, pointing to a spot no more than ten feet from where we stood.

"Oh yeah," I answered, not impressed.

"No, he did, with one punch," said Jake. Gary stood looking at me, as if looking for something in my eyes or in the way I stood. I ignored Jake and focused on Gary.

"Am I supposed to be impressed, Gary?" I asked.

"Well, I didn't like the way you treated me," he said again. The truth was I'd treated him very well, even going so far as to stand talking to him regularly at his range door.

"I'm going to my unit, Gary," I said. "We'll talk about this later, how's that?"

"Yeah, we'll talk later," he agreed. But I knew he couldn't be trusted, so I'd be watching my back.

Gary and his mob of guys had been fighting with the Natives over a racial issue which could become serious and deadly. Before Gary and I could get together, he and a half-dozen of his mob were locked up, and my problem disappeared. After the lockdown and scoop, we were all allowed out of our cells and a barbecue was held in the backyard. It was very relaxing and everyone seemed relieved that the muscle in the joint was now out of sight and out of mind. It was a beautiful day, and though I didn't like to see men locked in the hole, I felt removed from it and I was relieved too.

From what was alleged, Gary and his mob had been hustling many of the dope smokers for their drugs and cash. I'm sure those kids were feeling much better now that their tormentors were no longer around to rip them off.

I became very active, working as an elected committee member, and a clerk in the Corcan Prison Industries business office as well. I played tennis, worked out, maintained my marriage to Judy and commitment to Jeff and Debbie, my wife's children, and began to think of getting out and staying out.

I did what I could as a committee man; however, there were staff members who didn't like my approach to solving problems. The last thing some prison guards want to see is a prisoner who can read and write well, and who has the ability to put them on the spot by talking about inmate concerns in clear language. My approach was simple: file a grievance, outline the problem as I saw it, and request a corrective action which suited the situation. If a department head attempted to intimidate me, I usually found a verbal response which quickly cleared the air. The day the maintenance department received instructions to change the shelving arrangements in the cells was a good example.

I returned to my cell from the business office at noon, and discovered my personal property strewn about my cell. Photographs and personal papers, including protected documents, were scattered across my bed and floor. It looked like a cyclone had hit my cell. I filed a complaint and asked for a three-day suspension without pay for those responsible. The department head whose duty it was to answer the complaint came to see me in the business office a few days later. He held up the yellow form in his hand and looked at me very sternly.

"I haven't shown this to Ron yet," he said, "but when I do, he's going to be really mad."

"I understand you're a religious man," I replied.

"Well..." he began, but I cut him off.

"I'm not a religious man," I continued, "but I do get angry sometimes myself. And when I do, I get down on my knees beside my bed at night and I pray to God, asking that he make me a staff member for twenty-four hours so I can meet some of the abusive sons of bitches in the parking lot." His demeanor changed to one of conciliation so quickly it surprised me.

"I'll have the shelf put back in place before four o'clock today," he said. "You make some marks on your wall indicating where you want the shelf placed, and it'll be put there." I could clearly see he was sincere.

"You guarantee it?" I asked.

"Yes—you withdraw this complaint now and I'll have it done by the end of the day."

"Okay," I said. I signed the withdrawal, he picked up the papers and left the office. That evening I returned to find the shelf placed where I wanted it.

Like everyone else I was hoping for parole; however, I had a case manager who seemed unable to handle his personal feelings about me. On many occasions he would literally yell so loudly and so long at me that guards stationed in the security bubble at the top of the stairs would come knocking on the door, concerned about the intimidating noise.

I used to sit in his office, my hands on my lap, and I would focus my attention on keeping my fingertips gently touching each other. This allowed me to stay grounded, and at the same time it forced me to relax my body no matter what he said. His tone of voice and his insults were an attempt to trigger me into an irrational reaction, and though butterflies of fear were beating in my belly, I always managed to retain my presence of mind. I just bit my tongue and let him rant and rave; at times he became so excited, so angry, and so tense, that spittle would fly from his mouth. But, for some reason, after I told him I was going to serve my time, he decided to support me for a day parole. Little did I know where this would lead.

The prison had begun to change, and not for the better. Drugs were the main reason for the outbreaks of violence, and drugs caused many promises to be made to too many people.

The chairman of the Inmate Committee is the man the prison administrators rely on to solve most minor problems, and also the chairman holds signing authority for all money distributed from the Inmate Welfare Fund to the various groups within the prison. All prisoners have a compulsory deduction from their pay, and it's this deduction which fills the coffers of the Inmate Committee. As well, money is collected from the candy and pop machines in the visiting area of the prison.

The canteen, where prisoners buy their tobacco and other necessities, is the hub of the prison's economic wheel, and the committee also controls all canteen money and stock. Working in the canteen as a clerk is a sugar plum job where many deals can be made. Whenever a position in the canteen comes open, there's competition between prisoners for it. However, the committee chairman has a major say in who gets the job.

Lorne, the man across the hall from me, a relatively quiet man who minded his own business, had his eye set on working in the canteen. When a position came open, he approached the chairman and asked for it, and the chairman assured him he would get the job. However, the chairman also promised the same to other men and, as a consequence, a number of men were waiting to go to work in the same place.

Tempers flared, knives were drawn, and the tension in the courtyard rose to a critical level. I did what I could to diffuse the situation, but it was too far out of control. One evening my neighbour asked me if I could talk to the committee in an attempt to make peace between all parties. I reluctantly agreed. My day parole date was only days away, but I couldn't sit back and watch knife-play, perhaps even the death of a friend, if I could help it.

There were at least thirty men waiting for Lorne in the breezeway, and the fact that many of them wore heavy parkas, and stood with their hands buried deep in their pockets, told me they were ready to do him serious bodily harm. I walked to the committee chairman who stood between two of his guys.

"Lorne asked me to talk to you to see if this can be resolved peacefully," I said. I could see the effects of cocaine and valium in his eyes.

"He asked you to come here?"

"Yes, he wants to put it all to rest," I said. Just then another man stepped forward, his hand in his jacket pocket.

"You're taking his side," he said. His voice and eyes were belligerent, and his body language spoke of a readiness to pounce.

"I'm not taking sides," I said. "If this matter isn't resolved peacefully, there'll be hell to pay and many men are going to be in serious trouble." For a moment I saw a reflection of common sense flow across his face, as if he was considering the consequences to himself and others. But the committee chairman put a stop to that.

"You tell him he either checks in, or he's a dead man," he said, meaning Lorne had to get himself put into the hole for his own protection.

"That's your message?" I asked.

"Yeah, that's my fuckin' message to him." I left them standing there, most of them pilled up, and as I walked back to the unit to see my neighbour, I could feel the darkness of dread come over me. Somebody was going to die.

He snorted in response to the suggestion he check in. I knew somebody was going to be bleeding before too long.

The men in the breezeway were looking for a victim and they found one in Kevin May. Kevin was a friend of Lorne's. He'd lost an arm after a shotgun blast had ripped it apart in a Calgary parking lot some months earlier. As he walked through the gauntlet, he seemed a likely target. They grabbed him and threw him against the cement wall in the breezeway and delivered a few blows to his body and face. Though his feelings were hurt more than anything else, the unfair beating he took was fuel added to the angry, fearful flames of the problem.

Kevin came into the unit, and right behind him came a couple of men who'd played a role in roughing him up in the breezeway. My neighbour saw the blood on his friend's face and he walked down the range to straighten out the problem.

Al Casey was the man who received the blade in his body, and though he was rushed to the hospital, he quickly died from his wound. The prison was finally locked down.

Two days later, the Committee, acting on orders from the administration, gave a pep talk to each Unit to try to calm the atmosphere. It was difficult to understand how the administration could allow the very people who caused the problem to still hold their positions on the Committee, but they did.

It took a couple of weeks for the whole story to come out, and when it did there was a lockdown and search of the whole of the prison population, particularly the canteen which proved to be thousands of dollars short. Al Casey was a good man in many ways, and he certainly didn't deserve to lose his life for nothing.

I was released on day parole to a halfway house a few days later, and I caught the bus to Calgary.

When a man walks out of a prison and into the community, he has to be able to handle the slings and arrows he encounters on a daily basis. Most inmates are not so equipped; they tend to be self-centred men with a need for instant gratification, and most lack the necessary skills to survive in the most ordinary of social situations.

The means and methods one employs to socially survive inside a penitentiary, which usually involve at least some form of intimidation or threat of violence, do not have the same effect on the people in the community. An average law-abiding citizen doesn't think he'll be punched in the face, have his head crushed by a pipe, or be stabbed with a knife, by a man who holds an opinion contrary to his own. In prison this threat is always present and usually clearly understood, and it runs unseen beneath the surface like a hungry shark in the undercurrent every second of every hour of each and every day. And it works well, for it keeps mute those men who might otherwise dare to break free of the bonds of the con code. The "con code" differs from the moral social code of the community, for in the community an individual is expected to assist others in righting a wrong and speak out in order to help the community at large. The average person who follows this moral code receives recognition for his good work. In the penitentiary, one must regularly and consistently insist that he doesn't know what he knows and that he doesn't see what he sees, under the threat of violence. Not only can men do grievous harm in the penitentiary, the con code helps to ensure that they can escape retribution for their transgressions.

Therefore, when an inmate walks out of a penitentiary, he's a man with an attitude that's in direct opposition to the attitude prevalent in the community. And the longer an inmate has been inside a prison, away from the community, the more difficulty he will have in adapting. It'll take more than mere discussion to bring some light of understanding to the inmate's mind. An attitude entrenched through years of irrational thought, feeling and behaviour will go to great lengths to remain in comfortable darkness. Inmates with a history of substance abuse problems face even greater obstacles, for when alcohol, or drugs, or both, are added to this already potentially dangerous attitudinal mix, the inmate's chances for success are further reduced.

In 1992 I walked out of Drumheller and into a pre-release plan I knew nothing about, and even those things I expected were not the way I expected them to be. It began when I was scheduled for a Category One evaluation. A Dr. Weston was to interview me in his Calgary office. A series of interviews were set up and I was transported there in handcuffs and shackles to see him.

On the way to the first interview the van ride was fine. It was the first time in years that I'd seen the countryside and the trip afforded me a good view. It was spring, the world was just coming alive after a long winter, and I truly enjoyed it. It reminded me of growing up in Northern Saskatchewan.

Every spring I would unroll my goose-down sleeping bag and sleep in the walk-in closet in my room. My bedroom window overlooked the woods through which the Assiniboine river ran. The distance from my home to the river was no more than three city blocks. There was no need for an alarm clock to rudely jar me, and consequently everyone else, out of bed. The uncomfortable hardwood floor, combined with the sounds of the birds chirping through my open window, ensured that I would waken very early in the morning.

In looking back, I think my fishing the Assiniboine every morning was probably one of the main reasons I found school work boring. It's difficult to match the high excitement of a hands-on battle with an eight-pound Northern Pike, with the sterile, paper-dry reasoning of "You must have an education to be happy and successful." After all, a fish can be caught, cooked, and immediately eaten. To a boy, enjoying the capture of food and filling a hungry belly is sometimes the only real meaning to life.

The corrections van pulled into a hamburger stand for lunch. Just as it turned to enter the parking lot, it hit the curb with such force that I was lifted from my seat on the bench in the back. I was slammed against the back door and landed flat on my back in the slush on the floor. When I managed to untangle myself—no easy task when handcuffed to a belly-chain and shackled—I saw grins on the guards' faces in profile. I realized then that this was a trick they'd used on other occasions. Like boys, they enjoyed the prank. My hamburger and fries lost their flavour.

We arrived at the Foothills Hospital, and because there were no parking spaces, we had to park on a street in front of some apartment buildings. As I got out of the van I glanced up to see two little faces peering at me from a second-floor apartment, and I could hear them calling to their mom to come and look. Mom showed up behind them, and at the sight of me in shackles and chains, she quickly instructed the kids to get away from the window.

There was some distance from the van to the hospital's front door, which meant we had to pass many people on the way. They must have wondered who this mud-spattered individual was, but I remember thinking that if they did look past the prison greens, the handcuffs and the shackles, the mud on my clothes would mean little. I kept my head up and shuffled along as if I owned the street.

In the hospital waiting room there were three people seated, but in minutes two of them, showing obvious discomfort, left as if they had business elsewhere. The third man, brave soul that he was, lasted a couple of minutes longer before he too took his leave. I quietly sat there while the guards talked of ordinary things until the receptionist popped her head in to tell the guard nearest her that the doctor was ready now. I wanted to cut in and ask when the doctor would be ready to see me but I bit my tongue. I felt like an invisible man.

Doctor Weston sat behind a very cluttered desk. I still had the handcuffs and shackles on.

"How are you?" he asked. He looked at the paper inside the file folder he held.

"Fine," I replied. He glanced over his reading glasses to look at me.

"How did you like the ride here?" he asked.

"The countryside was nice," I answered.

"Yes," he agreed, "it's a beautiful day."

"Yes," I acknowledged. He went on to ask me some normal statistical questions, and he then began questioning me as to why I was there.

"The authorities must have some plans for you," he suggested. As he looked me full in the face I noticed he appeared skinny and pale.

"Yes, I guess they do. I'm not sure what they are, but they must," I replied.

"Well, this is part of a pre-release program, isn't it?"

"It may have something to do with getting me used to public humiliation and social degradation," I answered.

"You don't like being here?" he asked. He picked up his pen as if to make a note of it in the file folder.

"No, not particularly. I'd sooner be sitting in the dining room of the prison, eating at a table with a knife, fork and spoon like a normal human being, instead of trying to eat a burger in the back of a mud-spattered van with my hands attached to a belly-chain."

"I see a great many men here like this," he said, a bit perturbed, "and they enjoy their outing." The way in which he formed his sentences fit his English accent perfectly. His pen was poised over the paper.

"Yes, they probably tell you that, but I'm willing to bet they're lifers too."

"Well, yes, most are. But what's that got to do with anything?"

"They can't say shit if they have a mouthful," I replied.

"What do you mean?" He seemed interested now, and he lay his pen on the desk.

"If they spoke honestly to you, as I'm doing here, you'd probably write a report stating that they had a bad attitude and obviously weren't ready to be released—which might mean another five years inside." In my anger I was being frank with him.

"But you can speak your mind?"

"Yes, I can. I have two years to my release date and I don't believe that anyone can twist the facts enough to make me stay past my time."

"And what do you mean by that?" he asked.

"I believe that any psychological tests, or any objective analysis by a competent professional would show me to be quite normal," I answered.

"I see," he said. I couldn't read whether he did or did not see what I meant.

As our conversation went on I explained that, yes, it did bother me to see mothers telling their children that my face was the face of the bogeyman. I also explained to him that it was good that it bothered me to be seen by members of the community in chains. "Show me a prisoner who doesn't care what people think of him, and I'll show you a dangerous man," I said. He nodded his head as though he agreed with me.

However, like all good things, the interview came to an end and I was taken back to prison in the van. I had four such interviews.

In our last session Doctor Weston asked me what my plans were. I told him that I'd probably find a halfway house to accept me, that I'd find a job and get on with my life. He suggested that I look at Bedford House, of which he was a part, because he said, "We run a house that's less restrictive than most others." He mentioned the John Howard Society and I liked the sound of it. The John Howard Society is an organization committed to improving our social and criminal justice system.

"Sounds good," I said.

"We have a mandatory Life Management Skills Program," he added, "but you won't have any trouble with that."

I told him I didn't expect so, for a I'd been the clerk of the Life Skills in Drumheller.

"Fine," he said.

"So what is your report going to say?" I asked.

"That you should be out of prison," he answered. And, with that conversation, the die was cast.

Following my last meeting with Doctor Weston, I called Judy to tell her of the new developments. She accepted the collect call charges and after our opening how-are-you's I gave her the good news.

"Weston is recommending that I be released right away," I said. I felt great; I was full of new hope. I had dreams of a new life, and the promise of a future full of freedom seemed imminent. There was a dead silence at the other end of line.

"Are you there?" I asked.

"Yes," she said, "I'm here." Her silence was an indication that all was not what it appeared to be.

"Is there someone else, Judy?" Again silence.

"No," she replied. "I'm just shocked, that's all." But I knew that if I could see her eyes they would avoid any real contact with mine.

We talked briefly, saying nothing, and on June 25 I received the dreaded "Dear John" letter. "Dear Wayne," it began, "the thing I said I would never do, which is write you and tell you instead of seeing you in person, I'm doing now..."

She'd met a man whom she's been together with ever since.

I went ahead with my plans, but I learned that I would first have to go to Bow River Correctional Centre in Calgary, and take the Life Management Skills program in Bedford House while living in that provincial institution. This was set up by my case manager and parole officer at the time.

On November 17, 1992 I left Drumheller for Bow River. The bus ride was a pleasure, and even though it was sleeting, I found it a welcome experience. When I arrived in Calgary, I phoned my stepson Jeff to let him know that I was on day parole, and that I'd be in touch with him once I was settled. I had a hundred and seventy dollars in my pocket. Fifteen minutes later I was picked up by Bow River staff and a short time later I was booked in.

During the booking I was seated on a bench in front of the Admitting and Discharge area, which is situated by the back door, and I caught a movement in my peripheral vision. I looked out to see a large dog moving past. I asked one of the people nearby if I could step outside for a moment and I received a nod of approval.

I could no longer see the dog so I just whistled. To my amazement he came running around the corner to lay prone at my feet. I reached out to pet him and as my fingers ruffed the hair on his head, he turned his brown face into my hand. I felt I'd found a friend.

"We have two dogs," said a voice. I looked up to see that a male staff member had walked out the door behind me.

"What's his name?"

"Clyde," he answered, "and the other is a female we call Bonnie." He explained that they had to keep at least one of them tied, to keep the other one around. If they were both free they'd run around the countryside and get themselves arrested. I had to laugh at that. It fit though; after all, this was a jail.

In no time at all I had a room and I checked the place out. The place was co-ed, and though there were a few federal prisoners like myself, most were provincial prisoners on pre-release programs. I was interviewed by my new case manager, a man called Mark, and he explained that I'd be leaving on a bus in the morning for a job search. He explained then that the Life Management Skills program in Bedford House was not being offered until January 18 and, because that was two months away, if I could find a job I could go to work until the program started.

The next morning I left Bow River and went into the city. I made a couple of phone calls and a man I'd met inside some years earlier steered me to the owner of a service station. I called him and he told me to come to see him the following day. I then called Jeff and told him I would meet him at a restaurant and we'd go together to surprise his sister. We met, had a cup of coffee, and went off to see my stepdaughter Debbie who lived with a young man in a high-rise apartment building downtown.

When she opened the door she was delighted to find me standing there with Jeff, and after a short introduction to her boyfriend, I took both Jeff and Debbie out for lunch. We had a good meal, during which Debbie and Jeff communicated that they'd like to see me back with their mother. I told them to put that thought completely out of their minds.

We took in some sights downtown; they'd grown up in that area and knew them all. We spent a fully enjoyable day together, and when it was time for me to return to Bow River at five o'clock, they took the LRT with me to the bus stop which would carry me on the last leg of the journey back to the halfway house.

When I arrived back at the Centre I found Mark Becker waiting for me. He asked me how my day had gone. I told him about the job opportunity, and the pending interview next day. He said there was some problem with my day parole, but that I could go out the next day while they cleared it up.

The next day I took the bus to the service station and talked to the man who owned it. He said I could start work on Tuesday, explaining that he needed someone mature to supervise the six kids who worked there. He knew where I was living, and that I'd just been released from prison—he had no problem with that. I stopped off at the licence bureau and took the learner's test via the computer, and I then went to see Debbie who cooked me a meal in her apartment. Life seemed to be unfolding in a very positive way.

I walked in the door of the Centre at five o'clock to find Mark Becker once again awaiting my arrival. He told me that I wasn't going to be allowed to go on any pass downtown, and that I couldn't take a job until I'd completed the Life Management Skills program at Bedford House. I asked if I could go to see Doctor Weston on Monday morning and he agreed to that. I spent a rather depressing weekend in my room.

On Monday I took the bus and the LRT to the hospital to see Weston. I had no appointment and simply showed up at the receptionist's desk. Although he was busy, she managed to get me a few minutes.

"What is it?" he asked. I explained that I couldn't be in Bedford until the program started in January which was two months away.

"Then get a job," he curtly stated. He seemed harried.

"I've got a job," I replied.

"Then go to work!" He wanted to hear no more of this nonsense.

"You got it!" I said, pleased as could be. I went back to the Bow River and told Mark what had been said, believing that the good doctor's opinion would hold sway. But the parole service would not fluctuate, and he showed me the written ruling, which clearly stated that if I made any attempt to change the day parole conditions, my day parole would be immediately terminated.

I tried one last time to find some reason in the madness. I phoned Central Parole and talked to the parole officer who had originally, along with my case manager, set up the whole package, right down to the last final and fine-print detail. He actually laughed at my predicament. I then phoned Doctor Weston. He was not available, for he was leaving for England. It was not easy to accept, but I did.

I went to work cleaning the gymnasium in Bow River for fifteen minutes each morning for two dollars a day. I would rise early and have shower, go for breakfast, and then walk to the doghouse and pick up one of the dogs who always seemed happy to accompany me to the gym. They were both well trained, and Bonnie wouldn't even enter a building. She looked to be part wolf, for her hair was more like a wolf's pelt than dog hair. Clyde would come with me into the gym and lie on the rug inside the door until I was done. Other than my short outing to do my job, I had to remain inside until after supper. All day long I listened to staff calling each other on the PA system, for that was how they communicated, and it was like living inside a bus depot where the arrivals and departures of the buses were announced every few minutes.

Everyone else in the Centre, except for a couple of female cooks in the kitchen, left the jail in the mornings for the city and returned at night. Some had regular jobs and were seldom seen in the Centre at all. Others would travel here and there to take care of the lives they had, and I sat there for two months with no meaning, no direction, and no money. If it wasn't for the generosity of a man I met while I was there, I wouldn't have been able to support my tobacco habit. I admit to feeling desperate.

Each night I walked the dogs. By keeping one on the leash, the other could run about in the fields, yet would always stay close by. Bonnie and Clyde had a very strong bond. They became so familiar with me that I only had to call them once, and no matter where they were or what they were doing, the one without the chain would always come running. During my nighttime walks with the dogs, I'd stand on top of a snow-covered hill, sometimes for hours. I would gaze at the lights of the city, "the lights of life," I called them, and I'd imagine myself travelling in one of the cars driving down the street, sitting in an apartment, having supper with friends and having a normal conversation. One cold night as I stood there I came up with a name for the program I was involved in. I called it the Reintegration by Osmosis Program, for it was as if I was expected to grow accustomed to the community by absorbing all the emotional things I needed by just looking at the lights of the city through the snow.

I came to know all the women there, and each of them told me her story. Many of the tales they told were heart-wrenching; almost all had been used and

abused by men all their lives. They understood after a time that I was not interested in any kind of sexual relationship with them, which somehow enhanced
and deepened their trust and honesty with me. One of them, Linda, a quite
beautiful young woman, took me for a walk one night and suggested we jump
into the snowbank for a quickie.

"It's cold on the bum, but it's fun too," she said. She was hurt when I
declined her tempting offer, so I explained my situation this way.

"Do you know what imprinting is?" I asked her. She walked beside me, and
Clyde was tugging on the leash. Though it was cold, it was still a beautiful winter night with no breeze, and it was perfect for walking.

"No," she answered. The tone of her reply told me her feelings were smarting.

"When a chick bursts out of its shell, it seizes on the first thing it sees as if
that thing was instrumental in its birth. It will follow that thing, be it a man, a
woman, a child, a balloon, or its mother, forever. It's kind of like love at first
sight," I said. Her company was always pleasurable for me, and I didn't want her
to be hurt in any way.

"Um-hmm," she murmured.

"Well, a man who's done a lot of time is like that with women," I went on,
"and he falls in love with the first naked woman he sees, and he'll follow her to
hell and back." She laughed. "I try my best to avoid that happening," I said. She
laughed again.

Later on, every once in a while, one of the women would make a remark
about imprinting to me as we passed in the hallway, which told me Linda had
talked to them. I'd always smile and tell them it was the truth. Which it is.

Jeff and Debbie offered to visit, but after I explored how they would come
to see me, I learned that they'd have to walk the last couple of miles from the
bus stop to the visiting-room door. That made me nervous, so I discouraged
them from coming.

At New Year's, one of the federal prisoners I knew asked me what I would
drink if I had a choice. I mentioned Southern Comfort, more to answer him
than anything else, for I was on the phone at the time and thought he was just
making conversation before he left on a pass. Later that evening he stopped at
my room to put a bottle of Southern Comfort and a small bottle of champagne
on my desk. I had a good New Year's party because of his kindness, and I'm
grateful to him for it to this very day.

January 18 finally arrived and I was transferred in the van to Bedford House.
I liked it, for it had small but regular apartments, and though I had to share with
two other men, I found it quiet, peaceful, and liveable.

I put away my belongings, made myself a bed in the living room, and then
went shopping with a forty dollar food voucher supplied by the house. I

shopped carefully—no frills, no extras— chicken instead of the expensive beef and pork, and I looked for bargains in the Co-op market. Linda was already there in the house and I spent a few minutes talking to her.

That afternoon I was called in to see the parole officer and the first words out of her mouth were startling.

"What are *you* doing here?" she asked, implying something was wrong.

"I'm on a day parole," I answered. The manner in which spoke to me suggested I had somehow managed to sneak in the back door hoping to find a handout.

"Yes," she said, "I know you're on day parole, but *why* are *you* in *this house?*" She was an attractive blonde woman in her thirties, and with her hair tied back, she looked as though she was no one to mess with. We were in her office, which was small, and a number of people waited outside to see her. I thought she was asking me to give her a reason for wanting to be there, much like the parole board asks a man why he thinks he deserves consideration for release.

"I'm here to take the Life Management Skills program," I replied, somewhat defensively. "But I do have to admit that it puzzles me why I have to take a program which will help me find a job, but I can't take a job if it's offered." Some sarcasm seeped into my voice at this point, for I harboured a shipload of resentment for the two wasted months in Bow River.

"This house is for people with *very special needs,*" she said. "I don't think *you* fit in here."

"Well somebody obviously thought I did." I felt I was about to be sent back to walk the dogs in Bow River. That thought scared me.

"And there's more to Life Management Skills than getting a job," she said, curtly but controlled. She appeared ready to have me ushered out the door.

"What do you mean?" I asked.

"You'll see—tonight is the first meeting."

That night I attended the first group session and found that Life Management Skills was a psychodrama group in which each group member acts out his crime. The group leader asked each man to step to one side of the room if they wanted to be there, and if not they were to remain where they were. I found myself alone in the center of the room.

"Where would you sooner be?" he asked.

"Riding the LRT, having a sandwich downtown, talking to my daughter and son, or watching a movie," I replied.

"Why?" he asked.

"Because I've heard every horror story in prison, I've seen many years of nothing but cruelty and violence, and I just spent two solid months listening to women tell me their histories of physical, emotional, sexual and psychological abuse at the hands of men. I'd like to live normally," I answered. I'm sure my deepest, most heartfelt feelings could be heard behind my words.

"Well, try it, Wayne," he suggested, "and see how it goes." I did. After all, I did have a decent place to stay.

A few weeks later my friend Linda got involved with cocaine use, and she called me from the Remand Centre to tell me that someone had written a report saying that I'd supplied the coke to her. She said she just wanted to let me know that this had happened, but she wanted me to know too, that she had cleared up the misunderstanding and had completely exonerated me. I never thought any more about it.

In Bedford House all inmates were interviewed by a psychiatrist, accompanied by a psychiatric nurse. No one had told me this was standard practice. It was unexpected, and the interview I went through truly frightened me. An office had been set aside and both the doctor and nurse had file folders stacked in front of them. I walked in and sat down, thinking they had me mixed up with someone else.

"Carlson?" the doctor asked. He didn't look up. He was a very large man who appeared to be more suited for construction work.

"Yes," I acknowledged.

"How are you doing?" he asked.

"Fine," I replied.

"No problems?"

"None," I stated. He looked at his nurse, who glanced down at her file.

"Does this man require any medication?" he asked. I was having none of this and I cut in with my own answer.

"No medication for me," I protested. "I'm not a mental patient." I felt butterflies begin to desperately beat their wings in my belly. Neither the doctor nor the nurse seemed to hear my plea. *Of course,* I thought, *all mental patients say that.* There was a long pause before she answered, and before she did, she looked directly into my eyes as if appraising me, and stared. I could picture her hazel eyes searching for a convenient spot on my body in which to thrust a needle full of medication.

"No," she answered, "I don't think there's any required." I could've kissed her.

"Okay," said the doctor, making a note then closing the file. I took his okay to mean I was dismissed and I quickly, and with a great deal of relief, made my way out of the room and began breathing again.

One day I walked to the Co-Op store to pick up my food supplies and I ran into a personal situation, the kind which I thought I'd left behind in the prison. I'd selected my supplies and added one package of cigarettes, and one package of tobacco and papers. The line of people was quite long, both in front and behind me.

"You know you can't do that!" shouted the clerk when it was my turn at the till.

"I can't do what?" I asked. She'd surprised me. I was trying my best to slip through with my voucher and remain anonymous and unnoticed by the line of people, who, with their shopping carts full of goodies, appeared to be part of the affluent middle class. I did have some pride.

"You can only have *one* pack of cigarettes, *or one* pack of tobacco," she said. "You can't have *both*. You know that!" I could feel my face getting redder through each beat of my heart. I was not aware of that rule.

"I'll take the tobacco and papers," I replied.

"Okay," she snapped. I remember walking down the street with two plastic bags and cursing her, cursing my sad and sorry situation and how unfair life was. Most of all I was cursing my addiction to nicotine and the tobacco companies who grew the killer weed, all of which and whom I felt were responsible for exposing me as a voucher-carrying welfare case. My pride had suffered a serious blow. *Life sucks,* I thought, *and it can't get worse than this.* I was wrong.

A short time after that even the comfort I'd had in the house was stripped away. When I would return from a few hours away from the house, the staff on duty would jump into my face when I stepped inside the door. They'd be very demanding, and I felt they were extremely rude, and even abusive, toward me. At night the man on duty began sneaking up on me in my room in the early morning hours, to jump from around the corner and unexpectedly slap my face with the light from his flashlight. It didn't take long for me to be unnerved by it all. The few times I attempted to discuss it with staff members I was met with cold silences, in which I could find only one answer: I was a hated man. I felt that most people do not fully comprehend that even prisoners, welfare cases though they may be, do have some sense of pride and feelings of self-worth and that these are tender, sometimes fragile things that can be painfully bruised and damaged. *Nobody understands people like me,* I thought. My resentment began to build, I was angry all the time, I felt that straight people were hateful, and that life itself was totally unfair.

It wasn't until much later that I learned that the erroneous report Linda had spoken of on the phone had indeed been filed, and believed by all. And it wasn't until after I was arrested that it was admitted to as being false. There was another Wayne who'd supplied her with cocaine, but everyone had thought it was me.

Time passed, life stayed the same, and my resentments grew, until one day I was sitting in a house in downtown Calgary with a small group of people just as lost as I was, who were discussing their money problems. I only knew one man there but a moment later I changed all that and I made them all my friends. I had no life, I had no friends, I had no money, and I no longer even had a place where I could comfortably take a nap, for I was no longer wanted in the building where I made my bed. So I did what any irrational, ill-equipped inmate with no future before him would do: I just gave up trying.

I took a pistol from the hand of one of my new friends, and after another offered to supply the vehicle, I proceeded to rob three banks and pay their bills. Aside from a Chinese dinner I bought absolutely nothing for myself. I didn't need things where I was going. I'd demonstrated I was willing to sacrifice for my friends, which meant I was a pretty nice guy.

I returned to Drumheller and I wasn't back an hour when I was offered the mail runner's job. I jumped on it, because it was a job where I only had to walk a couple of miles a day with a mail bag. It suited me perfectly.

I began to deal in smoke dope. It was a quiet way to earn a few bucks and it paid for my high as well. In every prison a man goes to there are drugs, and some men spend the whole of their sentences looking for drugs, finding drugs, paying for drugs, and getting high in between. It's part of the nature of the prison beast.

At night, after the doors were slammed shut and the prison fell into a fitful, uneasy slumber, I would lie in bed staring at my flickering television screen and see that, with all of my running and all of my cunning, I'd arrived at the edge of a black hole.

REDEMPTION

The electric fan blades were pointed toward the open window of my cell and, with the curtain pulled back and hooked to the wall with a piece of string, silent ribbons of blue cigarette smoke wafted into the open air of the courtyard. Just to be on the safe side, a stick of incense, pilfered from the chapel two days before, had been stabbed into the corkboard on the wall. As it glowed and smoldered its perfumed scent into the air of the cell, Lance and I felt our activities would be well disguised.

The guards making a range walk would use their eyes to look for anything unusual, which might mean trouble, but the smart ones also used their noses to smell illegal activity. Dope smoking wasn't high on their list of concerns, for they'd discovered over the years that smoking itself did not present a danger to the security of the institution. In fact, many of the more seasoned staff veterans welcomed its use, for it seemed to mellow the men in the joint. Home brew was a different matter. Once prisoners "got wet," the threat of violence permeated the ranges, and the very smell of the alcohol seemed to rise from the floors of the prison and roll down the ranges like a west coast fog. It was one thing to handle an angry, resentful and irrational inmate under ordinary circumstances, and it was quite another to handle him when he was drunk.

"When was the last round?" I asked.

"She won't be around for another half-hour," said Lance. He was thirty, but despite his age, and his seemingly innocent blue eyes and blond hair which gave him an all-Canadian-boy appearance, he was well on the way to making a reputation for himself as nobody to mess with in the system.

"Okay," I said "But keep your eye on the flash and keep six anyway."

"I'm on point," Lance replied. He sat on the toilet and leaned forward to peer into the sliver of broken mirror, which we called a flash, and watched for anyone coming onto the range. There were seventeen cells in all, with the odd numbers running down one side and the even numbers running down the other. We were in cell seventeen, the last on the range, so the mirror commanded a full view of all the cell doors and the corridor as well. If any guard decided to make a quick, unexpected time clock punch, Lance would have ample time to give warning.

Feeling comfortable with Lance's vigilance, I reached into my pocket and pulled out twelve dillys and a red, marble-sized balloon in which I kept three grams of "wheelchair" pot. My thumbnail slit the knot as neatly as a knife, and as the weed spilled onto the white paper we could smell the rich, pungent odour of the marijuana. I quickly and deftly began rolling joints and gave further instructions to my partner.

"If it looks like any of the grinders are coming down here, let me know," I cautioned.

"Right," replied Lance. He then added, "Horse-face cut into me before lunch..."

"Yeah? What the fuck did he want?"

"He was lookin' for a toke."

"If he knows, the whole fuckin' joint knows."

"I know, I told him fuck all."

"That's all we need, Horse-face in the know," I muttered as I licked the glue on the cigarette paper. I crimped both ends of the joint so the weed wouldn't fall out, then continued.

"The last time I turned him on I had fifty guys paging me to the door, lookin' to buy—but of course he denied sayin' a fuckin' word." I laughed at how ludicrous the denial was, for I'd told nobody else.

"That fuckin' Horse-face," Lance snorted in derision, "somebody should fuck him up." His tone of voice implied he need only to hear the word from me and he would personally take care of him.

"No, he can't help himself. Besides I've known him for years. Just tell him nothing and we'll put him on the grease," I said. I had four joints rolled, two of them "pinners," a term used by disgruntled buyers meaning they were the size of pins, and yet, though they were as small as possible, they were still good enough to sell for fifteen dollars plastic each on the open and needy market. The other two were larger, and we'd smoke them immediately. Having served a good portion of my life inside one prison or another, I knew every game, had heard every story, had seen many men come and go, rise and fall, and if nothing else I considered myself a survivor. I carefully wrapped the remains of the three grams into a fresh piece of Saran Wrap, opened my desk drawer and pulled out a new condom. I walked to my door and called Willy, a man who did odd jobs for me. In a moment he was there.

"I want you to suitcase this for me," I said.

I opened the plastic wrapping, unrolled the rubber tube and dropped the dillys into it. I tied it off and then turned this inside out again, and continued to do so until there was only the ring of the condom left. I snapped this off by pulling on it and tossed it on the table. I handed it to Willy. He didn't hesitate.

Willy took the rubber bundle in the palm of his hand and spit on it twice. He unzipped his pants, opened the top button, and put his hand between the cheeks of his buttocks and a second later he had the package safely "suitcased."

"Later," he said, sliding the door partially closed.

"Pick up the flash," I instructed Lance, "and sit down by the desk." Lance picked up the mirror, stood to his feet and put it on the shelf beside the door. I stepped to the sink and turned on the hot water tap. I began to wash my hands while Lance moved to the back of the cell to sit in the chair alongside the bed.

The cell was a seven by ten foot cinder block room painted institutional green. A steel-frame bed complete with a foam mattress was stretched out along one wall, and a steel desk with three drawers, a red plastic chair, and a large tack board above it occupied the opposite wall. At the end of the cell stood a seven foot tall, grey metal wardrobe. A white porcelain toilet squatted beside the door and a sink sat above it. The window was covered with a white, see-through curtain, and an immovable fluorescent plastic-covered light fixture ran across the ceiling at the back of the cell. Steel bolts driven into cinder block and concrete held everything firmly in position. Without exception, when unoccupied, each cell in the prison was exactly the same.

When occupied, a cell took on the individuality of its occupant, and though the towels on the wire rack beside the sink were a standard-issue blue, as were the blanket and sheets on the bed, the man who occupied that small space would eventually make the place into his own private living quarters. There were basically three things which would determined how comfortable the home of his cell would appear. The first was free-world wealth, the second was directly proportional to how jail-wise the man was and therefore how much he could acquire within the joint, and the third was how much time the man had already served on his present sentence.

Most prisoners had no family, and most had only the clothes on their backs. But if a man had good family connections he might have a colour television set, a stereo, a coffee pot or kettle, a fan, a top-of-the-line computer, and his steel wardrobe would be full of street clothes and expensive sneakers.

The extra furnishings in each cell were arranged to suit the personality and the preferences of the prisoner, and wood shelves would be placed over the sink, over his desk, or at the side of his bed. A lamp, which would softly illuminate the room and eliminate the need for the harsh, glaring overhead light, would eventually find its way onto on his desk. Sometimes a light fixture would be hung over his sink as well. There would be large mirrors placed in strategic positions on his walls and over his sink, for these not only gave the illusion that his cell was much larger than it was, but it satisfied his ego to be able to see his own reflection no matter where he happened to be standing in the room. Many men worked out in the gym, and those men who dropped in to visit would usually pause and peer at themselves, vainly twisting this way and that in the mirror, eyeballing themselves critically while they discussed something of momentary importance.

There was also an extra coffee cup, and though coffee was one of the three most often sought after legal commodities, the others being tobacco and sugar, the well-to-do always had the kettle near at hand and close to the boiling point for any- one who happened to drop in for a chat or to do business. It was a mark of one's prison status to be asked if he would like a cup of coffee when he went visiting, and it was important too that the occupant of the cell had some to offer.

The only way most men could acquire the creature comforts they desired was to wheel and deal inside the joint. Drugs and cash money were the two most important currencies, and the plastic tokens—called "plastic"—which could be spent in the prisoners' canteen were a close third. Almost all prisoners lived beyond their means, which made for a hustling, bustling, needful but interest- ing life for everyone doing time.

I finished washing my hands, reached under my bed and pulled out a plastic bag into which I placed the soiled towel. I glanced at Lance who was surfing the channels with the remote control.

"Hand me a towel from the shelf," I said. Lance pulled back the curtain on the wardrobe, reached up and took one from the top of the neatly folded stack and handed it to me. I took it, folded it over the wire rack and proceeded to plug the kettle in.

"Are we going to do a doobie before count?" asked Lance, still looking through the channels. It was late afternoon and the count was thirty minutes away.

"We'll do two, and I'll flog two," I answered. "Carl will take 'em in a heart- beat, and nobody'll know he's got. He only smokes at night, after lockup." If a toker carelessly did a joint with no thought to the smell which would permeate the air, the grinders would be on point, tirelessly searching through every unit, like bird dogs on the scent in a field, looking for the source of the smell. If they found it, the grind would be on. The grind was a term applied to the manner in which some addicts sought relief. They'd start by asking for a cuff—or credit— involving every conceivable promise of future payment they could come up with. If this didn't work they'd resort to subtle and not so subtle forms of intim- idation, which meant that someone holding would have, at the very least, a minor but needless problem to deal with. Seasoned veterans knew full well the best way to avoid grinding hassles was to maintain complete and total secrecy. The men I dealt with knew that if they told someone, or if someone else even inadvertently found out that I was holding narcotics, their position of trust would no longer be held, and they'd be put on the grease without a word being said. Without words and discussion there would be no resolution—there'd be only the fact that one was on the dreaded grease. The Amish have a different name for the grease; they call it shunning, but regardless of the term, the effect was the same. The greased became invisible, unacknowledged men. Men who had been friends for a long time sometimes put each other on the grease for years, and all because of a slight, real or imagined.

The water was boiling, the coffee, cream and sugar was spooned into the plastic mugs and I popped my head out the door and took one quick look down the hallway. After finding it clear of movement, I lit one of the joints. I stood with my back to the door, which blocked the view should anyone pass by and curiously peer in. Casually I sucked in the smoke with three practiced drags and held my breath as I passed it to Lance, who stood to his feet. As we smoked we stood close together and blew lungs full of pungent weed into the stream of the whirling fan blades, and it was carried directly out the window where it wafted unnoticeably away. In less than two minutes we'd smoked both joints, each chewing and swallowing one of the roaches, and a few moments later we were feeling the euphoric affects. I picked up the remaining two joints, carefully rolled them like a firehose into a small circle, wrapped them in Saran Wrap and put them in a corner of my pants pocket. If I was forced by guards to undergo a search I had them ready to pop into my mouth and quickly swallow if need be. But I felt safe now, secure in my own space, and as I lay back on my bed we began watching downhill skiing on the CBC Sports channel.

The effects of the marijuana seemed to heighten our senses. We thought we could hear every sound in the prison: a voice harangued the guard in the security bubble, a stereo played headbanger music down the hall, and yells from a group of prisoners playing like kids in the courtyard floated in through the open window. In the distance, on the other side of the fences, a crow cawed a signal to one of his brethren and, as time slowed, I was kicked into a mood of reminiscence. Lance was always a good audience for my stories.

"I knew this kid who was probably as dangerous as they come," I started. I leaned back against the two pillows on my bed just below the window sill, interlaced my fingers and put my hands behind my head. With my legs casually crossed I'm sure I looked as if I was at home, which in fact I was, at least for the next ten years. We both looked at the television set and not at each other.

"Yeah?" Lance sat leaning slightly forward, as if attentive to the skiing, but he was listening closely to what I was saying.

"He was just a kid, nineteen in fact, when he killed a guy here."

"In this joint?"

"In this joint, and on this range."

"Shanked him?"

"No, he first smashed him in the head with a lamp, and when the man went down he used the bed leg to beat his brains out."

"The beds are bolted to the floor—so how?"

"They weren't then. After the killing they were nailed down."

"Why did he do it?"

"There was a rumour the guy was a skinner."

"Was he?"

"No, he was just an old man nobody knew anything about, and the kid wanted a reputation—the old man was available."

"Did the coppers catch the play?"

"No. It seems one of them smelled the presence of death."

"Death?" asked Lance.

"Yeah, the blood and shit when the man let go."

"What happened to the kid?"

"He got five years for manslaughter, and they transferred him to Stony Mountain after the trial."

"He got lucky," stated Lance, who thought the story was over. He leaned back in the chair, never taking his eyes off the screen.

"He killed a guy in Stony too."

"Really?" He leaned forward again.

"Yeah, shanked him for coming onto him, plunged him over twenty times. Do you know how much work it is to plunge a man over twenty times?" I turned my head to glance briefly at my visitor and reached to pick up my coffee cup on the shelf beside my bed. I took a sip.

"Yeah, a lot of work," Lance mused. He paused for a moment then asked, "What do you mean 'for coming onto him?'"

"Homo, faggot stuff."

"Oh."

"He got a fin for that one too."

"Jesus!" A fin was five years, small time for murder.

"Yeah—he then went on to the SHU in Prince Albert." The SHU, pronounced "shoe," was short for the Special Handling Unit.

"Yeah?"

"Yep, rumour has it he was suspected of strangling a man there with a shoelace—no evidence though. Then he transferred to Kent."

"So he's in Kent now?"

"Nope. He killed a guy there, in the gym with a ball bat. The guys say the kid beat him so bad his head was smashed to pulp and he was literally unrecognizable."

"Don't tell me—he got a fin," said Lance.

"No," I responded. "First degree, life twenty-five. I guess they got tired of him."

"He's fucked then."

"Yeah, that's one way of lookin' at it. But maybe he's happy now."

"Happy?"

"Yeah, I think he wanted that life sentence from the get-go," I suggested.

"He must be a fuckin' bug," ventured Lance. A bug was someone who was crazy. He took a sip of coffee and watched as the USA skier took a tumble on the downhill run.

"No, not really," I answered. "He's just one of those guys with no respect for life—not even his own. The last I heard he was in the Prince Albert Penitentiary SHU, still in phase one, and where other guys put up girlie pictures, he has the blown-up autopsy pictures of his victims on his walls."

"Fuckin' gruesome."

"Yeah, it's that alright. The last thing he sees at night are the bloody bodies, and it's the first thing he sees when he wakes up." I paused while I watched a skier race across the finish line before I added, "he's got two of them taped to his ceiling, so when he opens his eyes in the morning he's got a full view of his favourites." I was interrupted by a guard's voice blaring over the intercom. It was a demanding shout in the ears of the men in the unit, instructing us that we had one minute until the stand-to count. The stand-to count had been implemented years before, after a dead man had been counted twice, and it meant that each inmate had to now stand on his feet, and show his "living, breathing flesh" so the guards who counted him in his cell knew he was alive.

"Hanging the autopsy pictures on the wall—Jesus. Do you think he'll do it again?" asked Lance.

"Probably," I replied. "It's weird. I think about the guys who have porno pussy pictures on their walls, and when they get tired of them they want new ones. When this kid gets tired of lookin' at the same bodies, it seems he'll just make new ones himself."

"And you don't think he's a bug?" asked Lance.

"Hell no. If you met him, you'd like him. And he tells a good joke."

"A good joke?" he said, as if it were ludicrous that such a man could make someone laugh.

"He's got a great sense of humour," I said, "and when we've got time I'll tell you a joke he told me." The intercom blared out that it was time for the count.

"I gotta go," stated Lance. He stood up and looked down at me on the bed. "See you later," he said.

"Yeah, later," I acknowledged, and as Lance reached the door I added, "close my door will you?"

"You got it," said Lance. He closed the cell door and as it clumped shut I'm sure he found his head buzzing, both from the weed and the brutal mental images. He walked five cells down and turned into his own sparsely furnished space, and he slid closed the door behind him.

My case manager was a woman who seemed to enjoy keeping men in prison—me in particular. It was unpleasant being in the same room with her; other prisoners on her caseload, and even other staff members felt the same way.

One day she called me to her office, handed me a document, and told me I had an hour to make up my mind whether or not I'd agree to take part in it. I glanced at it quickly. It was a poop sheet on a new program. I knew if I didn't take part, she'd write me up as refusing to take programs. Such a report can have consequences later on.

I looked at it over lunch, and though there were many interesting items, I focused on one of them. Anybody who took the cognitive program was expected to keep a journal while they were there. I'd always wanted to keep a journal, and though I wrote a great deal, I'd never bothered to keep anything resembling a diary. It was that small thing that brought me into one of the best learning experiences of my life. In November, 1993 I took part in the Innovative Socialization Program in the Regional Psychiatric Centre in Saskatoon. It was an intensive six month cognitive program, consisting of separate modules on emotional awareness, human values, principles, moral reasoning, Rational Emotive Therapy, the importance of leisure activities, and in-depth group discussion and group activities. As well, as an integral part of the program, we were required to record our thoughts, feelings and activities in a daily journal. This journal was periodically read and reviewed by each participant's primary nurse, and any personal issues the participant might have, were discussed.

The program did not allow the participants to socialize with anyone outside of the group for the first three months. This effectively created a situation where any problems between the members had to be worked out between them; this was unique for almost all of us, for we'd grown accustomed to simply putting our antagonists on the grease. It's the prisoner's way of dealing with people in the penitentiary, and it's the way he continues to deal with people and problems once he's released.

One of the questions we were asked to supply an answer to in the beginning of the program was, "Why did you volunteer for this program?" Everyone had their own answer, and some of the responses involved parole, while others suggested they felt they had to take the program because their case manager suggested they do so. When it came my turn I said I was there in that chair, because I wanted to know why I was there in that chair, and I said I thought the program might supply me with an answer. All of the men who took that program learned a great deal about themselves and about other people. I came away with a much clearer understanding of who I was and why I was that way.

Over the course of the program I slowly became aware of how I thought, how I felt, and how I acted in different situations. I knew I had some intelligence, for I could read and understand fairly complicated passages in literature, I'd successfully studied electronics and complex circuitry was something I could grasp, yet there was something important lacking in my social being. Reading and learning in a cell where one is as solitary as an oyster is one thing, but applying that learning with people in a social situation is quite another. What changed in me when I walked out of my cell and into the community? If I disliked prison as much I believed I did, why would I place myself in situations which would in all likelihood put me back me back inside? Yes, I'd had some bad experiences when I was growing up, yet I had a brother less than a year younger than myself who'd managed not only to survive those experiences, but go on to become a successful man in the community. I had a conversation with him about that very thing many years ago.

"How do you feel about this, Roger?" I asked about a particularly difficult time in our lives. We hadn't seen each for many years, and as usual I was on the run.

"I don't think about those things," he answered. "In fact, I don't think about anything that happened to me before I was sixteen years old." He didn't elaborate and I didn't continue to explore the past with him. I never gave it further thought until the ISP program.

During my analysis of the meaning behind the psychological principle of reinforcement, a difference between my brother and myself began to slowly emerge. He no longer thought about those same things I hung onto and mentally chewed and regurgitated, over and over again. Why would I do this when it was so painful to me? The principle of reinforcement helped me answer that question.

A human being seeks pleasure, and seeks to avoid pain,
If an action bring pleasure, he will do so again.

There must have been a pleasure in the pain of my remembering the past to keep me returning to it in my mind, but what could that pleasure be? The answer to this began to flower in my mind, starting as a small bud and slowly growing until it became large enough for me to see. In remembering all the past transgressions against me, I was able to focus on how badly others treated me, and avoid thinking of my transgressions against others. I could always justify the things I did by looking at the things others had done to me when I was younger. I was extremely self-centred and, because I looked only at my own needs and ignored the needs of others, I acted in ways that hurt people badly, yet I never looked at that

In my self-centredness I wouldn't look at anyone's pain but my own. I had no understanding of what the word "empathy" meant; I was too busy walking in my own shoes and taking what I wanted from people to even pause and consider their feelings. I never saw people as giving me something out of kindness; if someone gave me something I perceived it as something I deserved. Therefore gratitude was something I knew nothing about. How can a man be grateful when whatever he receives he feels he deserves as a matter of right?

I met a young man by the name of Chris Hood, and though I wasn't to know it for some time, his suicide was to play a major role in my life.

As part of our program, we each had to write out three positive significant events in our lives. I was hard pressed to remember that many and I wasn't the only one. Chris wrote a short story, which talked about his upbringing with a stepfather, and when he handed it to me to read I immediately did so.

When he was at the curious age of two, his father began teaching him the names of plants, animals and things. But there was a twist to this educational experience — he was taught that a crow was a duck, a pig was a horse, a cow was a deer, an eagle was a pigeon, and so on. When Chris entered school, he began to get into fights with other kids in his class because he insisted he was right; after all, his dad had taught him and his dad knew everything.

Until the ISP, Chris had no idea of the effect this must have had on him. Most certainly he would have had a difficult time trusting any teacher or figure of authority. I began to spend time with him. He talked of his life and talked long about his mother, whom he dearly loved.

Chris was eligible for day parole, and he chose to take the St. Norbert's drug treatment program. I knew he had a problem with substances, but he'd just completed an intensive program and I thought he should go home to his mother and his sisters. He insisted on St. Norbert's.

He left for Winnipeg and that was the last time I saw him. He went unlawfully at large from the treatment centre, turned himself in to police in Kenora, Ontario and he was sent back to Stony Mountain Penitentiary.

Later, our program director, Dr. Cindy Presse, called us into a side room to tell us that Chris had hanged himself in his cell. It was devastating news. We were all affected and I knew his mother, Erna, would be suffering the torture of the damned. I called her on the phone and we spent hours discussing Chris and his life, and she came to see me a few weeks later. We remained friends from that point on. It was my relationship with Chris's mother that would later lead me to become involved in an inmate suicide prevention program, the Sams of Drum Pen.

I'd been writing with an old typewriter. There were times when the frustration of confinement made my life miserable, but I discovered an outlet in writing. One afternoon, when the frustration weighed heavily on my mind, I wrote a short piece I called The Way It Is. It was one of my first attempts at writing about the experience of being in prison, an exercise which eventually became this book.

During the time I spent in the ISP, a time in which human beings with feelings began to take shape before me, I learned about gratitude, and through personally experiencing that feeling I began to see the value of human kindness. To give such a pleasurable feeling to someone else was something I began to practice. I'd stop and listen to prisoners, knowing they'd appreciate my doing so. I'd talk to them and give them a sense of recognition, not because I needed something from them, but because I wanted them to feel accepted and as comfortable as possible.

I'd had my first experience as a gardener in Marion, and it had given me a wealth of knowledge. When I was offered a job on the yard crew in RPC I didn't hesitate, and I immediately went to work in the large flower garden with a man called Blue.

There were some plants that required special attention; at times it was a simple matter of overcrowding in one area, or the way the water ran during a rain. At other times we had no perceivable explanation for it, but transplanting them often helped. As we worked, other prisoners would walk by on their exercise period. Many of them, like some of the flowers, required special attention, and we'd come to know them by name and by disposition. Gary was one of them. As he approached, Blue called out to him.

"*Hey* Gary!" Gary walked over to where we were filling vases. "Give us a hand here Buddy." Gary had a sour look on his face, which spoke volumes for his feelings.

"*I'm* a *girl* you know," he said. He was a large, heavy man, who always said the same thing whenever he was having a bad day.

"*No*," replied Blue, "*you're* no girl. *You're* a man."

"*I am*, I'm a *girl*." Gary picked up a large yellow marigold and, with its stem in his hand, he looked for a place in a half-filled vase in which to set it.

"Here buddy," Blue pointed to a spot in the vase he was working on, "put it right there." Gary carefully placed it between two orange snapdragons. A nurse was strolling by on one of her rounds. It was Natalie, from Gary's unit. Off to the side a portable stereo system played Bonnie Raitt and the sounds drifted across the garden to us. The nurse stepped from the sidewalk and walked across the grass.

"Are you making flower arrangements?" she asked Gary.

"Yeah," he paused, his face was slack-jawed in concentration. He was inserting a difficult snapdragon into a bouquet, "*I'm* making arrangements."

"And a good job too," I encouraged. I'd been struck by Natalie's professional kindness over the past months whenever I'd encountered her in the hallway or courtyard. She had a way with prisoners who had difficulty functioning, and they responded to her in a most positive fashion. They became less suspicious, more open and friendly, and were drawn to her human warmth. I was unused to seeing such treatment of prisoners in any institution, and the first time I saw it, I was deeply touched by the sight.

A half-hour passed as we talked and lightly joked with one another, and soon it was time for Gary to leave. We all said our goodbyes and Natalie left with her group for the unit. As they walked away, I made a comment to Blue.

"Some of the guys in here *think* they have it tough," I said. I was thinking of the men from other units who were able to function, but chose not to, while Gary and others like him needed special attention. I tucked a bright white snapdragon into place.

"And our guys," responded Blue, "don't give them the time of day." "Our guys" were the patients from the regular prison environment. I agreed with his tone which implied it was a shame on us. On that note that we gathered up our containers and left the garden for our unit, which was called Assiniboine.

I was born a stone's throw from the Assiniboine river in northern Saskatchewan. My great-grandfather would swim across the river with a ploughshare on his back to take it to the only blacksmith for miles around for sharpening. He died after contracting pneumonia following one such adventure, leaving behind a wife and eleven children to run the farm and fend for themselves on undeveloped land. In 1903, it had yet to be declared a part of Confederation. From time to time I'd imagine my great-grandfather, my grandfather, and my father as well, rolling over in their graves if they knew I was now living inside a psychiatric centre in a unit named after the river running past their farmland.

Blue had a background far different from mine. Where I picked rocks and roots off the family farm in the heat of the Saskatchewan sun at a young and tender age, the big man picked pockets in the city of Winnipeg. It was Blue who'd laid out the garden and planted it in the early spring. I hadn't come into the picture until June when the flowers were already beginning to bud.

We'd become acquainted in the mid-seventies and we were such seasoned veterans in the system, we'd both, at one time or another, been written off as incorrigible. Blue had completed the Innovative Socialization Program in August of 1993, and I'd taken the program some three months later.

The sun shone brightly through the windows as we walked the main circular hallway, off which ran the doors leading to other departments and work areas. We passed staff members and prisoners, and at times, outside visitors. All seemed delighted by the beauty of the flowers we carried.

We stopped at the door leading to our unit, and as I set down one of the vases to open it, a male nurse walked by. It was Kevin.

"Flowers look great," he commented. He paused for a moment. He was a young, sandy-haired man of medium height, quite professional with the patients, and he had a wry sense of humour.

"Yes," replied Blue, holding up a vase to the sunlight. The freshness of the colours were remarkable.

"How do you guys do it?" asked Kevin.

"We care," I said.

"TLC?" suggested Kevin, meaning if someone cared for things, those things would grow.

"That's it," said Blue. Kevin smiled his agreement and he continued on his way. I pulled the door open and we walked through. As we sat down at a table, coffee cups in hand, I brought up Kevin's comment in the hallway.

"Remember what Kevin said, about TLC?" I asked.

"Yes?"

"Well, when I was debating on whether or not to come here," I explained, "a friend of mine in Drumheller said the same thing about this place."

"Mmm-hmm," Blue murmured over the lip of his coffee cup. He had a very direct way of looking into a speaker's eyes.

"He told me I'd never regret this experience," I said, pausing to drink from my cup, "and he was right." I put the cup back on the table and thought of how pleasant life could be if there were kindness in people.

"Yes," responded Blue, "it's a good atmosphere, but not everyone can handle it."

"Yeah. I noticed the difference in the way we were treated as soon as I stepped off the bus." I hadn't been in the centre as long as Blue, but I could recall my own adjustment period. I couldn't help but notice the difference between those who'd taken programs, and those who hadn't. New arrivals were more hyper and abrasive, and though some of it was due to where they had just come from, it was also due to their basic insecurities at being out of their comfort zone. As strange as it seemed, a man can become quite comfortable living in fear and hatred. Those two things can fill a man's mind and he doesn't have to think much, nor does he have to deal with his own personal problems.

Ignorance can be blissful, and as Thomas Gray said, *"Where ignorance rules, 'tis folly to be wise."*

"Remember that vase of flowers I gave Ed?" Blue asked, after another sip of coffee.

"Yes?" I did.

"Ed had visitors at his home, all the way from China. Professional people," said Blue. He seemed to be thinking about the distance. "It's as if our garden is now known worldwide." Blue sipped his coffee and went on. "Ed took them home, showed them to his guests, and they were impressed."

"Really?" I liked that idea. I never tired of compliments on the garden.

"Really."

"World-renowned gardeners—I like that idea."

"Even if the appreciation doesn't last that long, it was there, for a moment, and it does make a difference," Blue suggested.

The door opened and Kevin, whom we'd met in the hallway, appeared. He walked in, looked directly at us, and walked to our table.

"You're both invited to the stores area, tomorrow for lunch." he said.

"A dinner?" We were both pleased.

"Yes," answered Kevin, "In appreciation for the work you guys put into the garden."

"Great!" declared Blue.

"When the count's clear," said Kevin, "you can just go down there." We thanked him and he left.

I began to more clearly understand what it meant to be a social human being, which means that I began to see that people are very much the same under the skin. I knew what pain was, and once I began to comprehend that we're all subject to that pain, I no longer wanted to do or say things that would hurt others. As well, if people hurt me, it didn't hurt as much as it used to. If people let me down, I didn't write them off as being unworthy. I'd been far worse to others than they were to me. After a time, I found pleasure in small, everyday things. I spent a total of fifteen months in that kind and warm-hearted environment, and too soon it was back to Drumheller.

The day the bus pulled into Drumheller was a day to remember. Four men met me at the A&D door, expecting to see the wheeling, dealing man they'd come to know. I briefly talked to them and told them I'd be in touch. Later that night I took them for a walk and told them I'd no longer be doing those things that they thought I did better than anyone else.

I began to take part in worthwhile programs, including instructing my peers in first aid, and coordinating The Sams of Drum Pen, a volunteer group of prisoners who assist other prisoners who are under a great deal of emotional stress and anxiety. Part of the Sams philosophy is that a Sam must maintain confidentiality with any "contact" he has with someone under stress. I believe bringing compassion and human understanding into the prison system is one of the most worthwhile endeavors and undertakings a man can do. In the years I was a Sam in Drumheller, I never had a prisoner disagree with my belief. It was remarkable that Hilde Schlosar, the Executive Director of The Samaritans of Southern Alberta, could bring such a program into the penitentiary system.

After the Sams training, I began to listen to prisoners whom, in the past, I would have put on my "pay them no mind list" and ignored. One evening, a friend of mine, Dennis Maday, asked if I would visit a man in another unit who was in a great deal of emotional and psychological distress—he'd just been informed he had contracted HIV. He not only had to deal with the psychological reality of having the virus, he was very fearful other prisoners would learn he had it and he turned to the Sams. I sat in his cell with him on many occasions, and six months later he called me to his cell to thank me, not only for the emotional support I'd provided, but for keeping confidentiality.

I'd been writing off and on for years, and when the opportunity came to take part in a creative writing class instructed by Pat Quinn, I did so.

Pat had an approach completely different from other staff members in Drumheller. He wasn't trying to impress the men in his charge, he was intent only on helping them develop their creative talents. After I completed the first class he asked me if I'd co-facilitate the next one, and because I thoroughly enjoyed working with him, I agreed to do it. It was through Pat Quinn's encouragement that I realized I could be a writer.

Rick Lévesque and I developed and delivered our own material for a substance abuse program; we based it on the rational recovery philosophy.

Stephen Reid and I communicated closely during our struggle to defeat Bill C-220. The Bill, if passed, would mean that writers like Stephen and me, with criminal histories, wouldn't be able to make a living. I found Stephen to be a dedicated man and writer, and I'm grateful for his continuing support of me as a writer.

Committing myself to these endeavours not only helped others, it assisted me in that my involvement allowed me the benefit of being surrounded by the more positive attitudes in the prison.

I began keeping a regular routine which helped me to keep on track. If I found I wasn't maintaining it, I knew something was bothering me. I would then look for the reason, identify it, and deal with it in a rational and productive manner. I stayed away from drugs and I avoided users as much as possible. I discovered through observation of others that one who uses substances will not be able to successfully maintain any kind of regular routine, even weight pit workouts. I found a pleasure in looking back at the end of each day with a real sense of accomplishment.

I became reliable and dependable and I took seriously the things I said I'd do. I discovered too that in avoiding substances and those who use them, I avoided most of the daily stresses in my life. If someone came to see me, it was for legitimate purposes and I welcomed their company. If I could help them I would do so, and people understood I was doing so because I wanted to, and not because I had a hidden agenda. I could see they were grateful for it, which in turn made me feel I was a positive and productive man.

I had almost no confrontations with staff. I was able to deal with them as I dealt with prisoners, because people are people no matter what colour the clothes they wear or what they do for a living. Life was unfolding quietly and well, until one night when things went topsy-turvy. I was sitting at my computer writing a letter when it all began.

On January 2, 1997, at around 9:15 p.m., Dennis stopped by my cell door to tell me there might be a problem. I'd known him for many years. He was my workout partner and we were tight.

"What kind of problem?" I asked.

"Guards got into it with a couple of kids in another unit."

There are four units in Drumheller, each separate from the other, each housing a hundred forty men. The men from all units interact and socialize in the gym, the courtyard and the Back Forty, where tennis courts, ball diamonds and running tracks are laid out and surrounded by perimeter fences and gun towers. Although the prison is spread over more than eighty acres, a problem in one section can very well mean a problem for everyone.

"A beef?" I asked.

"Yeah, kind of a one-on-one. A guard was cut."

"So there's a lockdown coming?"

"There should be. And the kids are really talking it up in the courtyard—hey, can I borrow some cigarette tubes? I'll pay you back tomorrow."

I kidded him about telling me about the lockdown and then asking to borrow something until *tomorrow*, but I gave him the tubes anyway.

During a lockdown, all inmates are shut in their cells with no access to the areas that supply their daily needs. The wise stockpile soap, tobacco, cigarette papers, tubes, coffee, sugar, writing paper, pens, stamps and even toilet paper. When an unusual number of men are looking to borrow items, it generally indicates that something violent is going to occur. If those with influence—elected inmate reps and ethnic group leaders—miss these small indicators or fail to notice unusual gatherings of men, it means the storm will hit and catch them by surprise.

After my friend left, I took my nightly walk in the yard. I left the unit for the small track in the Back Forty, looking for signs of trouble. The ice and snow made the ground so slippery that I found it difficult to walk and I only made one round. There were about ten men scattered around the shared courtyard in front of the four units. Nothing unusual. I walked back into the unit and onto my range. I told the men there that everything seemed quiet in the yard.

Just before the nightly 10:30 lockup was called, a young friend of mine from another range dropped by to see me.

"I was just told to go to the yard," he said nervously. "I was told it's happening. They're tearing the joint down."

"Yeah, right," I said sarcastically. I didn't think the incident with the guard was enough to generate a riot. Drumheller is an open federal prison, and in terms of freedom inside the perimeter fences, it's second to none in Canada.

"No, seriously, everybody's being told to go to the yard. I don't know what to do."

"Just go back to your cell," I suggested. "Close your door when they call lock-up. It's what I'm going to do." My friend seemed to relax and he left for his cell. Seconds after the five-minutes-to-lockup was announced, a man showed up at my door. He was wearing a large, green prison-issue parka and he seemed rather puffed with self-importance.

"Well," he said, his hands hidden in his pockets, his body language and tone of voice meant to be intimidating.

"Well what?" I asked.

"Everybody's going to the yard. It's going down."

"What do you mean everybody?"

"There's a hundred guys out there now."

"A hundred men is not everybody," I said.

"We got to show some *heart*," he said, subdued, but playing on my convict guilt.

As he walked away I began shutting my computer down, and just as the last flash of light flared across the screen of my monitor, I heard an explosion of noise. "Get those cocksuckers—rip their fuckin' heads off. Yeah! You fuckin' goof!" I stepped outside my door and looked down the range toward the noise. A group of frenzied men wearing homemade balaclavas were pounding and hammering with makeshift clubs and sticks at the windows of the security bubble. Constructed of reinforced glass, the security bubble is held together by a solid steel framework, and is the location of the inmates' files and the electronic panels that operate and control the phones, cell doors and lights. The bubble is the brain and nerve centre of the unit and once breached and taken by rioters, the whole area is captured. I heard glass shatter, and suddenly there were more men with balaclavas using bars and what looked like wooden coat trees to smash at the glass. I watched for a moment, transfixed, hoping to get some idea of who they were. I took a couple of steps toward the cell across the hall and found Rubberneck and Randy, two friends of mine, in a state of near panic. They were busy helping each other put heavy magazines around their torsos. An old but effective penitentiary method of shielding the body, it might not stop, but will surely slow the penetrating blade of a shank.

"It's come," Randy said, his face white. "It's going down! And some people here hate me! Well, I'm fuckin' ready!" Turning and looking down the hallway I saw a balaclava-clad figure come up the stairs. He began walking slowly toward me. I stepped into the hallway to confront him.

"What's up?" I asked.

"I don't know," he said. Looking into the eyes peering at me through the slits of the balaclava, I realized he was just a kid playing dress-up, caught in the pan-demonium—no threat to my security. I refocused my attention on the people still determinedly smashing at the glass of the bubble. They too were young, dangerous and wild with a will to destroy.

I was going to have to protect my computer, stereo and television as best I could, so I walked toward the front of the range in search of some garbage bags. Once a riot's become full-blown it's like being in a hurricane aboard a mutinous ship. You can only batten down the hatches, protect yourself as best you can and wait for it to pass. To batten down my own hatches, I needed to cover my computer and other precious items. I stepped into the hallway and saw that fires had been lit and smoke had begun to billow up the range. My head was filled with the sounds of splintering wood, breaking glass and mindless, raging curses. Every once in a while, high-pitched maniacal laughter rose above the storm of violence. I knew staff had long since abandoned their security post through the escape hatch in the floor of the bubble. I also knew that once individual files had been snatched, there'd be bloodshed. The files contain information on every man's criminal record and if there's anything that points to him being a sex offender or an informer, the other prisoners would destroy him.

I walked down the range and saw hooded figures competing with one another to smash anything breakable. Passing by the staff computer room, I glanced in. Amid clouds of smoke, a man was smashing the office. The hot yellow flames of a fire licked at the pile of computers, printers, files, paper, chairs and desks that were trashed and stacked in the centre of the room. The water sprinklers had been triggered and though water poured over him, the tall, skinny kid ignored it and concentrated on piling more material on his makeshift bonfire.

"Is there a garbage bag in there?" I asked. He stopped to look at me, then bent down to pull a bag of garbage from the heap of destroyed material in front of him. "Yeah, here's one," he said calmly. He shook the paper from the bag into the flames and handed it to me. I took it and returned to my cell where I arranged the plastic over my keyboard and printer and planned to head outside. I called to my next door neighbour Mike, an old friend of mine, to get his warm clothes on. I also told Rubberneck and Randy that it was time to abandon ship. I locked my cell door behind me.

Outside, standing around the courtyard, were a dozen men wearing balaclavas, and they all seemed to know each other. One of them walked through the crowd to speak to me. I could see other men with balaclavas talking to barefaced men in the crowd. It was as if the rioters were looking for recognition, a pat on the back for a job well done, as if we should not only all agree with their actions, but applaud them. The man who approached me explained the incident that had lit the fuse of the explosion.

Earlier in the evening, two guards had become involved in a dispute with two inmates over a television set. One man was returning a borrowed TV to its owner and, after being confronted by a guard in front of the cell, a struggle ensued. The guard required stitches.

Sometime later, the correctional supervisor called some inmate reps to his office for a conference. The reps returned to tell the prisoners who'd been involved that they had to go peacefully to the hole. As soon as they complied, a few of the men in that unit decided to go to war. They felt their friends had been wronged; that it was the guard who had deliberately initiated the struggle when he should've let the inmate who owned the set place it in his cell. In short order they enlisted others, and because they were unimportant in the inmate hierarchy, their plans went unnoticed.

Over a two-hour period that night, a handful of the young and restless organized and dispersed into separate gangs in order to attack each unit's security bubble in concert. The five-minutes-to-count announcement had been the signal to act.

I glanced around the courtyard and saw fires outside each unit piled high with computer equipment, chairs, cardboard and plastic containers, the sparks crackling a hundred yards into the black winter sky. We milled around for a bit, avoiding the smoke and trying to find a place to stand out of the cold wind. It wasn't long before tinny voices could he heard issuing indistinguishable orders over loud hailers. After a few minutes, the gunfire began. I could tell by the flat sound that they were shotgun blasts. Then I saw a group of guards running down the breezeway carrying drawn weapons. One was shouting orders on the bullhorn, but his voice was distorted and the screaming of a hundred men drowned out his words. When they came closer I stepped forward to yell that we couldn't understand him.

"Go to the Back Forty!" This time his words were clear, and two dozen of us began walking toward the gateway of the big yard. The balaclava-clad men shouted to us to stay where we were. A number of us ignored them and edged our way forward. Slowly and deliberately a dozen armed guards spread out in a skirmish line to drive everyone into the yard and away from the buildings. Seconds later, a short series of explosions pumped into the sky. Tear gas wafted into the air nearly blinding us, but we managed to fumble our way through the gate and down the hill to the Back Forty. There were lifers and men with long sentences in the group. No one actually voiced their gut feeling that we'd all lost a great deal of work, but it was written in their pained expressions. Contrary to what the public might perceive, it's not the long-termers, the lifers, or the seasoned prison veterans who riot. Most long-termers have a vested interest in maintaining the status quo: parole hearings, visits, phone calls, recreational activities, work and school. The men around me were already feeling the loss of the things that keep them going.

From time to time, balaclava-wearing men waved at us from the courtyard on top of the hill that looks down on the big yard, exhorting us to join them. Although some men were intimidated, most of us saw their gestures for what they were: the hollow posturing of men whose resolve would quickly dwindle in the cold night air. We ignored them.

I made a point of looking for my neighbours. I found Rubberneck and Randy and told them to stick by me. My old friend and neighbour hadn't fared so well.

"Mike's toast," Rubberneck said.

"Toast?" I asked, shocked. "What happened?" Although Mike was sixty, he was a tennis player and tough.

"Heart attack."

"Just what we needed, a fuckin' riot," said one man wearily.

"There goes my trailer visits," another man cut in.

"We'll be locked down for months."

"All over a fuckin' black-and-white television set."

"I would've bought 'em both a fuckin' TV!" said a man who was known to have a few dollars stashed away. His comment brought half-hearted laughter from the others.

"My old lady told me if our next private visit was fucked up she was gettin' her ass into the north Alberta wind," said another man.

Suddenly another explosion of gunfire punched into the sky. A moment later, a mob of men came running down the hill. I walked slowly toward the perimeter fence, both to get away from the crowd, and to see if I recognized any of the men who'd found sanctuary from the wind behind the wall of the nearby handball court.

Before joining a crowd during a riot, a man should always know his companions. You wouldn't want to be caught in a group of sex offenders for instance, since you could quite easily fall victim to the idea that birds of a feather flock together. But I saw some friends of mine gathered on the handball court, and I decided to go over and join them. Some other men moved to the running track and after more than a few cold minutes, went to the skate shack and broke in. Soon, a fire had been lit and my crowd came to the general consensus that the skate shack with its bonfire was the place to be.

I knew from previous experience that the adrenalin rush in the rioters would now be greatly reduced and the cold would soon take its toll. If someone didn't step forward to try to bring closure to the incident, we'd all stand around in the yard looking at each other foolishly until the next morning. I had the support of Randy, who has the courage and skills to put up a good battle if he's pressed, and I also knew he carried a large shank. I decided to make a leadership move, so I stood out in front and talked to the men.

"I speak for myself when I say I don't want to be here," I began. "However, if the majority of you do, then here is where we'll stay." People started to come out of the skate shack to hear me. I waited a few moments, then went on "We'll stay here until we're frozen, starved or beaten into submission." I paused to let my words sink in. "But if you want to return to your cells, I'll take a couple men with me and together we'll go and talk to the coppers. What will it be?"

"Amnesty!" shouted one man. I didn't recognize his face but I knew his shout meant he was deeply involved. Most importantly, it meant I was being heard and accepted as a spokesman. Still, I didn't want to become involved in any kind of negotiations except the unconditional surrender of all of us—guilty and innocent.

Walking around the fire, I approached the man who'd called for amnesty. He was busy stoking the fire.

"The way it stands now, nobody's been identified," I told him. "Anybody who feels they need amnesty is going to be tagged."

"Yeah?" He stoked the fire with the jagged end of a broken hockey stick. Sparks flew.

"Yeah." I could see he didn't like losing the argument. He paused.

"Okay," he said finally.

Relieved, I walked into the shack and found it packed. "How many are wounded?" I asked. A dozen men put up their hands. The shotgun pellets were still in their bodies. One man had been struck in the arms and both legs, another had a leg wound, another had two wounds in his arm, including one in the elbow joint. Eleven men had been shot and though none of the wounds were life-threatening, they were painful and there was a danger of infection. Once the shock had worn off, the pain would get worse.

I suggested that my friend and I go to the fence and talk to the guards. Two others volunteered to go with us. As we moved across the snow toward the guards, the walkie-talkies came to life.

"Halt where you are!" came the order. We stopped.

"Do you want to surrender?" I could see six men, faces covered by white hoods, all cradling high-powered weapons with banana clips. They were spread out and ready for combat.

"We want to evacuate the wounded, then we all want to return to our cells!" I shouted over the wind.

"Do you want to surrender?" Our mission of mercy was clearly being misconstrued. They thought we were rioters. I saw another small group of guards moving toward us.

"We have men here who've been wounded. They should be allowed to leave first," I said. I saw one of the guards who'd just arrived walk closer to the fence, so we walked closer as well. I saw Mike, a unit manager I knew.

"Any dead bodies in there?" he asked, nodding his head in the direction of the skate shack.

"No, no dead," I replied.

"What are your demands?" The question surprised me, as did his tone of voice.

"Listen, we have no demands. I'm treating this whole thing as though none of the people down here were involved," I said.

"What do you want to do?"

"Get the wounded out for treatment, then the rest of us will follow."

"All right, come back to the fence in twenty minutes. The four of us agreed and returned to the skate shack.

The twenty minute delay lasted for many hours. At 7:15 a.m. the evacuation began. We were instructed to leave according to our unit. We gathered the walking wounded into one group, helped carry another man, and returned all of them to the fence.

It wasn't until the last two men stood beside me that I felt it was finally over. Just before he was frisked and whisked away to the unit, one of the last men turned to look at me. "I wonder if they'll give us breakfast," he said. I laughed for the first time that night. As he walked away with his hands on top of his head, I thought about the senselessness of the riot—burn the place down and then wonder if breakfast will be on the table on time.

Once in the unit I was abruptly released, ordered up the stairs toward the laundry room and then told to strip. I did. As I was putting my clothes back on, Darren, one of the guards, said, "So it wasn't good enough for you, eh?"

I couldn't help it, I laughed for the second time that night. In the minds of many of the administration, we were all to blame.

"Don't you think I would've stopped it if I could?" I asked.

"It happened too fast?" he asked, relaxing a bit.

"It happened too fast."

When I got back to my cell, I realized it had been nearly twelve hours since the riot began. My computer and personal belongings were intact. I considered myself fortunate. As it stood, at least eleven men had suffered gunshot wounds, almost a million dollars in damage was done, and some men had been badly beaten by the rioters. Once the rioters got hold of the files, inmates identified as sex offenders were attacked where they stood, or tracked to their cells and beaten there. In one instance, a man in my unit was severely beaten, but somehow managed to get away and lock himself in his cell. A failure in the locking mechanism saved him. His door could not be reopened, so his attackers began to smash their way through the cinder block wall of his cell. Just before the hole could be made large enough to enter, guards retook the unit and saved him. The man lived in a cell a few doors away from me on the other side of the hallway, and through the small window in my cell door, I could see that the hole in the wall of his cell was almost big enough for a man's shoulders. Although I have no affection for sex criminals, I could well imagine the terror he must have felt. He'd been lucky.

Over the month-long lockdown that followed, during which more than sixty men were either charged in street court, locked up in the hole, or transferred to maximum security institutions, some politicians publicly speculated or outright accused the lifers and the long-termers of being responsible for the damage caused by the riot. The press suggested inmates had it too easy, that a riot over a television set indicated a softness on the part of "the system." The logic behind such statements seems to be that if there were no television sets, there would be no riots. But the hard truth is that a great many inmates lost a great deal. Most inmates believe that nothing positive can come from such violent, riotous and senseless upheavals. The loss of personal and institutional property, the fear generated in inmates' families, the loss of visits, phone calls, pass programs and work hours, and the negative press that unfairly affects parole and educational programming, cannot be justified. The fact is, riotous acts by a few frustrated short-termers taint all inmates and cause a distorted, unrealistic perception of the system and the people in it. This leaves us all so wounded that it takes many, many years to heal. Sadly, following a riot, the best a prison and its people can hope for is a return to the way it was before it all happened.

Following the riot, I met as a Sam with Hilde Schlosar and with a writer, Moira Farr, who accompanied her. Moira was from Toronto, doing some research for a book she was writing. We talked about a variety of different things, and I took the opportunity to send Moira some of my work. It was through Moira and Hilde that the article on the riot was published by *THIS Magazine*.

Following the riot, during the lockdown, I was talking under the door—there's gap of two inches between the bottom of the cell door and the floor which allows for air ventilation, and if prisoners want to hold any kind of meaningful conversation from one cell to another, it's necessary to speak through this opening. To talk while standing at the door doesn't allow for sound to carry well, so we lay on our bellies with our chins resting on our hands.

It was just after the David Rutherford television talk show where the riot was discussed by a panel of people, including a Prisoner Committee member who was brought in via the telephone. Some of the guys on the range began talking about what they'd seen. One of them called my name to tell me he thought programs forced a man into prison activities that he really didn't need. I disagreed.

"A man has a choice," I said. "If he wants a parole or a pre-release program, there are expectations that he's learned something about himself and other people if he's to be considered. There are even professionals in place who view his past and other factors, and they then try to determine what the man's needs might be. If the man wants an early release he has to address those needs."

"Yeah, right. But they force the man to do them, even if he *doesn't* need them."

"So you think you know what you need and what you don't need?" I asked.

"Yeah, I do know."

"And when did this knowledge come to your mind?"

"As soon as I came to in the remand centre and was told I was under arrest for manslaughter."

"You just got out after serving a sentence here—right?"

"Yeah, I did a three-bagger for B&E."

"There were reports stating there was a possibility that your crimes might escalate in seriousness, wasn't there?"

"Well, yeah."

"Root cause—alcohol and drugs?"

"Yeah, and they tell me I have to take substance abuse programming now..."

"And you don't think you need it?"

"I took a program. Relapse Prevention," he answered.

"How did you make out in it?"

"Well, you know Darlene who teaches the program?" A question answered with another question usually means the gypsy-switch is coming—taking the attention off oneself by putting it on someone else's coming.

"Yeah, I know her," I replied. She was a reliable, dependable teacher.

"She kicked me out of the class." The resentment in his voice was obvious, and he seemed to blame her for his failing.

"Kicked you out? Why?"

"I got into an argument with her. She never did coke—she never did junk—what the fuck does *she* know? How can she teach *me*?"

"So you think you she has to do coke and junk before you can learn anything from her?" I thought if we continued he might arrive at some sort of understanding.

"Well *she* doesn't know what it's like. How can *she* tell *me* how to quit?"

"Well, if she did use drugs there's a good possibility she'd be just another dope fiend talkin' shit and you wouldn't listen to her anyway—true?"

"Well, maybe..."

"So maybe she has something other than drugs you can learn from her."

"What do you mean?"

"Square johns are different from us."

"Yeah right," he agreed, with a suggestion of contempt for square johns in his voice.

"How are they different?" I wasn't letting him up.

"Well *we* know how they're different." I could see that he would not, or could not, elaborate on the differences. I decided to explain it myself.

"They have a different value system. Darlene is probably a good parent, a good wife, and she works for a living just like most people do, and some of them in jobs they don't like. At the very least we know she manages to live her life without going to prison," I said.

"Yeah—so?"

"How do they do it?"

"They *have* to."

"How so?"

"They don't have the balls to steal," he replied. A few chuckles rolled across the floor from the other cells.

"No, there's a little more to it than that, I think. Aside from a social conscience, they do what they do because they find pleasure in small, normal things in life. They wouldn't risk their kids going without a mother or father, and they wouldn't throw away the life they have for the short-term, big-bang pleasure of the addict."

"Well, she pisses me off."

"Why does she piss you off?" I asked.

"Well, she wants to let me know she knows everything."

"Well she knows more than we do about living in the community. But you feel there's nothing she can teach you, because you already know all there is?"

"Well, not everything."

"No, not everything. Let's take me as an example."

"Okay," he agreed.

"Here I am, fifty-four years old, laying on my belly on the concrete floor in a prison talking through a crack in the floor to you; we're all in the same position and yet we know just about everything there is to know about life," I said. I always find it easier to use myself as an example because no one is offended. I knew there were many ears listening to this conversation. I went on. "And do you know why I'm here on my belly on this dusty cement floor?"

"Why?"

"Because of our value system. Because we never take the time to actually listen to anyone else, we know it all, and square johns to us are like helpless barnyard chickens."

"Chickens?" He laughed at my analogy.

"Yes—victims—or chickens from which we pluck the feathers then roast their meat for dinner. And when we're done, when we've taken all we can use, we use their feathers for pillows so our heads can rest easy at night."

"Well, yeah."

"And then, because they don't want us feeding off them, they react by calling for help and we find ourselves in prison. We want out of course, but to get out we find we're expected to listen to someone else, learn from someone else, and somehow come to an understanding of how other people think and feel if we want out early. But we're so fuckin' self-centred that we have a hard time coming to terms with having to listen to the very people we once victimized."

"Self-centred—that's on my file too..." he said. He seemed puzzled.

"Yes, self-centred, *me, me, me,* and we don't really give a shit for anybody else, we feel we're different, that we're the most important person in the entire world, and we'll go to any length and depth to get what we want. And all because we think we actually deserve it."

"I think of other people," he replied, "and I help people out." His tone of voice told me he was feeling defensive, and it wasn't my intention to humiliate him or cause him to think he didn't have some good qualities, for he did.

"Sure you do, but lots of us don't," I replied. It was always a good practice to let someone save face, but I continued to stress the point. "How many guys have you known who've beat their families and friends for money, made promises they can't keep, ruined people's lives, and even killed their own crime partners because of something they wanted?"

"More than a few," he agreed.

"And how do they justify it?"

"Well I guess they say they had to do it."

"Why did they have to?"

"Probably because they wanted something—and they were assholes."

"Yes, assholes. But they're self-centred assholes who have no value for friendships, no value for partnerships, and they're intent only on feeding their own needs at any cost. That's some of what self-centredness means—'feed *me* until I'm fat and fuck *everybody* else.' Let everyone else starve."

"Well, that kind of person is an asshole."

"And an asshole is someone who gives no thought to anyone else's needs, or feelings, correct?"

"Yeah, right."

"And if someone's feelings are hurt, they react?"

"Right."

"So if somebody's standing in front of a class, and you hurt them in any way, they'll react in a normal fashion, true?"

"Well, yeah."

"If somebody hurts you, you hurt them back—usually in a very bad way, right?"

"You bet," he replied, "smash 'em in the face."

"So when you found yourself kicked out of the class, maybe that was just a reaction to the pain you caused someone else...possible?" There was a pause while he thought about it before he answered.

"Well there are other ways to handle things," he finally replied. He meant, of course, that she should have found another way to handle him.

"Yes," I said, deliberately misunderstanding, "and it's up to you and me to find those ways without hurting other people and ourselves in the process. We have to look ahead and see the consequences for what we do."

"Okay, *okay*," he said, but he laughed when he did so.

"I'll let you up," I said, "and I'll get off the floor myself."

"Yeah, okay, we'll talk when we get out." His voice held a different tone than when we first began. I felt I'd at least started him thinking. I rose to my feet knowing that many of the men on the range had heard our conversation, and I knew that they'd also have picked up on some of the ideas behind what was said.

My case manager's attitude hadn't changed. The one thing that was becoming apparent was the fact she'd never be able to recognize anything positive in me. Initially this didn't bother me. I was just doing my time in the best new way

I knew how. She had no rational reason for treating me as badly as she did, but then she treated just about every man badly. Because I was unable to find a rational reason for her attitude and behaviour, I wrote a short story about someone just like her, called Not For Bread Alone.

It was the Not for Bread Alone story that brought home to me the full realization that writing allowed me to deal with strong emotions in a most productive, pro-social way. In answering why he hadn't taken the same path as his criminal friends, Jimmy Breslin said, "To write about crime, and commit crime, is redundant." I felt my writing was doing the same for me.

Her name was Gladys and she was given to wearing clothes that spoke to the possibility that she might have been colour blind. Lime green blouses, purple pants, black cotton stockings, and brown shoes with sensible heels were all part of her everyday wardrobe. Yet if one could get past her taste in clothing, she seemed normal in all other ways. The frameless and nondescript glasses she wore were as sensible as her shoes, and they gave her an academic appearance that was almost kind. She thought of herself as a psychologist, because that had been her major when she'd received her degree in sociology.

Gladys held an administrative position in a government institution. She was single and she seemed to enjoy both her work and her solitary life. Her family had moved away from her home years before, and though she got along with her neighbours, she was generally reclusive. She lived in an old house, in an old neighbourhood, and her neighbours left her alone. They might pause as they passed by on the sidewalk in front of her home while she worked on the small flower bed in her yard, and they'd ask how she was, they'd comment on the health of her petunias, and wasn't it a lovely day, and she'd always answer that she was well, and yes, it was quite nice for that time of year, and she always said "thank you" for their compliments on her gardening skills.

She had two small dogs and a cat who, because they were raised together since they were very young, had learned to live in harmony. There seemed nothing unusual about her or her life, and if one didn't know what her job entailed, anyone would believe her to be just another fortunate person who enjoyed a decent and regular income as an employee of the federal government. However, nobody knew she was a Protector, and Protectors were a different breed altogether.

She'd been disappointed when capital punishment was abolished, for she fervently believed that the only thing wrong with the practice of killing inmates was the fact that the law only applied to murderers, and not to ordinary thieves and other garden-variety criminals. She believed that anyone who broke the laws of the nation deserved everything they received. Every once in a while, whenever the issue of capital punishment was raised by the Reform Party, which was quite often over the last few months, she'd felt a deep and abiding sympathy for the man known as Mr. Ellis. Mr. Ellis had gone public after the abolition of capital punishment and his wife had left him, his small convenience store in northern Ontario went bankrupt, and his customers and his neighbours shunned him. Mr. Ellis had been the nation's hangman.

She kept a yellowed article, which contained Mr. Ellis's photo, in the drawer of her night table and each night she would carefully unfold it to read over once again. Each time she'd shake her head in dismay as she read of his sad and sorry plight.

"Tsk, tsk, tsk," she would say to her pets resting comfortably on her bed. "People are so ungrateful for the good that people do." Her pets would yawn and lick their lips, and Skippy, her favourite, would tremble and bark as if in agreement with her. She would then carefully refold the article and lay it on the linen cloth in her drawer. Long after she had turned off her reading light she would imagine how nice it would be to meet the man she knew as Mr. Ellis. He would certainly have some good stories to tell her about *them*.

Her career as a Protector began, long after the abolitionists had had their way in the nation, when a mysterious stranger came to visit her. Initially she was tempted to ignore his quiet knock, for when she peered out the peephole in her door and first laid eyes on him, she was repelled by the sight. He seemed so, well, *different*, yet there was something attractive and strangely compelling about him too. He was well-dressed, and he had a dark complexion which she found infinitely appealing in a man. So it was after only the briefest hesitation, during which she fluffed her greying hair and wiped the damp of her hands on her purple dress, that she opened the door.

"Yes?" she asked.

"Gladys?"

"Yes?"

"Your name came up on the federal government employee computer system, and I wondered if I might have a few minutes of your time." He smiled winningly.

"My name came up?" she asked.

"Yes," he said, "you're a special person."

"Oh!" she exclaimed, pleased.

"Do you mind...?"

"Oh, not at all! Please, do come in," she replied. She stepped to the side and the stranger brushed past her and into her home.

Over tea she learned that he was a government employee, just as she was, but his position was secret. He had worked closely with Mr. Ellis, when that man had been gainfully employed by the government, and since abolition the stranger now held a new position as Recruiter of Protectors. At the mention of Mr. Ellis's name her heartbeat quickened. She listened intently to his every word, and even before he brought out the contract from his inside suit-coat pocket, she had made up her mind to sign. And sign she did. He left a short time later, with the contract bearing her signature tucked safely in his pocket. After he had disappeared down the block, she remembered that it was the first time anyone had visited when she didn't have to tell her pets to stop barking, or to stay off their lap, and she realized too that she didn't even think to ask his name. He seemed, well, so perfectly *legitimate*.

Life went on and she loved her new position, secret though it was, as she had never before experienced such exquisite pleasure. Not even the few and far-between orgasms she had experienced when she was younger could compare to the pleasure she received daily in her job. She would have liked to tell her friends and family about her secret work, but the mysterious stranger had been explicit in his instructions, and those instructions were in fact written into her contract. She was to tell nobody about his visit, and she was *"strictly forbidden to tell a living, breathing soul about her life as a Protector."* She said nothing to anyone. Except of course to her dog, Skippy. He was her trusted, faithful confidant.

Inside the prison in which she worked she could be found working long after other staff had gone home, and many nights, in both winter and summer, she could be seen pulling her large suitcase on wheels behind her as though she were travelling through an airport terminal on her way to some exotic place and not just home. She was always asking the prisoners, seemingly innocently enough, if they were unwell.

"You look a little peaked today," she would say kindly. She would peer over her glasses at them, and slowly let her gaze run over their faces as if analyzing their skin colour and the whites of their eyes through a maternal concern about their welfare. Still, whenever a prisoner answered that they were fine, they always walked away from her scrutinizing gaze with the feeling that she was disappointed to learn they were indeed well. They noticed too that in the days before the arrival of the parole board she became quite intense and she seemed extremely busy writing out reports in her office, staying even later than usual. She could be seen through the curtain hanging over the window in her first-floor office, hunched over her desk with file folders spread out before her. Some curious prisoners paused briefly to peer through the curtain and noticed that she became almost frenzied at times, as she searched through the old files. Her writing and busyness took on an even greater intensity whenever it appeared a prisoner on her case load might receive favourable consideration from the parole board.

At the end of each and every day, at home in the late evening, when the sun had gone down, when her neighbours were getting ready for bed and all was quiet, she would pull open the top of her blouse and fished out a gold key on the loop of string around her neck. The key fit perfectly into an almost invisible slot in the mouth of a tiny, horrible-looking gargoyle on the wall in her bedroom. As she turned the key, a hidden door silently slid open to expose a staircase leading down into the basement, and as she descended the stairs into a green glow, her pets became excited as they heard her breathing quicken and rasp in her throat.

The light in the basement just seemed to *be*, like the glow from the sun below the horizon. Though there was no visible light source, the light was always just greenishly *there*.

In the basement, at eye level, a shelf ran completely around the room. On the shelf were many small, clear glass boxes. They were arranged side by side, like trophy cases, which is what in fact they were. Inside each case was a single and solitary human soul. They all looked the same: sightless, naked, miniature men without eyes, hair, or genitals. Each twisted and turned and fruitlessly scratched at the glass, as if blindly searching for some way to claw his way out. Their open mouths moaned and screamed horribly, but they were so small, and the glass case so tightly fused, that it was only by standing close to the case that a keen ear could actually hear them. She heard them well, lovingly resting her cheek and possessively placing her fingertips against the glass so she could not only hear them, but could feel the vibrations of their agony through the glass itself.

The contract given to her by the mysterious stranger hung in a frame, much like a favourite picture, on the wall at the end of the room. It read that as long as she kept the body of a man captive in a prison cell, she could keep the soul of the man in the glass case for her own personal pleasure in her basement. However, if the man was freed, so too was his soul. If the man died while in prison, she could keep the soul in the glass case forever. She had two dozen in her trophy cases now, three of which were hers forever. She dearly wanted more.

"Oh, my precious," she moaned, eyes closed, as she felt the delightful vibrations of the glass in her cheek and fingers. She shivered with the pleasure flowing through her body. "We will keep you all here, forever and ever, won't we Skippy? Won't we? If only Mr. Ellis could see us now he would be so pleased, wouldn't he Skippy?" She took Skippy's quick, high-pitched answering barks as evidence of his agreement. It was enough to let her know she was doing the right thing, and in her righteousness she felt totally and completely alive. After all, neither man nor woman works for bread alone.

After writing this story, Dennis stopped at my cell and I let him read it.

"When did you think of this?" he asked. Dennis was a seasoned veteran, but he was disturbed by what he'd read.

"The other day," I answered. "It's just a story."

"But what if it's true?" he asked.

I laughed, but I could see he was shaken.

Following the Riot article coming out in the magazine, I found guards had taken exception to it, and they made an attempt to cause me serious problems.

On Friday afternoon, August 22, the mail delivery went as usual. On Saturday at noon, I was told I had mail in the security bubble. It was my subscription copy of *THIS Magazine*. It was strange because there is no mail delivery on Saturday. Later on that night, a lifer walked across the courtyard to talk to me. He was a man with considerable influence in the population.

"I read your article," he said. I was sitting on the cement ledge which surrounds each unit, almost like a convenient bench, and the posture he adopted was almost, but not quite, confrontational.

"And where did you get that?" I asked. My calm attitude caused him to modify his stance, and he sat down beside me.

"Oh, you know how these things happen," he replied "It's a photocopy."

"The reason I'm asking is that I played that article close to the vest, and the magazine just came in today."

"Today?" He was surprised. We all know there's no mail delivery on Saturday.

"Yeah, at noon."

"A guard gave it to me," he said

"It strikes me as more than coincidental that I'm given the magazine on a weekend, and you end up with a photocopy of the article on the same day."

He then explained how the guard had slipped him the copy in his cell. I was under the distinct impression that the guard did not give it to him because he wanted me to be congratulated. The man who came to see me also suspected the guard's motives.

I made a few discreet inquiries and in a matter of minutes I found out what had taken place. Just before the mail delivery in the unit, the magazine had been taken out of the stack and photocopied later on that afternoon. Copies were quickly distributed. The best I could hope to accomplish at that point was some damage control, so I talked to one of the guards involved and halted any further distribution of the article. The next thing I did was allow a number of men to read it, but I made that reading a personal thing. I was lucky to have the respect of the men, and I was fortunate to have some influence with people in key positions in the prison population. If that hadn't been the case, I could have suffered some irreparable harm. But I was able to handle it and after that I let the matter drop, but it wasn't over yet.

On the morning of August 28, 1998 an emergency lockdown was called in all units and a short time later two guards came to my cell and took away my hard drive. They insisted on having all my security codes. Three other men in my unit also lost their machines but the computer-seizing business was restricted to the unit in which I lived.

The next day we were on regular status and I tried to get my machine back. I was told there were people suggesting that my hard drive be wiped clean and that I be forced to "start fresh." This caused me more than a little concern because I had four years' worth of work on my hard drive. It was a long weekend so it wasn't until Tuesday that I could get back into the struggle again. The committee was involved because I did all their written work, and still it wasn't until Wednesday that the matter was resolved.

I was sitting in the office of the Chief Security Officer with a committee member discussing my confiscated computer, when Mike's face appeared around the corner. In his hand was a brown envelope with my name on it. I knew Mike was not the kind of man who would deliver any prisoner's mail, so it was with some concern that I opened the envelope and pulled out some white sheets of paper. It was my story, Not For Bread Alone. It became clear to me that the riot article wasn't the only piece they'd taken exception to.

My cell door was fully open, which meant I wouldn't mind if someone dropped in for a visit. But still, good prison etiquette dictated that one should knock before entering. Lance always followed the rule, and after his quiet tap on the steel door announced him, I invited him to step into my small piece of personal prison territory.

"What's up?" I asked. I was sitting in my chair watching the local news. He stepped through the doorway and sat down on the end of the cot. The cot generally acts as a second chair in every cell in the prison.

"I read that article by Laird in *THIS Magazine*," he said.

"You did?" I'd given him the magazine to read a day earlier.

"Yeah."

"And?"

"I thought it was good." Lance held the magazine and a copy of the Calgary Sun in his hand.

"So did I, but there was something he said in it that bothered me too."

"What was that?" he asked. He handed me the magazine and because it was already dog-eared to the article in question I quickly found the page. I asked Lance if he recalled Laird discussing his five month employment in Bedford House. He did. I read the specific part of the article that troubled me out loud.

"'At the halfway house, I saw guys who'd hallucinate butterflies flying over your shoulder and stone-sober miscreants who once stabbed their own prison warden. Some enjoyed making the staff uncomfortable with their badass personae and nasty case histories, and we'd be forced to seem unfazed, disallowing them the pleasure of manipulating our emotions.'"

"There probably were guys like that there," offered Lance somewhat defensively, when I was done.

"Sure there were, I have no problem with that, it's when he says the staff were forced to 'seem unfazed' by the stories and histories told by some of them."

"Of the badasses?"

"Yeah, that's it. Not giving the badasses with the nasty case histories the pleasure of knowing how they were manipulating the emotions of staff."

"That bothers you?"

"Yeah, it bothers me. The only way some of these guys will have any idea of how they make people feel when they tell their horror stories, is for the people hearing them to point it out to them. How can counsellors truly help these men who've been in trouble and in prison for so long that they have compiled, 'nasty case histories' and yet not tell the men themselves how they affect people. How are these men going to relearn, be re-socialized, or readjust and reintegrate into a community if all they do is turn people off?"

"You mean, let the storyteller know he's a scary son of a bitch?"

"Exactly. Feedback. Only through regular and constant feedback are they able to get in touch with the feelings of ordinary people," I said. "Most them have no idea that their stories alienate average people from them—they have to be told."

"I've seen that myself; a man who's been in the SHU for years can't at first even fit into a regular prison environment. He's too full of the violence of the SHU."

"Yes," I agreed, "he has no frame of reference except that which he's just left behind. The system knows this full well."

"You think so?"

"Of course they know," I said. "They use the words re-socialize, readjust, and reintegrate all the time, and what's more, they know what they mean."

"Yeah, we've all heard them used enough," agreed Lance.

"A man who does hard time is so full of the prison it seems that's all he knows, and it also seems that he must tell everyone about his history. In some cases it comes down to trying to rid himself of the memories, or he finally feels free enough to talk about the unspeakable. The sad part is, Bedford House itself was created for the very badasses that Laird says he simply ignored. He just put them on the grease, and all because he didn't want to give the abrasive men needing his help what he thought would be pleasure."

"Well nobody really wants to listen to us," suggested Lance, "and if we didn't have each other, there'd be no real understanding at all."

"Yeah," I agreed, "and though some would say it's like the blind leading the blind, at least there's somebody trying to lead—better that than the sighted leading the blind down the wrong path."

"Ottawa needs to make changes," Lance stated.

"Ottawa has made changes," I suggested.

"Not enough of them," he argued.

"It might help you see my point of view if you see Ottawa as the brain of the system, and the people who work throughout the prisons across the country as the hands."

"Yeah, okay."

"Ottawa—the brain—tells the hands in the prisons to do things a certain way, but the hands can't seem to get the message right. In a way it's as though a spastic man or woman is trying to do very fine, very intricate work while suffering a disability, so of course there may be disastrous results," I said. My analogy brought a chuckle of laughter from Lance.

"That would explain it," he said.

"It's very close to the truth, buddy," I added.

"Is this coffee pot ready to go?" asked Lance. He was looking at my espresso machine and I could see he was ready to change the subject.

"It's ready—just hit the switch."

"Did you read the Sun?" asked Lance. He put the newspaper on the bed and reached forward to flip the switch.

"No," I replied, "I let my subscription to that rag expire. What's in it?"

"Section 745," he answered.

"Oh yeah, there's a couple of guys going up for their faint-hope reviews."

"Clifford Olson's mentioned again."

"Which just goes to show, as misled as the press is, they aren't stupid," I replied.

"Yeah?"

"Yeah, Olson's name generates feelings of revulsion, revulsion overrides reason, and the public can be kicked into a vengeful mood," I said.

"Olson's a skinner," Lance stated emphatically. Ordinarily this statement of fact inside prison would shut down a conversation in mid-sentence. However, because I'd known Lance for years, I wasn't concerned that he was going to run around falsely accusing me of being a skinner-lover.

"Oh yeah," I agreed, "he's every bit of that. But there's more to the story..."

"What do you mean?"

"He wasn't always a skinner," I answered.

"No?"

"Nope. He was just an ordinary, run-of-the-mill, garden-variety criminal who could crack a safe in a heartbeat."

"You knew him?"

"Many of us of who've been around the system did—way back when," I answered.

"What kind of guy was he?"

"Like I said, just an average guy, but he was half-tough too, and a good fighter. His nickname was Bobo, something he picked up because there was a Middleweight Champ by the name of Bobo Olson." This information was common knowledge among the "old-timers." It was also well recognized by prisoners that no penologist, sociologist, psychologist or psychiatrist had the moral courage to publicly ask questions about Olson's history.

"And he gave up safecracking for raping and killing kids?" asked Lance. "That's a big jump."

"Well, he actually went sour while doing a bit in the old BC penitentiary." Going sour meant he'd broken criminal mores and had screwed somebody, somewhere, and in many cases this meant a death sentence.

"How so?"

"He apparently gave up a drug smuggling operation in the joint out there," I replied. "Someone passed the word through the grapevine to the guys in Prince Albert Pen that he was a rat."

"Oh yeah?"

"Yeah, so some of the boys put the hoods on, picked up their shanks and trapped him in the card room. They stabbed him seventeen times. But he was tough. He got away by jumping over a ping-pong table before they could kill him."

"Did the guys get made for it?" he asked.

"A couple of them went down for it, and got a transfer down east," I replied.

"I know a couple of them. Gordie's one, and Pat's another. Pat's here—do you know him?"

"Pat?"

"Yeah, with the buggy eyes in unit eleven."

"Yeah—what about him?"

"He got four years for stabbing Olson."

"And Olson?"

"Olson was locked in the Penthouse, which is the hole on top of the prison, and he stayed there in solitary for over two years," I said.

"Two years in real solitary?"

"Yeah, two years—real solitary. Solid steel doors, no radio, no television—just a few discarded library books and the Bible. No windows—even the count-slot in the door was kept closed until a guard opened it briefly, to count a body inside and just as quickly slammed it shut again. Of course no convict talked to him under the door, even the guards just counted his body, and every con who ever went to the hole knew who he was, and in what cell. But nobody, and I do mean *nobody*, ever talked to him. He was a man who was as single and as solitary in his confinement as an oyster in its shell. He was totally on the grease."

"Good!" declared Lance. "He was a rat bastard. He gets no sympathy from me!" Just then a guard briefly peered through the doorway and into the cell, so I waited a moment until he left, then I continued.

"Well, there is that perspective. He was a rat, and we believe rats deserve to be killed or should be very severely fucked up, but that's not what the system believes. Sometimes I wonder if maybe, just maybe, this was a contributing factor to his later madness. I also wonder why I've never seen anything in print about it."

"What do you mean?"

"Well, the system has him on the grease now too, but you could ask why this is so."

"What do you mean?"

"Well, is it because the system doesn't want anyone to know the effect of solitary confinement on the human psyche? It's obvious that some people do realize that the way someone is treated today will have an effect on later behaviour. Could it be that people don't want to look at this?" I asked.

"Like maybe the system created the breeding ground for Olson?" asked Lance.

"Yes. Or is it because our revulsion prevents us from exploring, or delving into his history and looking for the cause?" I asked.

"It's food for thought," offered Lance, "especially today..."

"Yes, it is. But it seems we're the only ones who really dare to think such things, and if we speak of them, who'd actually lend us their ear? Who'd give us the pleasure?"

"Yeah, who would?" agreed Lance. The coffee pot began to burble and bubble a rich aroma into the cell, and we both fell into a comfortable silence while we waited to pour it into our cups.

After a long paper-work battle, Larry Simonson became my case manager, and my future brightened. In April I was given a pass to travel to Prince Albert Penitentiary to visit the Sams group there. I'd spent many previous years as a convict in P.A. Pen, beginning when I was eighteen years old. However, my return to the prison this time was quite different.

It was exactly a quarter after eight in the morning when I was called to the administration to begin my trip to P.A. I would travel under escort by Gary Storrs, and we'd be accompanied by Hilde Schlosar, the Executive Director of The Samaritans of Southern Alberta. Although we'd travel in a Correctional Service of Canada van, I would not be handcuffed or shackled, and I'd be treated as if I was just another passenger along for the ride, but of course Gary would closely monitor me.

We left Drumheller Institution at eight-twenty-five and stopped for coffee to go in a small store in Drumheller. Minutes later we were on the highway heading east to Saskatchewan. The sky was cloudy, looking as though it might rain at any given moment, but it didn't. Although there was no snow, the small sloughs were still frozen, and it wasn't until the van had carried us a considerable distance down the highway that we began to see ducks swimming in open water along the road.

The horizon showed a clear delineation between cloudy sky and clear. As the town of Drumheller receded, I could feel the reality of the prison begin to dim, like harsh glaring lights being turned down. As the clear sky on the horizon approached, I began to feel a freeing take place in my heart and mind. It was a gradual process, a melting away of the prison reality, like snow slowly melting in the burgeoning warmth of a spring day. With it came a deep feeling of gratitude for the trust the people in my life had shown.

At Oyen we passed a large field in which someone had made a humorous contribution to the art world. There was a large, circular hay bale with the front of a two-wheeled bike and two blue-jeaned legs sticking out of it; it looked as though someone had run their bike into the bale at high speed and was forever caught inside it. We were travelling the speed limit and the sight was visible for only a moment, and then we were past. We decided we'd take a picture of it on our return.

Soon we saw the Welcome to Saskatchewan sign on the right-hand side of the road and Gary pulled over so we could get a picture of me beside it. I went down on my knees, bent forward and kissed the grassy ground. Hilde snapped the photo and we laughed about it while we climbed back inside and continued on. At this point Hilde convinced me to ride in the front.

I absorbed the sights of freedom and I felt myself becoming fuller, like a dry sponge, softening and filling out as it soaks up liquid and returns to a more natural state. The stress of a prison environment can inhibit positive emotions, creating an emotional and psychological shell, so I concentrated on relaxing to allow the natural process happen to me. I was not a free man, but I was so much freer than I had been just hours ago. There were no fences, there were no inmates with seemingly insurmountable problems; there was only me, riding along in the van with two good people, heading east down the highway to our destination.

We stopped in Kindersley for an excellent breakfast. The orange juice with my breakfast tasted absolutely delicious. As I pointed out to Hilde, oranges were *verboten* in the penitentiary, because the guys have a tendency to cook up a potent brew from them.

Gary left the van to fill up at a service station, and though he stayed close by, Hilde and I were alone for a moment or two.

"It seems to me that Gary's nervous, as though he doesn't really trust me," I said, looking at her in the back seat.

"This is the first pass he's been on with you, Wayne," she said kindly.

"Yes, that's true," I replied, "but he knows me from work..."

"In there is one thing, out here is another," she suggested.

"Well, yes..."

"Trust is something we have to earn with people, and you do have a history of escape," she said. What she said grounded me. Over the past couple of years Hilde and I had come to know each other through her work with the Sams group. The escorted temporary absence was her idea. We were traveling to Prince Albert Penitentiary in an effort to help the P.A. Pen Sams group find ways to better organize their skills and abilities. Hilde had a lot of faith in the people in the P.A. Sams, including staff. She believed together we could bring them some insight into how to resolve their problems. The Sams of Drum Pen had been at it since 1996 while the P.A. Sams group was only three months old.

Although everything I was currently experiencing on the trip was familiar, everything also seemed new to me. I found a deep pleasure in the simple, everyday smells around the gas stations, the restaurants, in the scents of the open air, and it all somehow smelled richly like freedom to me.

We arrived in Prince Albert at four o'clock and stopped at an information centre for directions to the RCMP station. We had to check in with the police before we went for supper; I was a little concerned that I'd be taken inside and locked up when we did so. When we checked in it was decided that I'd be taken out for supper and brought back to be locked up at seven o'clock.

We picked a decent restaurant and we each had a fine meal. I was feeling somewhat subdued—I wasn't looking forward to spending an early night in a no-smoking cell in the bucket. But I felt even this was preferable to spending it in the penitentiary.

Gary and Hilde dropped me at the RCMP station around seven, and told me they'd be back in twelve hours.

It was not easy to sleep, but reading helped. At one point during the night I put my Grisham aside, and for a moment thought back to the first time I'd ever entered a cell in Prince Albert Penitentiary. Here it was, thirty-eight years later and I would again be entering the penitentiary right after breakfast. This time, though, I'd be walking right back out again in the afternoon. Hilde had been bothered by the idea that I'd spend the night in the RCMP cells and I hoped she wasn't worried about me. I felt a craving for a cigarette and once again I picked up my book, and lost my craving, and the rest of myself, in the pages.

Breakfast comes early in all jail buckets in the country because of early court appearances. At six-thirty the commissionaire made a move to put a plate in the serving slot of my cell, but I declined his offer. He then offered me a cup of coffee, which I accepted. Fifteen minutes later I heard Gary's voice. The commissionaire opened my cell door and I walked out, taking my book with me.

It was eight-thirty when we arrived at the penitentiary, and it was with mixed feelings that I entered that house of the dead. As I walked to the front door, I vividly remembered my first appearance at the entrance of the prison so long before. Although the layout had changed, and the front door had been modernized, I could still recognize the framework. I knew little had changed inside, as I had returned many times. This time was going to be my last time as an inmate.

We were immediately allowed in the front gate, the electronic door sliding open so silently that if I hadn't been watching, I wouldn't have known it was moving. Chaplain Chris Tolton, the Sams of P.A. Pen Liaison arrived and Hilde introduced us. I was taken to A&D to be strip searched, and when I returned Chris escorted us to the chapel to meet the Sams group. We walked in a group through a series of electronic doors to the large dome for which Prince Albert Penitentiary is famous.

The dome, the hub of the wheel from which all ranges formed the spokes, was exactly as I'd remembered it from years ago. I made a point of directing Hilde's attention to E-3 and F-3, which were ranges I'd lived on years ago; but then I'd lived on other ranges as well, some of them long since lost to renovations. I didn't see anyone I recognized, then, but I knew there were probably a hundred men I knew scattered throughout the prison. A short while later I did see a guy I knew and shook hands with him. His bearded face showed his stress and I was struck by his appearance. Although the penitentiary was rated medium security, and one would expect this to reflect a calmer, non-violent prison population, a horse by any other name is still a horse.

Chris took us through the dome to the side door leading to the inner prison yard. As we walked along the outside sidewalk to the back door, I noticed a gnarled old tree beside a building I'd once known as the carpenter shop. The tree had grown from a small, two-foot sapling into a large old tree. I suddenly felt my age.

Once we reached the chapel area, where I met some of the men I knew and was greeted with a great deal of respect, it felt good.

As the morning went on I was further impressed with the sincerity of the group. They were committed to the philosophy, and to aims and the goals of the Sams; that is, to help their fellow cons who were in emotional and psychological distress. After some discussion, Hilde and I focused our attention on giving them some assistance to help organize their group skills. Many of the problems they were currently experiencing were the same problems the Sams of Drum had encountered, which made our suggestions timely and appropriate. All of the P.A. Sams had many good points to make; Linda and Chris unhesitatingly contributed, both through their expertise and through their presence. It was obvious to me that all of the people, whether they were Sams or administrators, were sincerely involved in the Samaritan and prison Sams endeavor.

At one point during the group discussion I saw the Inmate Committee chairman through the window of the closed door. I immediately excused myself and left the room to talk to him. He and I had a history dating back almost thirty years, and I believed he could further contribute to the Sams. It's important to the delivery of the unique service which the Sams provide, that all prisoners in positions of respect in the prison population assist the Sams in promoting the service and the Sams philosophy.

Prior to leaving, I felt I had one last important thing left to do. I was walking across the dome with Virgil, one of the P.A. Sams, and I told him to wait for just a moment. I walked into the dead centre of the dome, stopped, looked around at the ranges and the people moving on the stairways and landings, and then closed my eyes for a moment. I imagined my soul floating above me like a butterfly, and I reached up as high as I could reach, and in a symbolic gesture, made as if I was snatching something out of the air. I closed my fingers over it, brought down my hand and slammed my open palm against my heart in my chest. Virgil and others were watching me.

"I just recaptured a missing piece of my soul," I said, "and I'm taking it with me."

"Good," declared Virgil. I shook hands with him and began to walk out with Hilde and Gary. I reached up again and pulled another invisible butterfly out of the air, and tucked it into my shirt pocket.

"That's for Freddy," I said. I walked out and I didn't look back until I was out the gate and away from the front of the building. Before we arrived at the van, Hilde took her camera and snapped a photograph of me standing alone, waving goodbye to the penitentiary.

As we drove away I felt exhilarated. There was a freeing within me, which sprang out of the realization that we'd accomplished all that we had set out to do. It was a most extraordinary experience, and I was naturally high as we headed south for Alberta and Drumheller Institution.

We stopped in Saskatoon for a nature call and a cup of coffee to go, and just as we climbed back into the van an older man with grey hair, walking with a slight limp and using a cane, strolled by on the sidewalk in front of the van. I was surprised by the intense look of animosity on his face. *Do I know this guy?* I asked myself. I held his gaze through the windshield as he continued on.

"Did you see the look on that guy's face?" I asked Gary and Hilde, nodding at the retreating figure.

"Yes, I did," replied Gary.

"I wonder what his problem was?"

"It's the van," Gary answered.

"The van?"

"Yes, he's probably been inside one of these."

"Oh, I see," I said. The man with the sour, intimidating expression on his face thought I was a correctional officer. *It figures,* I thought, *even when I'm mistaken as one of society's good guys, I run into a man who hates them too.* I couldn't help but wonder how many staff members ran into that kind of thing.

It was a long peaceful ride back to Drumheller. At Oyen, we paused on the highway to take a photo of me attempting to pull the man out of the hay bale.

We arrived at the front door of Drumheller Institution at eleven o'clock. My only regret was not asking if I could help Hilde carry her bags to her van, which was parked a distance away, before I turned away to walk through the front gate of the penitentiary.

Once back in the small confines of my cell, I found it took me some time to adjust to it again. My comfort zone had changed and my mind was still in the free world.

The next morning I walked up to Freddy, and without a word, I lightly touched my hand to his chest, over his heart. "There," I said, "I brought back a piece of your soul with me too." He laughed, but I could see he was pleased.

I immediately sat down and wrote out a warden's request for a temporary absence program to Lethbridge, Alberta, which was the start of my release plan.

My pass program was approved, but I was somewhat surprised to find that I'd be escorted by not one, but two, staff members on my temporary absence to Lethbridge to visit the Samaritans.

The three of us walked through the front gate and into the parking lot to find the vehicle that had been assigned to us. I rode in the back of the car and enjoyed the scenery.

The countryside had now become lush. On each successive pass I was seeing the deepening of summer; there was no ice on the water, the cattle and horses along the roadside were all grazing on rich green grass, and on this pass I could see the hazy image of the Rocky Mountains to the west.

When we arrived in the city of Lethbridge I was struck with the feeling that it seemed familiar. Lethbridge has very few high-rises; it looks a lot like Regina. I had once called Regina my home and because I now planned on making Lethbridge my home, I was pleased to find I truly liked what I saw outside the car window. There was a quiet casualness about the city that I instantly fell in love with.

Hilde and Nancy Graham, the Samaritan Program Director and John Thompson, the Rural Liaison, were waiting for us. They gave me a tour of Samaritan House. There was one Samaritan working, taking calls on the crisis line, and I was shown the office, which I would share with John Thompson when I went to work for the organization. The Samaritans had long since recognized my writing and organizational abilities, and I'd been offered employment as an office support person.

Following the tour of the house, we all sat down over coffee, and Hilde briefly outlined to me what had taken place during her visit to Ottawa the previous week. There was a good possibility that CSC would be introducing a peer support system in twenty-four institutions, and there was also a good possibility that the Samaritans of Southern Alberta would be a part of it.

Our schedule included meeting and having lunch with The Samaritans, followed by two separate interviews, one with Donna Geer, Area Director of Lethbridge Parole, and the other with the director of a halfway house.

Donna asked me many questions, which I attempted to answer as concisely and in as much depth as possible. I found her to be a professional and open parole officer. She stated that she felt my pre-release plan was a very good one.

I thought the interview went well and I walked away with the distinct impression that Donna Geer was someone I could easily work with, should I be granted parole. The fact that she was so familiar with all the people involved in my life, including my parole officer, Larry Simonson, gave me the feeling that our relationship would be a positive one, and would last for a long time.

We walked out of her office building to the halfway house.

The director told me about the mandatory group sessions in the house, and at the end of the meeting he told me I was an acceptable candidate and he showed me my name on his list of future residents. He took me on a tour of the facility and at the end of it I knew I'd be able to adapt quickly to the routine of the house. I felt too that all of what I'd planned over the years was now close to becoming a reality. It felt great.

We returned to Samaritan House where I met a number of Samaritan volunteers. They accepted me as if I were already a part of their Lethbridge community. It was almost time to leave when the phone rang and it was for me.

It was an editor from the *Globe and Mail*. She informed me that she was going to publish an article I had written months ago on Bill C-220, and when I explained to her that it was pure luck that I was there, she suggested it was fate. I could only agree with her. The money I would receive for the article would pay for a much-needed monitor for my word processor. It was a fine way to end my visit to Lethbridge. Too soon we had to leave to return to the prison, but even the ride back was an enjoyable experience.

It wasn't long after my pass that the CBC's *The Fifth Estate* program came to tape a segment on our Sams Program. They also wound up filming, and using as part of the show, my final release from prison.

On Tuesday morning, August 4, 1998, Larry Simonson told me my work release had been approved. I'd been anticipating it so I had most of my personal property packed, and I quickly packed the last of my seventeen boxes. By mid-afternoon I had them loaded on the wagon, ready for transportation to the Admitting and Discharge department. At quarter after three I took it to the admitting and discharge area and I was processed for release.

That night I said my "goodbyes" to my friends and by the time the ten-thirty count rolled around I was ready for the last long night in my now-empty, hollow-sounding cell. There's something about an empty cell that makes a man think of the first night he came in. It was a good feeling to know that I'd be travelling down the highway in the morning. There was a difference from all other releases I had experienced: this time I'd be going to a place where people would be glad to see me, and this time I knew I wouldn't be back.

I slept fitfully, waking up almost every hour, but I used the counting system to put myself back to sleep. Counting backwards from two-hundred to zero, imagining the numbers as I did so, was something which had proven valuable many times. I understand the reason it works: my mind focuses on the numbers which diverts my attention from whatever is bothering me—in this case the mental images of myself in the free world. However, the excitement would flow through me, even in sleep, and I'd awake to have to go through the system again. Finally, morning arrived.

At six A.M. my door opened and I walked down the range to the shower and started my last day inside Drumheller Institution. I could see by the sun shining through the open shower room door that it was a beautiful morning.

There was a delay while the *Fifth Estate* cameraman showed up at the front gate, so I used the time to talk to some of my friends who were early risers. There was no question in my mind that they were happy for me, and I knew they'd miss me when I was gone. Many of us had lived together for years on A range; we'd also played tennis, worked out together, and generally socialized with each other during all of that time. Some of them would not be leaving for many years, and some would not be leaving at all.

The intercom buzzed in my cell to tell me that Larry wanted to see me in his office. The cameraman was there. He hooked me up with a sound wire and he filmed me as we walked back to my cell. Then we walked into the courtyard.

There were some men sitting there already and a couple of them called out to me as we walked down the breezeway to the Keeper's Office, and to the cart holding my many boxes. Hilde was already there, sitting on the bench usually reserved for inmates. While she and Larry left the building to bring in her van to load my property, I was processed and given what I hoped would be the last strip search of my life. The camera was rolling all the while I loaded the van, and it continued right up until we left the property. We stopped for breakfast at Stavros restaurant and I thoroughly enjoyed my bacon and eggs. I took my time, savouring my food as I savoured the feelings of being free. At one point Hilde left the table for a few minutes and, when she came back, I told her that the short period of time she was gone was the first time I had been alone on the outside for more than five years. It was wonderful.

Hilde made a great travelling companion because she knew I was experiencing a wide variety of emotions and excitement. She had brought her camera and her binoculars, and she stopped on the highway and allowed me to look over the hills, valleys, rivers and sloughs with her glasses. Eagles, ducks, bluebirds, hawks, cattle, horses, llamas, and even farmhouses fell unknowingly under my gaze.

We stopped at Chief Crowfoot's grave, which had been made into a monument by the Siksika Nation, and I asked Hilde to take a picture of me beside the fence. Someone had stolen the plaque from the Chief's tombstone, which meant his history would no longer be clear to the people passing by. As I gazed out at the beautiful valley below, I felt I was looking out into forever.